International Political Economy Series

Series Editor

Timothy M. Shaw, University of Massachusetts Boston, Boston, USA;
Emeritus Professor, University of London, London, UK

The global political economy is in flux as a series of cumulative crises impacts its organization and governance. The IPE series has tracked its development in both analysis and structure over the last three decades. It has always had a concentration on the global South. Now the South increasingly challenges the North as the centre of development, also reflected in a growing number of submissions and publications on indebted Eurozone economies in Southern Europe. An indispensable resource for scholars and researchers, the series examines a variety of capitalisms and connections by focusing on emerging economies, companies and sectors, debates and policies. It informs diverse policy communities as the established trans-Atlantic North declines and 'the rest', especially the BRICS, rise. NOW INDEXED ON SCOPUS!

More information about this series at
http://www.palgrave.com/gp/series/13996

Tamás Gerőcs · Judit Ricz
Editors

The Post-Crisis Developmental State

Perspectives from the Global Periphery

palgrave
macmillan

Editors
Tamás Gerőcs
Institute of World Economics
Centre for Economic and Regional Studies
Budapest, Hungary

Judit Ricz
Department of World Economy
Institute of International, Political, and Regional Studies
Corvinus University of Budapest
Budapest, Hungary

Institute of World Economics
Centre for Economic and Regional Studies
Budapest, Hungary

ISSN 2662-2483 ISSN 2662-2491 (electronic)
International Political Economy Series
ISBN 978-3-030-71986-9 ISBN 978-3-030-71987-6 (eBook)
https://doi.org/10.1007/978-3-030-71987-6

Cover credit: Rob Friedman/Stockphoto.com

This Palgrave Macmillan imprint is published by the registered company Springer Nature Switzerland AG
The registered company address is: Gewerbestrasse 11, 6330 Cham, Switzerland

Contents

Notes on Contributors

László Csaba is Distinguished Professor of International Political Economy, The Central European University, Vienna and Corvinus University of Budapest, and a member of the Hungarian Academy of Sciences.

György Csáki is Professor, Faculty of Economics and Social Sciences, Szent István University (Gödöllő, Hungary).

Tamás Gerőcs is Research Fellow at the Institute of World Economics, Centre for Economic and Regional Studies, and a lecturer at the Sociology Department, State University of New York (Binghamton, US).

Christopher Hope is from University of Cambridge (Cambridge, UK).

Ekaette Ikpe is Senior Lecturer in Development Economics in Africa and the Deputy Director of the African Leadership Centre at King's College (London, UK).

István Kollai is Assistant Professor at the Department of World Economy, Institute of International, Political, and Regional Studies, Corvinus University of Budapest (Budapest, Hungary).

Ruvarashe Masocha is from the University of Iowa (Iowa, US).

Nazia Nazeer is from the National University of Computer and Emerging Sciences, FAST School of Management (Karachi, Pakistan).

Andrea Oliveira Ribeiro Programa de Pós-Graduação em Ciência Política, Universidade Federal Fluminense (Niterói, Brazil).

Judit Ricz is Research Fellow at the Institute of World Economics, Centre for Economic and Regional Studies and Associate Professor at the Department of World Economy, Institute of International, Political, and Regional Studies, Corvinus University of Budapest (Budapest, Hungary).

Roberta Rodrigues M. da Silva Programa de Pós-Graduação em Ciência Política, Universidade Federal Fluminense (Niterói, Brazil).

Andrea Szalavetz is Scientific Advisor at the Institute of World Economics, Centre for Economic and Regional Studies (Budapest, Hungary).

Miklós Szanyi is Professor at the Faculty of Economics and Business Administration, Szeged University (Szeged, Hungary), and Scientific Advisor at the Institute of World Economics, Centre for Economic and Regional Studies (Budapest, Hungary).

Tamás Szigetvári is Senior Research Fellow at the Institute of World Economics, Centre for Economic and Regional Studies and Associate Professor at the Institute of International Studies and Political Science, Pázmány Péter Catholic University (Budapest, Hungary).

Gábor Vigvári is Associate Professor at the Department of World Economy, Institute of International, Political, and Regional Studies, Corvinus University of Budapest (Budapest, Hungary).

Andrei Yakovlev is Director of Institute for Industrial and Market Studies (IIMS) at the National Research University: Higher School of Economics (Moscow, Russia) and tenured professor at Higher School of Economics (Moscow, Russia).

Abbreviations

AA	Association Agreement
ABCC	Brazilian Association of Commercial Banks
ACP	African, Caribbean, and Pacific countries
AD	Anti-Dumping
ADLI	Agricultural Demand Linkage Industrialisation
AFC	Asian Financial Crisis
ASEAN	Association of Southeast Asian Nations
BCB	Brazilian Central Bank
BNDES	National Bank for Economic and Social Development
CEE	Central and Eastern Europe
CENTO	Central Treaty Organization
CEO	Chief Executive Officer
CEPD	Council for Economic Planning and Development
CETA	Comprehensive Economic and Trade Agreement
CME	Coordinated Market Economies
COPOM	Monetary Policy Committee
CSGD	China-Specific Safeguards Database
CVD	Countervailing Duties
DCFTA	Deep and Comprehensive Free Trade Agreement
DME	Dependent Market Economies
DS	Developmental State
DSM	Dispute Settlement Mechanisms
DSP	Developmental State Paradigm
EAN	Economic Association of Namibia
ECB	European Central Bank
ECE	East-Central Europe

EMP	Euro-Mediterranean Partnership
EMU	European Monetary Union
EPA	Economic Partnership Agreement
EPZ	Export Processing Zone
ERP	Effective Rate of Protection
EU	European Union
EVTA	Employment and Vocational Training Administration
FDI	Foreign Direct Investment
Febraban	Brazilian Federation of Banks
FED	Federal Reserve System
FGC	Credit Guarantee Fund
FHC	Fernando Henrique Cardoso
FIA	Foreign Investment Act
FIESP	Federation of Industries of the State of São Paulo
FTA	Free Trade Agreement
GAD	Global Antidumping Database
GAP	Growth Acceleration Program
GATT	General Agreement on Tariffs and Trade
GCVD	Global Countervailing Duties Database
GDP	Growth Domestic Product
GFC	Global Financial Crisis
GIP	Green Industrial Policy
GNI	Gross National Income
GTP	Growth and Transformation Plan
GVC	Global Values Chain
HDI	Human Development Index
HYV	High Yielding Varity
ICT	Information and Communication Technologies
IFI	International Financial Institution
IIP	Infant Industry Protection
IMF	International Monetary Fund
IPE	International Political Economy
ISDF	International Cooperation and Development Fund
IT	Information Technology
JCRR	Joint Commission for Rural Reconstruction
JEE	Joint Entrance Examination
JUEE	Joint University Entrance Examination
LIG	Low Income Group
LME	Liberal Market Economies
MDC	Movement for Democratic Change (Zimbabwe)
MENA	Middle East and North Africa
MNC	Multinational Companies
MoE	Ministry of Education

MTI	Ministry of Trade & Industry
MVA	Market Value Added
NAFTA	North American Free Trade Agreement
NATO	North Atlantic Treaty Organisation
NEA	Northeast Asia
NEG	New Economic Geography
NIPA	Namibia Investment Promotion Act
NME	New Macroeconomic Matrix
NSC	National Security Council
NSDUA	New System of Diversified University Admission
NTM	Non-Tariff Measure
NUTS	Nomenclature of Territorial Units for Statistics
OECD	Organisation for Economic Co-operation and Development
OGL	Open General License
OPEC	Organization of the Petroleum Exporting Countries
PAC	Programa de Aceleração do Crescimento
PISA	Programme for International Student Assessment
PMDB	Brazilian Democratic Movement
PML	Pakistan Muslim League
PPP	Pakistan People Party
PROER	Program of Incentives for Restructuring and Strengthening the National Financial System
PROES	Program of Incentives for the Reduction of the State's Participation in Banking Activities
PSDB	Brazilian Social Democracy Party
PT	Partido dos Trabalhadores (Workers' Party in Brazil)
R&D	Research and Development
SACU	Southern African Customs Union
SADC	Southern African Development Community
SAP	Structural Adjustment Program
SCM	Subsidies and Countervailing Measures
SEATO	Southeast Asia Treaty Organization
SFN	National Financial System
SIA	Sustainability Impact Assessment
SME	Small and Medium-sized Enterprise
SOE	State-Owned Enterprise
SPRU	Science Policy Research Unit (at Sussex University)
STI	Science, Technology and Innovation
SV	Systemic Vulnerability
SVOC	State in Varieties of Capitalism
SWAPO	South West Africa People's Organisation
TFP	Total Factor Productivity
TPP	Trans-Pacific Partnership

TTIP	Transatlantic Trade and Investment Partnership
UK	United Kingdom
UNCTAD	United Nations Conference on Trade and Development
US	United States
USD	United States Dollar
USSR	Union of Soviet Socialist Republics
VoC	Varieties of Capitalism
VUCA	Volatility, Uncertainty, Complexity, and Ambiguity
WTO	World Trade Organization
ZANU PF	Zimbabwe African National Union-Patriotic Front

List of Figures

List of Tables

CHAPTER 1

Introduction

Judit Ricz

On the eve of the twenty-first century both the world economy and economics as a social science face important challenges, that call for paradigmatic changes, maybe even for new paradigms. First following the global financial and economic crisis (GFC) of 2008–9, and more recently amidst the COVID-19 pandemic crisis and the following economic and

This volume brings together a collection of selected original research conducted in the framework of the research project 'From developmental states to new protectionism: changing repertoire of state interventions to promote development in an unfolding new world order' (FK 124573) supported by the National Research, Development and Innovation Office (NRDIO) of Hungary.

J. Ricz (✉)
Department of World Economy, Institute of International, Political, and Regional Studies, Corvinus University of Budapest, Budapest, Hungary
e-mail: judit.ricz@uni.corvinus.hu

Institute of World Economics, Centre for Economic and Regional Studies, Budapest, Hungary
e-mail: ricz.judit@krtk.hu

T. Gerőcs and J. Ricz (eds.), *The Post-Crisis Developmental State*, International Political Economy Series,
https://doi.org/10.1007/978-3-030-71987-6_1

social consequences, we can observe rising state involvement in the economy throughout the world. Correspondingly, governments must act however under new constraints posed and/or intensified by new challenges, which require reconsideration of the repertoire of developmentalist policies and state interventions.

The starting point of our analysis is the fact (long recognized by different generations of development economics literature), that developing and emerging market economies differ from their more advanced counterparts both regarding the structures of their economy and society and also regarding the capacity and autonomy of their states to implement development policies. These differences might have important consequences not only regarding their options in crisis management, either in the wake of the GFC, or the most recent crisis related to the global COVID pandemic, but also in terms of the viability of a development-oriented approach based upon active state interventions on the longer term.

Before going into details with more recent debates regarding the developmental state concept and the need for its reconfiguration (and reconstitution) in the twenty-first century, we aim to emphasize that every crisis offers also an opportunity, and we know from the classic developmental state theories, that an extremely constrained environment (along the urgency views—see Ricz in this volume) might push incumbent governments to build developmentalist institutions which effectively promote both structural transformation and shared and inclusive growth. History will show whether the COVID-19 pandemic can be considered as a perfect storm (Djankov and Panizza 2020) in this regard. The theoretical possibility is there, whether governments will seize this opportunity, is yet to be seen. What is sure nevertheless, that debates surrounding post-crisis developmental states have once again got to the top of academic interest, and this is the endeavour we aim to correspond to also within the framework of this edited volume.

This volume is the continuation of our research on economic and developmental policymaking in the global semi-periphery in the post-crisis cycle (see our recently published book titled 'Market-Liberalism and Economic Patriotism in Capitalist Systems' edited by Gerőcs and Szanyi 2019). The Institute of World Economics formerly belonging to the Hungarian Academy of Sciences was one of the institutions which launched major research programmes on related topics, and among its efforts, special attention should be paid to a series of international conferences entitled, 'The Role of State in Varieties of Capitalism'. These annual SVOC conferences have attracted scholars from many different countries and have contributed to fruitful discussion around several major topics related to the different patterns of direct state involvement in various types of economies. The present volume focuses on the post-crisis developmental state as it aims to explore the possibilities and constraints that semi-peripheral states in the Global South and East face when seeking new developmental strategies to effectively respond to post-crisis challenges.

The starting point for the chapters of this volume was the narrow, rather strict definition of developmental states, built upon the experiences of East Asian countries (Japan, South Korea, Taiwan and Singapore) and their successful structural transformation (economic upgrading) along a growth-with-equity approach. The classic development state paradigm emerged out of the related works (Johnson 1982; Amsden 1989; Wade 1990; Evans 1995; Leftwich 1995), and has highlighted main institutional and policy elements of these success stories, while embedding these into the very unique and specific (global and regional) context of the postwar era (shaped by the geopolitical considerations of the Cold War, the context of late development and the relatively closed economic systems by that time).

At the latest, by the end of the last century major changes in the external and internal environments of classic developmental states took place, and have significantly altered individual states' possibilities to directly guide the market and stimulate the economy with the 'traditional tools and measures' that were applied during the mid-twentieth century. One of the most important implications is that, starting already in the 1980s, the liberalization process has undermined the internal coherence of the classical DS model, which was not able to adapt itself to either the new external conditions or to the changed internal settings (shaped by weakening state capacities and the ever-stronger private sector). Accordingly, the decline of the classical DS model has to be regarded as a systemic phenomenon (Woo-Cumings 1999; Benczes 2000, 2002; Beeson 2004; Low 2004; Ricz 2019). The story does not end here, however. As both in theoretical realm and economic policy practices we see recently the revival and renaissance of active state interventionism in the economy, even if it is claimed to substantially differ from its old (and demised) counterpart, and with this, the developmental state is back at the centre stage of economic debates.

Following the deductive line of argumentation, in the theoretical realm the need for rethinking the analytical concept for developmental states can be verified on the one hand with the fall of the classic developmental state paradigm at the latest by the end of the last century, and, on the other hand, with new challenges emerging (or intensifying) in the twenty-first century and presenting new circumstances (possibilities and limits) for governments to formulate and realize national developmental strategies.

In an economic historical scale we can date the most recent generation of developmental state literature back to the Millennium, however, following the global financial crisis in 2008–9 we can observe a so-called renaissance of the developmental state approach (Chu 2019; Evans 2014; Fine et al. 2013; Haggard 2019; Mazzucato 2013; Nem Singh and Ovadia 2019; Wade 2014; Williams 2014; Wylde 2017)—we can also refer to these most recent works as the post-crisis approach. While these most recent works tend to build upon the intellectual traditions of the classic DS literature, nevertheless, these also tend to deviate from it in several ways, such as by applying a broader geographical focus—extending beyond East Asia, and by combining the results and frameworks of both the political and economic school of the classic works (Fine 2013).

The starting point for post-crisis considerations is the new development paradigm (which is by now widely applied in development economics—see also the Economic Nobel Prize in 2019[1]). The broad, multidimensional understanding of development (incl. social, environmental, political and spatial dimensions) and the most recent structural changes of the economy (resulting from the fourth industrial revolution) undoubtedly underline that expanding human choices and capabilities becomes a primary goal and mean of development in the twenty-first century. In our understanding however, some continuities remain with the classic developmental states models, as those were also focusing on both the structural and social component of economic progress, as transformative changes in the economic structure (economic upgrading) went hand in hand with social improvements for the majority of the societies within the classic a growth-with equity models.

For the twenty-first century's interpretation of developmental states in structural terms we also have to revise the meaning of late development

[1] It was awarded to Abhijit Banerjee, Esther Duflo and Michael Kremer 'for their experimental approach to alleviating global poverty' and has shown clearly a consensus regarding the capability approach to development.

(or even late-late development). Today an even more complex structural transformation of the economy is taking place, with different implications at different levels of development. The ongoing restructuring of the global economy has not only led to an *open global economy* dominated by intense capital flows, and transnational corporations transcending national borders, and organized into global production networks and global value chains, but also to the rise of the service sector's weight, and the emergence of the *bit-based, knowledge economy* (Evans 2014). This led to the appreciation of human capital investments, access to information and innovation and networking activities. The sectoral case study by György Csáki in Chapter 7 of this volume aims to bridge post-crisis perspectives with the classic developmental state paradigm regarding the role of education and its paramount importance for developmental states' economic success.

Nevertheless, technological changes have not only affected sectors of the new economy, but have altered organizational forms of traditional economic activities as well as the modes of corporate governance (Gereffi 2014). The socio-economic and other consequences of the spread of the new IT-based economy or even the so-called green economy are uncertain yet, however, seem to differ at different stages of development (such as in the Global North versus South, and even differences within this latter group prevail). Andrea Szalavetz in Chapter 5 of this volume looks at a related question by focusing on green industrial policies (GIPs), and by proposing a life cycle analysis of green energy industries she tries to argue, that since the drivers of growth are bound to change in the coming transition-to-maturity phase, despite the current enviable global market position of some new developmental states, the 'game is not over in the ongoing global green race'.

Consequently, the geographical focus of the post-crisis developmental state approach has to be broadened, and instead of a narrow focus on East Asian economies, it shall incorporate emerging and developing countries, the peripheries and semi-peripheries of the world economy. This latter wide geographical focus is applied in the current volume, which brings together empirical analysis from practically all over the emerging and developing world, by including case studies among others from Pakistan, Brazil, the Central Eastern European region and also from the African continent, namely Ethiopia, Namibia and Zimbabwe. According to our preliminary hypothesis however the differentiation according to development levels (such as between the low and middle-income countries) remains reasonable in the twenty-first century, as well as to some extent challenges for large and small country governments might also differ in the light of the most recent development challenges and constrained policy space.

Looking at the recently emerging set of literature we might claim, that this new, post-crisis DS approach constitutes to cover a rather eclectic group of authors and works, and a new developmental state paradigm has not emerged yet (at least no theoretical breakthrough has been documented), but is still in-the-making (with some consensual direction of thinking and some common points of analysis to be already detected).

Looking at the more practical side of the story—following a more inductive line of analysis, we can say, that during the last years, at the latest since the 2008–9 Global Financial Crisis (GFC) we see the rise of state involvement in the economy worldwide. Nevertheless, as long as in more developed countries the recent rise of state interventionism was directly linked to the crisis management afterwards the 2008–9 GFC, and remained mostly a cyclical phenomenon, in the emerging markets and the post-socialist world the extensive state involvement in the economy seemed to be a more entrenched characteristic (and not a transitional phenomenon) with long historical roots (Kurlantzick 2016; Nölke et al. 2019; Szanyi 2019; Szelényi and Mihályi 2020). In some emerging countries, the recent rise of statism dates back to the late 1990s and early 2000s, while in others it has been revived in the post-GFC era. However, in most late developers the state has traditionally played a more active role and is historically more embedded in institutional and social memories (at least according to the path dependence views). Its current rise also seems to be less of a cyclical characteristic, and is also shaped by the new political-ideological turn globally towards populism, nationalism and patriotism (Gerőcs and Szanyi 2019). In the focus of the current analysis are the countries outside the core of the world economy, the Global periphery, consisting of mainly those emerging economies, which are considered as late-late developers by development economists.

Over the last few years in line with the changes in economic and political spheres a broad popular debate has started (both in media and in academic circles) around the steady and rising state involvement, also called *new developmentalism* affecting all economies over the world, but especially outstanding in emerging economies (and to some extent also on the related phenomenon of the democratic backsliding). These current tendencies have received extensive media coverage. The list of examples is long, but mostly referred articles were published in leading Western media, such as The Economist (2012) but successive articles also in Time, Businessweek and Reuters have followed suit. Academic interest was also vigorous, and different authors applying different definitions and interpretations started to analyse contemporary rise of *state capitalism* from different angles (Bremmer 2009; Kurlantzick 2016; Musacchio and Lazzarini 2014; Nölke 2014; Nölke et al. 2019; Naughton and Tsai 2015; Estrin et al. 2019; Ricz 2018).

The systematic analysis of these more recent statist experiments is still awaiting. Some outstanding examples of both country experiments and sectoral approaches can be found (Wylde 2017; Nem Singh and Ovadia 2019; Szalavetz 2015), and the consensus on the steady feature of the increased role of the state in these countries seems to be emerging. Forms of more permanent state activity vary from case to case and sector to sector, however these range in general from state ownership and indirect forms of influencing micro-level decisions, through active structural policies, meddling with prices to paternalism (and even prebendalism according to Szelényi and Mihályi 2020) and business-politics entanglement, and finally to increased corruption (as a systemic feature). Furthermore rising state activism in the economy goes more often than not hand in hand with changes in the political realm. Along with the democratic backsliding we see tendencies towards autocratic governance style, personalistic ruling, attacking checks and balances of political power and hurting independent agencies. In many cases, this extended role of the state has some historic parallels of modernization and catching up. Therefore activist states can claim substantial social and political support. This is often expressed in deliberate confrontations with the neoliberal political and economic agenda of the Great Moderation period (in the political realm the most often used label is 'illiberal' state, while in the economic sphere state capitalism and economic unorthodoxy became the new catchwords).

Along with these economic policy changes, a renewed interest and focus on the classic, East Asian developmental states can be detected in the political rhetoric of many developing and emerging countries. The earlier list of the so-called aspirational or to-be-developmental states (Routley 2012) consisting mainly of African countries (such as South Africa, Rwanda and Ethiopia) explicitly aiming at emulating the East Asian development models, has been extended recently by some other, semi-peripheral countries, most notably in Central and Eastern Europe, such as the examples of Hungary and Poland show.

The aim of this volume is to contribute to the debates around contemporary state capitalist varieties, by focusing and extending the developmental state (DS) approach based on the experience of the global (semi-)periphery in the post-crises cycle. We explore the possibilities and constraints that states in the region face when seeking to formulate and implement new developmental strategies. The novelty of this book is that it widens the perspective and scope of analysis to new terrains, which urges the expansion and reconsideration of classical modernization theories. On the background of the historical and cyclical nature of capitalist development, this book relies on the concept of Developmental State (DS) with its critical approach to the role of the state in the catching up strategies. Thus, the edited volume aims at enriching discussions about the state-led varieties of capitalism by expanding both its temporal and regional focus. The chapters throughout this volume bring together a great variety of these approaches in order to reconsider the role of the (semi-)peripheral state and the social context of development in the post-crises era.

The volume encompasses a critical political economy approach on multiple scales and within different time frames and regional focuses. The empirical case studies entail both sectoral and regional focus, while relying mainly on the experiences of (semi-)peripheral countries in an overall comparative framework. The volume provides a comprehensive overview on crucial policy areas to support inclusive, innovative and sustainable development in relation to cyclical changes in the world economy, such as international trade relations, industrial policies (including science and technology), education and social policies. The chapters of the volume feature some of the most current trends in this regard.

Finally, the book broadens the perspective on post-crisis development strategies in the global (semi-)periphery, and at the same time, it aims to overcome the dominant Western narrative within the comparative capitalism research, and to critically analyse the relevance of the DS framework in the post-crises cycle.

The Structure of the Book

The chapters of this edited volume provide a plurality of approaches, multiple perspectives and applies different methodologies addressing however the same and very related questions and challenges of developmental state building in the semi-periphery with the main focus on the post-crises cycle.

In this vein the edited collection is structured into three main parts. The first part consists of three chapters (besides this introduction) dealing with topics inherently linked to the development and the state problematic and related theoretical issues in the post-crisis cycle, especially the role of institutions and change in economic theory and the role of big cycles and technological change in the development of global capitalism.

The second part of the book consists of six chapters, which besides the first more theoretical one—focusing on the emergence of developmental states in the twenty-first century—provide empirical insights for post-crisis developmental states based on case studies from a rather diverse group of countries. While Chapters 6 and 7 offer a more sectoral focused analysis, as mentioned earlier, by looking at green industrial policies and educational policies, and exemplifying their arguments on the cases of China and Taiwan, respectively. The remaining chapters provide country case study analysis from Slovakia, Ethiopia, Namibia and Zimbabwe.

The third and last part of the book is made up of five chapters (inclusive of the concluding chapter). The first chapter dealing with the opportunities of state-led capitalism in the world trading system is also followed by regional and country case studies. The chapter (by Tamás Szigetvári) focusing on development and trade policies in North Africa offers a good starting point to enrich the developmental state approach with insights from the varieties of capitalism school. The next case study (by Andrea Oliveira Ribeiro and Roberta Rodrigues M. da Silva) sheds light on the role of finance in the demise of the new Brazilian developmental state. While the Pakistani case study highlights how the mystification of power can hinder development in the global periphery. The final chapter sheds light on the interrelatedness of these wide-ranging analyses and arguments and concludes.

References

Amsden, A. (1989): *Asia's Next Giant: South Korea and Late Industrialization*. New York: Oxford University Press.

Beeson, M. (2004): The Rise and Fall (?) of the Developmental State: The Vicissitudes and Implications of East Asian Interventionism. In: Low, L. ed.:

Developmental States: Relevancy, Redundancy or Re-Configuration. New York: Nova Science Publisher, pp. 29–40.
Benczes, I. (2000): Válság és átalakulás a Távol-Keleten (Crisis and Tranformation in the Far East). *Külgazdaság*, 44(3): 56–75.
Benczes, I. (2002): A fejlesztő állam válsága Ázsiában (The Crisis of Developmental State in Asia). *Külgazdaság*, 46(5): 23–40.
Bremmer, I. (2009): State Capitalism Comes of Age: The End of the Free Market? Foreign Affairs, Vol. 88, No. 3, pp. 40–55.
Chu, Y. (2019): Democratization, Globalization, and Institutional Adaptation: The Developmental States of South Korea and Taiwan, Review of International Political Economy. https://doi.org/10.1080/09692290.2019.1652671.
Djankov, S., and Panizza, U. eds. (2020): *COVID-19 in Developing Economies. Centre for Economic Policy Research*. London: CEPR Press.
Estrin, S., Liang, Z., Shapiro, D., and Carney, M. (2019): State Capitalism, Economic Systems and the Performance of State Owned Firms. Acta Oeconomica, 69(S1): 175–193.
Evans, P. B. (1995): *Embedded Autonomy: States and Industrial Transformation*. Princeton, N.J.: Princeton University Press.
Evans, P. B. (2014): The Developmental State: Divergend Responses to Modern Economic Theory and the Twenty-First Century Economy. In: Williams, M. ed.: *The End of the Developmental State*. New York: Routledge, pp. 220–240.
Fine, B. (2013): Beyond the Developmental State: An Introduction. In: Fine, B., Saraswati, J., and Tavasci, D. eds.: *Beyond the Developmental State: Industrial Policy into the Twenty-first Century*. London: Pluto Press, pp. 1–32.
Fine, B., Saraswati, J., and Tavasci, D. eds. (2013): *Beyond the Developmental State: Industrial Policy into the Twenty-First Century*. London: Pluto Press.
Gereffi, G. (2014): Global Value Chains in a Post-Washington Consensus World. Review of International Political Economy, 21:1, 9–37. https://doi.org/10.1080/09692290.2012.756414.
Gerőcs, T., and Szanyi, M. eds. (2019): *Market Liberalism and Economic Patriotism in the Capitalist World-System*. Cham: Palgrave Macmillan.
Haggard, S. (2019): *Developmental States*. Cambridge: Cambridge University Press.
Johnson, C. (1982): *MITI and the Japanese Miracle: The Growth of Industrial Policy, 1925–75*. Stanford, CA: Stanford University Press.
Kurlantzick, J. (2016): *State Capitalism: How the Return of Statism Is Transforming the World*. New York: Oxford University Press.
Leftwich, A. (1995): Bringing Politics Back In: Towards a Model of the Developmental State. *Journal of Development Studies*, 31(3): 400–427.
Low, L. ed. (2004): *Developmental States: Relevancy, Redundancy or Re-Configuration*. New York: Nova Science Publisher.

Mazzucato, M. (2013): *The Entrepreneurial State: Debunking Public vs. Private Sector Myths*. London: Anthem Press.
Musacchio, A., and Lazzarini, S. G. (2014): *Reinventing State Capitalism: Leviathan in Business, Brazil and Beyond*. Cambridge, MA: Harvard University Press.
Naughton, B., and Tsai, K. S. eds. (2015): *State Capitalism, Institutional Adaptation, and the Chinese Miracle*. Cambridge: Cambridge University Press.
Nem Singh, J. T., and Ovadia, J. S. (2019): *Developmental States Beyond East Asia*. Oxon, New York: Routledge.
Nölke, A. ed. (2014): *Multinational Corporations from Emerging Markets. State Capitalism 3.0*. Basingstoke: Palgrave Macmillan.
Nölke, A., ten Brink, T., May, C., and Claar, S. (2019): *State-Permeated Capitalism in Large Emerging Economies*. Oxon, New York: Routledge.
Ricz, J. (2018): New Developmentalism in the 21st Century: Towards a New Research Agenda. IWE Working Papers, 245. Budapest: Institute of World Economics, Centre for Economic and Regional Studies, Hungarian Academy of Sciences.
Ricz, J. (2019): The Changing Role of the State in Development in Emerging Economies: The Developmental State Perspective. In: Szanyi, M. ed.: *Seeking the Best Master: State Ownership in the Varieties of Capitalism*. Budapest, New York: Centre for Economic and Regional Studies, Hungarian Academy of Sciences, Central European University Press, pp. 237–273.
Routley, L. (2012): Developmental States: A Review of the Literature. ESID Working Paper No. 3.
Szalavetz, A. (2015): Post-Crisis Approaches to State Intervention: New Developmentalism or Industrial Policy as Usual? Competition and Change. *The Journal of Global Business and Political Economy*, 19(1): 70–83.
Szanyi, M. ed. (2019): *Seeking the Best Master: State Ownership in the Varieties of Capitalism*. Budapest, New York: Centre for Economic and Regional Studies, Hungarian Academy of Sciences, Central European University Press.
Szelényi, I., and Mihályi, P. (2020): *Varieties of Post-Communist Capitalism: A Comparative Analysis of Russia, Eastern Europe and China*. Series: Studies in Critical Social Sciences, Volume 157, Brill.
The Economist. (2012): The Rise of State Capitalism. Special Report, 21 January 2012.
Wade, R. H. (1990): *Governing the Market: Economic Theory and the Role of Government in East Asian Industrialization*. New Jersey: Princeton University Press.
Wade, R. H. (2014): 'Market Versus State' or 'Market with State': How to Impart Directional Thrust. *Development and Change*, 45(4): 777–798.
Williams, M. ed. (2014): *The End of Developmental State?* New York: Routledge.

Woo-Cumings, M. ed. (1999): *The Developmental State*. New York: Cornell University Press.
Wylde, C. (2017): *Emerging Markets and the State: Developmentalism in the 21st Century*. London: Palgrave Macmillan.

CHAPTER 2

Institutions and Change: New Horizons in Economic Theory

László Csaba

Introduction

Three decades ago when systemic changes started in the socialist world and the third wave of democratization swept across the developing world there was an overwhelming belief that poverty, oppression, and other forms of human suffering may easily be overcome. The change will not be easy, but is within reach, if only we rely on good textbooks,

Keynote to the 5th *State in the Varieties of Capitalism* conference series of the Institute for World Economy of the Hungarian Academy of Sciences and CENS entitled *Institutions and Change*, Budapest, 28–29 November, 2019.

L. Csaba (✉)
Department of International Relations, Central European University, Vienna, Austria
e-mail: Csabal@ceu.edu

Department of Comparative and Institutional Economics, Corvinus University of Budapest, Budapest, Hungary

T. Gerőcs and J. Ricz (eds.), *The Post-Crisis Developmental State*, International Political Economy Series,
https://doi.org/10.1007/978-3-030-71987-6_2

borrowed from the United States, and on the wisdom of the international financial institutions (IFI), as summarized in the Washington Consensus (Williamson 1994). Let us add although we did have cautioning voices from both academia and policy-making from the very outset (Winiecki 1993), the overall mood was by and large that of hope and favorable expectations, which were to become self-fulfilling. Large-scale institutional transformation was presented both as necessary and feasible at the level of theory and policy alike.

Thirty years after, the emerging new consensus, both in policy-making and in theorizing, seems to be by and large the opposite. Criticism on both levels abound (cf e.g. the special issue of *Cambridge Journal of Economics* with authoritative contributions from various periods and written from many angles of analysis[1]). While on the onset of changes the role of institutions was though acknowledged, but tended to be subordinate and technical in nature (what is the optimal way to here or there, be that privatization or pension system), by knowing the complexity, even the trickiness of institutional change counts among the platitudes of the profession.

Institutions Matter: Heterodoxy in Policy-Making

One may draw various borders in the history of economic thought. Staying at the level of policy-relevant theorizing, that we call for shorthand international political economy, we may perhaps take the thin but influential and insightful volume of Nobel winner Douglass North (2005) as a watershed. By that time there were ample lessons from the rather unsuccessful attempts to change postcommunist economies in Central and Eastern Europe (Kolodko 2000), from the Asian and Latin American crises of 1997–99 (Eichengreen 2002; Lámfalussy 2000) and even from the burst of the dotcom bubble in the United States in 2001, that regulation and institution building should not be taken as marginal side-assignments of the broader task of inflation stabilization and overall liberalization in emerging markets.

From that time on—with the very partial exception of the United States under the George W. Bush Administration—the role of institutions

[1] Thirty years after the fall of the Berlin Wall/virtual special issue, edited and introduced by Michael Ellman/April, 2019—last retrieved from https://academic.oup.com/cje/pages/berlin_wall on 18 November 2019.

as being focal to major policy changes were consensually appreciated. If not in pure theory, but definitely in the policy-making literature following—and even more in the one critical of—the line of IFIs. To put it in the language of the IFIs, sustainability of solid policies requires anchoring in the lasting and formalized rules of the game, which are institutions. This insight has been powerful and practical, finding its way in the policy advice of both the European Union and the IMF. The doctrinaire approach of the 1990s has been gradually giving way to what Ilene J. Grabel (2017, pp. 29–53) aptly describes as '*productive incoherence*.' This means not only accepting that it is not always the smallest fiscal deficit, which is best, or that faster privatization does not necessarily and inevitably be deemed superior to slower ones.[2] It also implied that IFIs and the EU accepted both the need and the time dimension of institution building, provided this was a side condition for solid policies to sustain. In all, a paradigmatic change occurred, but not via revolution, of revoking previous doctrines in the open, but through step-by-step modifications adding up to an entirely new worldview and also novel practices.

In pure economics of the high-brow theoretical departments, like those in the Ivy League, but increasingly also in continental Europe including Germany and much of Central Europe, the neoclassical synthesis as hammered out by Samuelson and developed further by Lucas and Blanchard with its institution-less view of the economy triumphed. By contrast, in policy-making heterodoxy has found its way. No government in any major economy of the globe has ever subscribed to a hands-off stance or would have restrained its intervention in the economy to monetary policy in normal times, coupled with a bit of fiscal stimulus during rainy days (Csaba 2009; Tanzi 2018). Therefore, as it could be established already prior to the Great Recession of 2007–2009, *heterodoxy has become a norm rather than an exception in policy-making and the theories shadowing reality* rather than aiming at placement in top ten academic journals.

In the majority view of the period institutions and thus institution-building was seen as *something inherently benign in nature,* enhancing

[2] This consideration had some political- though by no means professional—justification owing to fears of return of the Communists. Indeed, countries dodging privatization, primarily the new Independent States and countries of Southeast Europe have been faring much worse than their Central European fellow travelers, who privatized and liberalized faster.

individual and social well-being over and above the trivial levels of excluding predatory behavior and misuses of monopoly positions, two factors appreciated even by 'neoliberals,' or as they tended to be called in the antebellum period, the Manchester School. Institutions tended to be portrayed as the bridge between individual and social, national and global concerns, overcoming class and situational conflicts, as between seller and buyers, employers and employees. This holds for the heterodox schools, as Keynesianism, old institutionalism or critical approaches (Marxism-inspired views more than to the Austrian school and public choice). However, given that political economy scholarship, and policy-making, in particular, tends to be eclectic all the times and in all corners of the world, we do not run a high risk if we interpret the huge policy literature of the 1999–2008 decade in this simplifying manner. Starting with World Bank papers issued during the Wolfensohn Presidency to increasingly even the output of the IMF the 'productive incoherence' take on economic reform has become predominant.

What did acceptance of the 'institutions matter' paradigm imply? First and foremost, that only the building of institutions was important, and even *lapses in improving fiscal performance tended to be tolerated in exchange for a more radical stance on structural reforms.* True, China with its de-emphasis of any formal institution, especially the judiciary, in favor of pragmatic and regionally diverse solutions that differ both from Western and other local options, never fitted in this picture (Xu 2011). But at the end of the day, the idea was that institutions—especially formal ones—are intrinsically good, and lack of them is fundamentally wrong, a shortcoming to be remedied.

The role of regulation and of institutions, cementing and enforcing these have only been underscored by the experiences of crisis management. One of the broadly accepted narratives, circulated in part in the banking community, has been the blame put on the regulators, who allowed the bubble to build up and did nothing to prevent excessive risk-taking. This claim counts among the items of common wisdom in the financial literature other than mathematical modeling. In his latest book Robert Shiller (2019) of Yale, Nobel in Economics (financial markets, as of 2013 vintage), claims that the inability to control the validity of information, especially in the public domain, including rumors, gossips, and openly manipulated pieces of news, has played a role comparable to those of viruses in epidemics on the spread of crises/panics in the capital markets. He proposes new analytical techniques and institutions to try to prevent or at least limit these infectious influences.

It is perhaps unnecessary to remind the Readers of the return of the state as a major player that in the decade since the Great Recession this view has gained currency. Not only do most analysts accept the enhanced role of regulations, of active fiscal policies, of discretionary interventions in order to achieve redistributory objectives as given. Similar to the 1930s and the 1950s and 1960s, state interventionism is anew considered to be not only necessary but oftentimes even virtuous in order to overcome market failures. Let us not be deceived: while pure economics departments continue to preach free markets, the Trump Administration of the United States from 2016 to 2020 has clearly taken a stance against free markets and of the multi-lateral trading régime, from TTIP to NAFTA for that matter. Protectionism is back in vogue, and so is the extra-territorial use of trade sanctions to promote political targets, from punishing Iran to contain Chinese expansion in various walks of life, from the university business to banking and information technology firms. The Republican administration is a far cry from being a supporter of free markets, domestically or abroad.

Let us note in concluding this section: *being statist and being in favor of institution-building are two distinct cups of tea.* Someone with a German ordo-liberal conviction may well be in favor of strong—and accountable—institutions and against petty interventionism and discretionary policies. And in contrast: Post-Keynesians or Structuralists may be in favor of state decisions over major investment projects, over macro-economic magnitudes, without necessarily emphasizing the role of institutions. If one takes Singapore from among the successful catching up countries, we see very little of transparent, rule of law guided institutions, but very strong central direction of affairs. Japan—once the archetype of classic developmental states—with its super-Keynesian policies is not a prime case for efficient institutions. Thus, it can easily be, that more statism goes hand in hand with weakened institutions—an outcome we shall return later.

Institutions as Impediment to Change

This insight counts among the better known ones in one part of the literature, and also among the most forgotten ones in the meantime—in a different literature. Coming from a postcommunist country one cannot but think about the *opus magnum* of János Kornai (1992), which counts among the most cited monographs on the field, despite its bulky volume. In this work—building on his previous empirical investigations as well as synthetizing previously available knowledge on diverse country experiences—he demonstrates with exceptional rigor the decisive role of institutional arrangements in bringing down the once invincible Soviet Empire. Looking from the theoretical perspective it is worth mentioning, that this reading runs counter to two equally widespread—though much less substantiated—explanations of the collapse in 1989–91. One blames the—unquestionable—errors and omissions, at the end of the day of lack of comprehensiveness in the Gorbachev line of *perestroika,* which aimed at saving the régime through incremental changes in policies and also to some extent in institutions (Aslund 1991). While it has not gone as far as contemporary Chinese reforms—let alone later changes—the logic and mindset were by and large the same: to combine one-party rule with partial marketization. Let us note: with the benefit of hindsight it is clear, that the idea per se had not been abortive, as it has been working in China and also in Vietnam in the following thirty years or so. The second competing interpretation blames the West for not having provided more forthcoming an international environment for Soviet and later Russian reformers (Sakwa 2019).

Similar stories are being told about the reasons for stagnation in Sub-Saharan Africa and Latin America, which we shall not enter into. This broader narrative is masterfully summarized in the best-selling book by Daron Acemoglu and James A. Robinson (2012). In their view, it is the inclusiveness versus the predatory nature of institutions which is decisive, and those institutions are to a large degree derivative of their colonial origins. This interpretation prevails today, though has also invited sweeping criticisms both from economic historians and economic theorists. The first group tended to finger-point to the perceived or real shortcomings of the bits and pieces of descriptive parts of the book. The second group tended to question if institutions on their own, without help from policies and the global environment, can be proven to be the only mover of changes, especially if and when this claim is to be substantiated in an econometrically sound manner. While it would take a separate review article to analyze the claims and counter-claims, our purpose was to show that this narrative has developed into a reigning one for the second decade of the current millennium, irrespective of its potential incoherence or imprecision.

A third major narrative where institutions play a pre-eminent role has been the revival of *the middle-income trap literature,* observing its syndromes in the 2000s (Eichengreen, Park, and Shin 2014; Kang and Paus 2019). This term is a modification of the broader concept of the institutional trap as a form of lock-in phenomena, discussed in the broader theoretical literature (Polterovich 2019). First diagnosed by the now-forgotten Nobel winner Simon Kuznets, countries with high rates of growth often enter into a period of low growth, even stagnation, owing to their institutional configuration, which hinders or preclude reforms, even if those are cognized by decision-makers. First diagnosed in Russia and the United States, the concept has become extended and widely used for explaining the slowdown in countries which do not yet enter the stage of Japanese sclerosis, still lose out of their previous dynamics without any good reason or trivial explanation as war or revolutionary breakup.

True, a significant body of literature claims—including the neoclassicals—that mature economies grow slower or nothing due to their structural and technological characteristics.[3] In this case, there is nothing to be explained. Radicalizing the pessimistic view of Gordon cited above, Vollrath (2020) openly proposes that stagnant output is a feature of high level of development, or as he puts it, when the economy is 'fully grown.'

The trouble with this claim is that in real-world scenarios we have an equal amount of cases, like Luxemburg and Singapore, with no signs of a slowdown, as compared to Japan and the United Kingdom, where slowdown seems to be a secular trend. Thus we need to attempt alternative interpretations, not based on a single case observation and generalization thereof. In a comparative perspective, stagnation is not to be equaled to normalcy, once a certain level of maturity is attained. Let us add: the examples analyzed in the *New Palgrave* entry cited above account for countries which would equal to medium level of development as of today, or middle-income countries to use the term our sources do.

The concept of the middle-income trap describes a widely observed phenomenon that has long been intriguing students of catching up and development. Namely, that *good policies and good institutions seem to be*

[3] Cf. recently with much influence in Gordon (2016).

eroding in the sense of getting less and less efficient with the time passing. As a result, registered rates of growth, but also the efficiency of allocation, innovation, and growth of employment/inclusiveness of the economy deteriorate. This may not automatically lead to the first becoming the last, but it often does mean that growth ebbs out before catching up would have been complete.

Some observers, such as the by now largely forgotten Mancur Olson (2000) highlight the impact of vested interest politics and the ensuing *ossification of social and economic structures* that create impediments to continuous adjustment and change, conveniently postulated by mainstream/neoclassical accounts of growth and development. The concept of middle-income trap goes a step further in specifying the causes and relates the *recurring delays in implementing already accepted structural reforms to specific political and communications channels*. These include the issue of visibility as well as the long-established rule of the short run. The latter means that measures with no immediate popularity gains, such as investment in human infrastructure, or improving legal and institutional arrangements that bear fruit only in the long run, and mostly not for the government introducing them, will be pushed to the background as useless or not being really urgent. What seems to be an innocent delay today becomes a major blunder in the medium to long run, long before 'we are all dead' as Keynes quibbled. These factors are magnified by the internet age and the advent of post-truth politics and the rule of social media, where *validation of claims is usually lacking*.

This insight has been supported in many ways by the emerging new theories of growth and development, all stressing the relevance of issues like rule of law, trust, transparency and accountability, the security of civic and property rights, that is the usual list of commandments for sound economic policies offered by various schools of thought.

While the Olsonian view focuses on institutional and social rigidities, as the final mover, the middle-income trap approach highlights *the role of policies and incremental action as well as non-action* in bringing about unintended consequences that dominate the intended ones.

It seems that the middle-income trap view is more encompassing as long as it covers *dictatorial and democratic regimes alike*. In the case of the former, the most recent and perhaps most relevant in the global perspective is the reversal of Chinese reforms under the Xi Presidency, particularly since 2012 (Lardy 2019). But the more traditional cases, as those in the European Union, with reforms preached but not practiced in several peripheral countries, from Portugal to Poland may be cases in point.

All in all, the middle-income trap—similarly to the resource curse and many other ills in development—may well be overcome. *There are remedies offered by economic theory, and there are successful cases* of breaking out developmental, institutional, or political deadlock. What we do not have is perhaps the naïve enthusiasm and belief of three decades ago in the quasi inevitability of the triumph of democratic and market-oriented solutions. At the end of the day, the big surprise in the decade which followed the Great Recession was precisely the lasting presence of state interventionism in its various forms and also in its condoning by a very large part of theories and of the public alike. Put it differently: while knowledge of how to handle what we would still describe as economic illnesses is solid and is also available (not least owing to open access and the internet), *the willingness to apply proper medication is not necessarily there.* Anti-vaccination movements do abound, in advanced and emerging economies alike.

Can Institutions Become Hollowed?

In the third section, we reflect upon a relatively new development. While certainly, at one level of abstraction 'there is nothing new under the Sun,' but the institutionalist interpretation tended to be the mainstream view, if not in the theoretical economics departments, but definitely in development studies. The latter is reflected in the fact which is easy to check, that most influential fora on development are by no means pure economics journals. They tend to be rather multi-disciplinary outlets, with contributions including as diverse fields as sociology or infectology, plantation studies, and demographics.

Development studies tended to be holistic in their diagnoses and therapy alike, from Gunnar Myrdal to Amartya Sen and more recently the Banerjee-Duflo-Kremer trio of Nobel winners of 2019 in Economics. What we are concerned about at this stage, not the broader methodological issue which is at the center of debates in the economics profession over the need for cooperation with sister disciplines or the redundancy of inter-disciplinary approaches. Our claim is that owing to their broader focus development studies have long discovered what has become a fashionable topic for the mainstream of international political economy by the current decade, namely the *hollowing of institutions*.

In short, it counted among the platitudes in development studies to claim that institutional transfers may though work, but in reality it is quite rarely the case. Furthermore, there is a tendency for the drift between developmental poetry and reality to be deeper than customarily acknowledged (Bird and Mandilaras 2012). This insight, supported by libraries of writings on the failed experiences in transplanting elsewhere successful arrangements in emerging and postcommunist environments, has been running counter to development thinking of the current millennium, which has changed emphasis. If in the preceding decade the creed was by and large the Washington Consensus in its first, second and third editions, the *post-crisis era* tended to be a period of revival regulation school and of highlighting institutional preconditions for successful adjustments.

The big turn against this latter tide has been made in the post-2010 period, with Central and Eastern Europe in its bulk turning against the previous tide of marketization and democratization. It has been a subject of insightful and colorful debate if this turn added up to the emergence of classical mafia states (Magyar 2019), or rather what we observed was a milder, local version of a global trend of the state reclaiming its lost territories in economic development, both in terms of ownership and micro-management of the cycle (Szanyi 2020).

Without re-iterating the literature cited in these extensive empirical volumes and our own reading of Hungarian reversals (Csaba 2019) let us posit the major puzzle. In Hungary—but also in Poland and to a much stronger degree in Russia and Ukraine—formal institutions of the market economy and of pluralist democracy have remained in their place. However, *their functioning has been modified, to the point of crippling,* by way of arbitrary appointments and by way of eroding the systems of checks and balances. For instance, by appointing individuals unconditionally loyal not only to the Party, but to the supreme leader's person to key positions, as the Governor of the central bank, the High Prosecutor, or heads of secret services and the public media (while undermining and closing down critical media and independent institutions, or turning them subordinates to the ruling party) the name of the game changed. Formally speaking there continues to be a system of checks and balances, but if the State Audit Office tends to be regularly more optimistic than the Treasury on macro-economic trends, while is diligent in persecuting opposition parties, the entire division of labor among the players undergoes a change.

To take the Polish example: if members of the Constitutional Court are nominated, as in reality since 2015, *en masse* and without broader inter-party consensus exclusively and single-handedly by the governing party only, and the Supreme Court is cleansed from judges openly critical of the government, *the balance between legislative and executive obviously changes in favor of the latter, without any formal systemic change*. Similar changes in a much more radical manner are documented in the collections cited above for Ukraine and Russia, as amply documented in the volume of Magyar (2019) cited above.

Yet another under-explored subject in this respect has been *the changing role of business-government relationship*. Central and Eastern Europe never experienced a power vacuum, and the claim of neoliberal excesses and giving up state regulation has often been voiced, but never convincingly substantiated by factual material.[4] The *state has never 'withered away,'* it has remained decisive as an employer, owner, regulator and re-distributor in each and every country, including the most liberal Baltic States. For instance these countries have joined the Euro-zone, while the Central Europeans—save Slovakia and Slovenia—have not and perhaps also will not. Joining the Economic and Monetary Union (EMU) has always been a strategic decision, staying out too. Joining in requires orchestration, meeting fiscal and monetary targets, keeping 'all options open' too. In sum, neoliberalism might well have been preached, but never practiced on the ground.

We do not assert, that staying out of EMU was an act of statism or illiberalism. If one takes Denmark or Sweden, we may observe two countries with tough economic policies, much in line with what critics would term 'neoliberal' in France, Italy, Spain, or even Germany, including the famous flexicurity arrangements, compelling workers for retraining in exchange for lavish unemployment benefits. Our claim is that the legal obligation to join EMU, taken up at the 2004 accession, has never materialized. And the explanation lays well beyond the customary technical explanations provided by central bankers in each of the countries concerned.

Non-membership in the EMU complements a series of other 'mishaps,' pertaining to security of property, equal treatment of foreign and local enterprises, or ensuring competition as a level playing field in all markets stipulated by EU law. In general, rule of law, implying even-handed and impartial administration of justice has been pushed to the background in favor of open favoritism, and far not only in agriculture. Banking,

[4] For a recent ideological re-statement of this old claim from the early 1990s cf. Appel and Oreinstein (2018).

media, energy sector, even sports as an important economic activity (building stadiums, organizing global sports events, etc.) all show signs of preferential treatment of those 'truly close to us', i.e., of power centers.

The fundamental difficulty in interpreting what we observe is exactly the lack of formalization, or *the increasing drift between form and substance.* To give but a few examples: if out of 1200 initiatives of the opposition not a single one is adopted in the legislation, it does not abolish the parliamentary nature of government. However, it would be hard to pair it to the US practice of say, the 1950–2000 period, when bipartisan arrangements and solutions were not the exception, but the rule. Likewise, if EU funds are allocated by a procedure in which the best bidder is chosen out of one, this may formally be law-abiding, but in substance it is a mockery of what this instrument is meant for. Likewise, if public media lacks pluralism and becomes a mouthpiece of power much to the same degree as it used to be under one-party rule, media pluralism becomes gradually extinct even without full nationalization. In short, *style becomes substance,* and a formally liberal market order is transformed into a highly coordinated one, without changing the law but modifying its implementation. Documenting these changes and proving claims against contesting, self-justifying propaganda is anything but a trivial task for analysts. By the same token, the dividing line between 'hard facts and soft interpretations' fancied in American social science becomes porous at least.

In all, one of the new developments of the current decade is the *changing interface of formal and informal institutions.* The phenomenon per se is nothing new in development studies. What is new is the re-emergence of this issue in advanced countries like the United States under Trump or the Czech Republic under Andrej Babis. In short, the hollowing may render institutions marginal rather than focal points in setting the features of the system as it works on the ground.

An Overview: What Makes Institutions Relevant for Change?

This section aims at incorporating the insights from the previous three into a broader theoretical framework and relates these to the new trends in thinking in global economics and international political economy. Perhaps one of the more perplexing trends has been the *de-emphasis of traditionally pre-eminent material factors and the appreciation of intellectual*

and emotional ones, that is highlighting the role played by typically non-material factors in explaining outcomes and also in shaping the normative view.

We may refer first and foremost to the literature on financial crisis and crisis management, where both bankers and regulators tend to highlight the focal role of moral standards and accepted models of individual and collective behavior. To cut a long story short we may refer to the fall 2019 'long read' series in the *Financial Times* on the imminent need to *re-think capitalism* in its present shape. Contributions voiced the requirement to find purpose over and above incessant increases in the consolidated asset value of firms, the inevitability to adopt broader objectives than shareholder value maximization, the urgency of remedying wealth polarization and slowdown or even stagnation in social mobility, as well as the need to include environmental sustainability concerns among the objectives of the firms, including the parameters deciding over bonuses of management. The above-listed issues, which we present as a selection of topics only, would have qualified as empty moralizing in the period between 1990 and 2010 not only in the media, but in most of the management, finance and economics departments of good universities and business schools.

A book chapter is not the place to come up with a new vision of the discipline. But our *tour d'horizon* may allow reflecting on some of those new developments, which may result in ***an incremental but fundamental renewal of thinking about the economy***.

First, the very fact that institutions and their role have become so pre-eminent in global economic scholarship is a sign of a gradual re-assessment inside the profession of what matters in terms of explanatory power. The literature we surveyed may have been considered to be marginal at certain points in time, especially at the level of both public policies and corporate management. This is no longer the case. We have cited the recent book by Robert Shiller above, but it would be hard to find any major analysts, regulator or policy-maker who would not invoke in his or her analysis among the root causes of crisis and among the milestones of avenues for betterment the need to restore conservative and often not quantifiable values of solidity.

As a consequence—*second of all*—in terms of management practices, one of the most intricate consideration is how to define and even more how to enforce such broad and non-parametric items like solid behavior, trustworthiness, responsibility for stakeholders, and the broad—natural and social—environment. In terms of German ordo-liberalism we are back to square one: a free market *pre-supposes a set of values* to which players are explicitly committed, by law and internal convictions/set of values alike.

Third, we may refer to a re-emerging trend in economic thought, which underscores the *role of public discourse* in shaping values and setting standards for socially appreciated forms and ways of success. Perhaps Deirdre N. McCloskey (2006–2016) of Chicago has gone the farthest in advancing this claim in her historical and logical explanation of capitalism and its innovativeness and ability to change and also generate shared prosperity against tendencies to monopolization of power and wealth. Under this angle, the rule of social media and generally the flow of uncontrolled and uncheckable pieces of information (to the point of deliberate manipulation) pose major and direct challenges to democracy and market economy, both built upon open exchanges and deliberation based on rational assessment of pros and cons. What becomes crystal clear supports our previous knowledge: *institutions do not act on their own,* as 'independent variables' in an equation. They exert their impact in the context created by societal values, that include discourses over what is and is not acceptable and commendable. Therefore the same arrangement may work in one place and totally fail in another one.

Fourth, as has traditionally been emphasized by Douglass North (2005), all institutions matter as much as they *are enforced on the ground.* As we have seen, institutions may be completely transfigured by way of a changed interpretation. To bring but one example: while Russia under Yeltsin counted for many as a normal country at a medium level of development with an overgrown military, under Putin few would share this conviction outside the official academics in Moscow. And this despite the fact that the constitution, land law, civil law, and many others are either the same as in the 1990s, or have been technically updated to conform to global standards. It is the implementation that changed.

Fifth, one more traditional debate, that of *sequencing* has gained new policy relevance for the contemporary world. Should institution building precede or conclude systemic transformation? Those believing in social engineering would opt for the first, those adhering to trial and error for the second option. Russia usually counts as a case for the first, China as the second, thus the issue seems to have been settled for some time. But it seems to be open again by now, with the marked and irreversible decline in the economic performance of mainland China.

In short, conventional wisdom went as follows in 1990–2010. Trial and error is superior to social engineering. The People's Republic of China with its profoundly a-theoretical, experimental approach has long been perceived by many a showcase for success. This is no longer the case in the post-Covid period, but not only and not primarily because of the epidemic-induced slowdown (Csaba 2020). By contrast, Russia shows that plans designed on computer remain dreams once experience disproves them, or if they turn out to be too abstract or be heeded.

In the current decade Russian economic performance deteriorated, not least owning to the stagnation of oil prices on global markets. The country has though recovered from the recession of 2015–16, but GDP growth remained sluggish, below two per cent p.a. in the subsequent periods. Retail sales peaked in 2010 and never regained that level in the following decade. The economic base for the revival of Russian great power interests, as illustrated by the annexation of Crimea in 2014 and the involvement in helping to victory Syrian president Bashir Assad in 2019 render the Russian experience contentious. Chinese slowdown, on the other hand, points toward the limitations to institution-less evolution.

If we are to consider true success stories, from Estonia to Israel and Ireland we do see a considerable degree of *social engineering, perhaps in reverse*. This term tended to be retained for move toward more state-managed options in the economy. In the above-listed cases, the move of the shuttle is though opposite, still it would be hard to deny: most of the changes were man-made, or at least initiated by human action. Is not deregulation or fiscal balancing not a form of social engineering?

In all of the above cases, our broader approach seems to have been substantiated. Particularly if we take the Baltics and Ireland social consensus is shown to play a formative role in laying the groundwork for sustaining solid policies (Győrffy 2018, pp. 79–112). By contrast, derailments in countries like Cyprus, Portugal, and Spain have been shown (i.a in op.cit., pp. 113—146) to be rooted in lacking social support for sensible economic policies and the actors aiming at implementation of these, lacking trust, and the ensuing weak functioning of available institutions, no matter how nicely elaborate the latter might have been.

We are, to a large degree, moving in darkness in our quest for the determinants for social trust and efficient institutions. This is an issue for political science, social psychology and international relations, sociology and media studies to study and come up with *propositions more subtle than the usual suspects,* as 'credibility of government' and 'coherence in institutional setup,' long in use in the literature on structural adjustment.

Conclusion

We have not promised to solve the one million dollar quiz question at the very outset. Thus, we are somewhat relieved. Mission accomplished in the sense that we produced an overview of the competing approaches to institutions and their role in producing change for the better and for the majority, as is usual in the policy-relevant literature. We have shown some lines of reasoning to be more convincing, more robust than others. Still, *most of the big questions remain open* and require further study, both empirically grounded and theoretically oriented.

One of the most intriguing issues that we dodged may be the definition: what counts as an institution? We have much less trouble with the formal ones and more with the informal ones. How far should we include habits, customs, perceptions, and beliefs especially in our new IT-dominated world, where the borderline between perceived and real, virtual and material is about to disappear, or become permeable at least? *How can we test if certain claims hold true or not, especially on the role of non-material factors* and other items, usually outside the scope of economic analysis? In short, there is a lot to be reflected about in more than one plane of research.

If we are to wrap up what is to be taken home from this particular overview of the evolution of global thinking on the role of institutions in fostering change for the better (meaning well-being for as many people as possible) we may come to a somewhat agnostic finding. Institutions do matter, as the limitation of institution-less pragmatic evolution—in China—and of weak institutions—as in Russia, Latin America, and Sub-Saharan Africa—indicate. There is no sustaining progress in human conditions without good quality institutions (quality not being standardized, nor subject to quantitative indicators, to the regret of much of the profession). On the other hand, our review of the potential and actual hollowing of institutions caution against believing they are everything. *Institutions as outcomes of human action do not act in empty space*[5]: they are surrounded by values, discourses, policies, collective action, natural

[5] This insight was elaborated first and in a most profound manner by the now forgotten classic of Ludwig von Mises (1949/2012).

and social environment which may be favorable or harmful to their functioning, and not least complemented or contradicted by policies employing them.

Thus, we are well-advised to pay due attention to the nature, coherence, inclusiveness, and the overall quality of institutions if we are to see economic betterment in service of most people. On the other hand, we should avoid the naïve belief in the omnipotence of good quality institutions, as if they were to save the strenuous efforts of trials and errors in the process of economic change.

In a recent authoritative volume (Nayyar 2019) disciples of the 1974 Nobel winner Gunnar Myrdal have asked the intriguing question: how come that their mentor, a great thinker in many disciplines, could get Asian development so wrong in his opus magnum, the three volumes strong Asian Drama, with its doomsday vision of the continent? Without pre-empting the richness of the tour d'horizon, we may approvingly cite the insights by Evans and Heller (2019), who underscore diverse national arrangements, conditioned by local endowments, translate into distinct qualities in institutional development. The latter, in turn, may and indeed must be invoked as immediate explanatory factors for economic outcomes in the longer run.

So what may be generalized for broad economic theory? The *developmental state is alive and well*, not least because it has been able to move away from its militaristic and exclusively top-down approach of picking winners. A *new brand of developmentalism* emerged in Korea and Singapore on the one hand, and in India and Indonesia on the other. They do not follow the 'one-size-fits-all' type of theorizing. Instead, they seem to be ruled by a fair degree of pragmatism. On a higher level of abstraction: they both succeed in *integrating institutional factors in the series of explanatory variables* of economic change, and that in a manner consistent with facts and fundamentals of institutionalism alike.

References

Acemoglu, D., Robinson, J. A. (2012): Why Nations Fail: the Origins of Power, Prosperity and Poverty. New York: Crown Publishers.

Appel, H., Oreinstein, M. (2018): From Triumph to Crisis: Neoliberal Economic Reform in Postcommunist Countries. Cambridge (UK) and New York: Cambridge University Press.

Aslund, A. (1991): Gorbachev's Struggle for Economic Reform. London: Rances Pinter Publishers.
Bird, G., Mandilaras, H. (2012): Is there a Beijing Consensus on International Macroeconomic Policy? World Development, 40(10): 1933–43.
Csaba, L. (2009): Orthodoxy, Renewal and Complexity in Contemporary Economics. Zeitschrift für Staats—und Europawissenschaften, 7(1): 51–82.
Csaba, L. (2019): Unorthodoxy in Hungary: An Illiberal Success Story? Post-Communist Economies. https://doi.org/10.1080/14631377.2019.1641949.
Csaba, L. (2020): China at the Crossroads. Acta Oeconomica, 70(1): 1–13.
Eichengreen, B. (2002): Financial Crises and What to do About Them. Oxford-New York: Oxford University Press.
Eichengreen, B., Park, D. H., Shin, K. H. (2014): Growth Slowdowns Redux: New Evidence on the Middle Income Trap. Japan and the World Economy, 32(1): 65–84.
Ellman, M. (2019): 30 Years After the Fall of the Berlin Wall. Virtual Special Issue in Cambridge Journal of Economics, April, 2019. Available: https://academic.oup.com/cje/pages/berlin_wall.
Evans, P., Heller, P. (2019): The State in Development. In: Nayyar, D. (2019), pp. 109–135.
Gordon, R. J. (2016): The Rise and Fall of American Growth. Princeton (NJ): Princeton University Press.
Grabel, I. J. (2017): When Things Don't Fall Apart: Global Financial Governance in an Age of Productive Incoherence. Cambridge (MA)—London: The MIT Press.
Győrffy, D. (2018): Trust and Crisis-Management in the European Union. London: Palgrave Macmillan.
Kang, N., Paus, E. (2019): The Political Economy of Middle Income Trap: The Challenges Advancing Innovation Capabilities in Latin America, Asia and Beyond. Journal of Development Studies, 56(4): 651–656.
Kolodko, W. (2000): From Shock to Therapy. Oxford—New York (NY): Oxford University Press.
Kornai, J. (1992): The Socialist System: The Political Economy of Communism. Oxford: Clarendon Press.
Lámfalussy, A. (2000): Financial Crises in Emerging Markets. New Haven (CT): Yale University Press.
Lardy, N. (2019): The State Strikes Back: The End of Economic reform in China? Washington (DC): Peterson Institute for International Economics Press.
Magyar, B. ed. (2019): Stubborn Structures. Budapest—New York (NY): CEU Press.
McCloskey, D. (2006–2016): The Bourgoise Era, vol. I–III. Chicago (Ill): University of Chicago Press.

Nayyar, D. ed. (2019): Asian Transformations. Oxford—New York (NY): Oxford University Press.

North, D. (2005): Understanding the Process of Economic Change. Princeton (NJ): Princeton University Press.

Olson, M. (2000): Power and Prosperity: Outgrowing Communist and Capitalist Dictatorships. New York (NY): Basic Books.

Polterovich, V. (2019): Institutional Trap. In: The New Palgrave—A Dictionary of Economics—3rd, online edition. Cham: Springer International, online edition, last retrieved on 12 November, 2019.

Sakwa, R. (2019): Russia's Futures. London: Polity Press.

Shiller, R. (2019): Narrative Economics: How Stories Go Viral and Drive Major Economic Events. Princeton (NJ): Princeton University Press.

Szanyi, M. ed. (2020): Searching for the Best Master. Budapest—New York (NY): CEU Press.

Tanzi, V. (2018): Termites of the State: Why Complexity Leads to Inequality. Cambridge and New York (NY): Cambridge University Press.

Vollrath, D. (2020): Fully Grown. Chicago (Ill): University of Chicago Press.

von Mises, L. (1949/2012): Human Action: A Treatise on Economics. Mansfield Center (CT): Martino Publishing. pp. 143–200.

Williamson, J. ed. (1994): The Political Economy of Policy Reform. Washington (DC): Institute of International Economics.

Winiecki, J. (1993): Knowledge of Soviet-type Economy and "Heterodox" Stabilization-Based Outcomes in Eastern Europe. Weltwirtschaftliches Archiv, 129(2): 384–410.

Xu, Ch. (2011): The Fundamental Institutions of China's Reform and Development. Journal of Economic Literature, 49(4): 1076–1151.

CHAPTER 3

On Big Cycles in Development of Global Capitalism

Andrei Yakovlev

Introduction

In the beginning of 2020 the *Foreign Affairs* magazine published a large collection of articles by prominent economists and political scientists under the common title "Future of Capitalism." These articles illustrate the recognition by representatives of the social sciences mainstream of the crisis in the global capitalism model that shaped out in the last

The article was prepared within the framework of the Basic Research Program at the National Research University Higher School of Economics (HSE). The author is grateful to Amanda Zadorian, Viktor Polterovich, Mikhail Komin, Andrei Melville, and Ilja Viktorov as well as to participants of the 4th conference "The Role of State in the Variety of Capitalism" in Budapest in November 2018 for their comments and remarks.

A. Yakovlev (✉)
Institute for Industrial and Market Studies (IIMS), National Research University—Higher School of Economics, Moscow, Russia
e-mail: ayakovlev@hse.ru

T. Gerőcs and J. Ricz (eds.), *The Post-Crisis Developmental State*, International Political Economy Series,
https://doi.org/10.1007/978-3-030-71987-6_3

two decades of the twentieth century, based on the arguments about the 'end of history' against the background of the victory of liberal ideology (Fukuyama 1989) and criticized during a long time only by radical left-wing intellectuals (Wallerstein 2000).

Economic uncertainty, terrorism and political instability, a rise in nationalism, and continuous eruption of new armed conflicts evidence that the model of global neoliberal capitalism in its present-day form is near exhaustion. What prevents it from collapse? First of all, a high level of economic and financial interdependence of countries—one of the products of globalization. Other deterring factors are the need to ensure collective security and resist terrorist threats, and control the environmental risks. But all the above are merely "protective functions" which do not remove tension factors and do not drive any progress toward a new model.

There is another important factor for development of capitalism: new technologies innovations related to digital economy and Industry 4.0. Continuous information technology (IT) innovations bring about the emergence of new players and new forms of organization of business. Many national states integrated in global economy lost their sovereignty in the field of economic policy and many independent firms integrated in global value chains lost their autonomy in decision-making. At the same time, the role of urban agglomerations as centers of economic activity is growing. These shifts are associated with vast opportunities but at the same time they generate high risks. New technologies posing a threat to existing players and incumbent organizations will, most probably, cause their resistance with resort to both economic and political "power" levers. This alternative has another important feature: it objectively provides more opportunities to developed countries with their large markets and a more sophisticated legal, economic, and technological infrastructure. At the same time, the readiness of new players to somehow "share" their gains is quite doubtful. This means a fresh increase in polarization between rich and poor countries and creates new challenges for national governments and elites in countries of global (semi-)periphery.

The economic crisis triggered by the Covid-19 pandemic, mass-scale antiracist protests in the United States, a fresh aggravation of confrontation between the United States and China has only intensified the feeling of tension and indefiniteness that has been building up in the world economy for the past dozen years after the global financial crisis in 2008–2009. Criticism of the current model of global capitalism sounding today both from the left and from the right stirs heated debates about the relationship between economic deregulation and growing inequality, about the impact of new technologies and business models and controllability of major corporations by national governments, about a quest of a new balance in relations between developed and developing countries and the search for new developmental agenda. The main aim of this chapter is to understand the possible logic of the future changes of global capitalism in the context of the challenges it encounters.

Basic Definitions and General Trends in the Evolution of Models of Capitalism

After the book Hall and Soskice (2001) literature has traditionally been distinguishing two models of capitalism: liberal market economies (LME) and coordinated market economies (CME). At that, LME descriptions in the initial concept were based on the cases of the USA, UK, and other Anglo-Saxon countries, CME—on the cases of continental Europe and Japan. However, these two models were not relevant for many countries outside of this traditional core of the world economy. Therefore in 2000s, two other models were suggested in literature for emerging markets: dependent market economies (DME) with reference to the experience of small countries of East Central Europe (Nölke and Vliegenthart 2009) and state-led (or state-permeated) capitalism for largest developing countries including China, India, Brazil, and Russia (Lane 2008; Nölke 2018).

These four models explain the current differences in economic systems of most countries of the world, but they do not reflect the changes in these differences over time. Both DME model and state-led (or state-permeated) capitalism model have only shaped out during the past three decades against the background of a new wave of globalization. A wider historical outlook on the evolution of capitalism is needed to make an adequate assessment of the future of these models.

The formation of a particular model of capitalism in a certain country depends on its institutional, cultural, and geographic features, whereas its evolution is driven by universal patterns of economic development. In this context, an important contribution was made by the recent work Nölke and May (2019), presenting a classification of stages in the development of global capitalism (see Table 3.1).

Table 3.1 Stages in development of global capitalism according to (Nölke and May 2019)

Period	*"Label"*	*Type of capitalism*	*Ending point*
1900s–1920s	Progressive Era	Liberal	Ended by the Great Depression
1930s–1960s	Fordism	Organized	Ended by stagnation crisis of the 1970s
1970s–2000s	Financialization/Neoliberalism	Liberal	Ended by the Subprime/Fiscal Crisis?
2010s–...	...	Organized?	

According to Andreas Nölke and Christian May, development of the market economy during the past century has covered three consecutive stages: liberal capitalism of the early twentieth century associated with the "Progressive Era," organized capitalism of the 1930–1960s that originated from mass production technologies, and neoliberal capitalism of the late twentieth century resting on financial technologies and dominance of the financial sector. Every such change was accompanied by a serious system-wide crisis: the Great Depression in 1929–1933 and stagflation of the 1970s. The 2008–2009 global financial crisis is regarded as a turning point in the global economy's movement toward a new stage: "we may argue that we are witnessing the beginning of a new phase of capitalism that will be less liberal and more organized" (Nölke 2019, p. 143).

Such an approach reveals a variety of diverse models of capitalism in space and their evolution over time. However, it does not clarify the role and place of developmental state as a specific form of economic and social organization. To answer this question we should turn to the characteristics of developmental state.

The concept of "developmental state" (DS) was introduced for the first time in the analysis of catch-up development of East Asian countries (Johnson 1982; Amsden 1989) that peaked in the 1960–1970s, and was related to the stage of "organized capitalism" in terms of Nölke and May (2019). Robert Wade considers developmental state as a specific model of capitalism and contrasts it with neoliberal model. However, he sees the main distinctions of the DS model in an elite consensus on high priority given to achieving high and sustained economic growth rates; very high rates of investment to GDP; coordination of the catch-up strategy by the state; restrictions on the growth of consumption by the urban labor force and farmers; promotion of exports combined with the feasible replacement of imports and concentration of foreign exchange on imports of capital goods, intermediate goods, and raw materials instead of consumer goods (Wade 2017, pp. 525–526).

Therefore, the point at issue is not so much the institutional specificities of a market economy of a relevant country as the ideas and political agendas used by those countries' national elites at a concrete stage of their development. In other words, DS is not a model of capitalism but rather a set of economic policy measures providing less developed countries with an opportunity for catch-up development. Within this context, the assumption about "the end of the developmental state" in Korea and Taiwan is quite characteristic once they have reached the development level of OECD countries (Pirie 2018).

Moreover, a certain cycle in political request for DS can be presumed, similar to the cycles in capitalism development stages. Specifically, the failure of attempts to repeat East Asian success stories in other developing countries[1] has sparked profound skepticism among economists in respect of active industrial policy. Consequently, the ideology of the liberal phase in development of capitalism that began in the 1980s implied that integration of the national economies in the global market on the basis of liberalization of trade and removal of barriers to capital flows would create the necessary conditions for economic growth of developing countries.

In reality, however, the gains from the new wave of globalization spread quite unevenly. The main beneficiaries were multinational companies (MNC) playing the lead role in the management of global value chains (GVC) with headquarters located in developed countries. Only a few major developing countries managed to swing the balance of cost and benefits in their favor as they retained control on the capital flow and currency exchange rates against the advice of international financial institutions and therefore remained capable to act strategically in bargaining with MNC. The majority of developing countries, on the contrary, are disappointed with the liberal policy of the past decades, and this explains their growing interest in the developmental agenda. Therefore, for the

[1] As noted Dani Rodrik (2009, p. 50) "for every South Korea, there are many Zaires where policy activism is an excuse for politicians to steal and plunder."

logic of forming different models of capitalism and change in economic policy priorities instead of international comparisons valid at a specific point in time there is a need to analyze capitalism models via intertemporal (historical) comparisons aiming to define and characterize historical phases (rather than simply building valid models for certain countries or world regions).

The change of phases does not proceed according to a strict sequence. Elements of a new stage emerge or "sprout" from the inside of the old one. This is what happened with institutions of state capitalism in Italy in the 1920s or with radical liberal experiments in the Chilean economy in mid-1970s. Presumably, state-permeated capitalism started taking shape in large developing countries in the 1990s precisely in this logic (Nölke et al. 2019). This new model can be perceived as a response to global dominance of liberal capitalism and a possible reaction to the manifested development limits within DME model formed in East Europe after the collapse of the Soviet bloc (Nölke and Vliegenthart 2009; Myant 2018).

Of no less importance is the recognition of the fact that the next phase of capitalism will be an organized, but not necessarily a social one (Nölke and May 2019, p. 31). In this respect the opinions of Andreas Nölke and Christian May coincide with the judgments of Branko Milanovic, a well-known expert on inequality analysis. In his latest book on the future of capitalism he compares two models (Milanovic 2019). The first one is liberal capitalism represented first of all by the United States and Western Europe.[2] The second one is a state-led, political model of capitalism, which is exemplified by China but also surfaces in other parts of Asia as well as in some countries of Europe and Africa.[3] However, Milanovic believes there is a risk of plutocratic convergence of these two models—if liberal capitalist systems fail to address the problem of growing social inequality. In my opinion, precisely this feeling of inequality—not only in social but also in geopolitical terms—is one of the factors of new request for DS. The critical role in implementing this request will again—like 50 years ago—be played by incentives and time horizon of elites as well as quality of government and state capacity to implement the set of relevant policies.

[2] In terms of VoC approach it will include LME, CME, and DME.

[3] It is close to state-permeated capitalism.

However, to understand the way the forms of organization of economic activity will be changing within the scope of this common transformation vector, we need to answer several additional questions: What are the advantages of the current phase of global capitalism? What actors can be considered as its drivers? What challenges confronted capitalist system and to what extent is organized capitalism capable of meeting these challenges?

Key Advantages, Drivers, and Challenges of the Current Phase of Global Capitalism

Throughout centuries on end, capitalism, resting on trade and finance, coexisted with other noncapitalist forms of economic activity in the industry and agriculture. Capitalism became truly global only in the twentieth century due to high-throughput technologies and mass production (Piore and Sabel 1984; Langlois 2003). Owing to dramatic increase in labor productivity, these technological changes led to the ousting of other forms of production organization from industry, the services sector and agriculture and ended in global dominance of capitalism. Another factor of globalization was the need to expand markets for the sale of mass-produced goods, as already at the turn of the twentieth century the national markets became too narrow for major companies.

However, transition to mass production had other consequences as well. In particular, it required considerably larger upfront investment in technologies and equipment leading to growth in the share of capital investment in the overall costs structure and entailing greater losses of entrepreneurs during the periods of cyclic crises that characterized the liberal "laissez-faire" capitalism in the second half of the nineteenth to early twentieth centuries. These destructive consequences manifested themselves especially strongly during the Great Depression in the 1930s. The crisis demonstrated the need for state interference in the economy—involving regulation of banks and financial markets and granting basic social guarantees to workers. Higher government expenses and broader rights of trade unions followed by growing share of wages in the GDP structure and formation of a wide middle class became an important factor of supporting demand and an incentive for further boost of mass production.

This difference of the phase of global organized capitalism consisted in location of production in the most developed countries. The other countries (described now as a "Global South") acted generally as a source of raw materials. In addition, demand was also concentrated in developed countries—due to the emergence there of a wide circle of solvent mass product consumers. The positive effects of this model based on market regulation and cooperation between labor and capital in developed countries, leading to stabilization of the economic situation, transpired especially vividly in the 1950–1960s. However, quite soon its constraints also became obvious. In particular, the mass production was faced with objective limitations, as by the end of the 1960s practically every family in developed countries already owned a set of basic consumer goods (a house or apartment, refrigerator, television set, car, etc.). Global organized capitalism based on mass production needed access to developing markets to ensure its further growth. It also needed a significant cut in costs and prices to continue doing business with traditional consumers in developed markets.

Satisfying this demand of global capitalism for further expansion was possible due to a combination of several factors including intensive development of standardization and unification of products and components and implementation of information and communication technologies (ICT) providing the possibility of remote control of the production processes quality. A significant role was played also by development of transport networks and lowering the costs of products and components haulage. Finally, another extremely important factor was deregulation of global trade that began in the 1980s, including the lowering of import tariffs, liberalization of currency exchange and capital flows, lifting administrative restrictions to direct investments from developed countries (Hillman and Ursprung 1996; Wacziarg and Horn Welch 2008).

These changes in economic policy that became possible due to the preceding technological innovations have driven the transition from organized to new liberal stage of global capitalism. An important part of this process was the development of new business models relying on global value chains (Humphrey and Schmitz 2001; Gereffi 2005). A fundamental organizational innovation was the separation of individual stages of the mass production process that previously were concentrated in one country and one company. Now these stages became dispersed. The starting and final elements of the GVC (basic and applied research and development—R&D, design, branding, advertising, marketing, specialized logistics, after-sales services) generally remained under direct control of multinational companies (MNC) based in developed countries. At the same time, most of the manufacturing and standardized services were outsourced, as a rule, to subcontractors in developing countries.

With relocation of production facilities to other countries MNC could reduce payroll costs and related taxes. Also it enhanced the flexibility of business processes because refusal from the production of certain products no longer involved obligatory unemployment benefits for fired workers. The result was a considerable cheapening of mass products. They became available to new consumers in countries of (semi-)periphery while traditional consumers in developed "core" countries could afford to replace their old cars, household appliances, and other durables much more frequently. Simultaneously, former socialist countries, including China, started opening in the late 1980s. For MNC this meant access to cheap raw materials and cheap labor, as well as new sales markets. This made possible further mass production and continued expansion of global liberal capitalism. But these technological and organizational shifts brought about a change in the social base of capitalism.

Organized capitalism of the 1930–1960s rested on regulation of markets by the national governments and a balance between trade unions expressing collective interests of employees and business represented, first and foremost, by industrial companies that needed qualified workers and sustainably operating production facilities. In the 1980–1990s, technological and organizational shifts contributed to higher performance of production processes and accelerated economic growth all over the world that continued for nearly 20 years. The architecture of global governance started shaping out at the same time on the basis of International Monetary Fund (IMF), the World Bank, World Trade Organization (WTO), and regular G7 meetings.[4] This supported the feeling of global victory of ideas of liberal democracy.

Branko Milanovic wrote in his book in 2016 that from the social perspective globalization and liberalization processes in the past decades

[4] G7 or "group of seven" is the organization of 7 most developed countries including USA, UK, Germany, France, Italy, Japan, and Canada. Since mid-1970s their leaders meet at annual summits to discuss the key problems of economic development and coordinate their international activities. In 1998 Russia was invited to join this political forum but the membership of Russia was suspended after Crimea accession in 2014.

had two principal beneficiaries. The first group were representatives of the emerging middle class in large developing countries to which companies from developed market economies moved their production facilities. From 1988 to 2008 the incomes of the middle class in China, Vietnam, and Thailand have more than doubled (Milanovic 2016, p. 35). As a result, the global income inequality has dropped significantly from 0.70 in the 1990s to roughly 0.60 today (Milanovic 2020, p. 13). The second group consisted of owners and managers of major companies that govern the global value chains and accumulate the main benefits from implementing a new model of their organizations. The distribution and comparison of the entire 100% global income gain in 1988–2008 will show that 44% of the aggregate gain was received by 5% of the wealthiest people and 19% can be attributed to the richest 1% over half of whom, or 36 million people, were Americans (Milanovic 2016, p. 41).

If we consider the political and economic aspects, the beneficiaries were, firstly, large developing countries demonstrating in average considerably higher economic growth than developed countries and, secondly, major MNC whose economic potential has overwhelmed the governments of many countries. According to (Babic et al., 2017), in 2016 the list of 100 top players of the global economy included 29 countries and 71 companies. The American Walmart was 10th in the rating, which means that its annual revenue exceeded the gross national product of 20 out of the 29 countries on the list. The total revenue of all US companies on the list surpassed the GDP of any country, including the United States, and the total revenue of Chinese companies on the list was inferior only to the US GDP.

These processes brought about a change in the balance of forces that ensured relative social and political stability of capitalism since the late 1940s. In particular, workers' bargaining positions in negotiations with business have become much weaker, as unlike labor, capital has become more mobile making companies much less dependent on the offer of labor force in concrete national markets. As a result although global inequality between countries has lessened, social inequality within countries has grown. According to Branko Milanovic, the United States' Gini coefficient has risen from 0.35 in 1979 to about 0.45 in 2018. This increase in inequality within countries effects the more developed economies in the West due to the flight of manufacturing jobs and wage stagnation.

One of the consequences of production capacity relocation from developed to developing countries consisted in negative social phenomena.

Case and Deaton (2015) state that all-cause mortality rates among white non-Hispanic men and women in middle age stopped falling in the United States, and began to rise after 1998. That is largely accounted for by increasing death rates from drug and alcohol poisonings, suicide, chronic liver disease, and cirrhosis.

Nevertheless, until a certain point such negative trends did not cause acute social tension. On the one hand, the differences in consumption levels in developed countries were mitigated by stormy development of consumer credit (giving the middle class an opportunity to finance current consumption from future incomes). On the other hand, the dominance of liberal ideas in mass consciousness combined with sustainable economic growth created the impression that "everyone has a chance," suffice it to make an effort.

The global crisis in 2008–2009 became a turning point in perception of the existing liberal phase of global capitalism. Despite the differences in the forms of anti-crisis policy, the reaction to the crisis in all countries ultimately boiled down to "extinguishing the fire" by injecting money into the economy. The common goal was to maintain stability. Owing to this we have experienced a "global recession" instead of a "global depression." However, this was not accompanied with real changes in the overall models of organizing economic life including, inter alia, mass-scale tax evasion by MNC and their avoidance of other national regulation. The awareness of those imperfections and related risks led to a change in the expectation of firms and reach individuals. Under conditions of increased uncertainty many of them started refraining from investments in new projects. It, in turn, translated into considerable slowdown of growth paces in the wake of the crisis.

Slower economic dynamics had political implications. Growing polarization of society and absence of chances to advance their social status under new post-crisis conditions created negative expectations among active representatives of non-elite groups. These perceptions and especially perceived inequality—not the actual income distribution—correlates strongly with demand for redistribution and reported conflict between rich and poor (Gimpelson and Treisman 2018). The result was the buildup of social tension manifesting in different forms including Brexit in EU and Donald Trump's victory at the US presidential elections in 2016.

However, the circle of losers from the new model of liberal capitalism was not limited by representatives of the middle class. Many merchants and craftsmen in the Middle East and African countries where patriarchic relations dominated at the time of onset of a fresh wave of globalization lost their business and jobs. Some of these countries (including Afghanistan, Sudan, and Somali) could not blend into the new global world order and turned into failed states. The disadvantaged population of those countries was particularly strongly exposed to ideas of extremist religious factions and international terrorists who received support from fundamentalist elites in wealthy developing countries trying to resist the spread of "Western values."

A special role is played by the elites in big developing countries who gained significant economic benefits from the new wave of globalization but remained dissatisfied with their place and role in global decision-making. Those particular countries started implementing the model of state-permeated capitalism in the terms of Nölke et al. (2019) or political capitalism in the terms of Milanovic (2019). Some scholars define them as "rising powers" (Lee and Gereffi 2015).[5] These countries have developmentalist aspirations and their policy represents the shift toward organized capitalism. However, there is a question about the capacity of "rising powers" to manage all systemic imperfections inherited from the previous liberal phase of global capitalism.

Global Market and Limits of National-Level Organized Capitalism

During the first phase of organized capitalism in 1930–1960s, the governments of developed countries should confront large-scale political corruption and state capture typical of liberal capitalism of the early twentieth century (Olson 1965; Stigler 1971). They did it by leveraging the national legislation including antitrust regulation. Control on business within national borders allowed them to collect taxes and provide public goods and support the welfare state.

[5] The main attributes of "rising powers" are the large-scale, economic dynamism, deep involvement in international trade as well as the presence of strong state and an engagement between the public sector, private capital, and civil society (Navdi 2014, pp. 140–141).

Economic deregulation and liberalization of markets since the 1980s opened the possibilities for relocation of business activities to other jurisdictions. On the one hand, it boosted business efficiency (first of all, for major MNC governing GVC). However, on the other hand, it noticeably undermined the bargaining power of the national governments (especially in small countries) in their relations with the biggest MNC (Wade 2017). Under disappearance of the barriers to international capital flows and acute tax competition the national governments became much more limited in their capacity to restrict opportunism of MNC (including avoidance of environmental and other regulations). Moreover, the countries that will attempt to "close their borders" risk to lose in the competition struggle—not only because of capital flight but also because of the value chains becoming global. Achieving effective economies of scale in industry and the high-tech sector requires access to external markets even for medium-size companies, with a rare exception of a handful of the biggest countries.

Thus, there is contradiction between the market forces that have become global over the past 30 years and market regulation mechanisms that remain predominantly national. The possible response to this contradiction is regional economic integration. The European Union with its supranational market regulation mechanisms is the most progressive example of this sort. Other examples include ASEAN, the Trans-Pacific Partnership, the Eurasian Economic Union, and to a certain degree also the Belt and Road Initiative promoted by China since 2013. However, development of such integration mechanisms is a long-term process that does not proceed smoothly and requires constant coordination of interests of their participants. Even relative success of supranational associations (which has for a long time been the case with EU) does not solve the two other groups of problems generated by the contemporary model of liberal capitalism.

First one is ecology and climate change. Proper implementation of new ecological standards can be managed only through collective action of largest countries—but national elites in the United States and China are not ready to it. The second key problem underlying destabilization of the global capitalism is the growing inequality (Piketty 2014; Milanovic 2016). It is meaning not only about unequal distribution of incomes but much more about inequality of opportunities. However, as Andreas Nölke and Christian May note, the next phase of capitalism will be an organized, but not necessarily a social one. History has already seen such phenomena: in part, they compare the socially "embedded" form of the New Deal against the Fascist economic organization in Italy and Germany (Nölke and May 2019, p. 31). The same watershed is stressed by Branco Milanovic, describing the models of liberal meritocratic capitalism and political state-led capitalism and the risks of their plutocratic convergence (Milanovic 2020, p. 21).

Disintegration of global markets (promoted by some populists) is not the solution due to high interdependence of national economies. To manage the key problems of global capitalism there is a need for cooperation between countries at international level and between main elites at national level. What kind of factors can provide necessary incentives for such cooperation?

External Threats and New Ideas as a Factor of Development

National political and business elites are the main actors responsible for choosing development path and creation of relevant institutional environment. However very often they are driven by short-term selfish interests. Usually they got incentives to think strategically and to cooperate with each other only in the face of serious external or internal threats. It took two catastrophes—World War I and the Great Depression of 1929–1933—for the elites of developed countries to start reacting to the challenges of liberal stage of global capitalism in the early twentieth century. But these threats were not enough without alternatives. An important part of this story was the emergence of alternative social models directly opposing liberal democratic ideology: the proletarian dictatorship and planned economy in the Soviet Union and fascism in Italy and Germany.

In other words, to the military and geopolitical competition between world powers the twentieth century added one more important factor—ideological competition. The elites from capitalist countries needed to substantiate their adherence to the values opposing the other model of organization of economic and social life that relied on the communist ideology. For this purpose, the elites had to agree to self-restrictions and cooperation with other social groups in their countries, which has become key to development of social organized capitalism. At the international level, this ideological confrontation also stimulated cooperation with other countries adhering to the same ideology.

Now the world is at a similar stage. Like in the early twentieth century, the last liberal stage of global capitalism was associated with rapid development of technologies and economic growth but at the same time it brought about new geopolitical and social imbalances. Moreover, the current liberal stage in development of capitalism led to serious ecological problems. But the future calamities alone will not produce a sobering and sanative effect. The growth in the influence of right-wing populists with the support from the social groups perceiving themselves as losers from globalization was a consequence of devaluation of liberal ideas. However, migration restriction measures and raise in import tariffs, new preferences to big business, and increasing the state debt do not lift social tension. The problem is that in its opposition with right-wing populists the liberal camp focuses on identity politics with the protection of the rights of different minorities regarded as separate groups—instead of a search for and public promotion of solutions eliminating the root causes of the escalated inequality of opportunities (Fukuyama 2018).

It looks now like a trap but the solution can be found in new ideas on development. Rodrik (2014) showed that new ideas about policy can change the equilibrium of political outcomes—as new technologies are doing it in the economy. From this point of view, high attention should be paid to the ideas of "entrepreneurial state" and cooperation between public and private sector in the process of market creation (Mazzucato 2013, 2018). New economic growth opportunities emerge at the public/private sector boundaries. As a rule, such opportunities evolve in the course of experiments, by trial and error. This can be seen from the industrial policy experience of Chile (salmon breeding and wine production in the 1980–90s), Israel (launch of high-tech industry in the 1990s), and Malaysia (manufacture of computer parts in the 1990s and implementation of major infrastructural projects in the 2000s). These success stories show the way of progress toward the new developmental state. Just like 50 years ago, DS depends on a meritocratic bureaucracy with a strong sense of corporate identity and a dense set of institutionalized links to private elites (Evans 1989). But other aspects of new DS become much more important today: private–public dialogue and fair distribution of outcomes between all stakeholders participating in value creation. Another important feature is that the need for developmental state (increasingly perceived as "entrepreneurial state") is particularly acute today not only in developing but also in developed countries. As a matter of fact, often it is precisely developing countries that initiate new policy tools, which can be considered as elements of new DS.[6]

Another distinction from previous transitions to new stages in development of capitalism consists in the fact that throughout the twentieth century such transitions proceeded against the background of competition between blocs of countries that adopted different models of economic and social organization. East Asian developmental states in the 1960s, having embarked on a path of a market economy, took into account the experience of the centrally planned economy in the USSR. This experience was used even more actively by China in the 1980–1990s. However, following the collapse of the USSR and a last wave of globalization the world became integrated, and addressing the current problems has become possible not through competition of economic systems but only through cooperation between the largest developed and developing countries.

Global cooperation will require new ideas capable to unite people in the name of their common future. But a no lesser role will be played by another factor. As always at the watersheds in history, the personalities of leaders will play a tremendous role. And this means that compromises will be possible if people capable of conducting dialogue and, if necessary, resisting vested interests of their national elites come to power in the biggest countries of the world at the same time.

References

Amsden, A. (1989) *Asia's Next Giant: South Korea and Late Industrialization*. N. Y.: Oxford University Press.

Babic, M., Fichtner, J., Heemskerk, E. M. (2017) States Versus Corporations: Rethinking the Power of Business in International Politics. *The International Spectator*, Vol. 52, no. 4, pp. 20–43.

Case, A., Deaton, A. (2015) Rising Morbidity and Mortality in Midlife among White Non-Hispanic Americans in the 21st Century. *Proceedings of the National Academy of Sciences*, Vol. 112, no. 49, pp. 15078–15083.

Evans, Peter B. (1989) Predatory, Developmental, and Other Apparatuses: A Comparative Political Economy Perspective on the Third World State.

[6] For more details, see Sabel and Jordan (2015) on new mechanisms of implementing large socially important projects in Malaysia.

Sociological Forum, Vol. 4, No. 4, Special Issue: Comparative National Development: Theory and Facts for the 1990s (Dec. 1989), pp. 561–587.

Fukuyama, F. (1989) The End of History? *The National Interest*, Vol. 16 (Summer 1989), pp. 3–18.

Fukuyama F. (2018) Against Identity Politics: The New Tribalism and the Crisis of Democracy. *Foreign Affairs*, Vol. 97 (no. 5, Sept–Oct. 2018), pp. 90–115.

Gereffi, G. (2005) The Global Economy: Organization, Governance, and Development. In: Smelser N. J., Swedberg R. (eds) *The Handbook of Economic Sociology*. New York, NY: Princeton University Press, chapter 8, pp. 160–182.

Gimpelson, V., & Treisman, D. (2018) Misperceiving Inequality. *Economics and Politics*, Vol. 30, no. 1, pp. 27–54.

Hall, P. A., & Soskice, D. eds. (2001) *Varieties of Capitalism: The Institutional Foundations of Comparative Advantage*. Oxford: Oxford University Press.

Hillman, A. L., & Ursprung, H. W. (1996) The Political Economy of Trade Liberalization in the Transition. *European Economic Review*, Vol. 40, no. 3–5, pp. 783–794.

Humphrey, J., & Schmitz, H. (2001) Governance in Global Value Chains. *IDS Bulletin*, Vol. 32, no. 3, pp. 19–29.

Johnson, C. (1982) *MITI and the Japanese Miracle: The Growth of Industrial Policy, 1925–75*. Stanford, CA: Stanford University Press.

Lane, D. (2008) From Chaotic to State-Led Capitalism. *New Political Economy*, Vol. 13, no. 2, pp. 177–184.

Langlois, R. N. (2003) The Vanishing Hand: The Changing Dynamics of Industrial Capitalism. *Industrial and Corporate Change*, Vol. 12, no. 2, pp. 351–385.

Lee, J., & Gereffi, G. (2015) Global Value Chains, Rising Power Firms and Economic and Social Upgrading. *Critical Perspectives on International Business*, Vol. 11, no. 3/4, pp. 319–339.

Mazzucato, M. (2013) *The Entrepreneurial State: Debunking Public vs. Private Sector Myths*. London: Anthem Press.

Mazzucato, M. (2018) *The Value of Everything: Making and Taking in the Global Economy*. London: Allen lane.

Milanovic, B. (2016) *Global Inequality: A New Approach for the Age of Globalization*. Cambridge, MA: Harvard University Press.

Milanovic, B. (2019) *Capitalism, Alone: The Future of the System That Rules the World*. Belknap Press of Harvard University Press.

Milanovic, B. (2020) The Clash of Capitalisms: The Real Fight for the Global Economy's Future. *Foreign Affairs*, Vol. 99, no. 1 (January-February 2020), pp. 10–21.

Myant, M. (2018) Dependent capitalism and the middle-income trap in East Central Europe. *International Journal of Management and Economics*, Vol. 54, no. 4, pp. 291–303.

Nölke, A. (2018) Dependent Versus State-Permeated Capitalism: Two Basic Options for Emerging Markets. *International Journal of Management and Economics*, Vol. 54, no. 4, pp. 269–282.

Nölke, A. (2019) Comparative Capitalism. In: Shaw T., Mahrenbach L., Modi R., Yi-chong X. (eds) *The Palgrave Handbook of Contemporary International Political Economy*. Series: Palgrave Handbooks in IPE. Palgrave Macmillan, London, pp. 135–151.

Nölke, A., Vliegenthart A. (2009) Enlarging the Varieties of Capitalism: The Emergence of Dependent Market Economies in East Central Europe. *World Politics*, Vol. 61, no. 4, pp. 670–702.

Nölke, A., May C. (2019) Liberal Versus Organised Capitalism: A Historical-Comparative Perspective. In: Gerőcs T., Szanyi M. (eds) *Market Liberalism and Economic Patriotism in the Capitalist World-System*. International Political Economy Series. Cham:P Palgrave Macmillan, pp. 21–42.

Nölke, A., ten Brink, T., May, C., Claar, S. (2019) *State-permeated Capitalism in Large Emerging Economies*. RIPE Series in Global Political Economy. Routledge.

Olson, M. (1965) *The Logic of Collective Action: Public Goods and the Theory of Croups*. Cambridge, MA: Harvard University Press.

Piketty, T. (2014) *Capital in the Twenty-First Century*. Cambridge, MA: Harvard University Press.

Piore, M. J., Sabel, C. F. (1984) *The Second Industrial divide*. New York, NY: Basic Books.

Pirie, I. (2018) Korea and Taiwan: The Crisis of Investment-Led Growth and the End of the Developmental State. *Journal of Contemporary Asia*, Vol. 48, no. 1, pp. 133–158.

Rodrik, D. (2009) *One Economics, Many Recipes: Globalization, Institutions, and Economic Growth*. Princeton, NJ: Princeton University Press.

Rodrik, D. (2014) When Ideas Trump Interests: Preferences, Worldviews, and Policy Innovations. *Journal of Economic Perspectives*, Vol. 28, no. 1, pp. 189–208.

Sabel, C., Jordan, L. (2015) Doing, Learning, Being: Some Lessons Learned from Malaysia's National Transformation Program. Washington, DC: World Bank.

Stigler G. J. (1971). The Theory of Economic Regulation. *The Bell Journal of Economics and Management Science*, Vol. 2, no. 1, pp. 3–21.

Wacziarg, R., Horn Welch, K. (2008) Trade Liberalization and Growth: New Evidence. *The World Bank Economic Review*, Vol. 22, no. 2, pp. 187–231.

Wade, R. H. (2017) The Developmental State: Dead or Alive? *Development and Change*, Vol. 49, no. 2, pp. 518–546.

Wallerstein I. (2000) Globalization or the Age of Transition? A Long-Term View of the Trajectory of the World-System. *International Sociology*, Vol. 15, no. 2, pp. 249–265.

CHAPTER 4

Catching-Up Opportunities of East-Central European States in the Context of Technology Cycles

Miklós Szanyi

Introduction

Countries of East-Central Europe (ECE) shared important systemic legacies that positioned them somewhere between the West (Atlantic model of capitalism) and East, Southeast in Europe (Byzantine model of Russia and the Ottoman Turkey). Periods of rather campaign-like modernizations, taking over Atlantic institutions, social order, and production technology were mixed with periods impressed by motives of the other two models (Szűcs 1983; Szanyi 2020). However, ECE countries usually compared themselves and their level of development with the West and aimed to catch up even if not by means of copying the Atlantic model.

M. Szanyi (✉)
Institute of Finance and Foreign Economic Relations, Faculty of Economics and Business Administration, Szeged University and Institute of World Economics, Centre for Economic and Regional Studies, Szeged and Budapest, Hungary
e-mail: szanyi.miklos@krtk.hu

T. Gerőcs and J. Ricz (eds.), *The Post-Crisis Developmental State*, International Political Economy Series,
https://doi.org/10.1007/978-3-030-71987-6_4

In analytical papers the issue of catching-up is usually restricted to the measurement of convergence of one or another development measure. Nevertheless, these results provide important information also for more complex comparative analyses of different economic systems. The classic East-Asian developmental state experience, for example, is often cited in government rhetoric. ECE governments try to justify the increased state economic involvement with the success stories. Thus, it is highly relevant to compare the process of convergence with changes and differences in some internal factors of economic models or the modifications of external conditions. These insights may provide information about the limited applicability of the developmental state models in other regions and periods of time. In this sense most relevant for the ECE countries could be intensive convergence with the West-European benchmark countries. Such convergence would then mean success of their internal institutional solutions compared to others. Similarly, successful convergence in a given type of external factor conditions means better endowments for economic and social progress. In this paper the historic convergence performance of the ECE region is interpreted in the framework of technology cycles.

The main question is whether the region's socioeconomic model (which is a mix of elements from other more fundamental European systems) performs better in the periods of accelerating technological development or can benefit rather from the widespread deployment phase of cutting-edge technologies? Quick technological development requires massive investments in innovation inputs (mainly human development). The business utilization of new technologies on the other hand requires capital investments in production capacities and adequate supply of skilled labor. Quick technological development provides unique opportunities to leapfrog development stages because much of the sunk costs of preceding technology applications can be spared. On the other hand, the technology deployment periods provide opportunities of large-scale capital accumulation from the evolving big business, provided the countries are plugged in the international division of labor. Obviously, the two technology development phases require different endowments. But they can be connected over time as it is shown by the few successful international catching-up stories (the East-Asian tigers, Ireland, Finland, or historically Japan, Germany, or the USA).

The right measure of development success is always historic. The main issue is if countries can launch an accelerated but still sustainable development path that will boost their economies and place them into the club of higher developed counterparts. This paper compares ECE convergence patterns with highly developed West-European countries' average figures. The Maddison database provides the necessary data for the historic period (1870–2016), which is divided into 7 shorter, a few decades-long sections that are adjusted to technological life cycles. The paper evaluates the ECE convergence performance in these shorter periods and draws some conclusions whether accelerating technological progress or rather the more widespread utilization of new technologies provided better opportunities for catching-up.

The section is organized as follows. First the convergence measurement method is briefly summarized which is based on the Jánossy concept. Ferenc Jánossy was a Hungarian economist who analyzed historic development patterns and differentiated between short- and medium-term quick recoveries (reconstructions) and longer term sustainable development trend lines. In the second part the historic period between 1870 and 2016 is sequenced according to the technological development features. The main part of the paper evaluates the ECE countries' convergence performance in the 7 sections of global technological development. Finally, the results are summarized and conclusions are drawn.

The Measurement of Convergence

In this paper, six East-Central European countries' per capita GDP averages are compared to the average indices of ten highly developed West-European countries. The so-called Jánossy trend lines are calculated to show long-term tendencies of development (see: Szanyi and Szabó 2020). These trend lines are connecting the local maximum points of the per capita GDP measures as an enveloping curve. They are interpreted as long-term development potentials. The actual figures are below this trend line. Jánossy (2016/1971) interpreted swings in historic development trends as temporary deviations caused by political or economic shocks. The negative impacts of the shocks were counterbalanced by accelerated growth of the succeeding recovery periods. But quick recovery lasted only until the historic trend line was achieved, then development pace was reduced to the "usual" level. Obviously, absolute convergence among countries or country groups happens if the slope of their historic development trend lines differs, as it is shown in Fig. 4.1. Here the Western benchmark countries' average is taken over by a group of selected successfully catching-up countries (Finland, Austria, and Greece). The six ECE

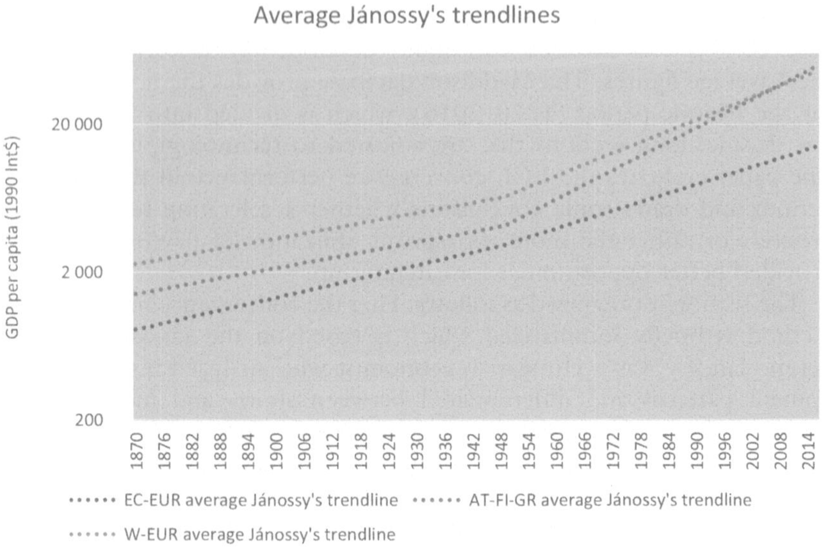

Fig. 4.1 Average Jánossy's trendlines (*Source* Own construction based on Maddison project database 2018)

countries show moderate catching-up in the first period and virtually no convergence after the Second World War.

The literature on economic convergence (for a good summary see: Monfort 2008) distinguishes absolute and conditional convergence. Absolute convergence is achieved as seen in Fig. 4.1 if the per capita GDP indices of a country catch up with the similar figures of more developed ones: the distance between them disappears. Conditional convergence on the other hand means closing the gap between the actual figures and countries' own long-term development trend. In this paper, Jánossy's historic trend lines are used as the basis for this comparison. Conditional convergence is obviously a less rigorous condition. Catching-up in development by definition means narrowing the development gap that can happen if the slopes of the long-term development trend lines continuously differ in favor of the less developed country.

As is seen in Fig. 4.2 the slopes of the 7 periods vary. In some periods they exceed the slope of the ECE region' historic trend line, in others they do not: in these later periods for sure no convergence occurred, since the

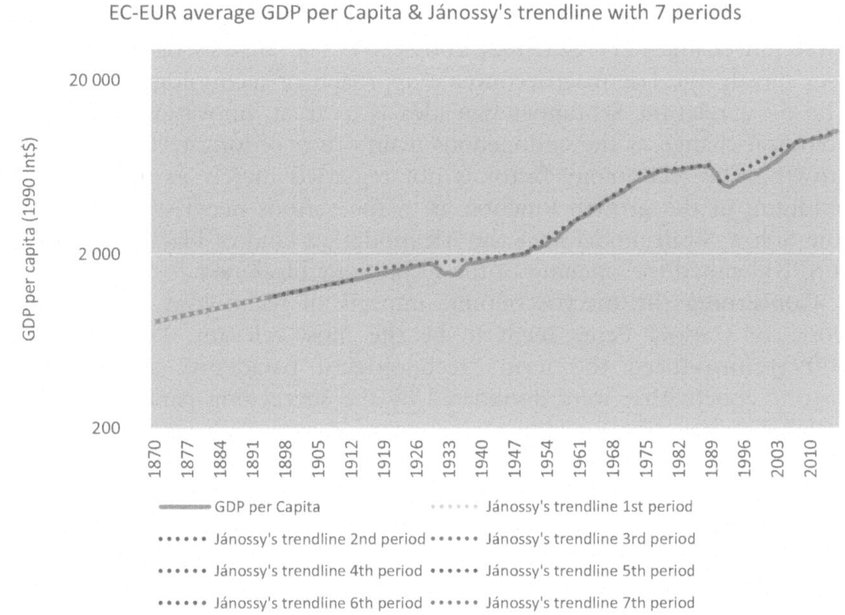

Fig. 4.2 EC-EUR average GDP per Capita and Jánossy's trendline with 7 periods (*Source* Own construction based on Maddison project database 2018)

historic trend line of the region was more or less parallel with the West-European benchmark. The slopes of the 7-section trend lines and the 2-section historic one are included in Table 4.4 for the ECE, Western developed, and the selected successfully catching-up countries.

Time Sequencing According to the Technology Cycles

The concept of technology cycles was developed at the Science Policy Research Unit at Sussex University. Work there covered a most comprehensive range of evolutionary theories of technology change and innovation from microeconomic aspects (Nelson 1981; Nelson and Winter 1977; Dosi 1988; Lundvall 1988; Pavitt 1999) through industry life cycles and market development (Abernathy and Utterback 1978; Dosi 1982; Dosi and Nelson 2013; Rosenberg 1982; Freeman 1982; Mowery and Rosenberg 1979) to the macroeconomic impacts of technological paradigm changes (Perez 2002, 2009a, b). The analysis of this section uses mostly the last macroeconomic approach of technological change. The most relevant Schumpeterian idea is to treat innovation and technological change as the endogenous main driver of long-term economic growth. The technology factor is not regarded merely as unexplained residuum of the growth function as in the various neoclassical theories (the Solow-Swan model later the AK model), a kind of black box. Work at SPRU aimed the opening of the technology black box.

Concerning the macroeconomic impacts of technology change the works of Carlota Perez seem to be the most relevant. Perez (2002, 2009a) introduced the term "technological paradigm" and defined historic epochs that were dominated by the succeeding paradigms. The switch between two paradigms was regarded as a deep rooting process of changes not only in technology, but also in economic structure, relevant communication, transportation and energy supply networks, changes in economically successful business concepts, and the institutional, regulatory, and legal frames of business conduct. Such fundamental changes could easily lead to major changes in international power relations, since the leading economies of one paradigm found the paradigm shift very burdensome due to high sunk costs in the old technology and failed to support technological renewal. This feature could support the leapfrogging of various countries which took the lead in the early phase of the development process of the new technologies. Table 4.1 contains some basic information about the five major historic technology paradigms.

The technological paradigms' life cycle consists of two phases. Following Nelson and Winter (1982) the evolutionary theory originates a systemic increase of innovative activities from the intensifying search of the firms for new business solutions in periods of economic slowdown. This is the time when the old technological paradigm's development potentials are exhausted. They usually hit a physical barrier of further development, as for example in the combustion engine-powered aircraft development toward the end of the Second World War. It was simply physically impossible to achieve higher aircraft speed with the old technology. Hence a new concept of the jet engines needed to be developed. The pervasive nature of the spreading new technologies can be illustrated by jet aircraft development, since it also contributed to the establishment of the new airspace industry revolutionizing both civilian and defense applications. It also merged with major innovation breakthroughs in radio

Table 4.1 Five technological revolutions: main industries and infrastructures

1. Technological revolution	*2. New technologies and new or redefined industries*	*3. New or redefined infrastructures*
FIRST: *The 'Industrial Revolution'*	Mechanized cotton industry Wrought iron Machinery	Canals and waterways Turnpike roads Water power (highly improved water wheels)
SECOND: *Age of Steam and Railways*	Steam engines and machinery (made in iron; fueled by coal) Iron and coal mining (now playing a central role in growth)* Railway construction Rolling stock production Steam power for many industries (including textiles)	Railways (Use of steam engine) Universal postal service Telegraph (mainly nationally along railway lines) Great ports, great depots, and worldwide sailing ships City gas
THIRD: *Age of Steel, Electricity and Heavy Engineering*	Cheap steel (especially Bessemer) Full development of steam engine for steel ships Heavy chemistry and civil engineering Electrical equipment industry Copper and cables Canned and bottled food Paper and packaging	Worldwide shipping in rapid steel steamships (use of Suez Canal) Transcontinental railways (use of cheap steel rails and bolts in standard sizes) Great bridges and tunnels Worldwide Telegraph Telephone (mainly nationally) Electrical networks (for illumination and industrial use)
FOURTH: *Age of Oil, the Automobile and Mass Production*	Mass-produced automobiles Cheap oil and oil fuels Petrochemicals (synthetics) Internal combustion engine for automobiles, transport, tractors, airplanes, war tanks, and electricity Home electrical appliances Refrigerated and frozen foods	Networks of roads, highways, ports, and airports Networks of oil ducts Universal electricity (industry and homes) Worldwide analog telecommunications (telephone, telex, and cablegram) wire and wireless

(continued)

Table 4.1 (continued)

1. Technological revolution	*2. New technologies and new or redefined industries*	*3. New or redefined infrastructures*
FIFTH: *Age of Information and Telecommunications*	The information revolution: Cheap microelectronics Computers, software Telecommunications Control instruments Computer-aided biotechnology and new materials	World digital telecommunications (cable, fiber optics, radio, and satellite) Internet/Electronic mail and other e-services Multiple source, flexible use, electricity networks High-speed multi-modal physical transport links (by land, air, and water)

Source Perez (2009a, p. 12)

control and communication systems later with the main driver of the new paradigm: microelectronic solutions.

The first phase of the technological paradigm is earmarked by intensive search activity and the coexistence of competing technological solutions for the same type of new demand. Later competition process crystallizes the technically and economically most viable solutions, the “dominant design” (Abernathy and Utterback 1978) that becomes industry standard. This process unfolds in the core industry of the given paradigm producing such basic solutions (new power generation systems, construction solutions, communication devices), that are applied generally in all industries. Thus, the underlying main technological bricks of the production and all kinds of activities (including personal and social ones) redesign the corresponding business models, organizational forms, and legal institutions. This pervasive application is the second phase of the technology paradigm: the deployment phase (Perez 2002, 2009b).

From the viewpoint of this paper the periodization is rather crucial, in order to see the fit of technology cycles and growth performance of the countries. Perez (2009b) suggested that the introduction phase can be separated from the deployment section via monitoring the characteristics of the financial markets. In the introduction phase venture capital plays a crucial role. New technological solutions pose a high risk of failure, but the winner takes it all. Exceptionally high returns can be achieved with a selected number of companies. Nevertheless, the introduction phase usually provides an investment euphoria and much of the capital market finances risky small business development. Then, the euphoria ends, the ties change the investment bubble busts (Perez 2009b). The few remaining companies of the new business will take the whole market, therefore, strong market concentration starts. This too needs a lot of investments, however, this time it is more regular business development that takes the lion's share. Thus, the switch between the introductory and the deployment phase is signed by major capital market breakdowns and changes in its structure.

Another important question of the sequencing is of course the definition of the starting and ending date of the technology cycles. The previous discussion already suggested that the cycles may overlap. The outgoing paradigm is taken over by the new one only gradually. Development of the core technologies of a new paradigm starts much earlier than the old technologies become hopelessly obsolete. Therefore, the dates of changes in the technology paradigm are usually arbitrarily chosen by the analysts. They are usually bound to the date of a symbolic innovation. For example, the fifth paradigm's starting point is the date of the announcement of the first commercially utilized semiconductor by Intel in 1973. Semiconductors are treated as the basic LEGO bricks of the paradigm: their usage is pervasive, they are cheap, their production costs have decreased very quickly, their supply seemed to be unlimited.

Many other broader economic and political issues show the crisis of the previous paradigm. In case of the fifth revolution we saw fundamental political and social changes, the collapse of the Bretton Woods financial system, the economic and political climax of the two superpowers. The switch from introduction to deployment phase is placed somewhere around the year 1990. The 2001 dotcom crisis of the capital markets can also serve as a yardstick. We are now in the second phase of the fifth technology paradigm. More recent crisis events and the rise of China as economic superpower clearly show the negative processes typical for the paradigms' second phase. We do not know yet what will be the core component of the next paradigm: it is just being developed right now.

Using this theoretical framework we can create a rough periodization of the 5 technological paradigms of the last 250 years. Table 4.2 contains this information together with some economic growth indices

Table 4.2 Historic economic and technology cycles

Economic cycles			*Technology cycles*	
K-wave	*K-wave section*	*Period*	*Techno-economic paradigm section*	*Period*
1. Kondratiew	Upswing	1790–1810/17	1. First industrial revolution deployment	1793–1820
	Downswing	1810/17–1844/51	2. Age of steam and railways introduction	1821–1847
2. Kondratiew	Upswing	1844/51–1870/75	2. Age of steam and railways deployment	1848–1875
	Downswing	1870/75 – 1890/96	3. Age of steel, electricity introduction	1876–1895
3. Kondratiew	Upswing	1890/96–1914/28	3. Age of steel, electricity deployment	1896–1913
	Downswing	1914/28–1939/50	4. Age of oil, auto, mass prod. introduction	1914–1945
4. Kondratiew	Upswing	1939/50–1968/74	4. Age of oil, auto, mass prod. deployment	1946–1973
	Downswing	1968/74–1984/91	5. Age of information, telecom. introduction	1974–1990
5. Kondratiew	Upswing	1984/91–2008/10	5. Age of information, telecom. deployment	1991–2008
	Downswing	2008/10–??	6. ??? introduction	2008–??

Source Own compilation based on Korotayev and Grinin (2012) and Perez (2009a)

based on the Kondratieff cycle theory (Korotayev and Grinin 2012). The Kondratieff cycle theory provides information about the speed of economic growth in various historic periods. The comparison of the technology and growth cycles shows a considerable fit. This is an important proof of the coevolution: technological change and business cycles influence each other. It is nicely shown in Table 4.2 that the technology cycles always start in the downswing period of the growth cycle: an important evidence of the rationale of evolutionary theory. On the other hand, after having achieved the dominant design the spread of new technologies provides a wide range of application possibilities producing a waste amount of business opportunities that fuel rapid economic expansion. Here the main question of this section needs to be asked: Can catching-up countries of the periphery participate in this process? Can they grow more quickly than more developed countries? There is no space in this chapter to go into the details, also including enabling policies or the defensive policies and tactics of other countries. A simple comparison is made: ECE countries' development patterns (per capita GDP indices) are compared with the technology (and growth) cycles.

ECE Development Patterns

The calculations of the per capita GDP indices are based on the 1990 Geary-Khamis International Dollar data of the Maddison database (the 2018 version). This is the most widely used source of comparative historic data. Despite its flaws (for example it defines country average figures for countries having significantly changing territories, or ones that were created and eventually also vanished during the observed period) we have no better option and must rely on the several decades-long, significant efforts that the Groningen Institute made for cleansing and refining the database. Nevertheless, some of the data obtained from this source seems odd. The description of the calculation of the Jánossy trend lines is detailed elsewhere (Szanyi and Szabó 2020).

The relative development level of six ECE countries in percentage of the average per capita level of ten developed West-European countries is shown in Table 4.3 for selected years of the period 1870–2016. Big differences of the relative development level are seen that also changed

Table 4.3 Relative development level of selected countries (per capita GDP in % of West-European developed countries' average)

	1870	*1913*	*1929*	*1937*	*1950*	*1974*	*1989*	*2001*	*2008*	*2016*
Austria	84	87	75	61	63	88	94	98	100	100
Finland	52	53	55	66	72	86	97	96	104	96
Greece	55	51	47	53	32	56	58	58	65	49
Czechosl.	53	53	62	56	59	55	50	43	36	62
Hungary	49	53	50	49	42	43	40	32	37	40
Poland	45	44	43	37	41	42	33	34	42	53
Bulgaria	38	30*	25	29	28	41	36	24	36	41
Romania	10	12	9	9	9	21	21	16	24	24
Yugosl.	25	24	25	23	24	37	36	23	29	33

Source Authors' own calculation based on Maddison (2018) database *: 1911

significantly over time. In the first decades of observation the various parts of the Austro-Hungarian Empire featured higher relative development levels (45–53%) than Romania, Bulgaria, and Yugoslavia (Serbia) featuring 10–45%. At the same time Austria already stood at 84%, the successfully catching-up Finland and Greece scored 52 and 55%, respectively. ECE countries could not improve their positions in the first decades until the First World War. The shocks of the war threw back Austria, but winners and losers alike suffered. Czechoslovakia could increase the relative development level in the interwar period. All other ECE countries could recover to the previous levels at best in the postwar reconstruction period.

A striking difference is seen between the post-Second World War development performance of the successfully catching-up countries and the ECE region up till 2001. This image seems to contradict the widespread knowledge of the intensive industrialization programs, large-scale housing projects, and infrastructural development efforts in the region. There was significant development. Nevertheless, it seems that the Western reconstruction was more robust when powered by the Marshall plan and the construction of the European integration. Moreover, this development trend seemed to be less vulnerable than the ECE programs that ended up in losing the economic and military competition of the two superpowers and their allies. The resulting political changes in the transition process largely eliminated much of the economically unviable, not competitive parts of the ECE economies leading to an exceptionally deep economic crisis, the transformational crisis. This threw back the relative development level of all ECE countries. The fairly quick reconstruction period after this shock featured very quick expansion based mainly on foreign direct investments. Most recently the catching-up continued, however, as it is shown in the following analysis, narrowing of the gap occurs mainly because of the drastic slowing down of the West-European economic development.

The relative development level is established through timely development which is illustrated by data of Table 4.4. It contains the slope figures for the 2-sections, long-term trend lines of selected countries, as well as the slopes of the 7-sections trend lines. As indicated earlier, differences in the slopes of the various countries may mean absolute convergence or divergence. Differences of the slopes of the individual countries compared to their long-term trend line slope may mean conditional convergence or divergence.

Table 4.4 Slopes of 7-phase and 2-phase Jánossy trend lines

	1870–1895 K.II down T3 introd. (%)	*1896–1913 K.III up T3 deploy. (%)*	*1914–1949 K.III down T4 introd. (%)*	*1950–1973 K.IV up T4 deploy. (%)*	*1974–1990 K.IV dow T5 introd. (%)*	*1991–2008 K.V up T5 deploy. (%)*	*2009–2016 K.V down T6 intro. (%)*	*1870–1949*	*1950–2016*
West-Europe	1.06	1.47	0.95	3.48	1.84	2.05	0.50	1.33	2.97
Austria	1.28	1.75	1.15	4.31	2.07	2.16	0.28	1.46	2.65
Finland	1.67	1.58	2.46	4.11	2.70	2.87	2.10	1.70	4.00
Greece	1.47	2.12	2.12	6.27	1.28	2.66	NA	1.07	3.79
Czechoslov.	1.31	1.47	2.62	3.85	1.07	3.45	1.87	1.64	2.20
Hungary	1.51	1.63	1.33	3.82	1.29	2.91	2.00	1.53	1.90
Poland	1.96	0.20	1.24	3.45	1.71	4.99	2.61	1.70	1.79
Bulgaria	1.37	0.56	1.72	4.98	1.44	3.01	2.35	1.37	3.39
Romania	4.72	1.28	2.09	6.38	2.39	3.83	2.25	1.21	5.07
Yugoslavia	1.73	1.34	1.04	5.69	0.38	2.12	1.09	1.24	4.60

Source Authors' own calculation based on the Maddison (2018) database

The data shows relatively stable development trends of the Western countries up till the last period after the 2008 crisis. The exceptionally low value indicates an even deeper crisis than the times of the Great Depression during the 1930s. The postwar development trend was especially smooth. When compared to the successfully catching-up countries we can see that these countries' slope figures always succeeded the benchmark countries' values. The development gap continuously narrowed until 2008 when it virtually disappeared. But the 2008 crisis hit also these countries rather badly. These countries performed quickest convergence in the post-Second World War decades.

Compared to this impressive convergence performance ECE countries' figures show important oscillations. Most of them had only limited, albeit clearly existing catching-up potential before the First World War. The interwar period's data consists of relatively few observations, hence the evidence on this period is not very robust. Based on this data and also concerning Tomka (2011) we may state that Czechoslovakia continued convergence, Hungary most probably recovered to the prewar development level. All other ECE countries' development gap increased after the war shocks and they could not fully recover in the interwar period despite the slightly quicker development than in the West.

The post-Second World War boom period was utilized by all observed countries. Hence, it is rather difficult to achieve absolute convergence. Nevertheless, ECE countries could achieve some gains in the trend line slopes. However, the general impression of the period was different. As Tomka (2011) explained the enforced industrialization did not result in equally big increases of the living standards. Much of the excess GDP served military purposes and other "regrettable necessities" and deprived the population the welfare gains of economic expansion. This was in sharp contrast with the West, where also private consumption, various areas of welfare services boomed. There was a sharp detour in the living conditions and lifestyles, not so much in the measure of development expressed by the per capita GDP index. The relatively lower level of welfare gains in the ECE region was however distributed more evenly, hence social inequality decreased. This policy was continued also in the more troubled crisis period of the 1970s and 80s. Hungarian goulash communism for example made important efforts to maintain the level of private consumption even if the sound economic background ceased to exist. This was in fact the least successful period for all ECE countries when the development gap increased to historically unprecedented levels (especially if we count with the transitional crisis as an unavoidable legacy of the previous period).

Data in Table 4.4 also provides information about the conditional convergence of ECE countries when slope data is compared to the 2-section trend line figures of each individual country. If figures in columns 2–4 are larger than the data of column 9 (1870–1949 period Jánossy trend line slope), it means that during these sections conditional convergence occurred. Similarly, if slope data of columns 5–8 is larger than the figure in column 10 conditional convergence occurred in the second (1950–2016) section of the observed period. In other words this means that the development performance of the given country approached the historically determined long-term trend line. The historic trend line can change shape over time. Jánossy (2016) indicated that significant and long-lasting changes in the conditions of operation in rare cases fundamental changes of a country's economic system can reshape the historic trend lines. The thorough analysis of the database suggested that such a change occurred in the working conditions after the Second World War. Development accelerated in all the observed countries. Therefore the 2-section historic trend lines were calculated for each country.

The developed benchmark countries' development pattern was rather stable until 1913 and the interwar section could be also fitted to the previous patterns. The three major shocks of this period were followed by significant recoveries thus, the overall development tendency did not decline in the long run but remained fairly close to the historic trend line. In the second section, exceptionally quick recovery continued and speedy development lasted until the 1970s pushing the historic trend line upward. Since then a steady deceleration can be observed with lower and ever decreasing slope figures for the shorter time sections. Compared to this general picture Austria's catching-up was thwarted to a much larger extent in the interwar period when the slots of recovery could not propel the country back near the historic trend line. This happened only after the post-Second World War recovery period. Perhaps even more interesting is the country's further development trend that was not depressed until the 2000s. Even the oil shocks of the 1970s could not push back the country's outstanding development record. This happened only in the last 2009–2016 period. In the case of Finland similarly strong performance is observed that started after the First World War, the gaining of independence from Russia. Interestingly, the remaining strong economic ties to the Soviet Union exercised a significant drop in the Finnish economy by the late 1980s when the Soviet market collapsed. Thereafter, the Finnish economy was not brought back to the historic trend line any more. The 2008 crisis hit the economy again rather badly with the collapse of the national champion company Nokia, that produced a significant drop in the production of the GDP (Nokia effect). The Greek data shows more significant oscillation, but the recovery periods returned the country back to the historic trend line in the first long period of the observation. More significant catching-up occurred after the Second World War, but especially during the 1949–1973 period. Afterward the convergence decelerated up until the last period that produced a lasting decline in the per capita index of the country.

Turning to the ECE region the Visegrad countries (Poland, Czechia, Slovakia, Hungary) show fairly similar development trends. Most importantly, the slopes of the first and second phase of their historic trend lines did not differ much (the second phase was only moderately stronger than the first). Moreover, the three trend lines had similar slopes (1.53–1.70 in the first period, 1.79–2.20 in the second). At the same time shocks caused more limited oscillations in the development levels than in case of the Western benchmark countries. On the other hand, due to the less robust recovery performance post-crisis recovery periods proved to be significantly longer. This stability of the development trends also meant less convergence potential. The slopes of the first historic period's trend lines still showed modest convergence (e.g. in case of Hungary 1.53% compared to the Western 1.33%). This potential disappeared altogether for the second period (1.90% for Hungary vs. 2.97% for the West). No convergence but divergence occurred. The Visegrad countries could not join the overall accelerating development trends. This rather disappointing performance was based mainly on the exceptionally poor development trends of the 1974–1990 period that eventually led to the collapse of the ECE economies culminating in the transformational crisis of the early 1990s. The convergence premium that was achieved during the 1950–1973 period vanished. The recovery of the three countries accelerated especially from the mid-1990s with the overwhelming recalibration of their economic systems. Conditional convergence was observed until the 2008 crisis. Afterward catching-up continued since the benchmark Western economies' development lastingly decelerated. The slopes of this last section are more or less identical with the historic trend line slopes. In Poland, convergence to the historic trend line continued even after 2008 (2.61% compared to the historic 1.79%).

The development pattern of the three Balkan countries differed substantially. Their economies did not show the relative stability of the three Visegrad countries. They were hit by crises much more seriously (in the first historic period mainly Bulgaria and Romania). They also started development from a much lower level. The three countries historic development trend line featured fairly low slopes in the first period, lower than the Western benchmark countries. This meant the bad news that the initial big development gap generally did not narrow, despite slightly better performances in the 1870–1895 period and the interwar decades. Very much to the contrary of the surprisingly sluggish new trend of the Visegrad countries after the Second World War, the Balkan countries' historic trend line featured very significant convergence potentials with their new slopes of 3.5–5.0%. The basis of these slopes was the exceptionally quick recovery after the Second World War that continued into the 1970s. The rapid growth was then replaced by very significant deceleration. Bulgaria and Romania slowed back to the level of the Visegrad countries, Yugoslavia even below. They were also thwarted by the transformational recession to a larger degree, than the other three ECE countries. Their recovery lasted longer and could not achieve the historic development trend line. Due to the very sluggish growth performance of the Western benchmark countries the three Balkan countries could narrow their development gap most recently.

Conclusions: Linkages Between ECE Convergence and the Technology Cycles

The Maddison (2018) database provides comparative data for the observed countries starting from the 1870s. This is the introduction period of the third technological paradigm with new technologies in the steel and electrical industry. Data of Table 4.4 indicates that the ECE countries scored above average compared both with the Western benchmark and their own historic trend lines. The introduction phases of the technology cycles are bound to more sluggish economic growth (downswing phases of the Kondratieff cycles). This data can be interpreted therefore as a sign of stability: no intensive search is necessary, business goes as usual. On the other hand, it is also well known that the ECE region produced a few outstanding engineers and innovations in this period. For example, the nowadays strongly hyped Nikola Tesla was a Serb educated in Budapest and Graz University before leaving for the USA.

Another example can be Tivadar Puskás, the inventor of the telephonic media news broadcasting service, who also lived for some time in the USA. The ECE region contributed to the technological paradigm, albeit the realization and business utilization of most contributions occurred in more developed countries. The deployment phase of the third technology paradigm boosted the world economy at higher speed than what ECE regions could achieve. The ECE region could not utilize its technological opportunities in new businesses: their results were used by the more developed countries' corporations. An important difference to the successfully catching-up countries is that they could better utilize the business opportunities of the deployment phase.

The interwar period provides a less straightforward picture of the observed countries. The two world wars and the Great Depression caused severe shocks and much of the period was spent with Jánossy's reconstruction phases. The shocks threw back Austria's catching-up process, but they did not cause harm so much to Finland and Greece. In the ECE region we can observe similarly mixed growth performance with significant convergence of Czechoslovakian and Romanian trend lines. Other countries' trend line slopes also exceeded the Western average, nevertheless, as the relative development levels of Table 4.3 show they could not really utilize the opportunity due to the deep and long-lasting shock periods. This is in sharp contrast with the 1870–1895 introduction period of the third technology paradigm. Obviously, the very repressive world economic environment (protectionist trade measures, uncertainty of capital markets, etc.) could play an important role in this. Western benchmark countries also suffered of course scoring a historic low trend line slope for the period. Due to the shocks ECE countries could hardly surpass the relative development level of the 1910s, except Czechoslovakia.

The immediate post-Second World War period propelled the world economy to a new, steeper development path. This was the deployment phase of the fourth technological paradigm featuring car industry, massive urbanization, petrochemical industry, and Taylorist mass production. All ECE countries launched a new growth path with the support of the Soviet Union. The slopes exceeded the Western average, however just as it happened in the interwar period the actual growth performance lagged behind, especially in the Visegrad countries. More importantly, the massive deployment of selected key technologies of the time resulted in fairly one-sided development pattern. Heavy industry, petrochemicals, and military equipment production scored above-average growth figures, but much less development was achieved in civilian production. For example, the level of public utilities remained basically on the same level than several decades before, private automotive usage, travel, mobility did not change much either. Tomka (2011) explained with many concrete examples how consumption patterns, the way of life started to evolve in strikingly different ways in the East and the West. This qualitative departure is not really seen on the statistical figures, but produced serious social and political tensions that stroke back in the next period's severe economic and social crisis. Yet, in the statistics the period between 1950 and 1973 showed the steepest rise in the development trend line of ECE countries, and much of the development potential was actually utilized, even if not in a balanced way. Nevertheless, convergence hardly occurred because this was an exceptionally strong upswing period in the West as well.

The fourth technology paradigm ended in chaos with rapidly increasing prices of the core product of the period: crude oil. Social tensions, wars, and the advance of East-Asian countries in the world economy also heralded the crisis of the paradigm. In the background, however, the nucleus of the new fifth technology paradigm was discovered and evolved to the stage of becoming the main driver of the next paradigm: semiconductors and various microelectronic devices. Despite the general decline of the growth patterns in the 1974–1990 period ECE countries could underperform rather significantly the lower Western average. This was not the case in previous epochs: ECE scored relatively better in the introduction phase. This time their slope figures were significantly lower than the Western average, except for Romania. The production capacities that were created in the postwar boom period became obsolete and posed huge sunk costs unlike in the previous epochs when development was more balanced. The technological renewal was blocked, ECE countries did not get access to the novelties of the new technological paradigm because of the politically motivated technology ban on the socialist block's countries. The Soviets and their allies were not capable to keep pace with the development of the new paradigm's technologies. This failure eventually led to the economic collapse and military defeat of the block. This is an important lesson for this chapter: the ECE region even if backed by other technologically not strongly developed superpowers is not self-supplying. The ECE region, but perhaps every small- and medium-sized country can perform better if plugged into the world economy, to the technology exchange and transfer processes. This can keep their own scientific and engineering potential up to date and strengthen their national innovation systems. Even if much of the potential business benefits are reaped elsewhere.

The 1990s until the 2008 crisis were the years of the "Great Moderation" in the West. Relatively stable albeit not exceptionally high economic growth rates were recorded. Moreover, the developed world seemed to solve the problem of macroeconomic imbalances, at least in the OECD countries. The period is the deployment phase of the fifth, electronics-based technological paradigm. We do not know much about the basic features of the next paradigm yet. Therefore, the ending point of the paradigm is unclear. For the time being the big 2008 financial crisis serves as a milestone since it inevitably ended the time of the Great Moderation. The social, political, economic disturbances which are typical for the introduction periods are also seen. Economic performance of the West is also continuously troubled resulting in a very modest slope for the last section of our time series. What is even more interesting, the successfully catching-up countries (Greece but also Austria and Finland) also suffer. After having surpassed the Western average and becoming members of the developed countries' class they seem to have lost the previous thrust after 2008.

The ECE countries were put back on the table in the 1990–2008 period. Their unsuccessful experiment with technological autarchy came to an end. They became integrated into the global value chains of leading multinational companies thus getting access to most up-to-date technology inputs. Also scientific research and education was plugged into the global systems. It seems that the typical trends of several decades ago reappear and the ECE countries become primarily as innovation and human suppliers of global firms. If this is the case, then the coming years' development pattern will show relatively good local performance, modest convergence but no major breakthrough. For this a fundamental change in the science and technology policies, as well as viable development programs, industrial policy would be necessary. The local usage of technological inputs would require strong, competitive local companies. Unfortunately, the current picture of the ECE economies is not rosy. They are deeply involved in corruption and rent-seeking, which is a kind of orientation that does not favor innovation. If no systemic change from rent-based to competition-based economy occurs, the convergence chances of the ECE countries remain weak. They can catch up mainly if the Western benchmark countries decline. Not to mention the new emerging economies most importantly China. The new dependence on Chinese investments and to some extent also technologies is being observed in the ECE region.

References

Abernathy, W.J. – Utterback, J. (1978): Patterns of innovation in industry. *Technology Review*, 80:7, 40–47.

Dosi, G. (1982): Technological paradigms and technological trajectories: A suggested interpretation of the determinants and directions of technical change. *Research Policy*, 11:3, 147–162.

Dosi, G. (1988): Sources, procedures and microeconomic effects of innovation. *Journal of Economic Literature*, 26:3, 1120–1171.

Dosi, G. – Nelson, R. (2013): The evolution of technologies: An assessment of the state-of-the-art. *Eurasian Business Review*, 3:1 3–46.

Freeman, C. (1982): *The economics of industrial innovation*. London, Frances Pinter.

Jánossy, F. (2016): *The end of economic miracle: Appearance and reality in economic development* (reprint, first edition by International Arts and Sciences Press, 1971). Routledge, New York.

Korotayev, A.V. – Grinin, L.E. (2012): *Kondratieff waves in the world system perspective*. In: Grinin, Devezas, Korotayev: Kondratieff waves. Dimensions and prospects at the dawn of the 21st century. Russian Academy of Sciences Volgograd Center for Social Research. 23–64.o.

Lundvall, B.A. (1988): *Innovation as an interactive process: From user-producer interaction to the national system of innovation*. In: Dosi és társai (szerk.), 17. fejezet.

Maddison (2018): *Maddison Project Database 2018*, 1990 Benchmark: https://www.rug.nl/ggdc/historicaldevelopment/maddison/data/mpd2018_1990bm.xlsx (letöltve: 2019.05.06).

Monfort, P. (2008): *Convergence of EU regions: Measures and evolution*. EU DG Regional Policy Working Paper No. 01/2008.

Mowery, D.C. – Rosenberg, N. (1979): The influence of market demand upon innovation: A critical review of some recent empirical studies. *Research Policy*, 8:2, 102–153.

Nelson, R.R. (1981): Research on productivity growth and productivity differences: Dead ends and new departures. *Journal of Economic Literature*, 19:3, 1029–1064.

Nelson, R.R. – Winter, S.G. (1977): In search of a useful theory of innovation. *Research Policy*, 6:1, 36–76.

Nelson, R.R. – Winter, S.G. (1982): *An Evolutionary Theory of Economic Change*. Harvard Univerity Press, Cambridge, London.

Pavitt, K. (1999): *Technology, management and systems of innovation*. Cheltenham, Edward Elgar.

Perez, C. (2002): *Technological revolutions and financial capital: The dynamics of bubbles and golden ages*. Cheltenham, Elgar.

Perez, C. (2009a): *Technological revolutions and techno-economic paradigms*. Working Papers in Technology Governance and Economic Dynamics No. 20. Tallin University of Technology.

Perez, C. (2009b): *The double bubble at the turn of the century: Technological roots and structural implications*. CFAP Working Paper No. 31. Centre for Financial Analysis & Policy, Cambridge University.

Rosenberg, N. (1982): *Inside the black box: Technology and economics*. Cambridge University Press, Cambridge.

Szanyi, M. (2020): *The three archetype European historic development models and their impact in East-Central Europe*. Institute of World Economy Working Paper No. 261, August.

Szanyi, M. – Szabó, G. (2020): Defining the long-term development trends of countries in East-Central Europe in the context of political cycles. *International Journal of Public Administration*. Published online on 14 April 2020.

Szűcs, J. (1983): The three historical regions of Europe: An outline. *Acta Historica Academiae Scientiarum Hungaricae*, 29:2–4, 131–184.

Tomka Béla (2011): *Gazdasági növekedés, fogyasztás és életminőség*. Akadémiai Kiadó, Budapest.

CHAPTER 5

On the Emergence of Developmental States in the Twenty-First Century: Urgency or Agency?

Judit Ricz

Introduction

During the last decades, at the latest since the 2008–9 Global Financial Crisis (GFC), and even more pronounced after the spread of the

This research was conducted in the framework of the research project "From developmental states to new protectionism: changing repertoire of state interventions to promote development in an unfolding new world order" (FK_124573) supported by the National Research, Development and Innovation Office (NRDIO) of Hungary.

J. Ricz (✉)
Institute of World Economics, Centre for Economic and Regional Studies, Budapest, Hungary

Department of World Economy, Institute of International, Political, and Regional Studies, Corvinus University of Budapest, Budapest, Hungary

T. Gerőcs and J. Ricz (eds.), *The Post-Crisis Developmental State*, International Political Economy Series,
https://doi.org/10.1007/978-3-030-71987-6_5

COVID-19 pandemic since the early 2020 we see the rise of state involvement in the economy worldwide. Notwithstanding these recent statist experiments, we claim that most of these deviate in almost all terms from the revised, new developmental state concept of the twenty-first century emerging from most recent theoretical considerations as presented in the introduction and throughout the chapters of this volume (see also Haggard 2018; Ricz 2016; Wade 2018; Williams 2014). In this vein, the new developmental state model represents rather theoretical (deductive) construct (a wishful thinking), and not a role model based upon real world experiences (along inductive reasoning).

In this chapter our focus is however much more narrow: we concentrate on the question how successful developmental states (and developmentalist institutions) have emerged and try to answer this question from the political economic perspective. We aim to look at the emergence of most recent statist experiments of the twenty-first century via the perspective of the classic developmental state paradigm. For this we first recall the origins of catching up success stories of the twentieth century, by focusing on the East Asian developmental states. As the often cited World Bank (Agénor, Canuto, and Jelenic 2012) study has shown, from 101 middle-income economies in 1960, only 13 have managed to reach the high income status by 2008, and this picture has not changed significantly since then (not even China has reached the high income status, even though its economic performance is often dubbed miraculous[1]).

Looking at the development state literature two main lines of argumentation on the origins of developmental states stand out. The first line stresses the role of elites as agents of development (for an overview of this literature see Amsden et al. 2012), we call this, the *agency view*. We argue that this traditional line of argumentation might become more and more popular recently with the ascendance of strong leaders along the global populist tide promising magical solutions for pressing and intensified social and economic challenges (see also Gerőcs and Szanyi 2019; Szelényi and Mihályi 2020). The other line of interpretations argues, that economic success throughout history tends not to arise from the geniality of strong leaders unconstrained from coalitional demands and social pressures, but rather developmental success emerges in extraordinarily

[1] Wide-ranging debates surround the Chinese growth story and whether it can be considered as a developmental state (see e.g. Boltho and Weber 2009; Knight 2014; Naughton 2017; Székely-Doby 2020). For a rather narrow focus on the new Chinese developmental state and its green industrial policies see Szalavetz, this volume.

constrained political environments, where political elites' own survival depends on successful economic upgrading (Doner et al. 2005). We call this latter, the *urgency view*, as political leaders under such constrained (*systemically vulnerable*) conditions are urged to build developmental institutions to promote economic transformation leading to sustainable and inclusive economic development on the longer term—in line with the growth-with-equity approach (for the institutionalist view see also Rodrik 2004 and the chapter of Csaba and Vigvari in this volume).

Before mapping out new challenges of to-be-developmental states in the twenty-first century, we first look back on the experiences of the classic developmental states, the model-cases of the Northeast Asian region, which provide our point of reference, and recall the specific global and regional context, in which these success stories emerged. From the wide-ranging academic literature on the emergence, rise and fall of the classic DS, we highlight the political economy explanation of Doner et al. (2005), also called systemic vulnerability concept. In the second part of this study we devote our attention first to recent and ongoing changes in the global level, which provide very different circumstances for states with developmentalist aspirations in the twenty-first century. In this regard we have to look at the global economic and political changes in a dynamic perspective, as even in the post 2000 era constant changes in the global arena are under way. While our main focus regards primarily the most recent (post 2014/16) years, we also shed light on the early 2000 years, and the effects of the GFC in this regard (to reveal the cyclicality and dynamism of changes) (Szanyi 2019 and this volume, and Yakovlev's chapter this volume). Finally after exploring new external constraints and potentially enabling factors for to-be-DS in the twenty-first century, we focus on the domestic factors, especially on the difficulties of building broad coalitions. By looking at the domestic arena we aim to provide a political economy interpretation on the challenges of building developmentalist institutions in the twenty-first century, or to put it differently to answer the question, why it is so difficult for DS to emerge under the current circumstances. According to our hypothesis the role of urgency is on the rise in the external front (mainly due to the GFC and the current crises related to the COVID-19 pandemic), yet urgent pressures on the domestic political leaders are less present (or at least less able to organize and unify themselves) in the domestic arena in the twenty-first century's state capitalist economies. These imbalances might lead to re-emerging views on the pivotal role of elites (with a particular emphasis on the role of strong leaders) or as we call it throughout this paper, the agency views might come back and offer a fertile ground for further research.

The (North-)East Asian Developmental State Model

In the mid of the twentieth century, during the decades after the Second World War some East Asian countries became role models of post-war reconstruction and late development. Their state-led development model based on dirigiste policies and institutional arrangements was mostly captured under the notion of "developmental state" (DS) as coined by Chalmers Johnson (1982) in his book on the Japanese miracle. The term was then taken over by many scholars (among many others by Amsden 1989; Wade 1990; Onis 1991; Evans 1995; for an excellent overview on the classic DS approach see Woo-Cumings 1999 or more recently Haggard 2018) and also applied for other, mainly Northeast Asian (NEA) states, such as South Korea and Taiwan (later Singapore from the Southeast-Asian region also joined the group).

The NEA region became a reference point regarding its novel state-led policy implementation and experimentation, also dubbed as the classic DS model or paradigm (DSP), which seemed to challenge both the liberal and Marxist postulates of the time regarding development within capitalist system. The so-called East Asian Miracle was not only based on impressive growth rates and successful economic catching up in terms of GDP per capita levels, but also social improvements (decreasing poverty rates, increased social mobility and the rise of the middle classes) and structural advancement (dynamism of new industrial and manufacturing activities and productivity gains) were integral part of it. These have led to the emergence of the growth-with-equity approach, which provided an optimistic narrative on the development potentials of the peripheries, contrasted to the more pessimistic postulates of the classic development theories (such as the dependency or the structuralist school).

The final decades of the twentieth century have however witnessed the fall of the classic developmental state paradigm (for this see Woo-Cumings 1999; Benczes 2000, 2002; Beeson 2004; Low 2004; Ricz 2019) and the Asian Financial Crisis (AFC) proved to represent a critical juncture for the state-led developmentalist approach.

Substantial changes have taken place already during the 1980s and 1990s and these have not only led to a different external context, but at the same time also undermined the internal coherence of the classic

DS model, which was not able to adapt itself neither to the new external conditions nor to the changed internal settings (shaped by weakening state capacities and the ever stronger private sector). Accordingly (as we have argued elsewhere, see Ricz 2019), the decline of the classic DS model has to be regarded as a systemic phenomenon, and the AFC has only put these internal controversies to the fore.

Before turning towards analysing the new global economic and political circumstances of the twenty-first century, we first shortly recall the time- and region-specific institutional and policy context that has enabled the successes of traditional East Asian developmental states in the mid of the last century.

The (North-)East Asian Developmental State Model as the Child of Its Era

A historical interplay of—political, economic, institutional, ideational, social, regional and geopolitical—forces has contributed to the East Asian economic miracle, part of these were time-related, while others were geographically determined and more region-specific.

We distinguish three elements of the general environment: (1) The *global political context* of the post-war period (national capitalist development concept, economic nationalism and Cold War geopolitics). (2) The *global economic context* of the post-war period (neo-mercantilist approach, growing protectionism, relatively closed economic systems and development models). (3) The *context of late-development* (national-based Fordist capitalism, promotion of strategic national industries, and in the context of underdevelopment, mass poverty and infrastructural deficiencies caused by the destructions of the war, economic catching up as first priority supported by wide social consensus). These *permissive global conditions* meant that national economic performance depended to a large degree on competitiveness of large national firms, the so-called flagship companies (state-owned and semi-private companies, national champions), and created the basis for national dirigiste state-led development policies.

In addition, three region-specific conditions have also substantially contributed to the unique context of the Northeast Asian developmental experience: First *Japan's outstanding role* within the region: (a) as former colonial ruler (laying down important institutional setting); (b) as important economic donor, providing development aid, and later on capital; (c) in more general terms, as regional economic leader (providing market and being an economic partner) and (d) last but not least as a role model for economic development to follow. Second the *complex role of the USA* in *security and economic policy terms* as providing (a) development and military aid based on geopolitical considerations; (b) foreign direct investments; (c) preferential market access; (d) in more general terms, the commitment of the USA to secure the stability of the region by all means (as to stop the spread of socialism-communism, and to secure the borderline between the two poles in the Cold War). As a third special condition, we highlight *historical and cultural factors*: most East Asian developmental states have relatively *homogenous societies* (with rather small ethnic, religious, racial, linguistic or other differences),[2] have inherited *extensive and good quality institutional systems* from the colonial period (for example strong and well performing core administration, extensive and good quality educational system). *Asian social and cultural values have* also played pivotal role by placing community and its priorities above individual interests, leading to wide-ranging economic consequences.[3] Just to give two examples, we first highlight the *very strong individual commitment* and maximizing efforts to contribute to the implementation of community priorities (resulting for example in extremely long working hours compared to European standards); and second, the provision of social security and welfare primarily through the channels of family, community and business enterprises has freed up important state resources (which thus could be spent on the aggressive implementation of developmentalist policies).

Finally, this unique set of historic and institutional factors have also contributed to the facts, that the classic DS model was non-transferable and not-repeatable in other times and places (Johnson 1999: 39–40;

[2] Though obviously even these societies reveal social stratification and can be clustered around social classes, the argument here is, that social (ethnic, racial, religious) cleveages were much smoother in the cases of classic developmental states, than is usually the case in Latin America, Sub Saharan Africa, or even in many countries in South Asia.

[3] The reference here is not to the exclusive and decisive role of Confucianism (as many critics to developmental state highlight that Confucianism was present in these communities even before the World War II, and that Confucianism is also present in other countries in Southeast Asia, such as in Thailand and Malaysia, which did not experience comparable economic miracles), however communitarian values such as obligation and loyalty to the family, obedience to legitimate authority, high value placed on hard work, education and self-discipline have played an important role in the social constructs of classic developmental states (see Pye 1985; Stubbs 2005).

Pempel 1999: 180). However at the latest by the 1990s (with some processes starting even well before that) these general and specific conditions have substantially changed and disintegrated the internal and external coherence of the model, leading to the decline of the classic model of developmental states (Benczes 2000, 2002; Woo-Cumings 1999; Ricz 2019).

The Systemic Vulnerability Approach

To highlight the very specific interplay of the elements of this general context in which the classic DS model and its unique institutional arrangements emerged we recall the political economic interpretation of the origins of developmental states, the so-called systemic vulnerability approach. Doner, Ritchie, and Slater (2005) plausibly argued, that developmental states only emerge when political leaders confront extraordinarily constrained political environments. This concept is basically denying and rewriting the traditional *agency* views on the political origins of DS, claiming that developmental states arise from the geniality of strong leaders (such as the Singaporean Lee Kuan Yew, often considered as the grounding father of modern Singapore) basically unconstrained from any coalitional demands and social pressures. The traditional view on the political origins of DS goes also back to Johnson (1982), who argued that in the Japanese case (the archetype of the classic DS) politicians "reign" while the bureaucrats "rule". Onis (1991) makes a similar differentiation between the political elites and the bureaucratic elites, by claiming that "*the objective of the political elite is to legitimize the actions of the elite bureaucratic agencies and make space for the latter's actions*" (Onis 1991: 111). The agency view is also in line with traditional interpretations of the East Asian miracle, such as the embedded autonomy[4] concept of Evans (1995), that described classic developmental states as highly autonomous entities, unconstrained by coalitional demands (in this narrative the role of the organized labour class was not explicitly highlighted, as wide masses of the labour force were either politically repressed

[4] According to the embedded autonomy concept the meritocratic bureaucracies of the classic DS are not insulated from the society (in Weberian sense), "*on the contrary they are embedded in a concrete set of social ties that binds the state to society and provides institutionalized channels for the continual negotiation and renegotiation of goals and policies*" (Evans 1995: 12).

or economically co-opted by improving well-being, or both at the same time).

Doner and his coauthors in contrast argued, that the impressive capacities of the classic developmental states (such as South Korea, Taiwan and Singapore) have emerged from the systemic vulnerability (SV) conditions, which resulted from the simultaneous co-existence of three interactive constraints (which have never applied to other *intermediate* cases, such as the Southeast-Asian countries, Indonesia, Malaysia, the Philippines, or Thailand): "*(1) the credible threat that any deterioration in the living standards of popular sectors could trigger unmanageable mass unrest; (2) the heightened need for foreign exchange and war material induced by national insecurity; (3) the hard budget constraints imposed by a scarcity of easy revenue sources*" (Doner et al. 2005: 328).

The cited authors convincingly argue that amid this extraordinarily constrained political environment "*these states' impressive capacities actually emerged from the challenges of delivering side payments to restive popular sectors under conditions of extreme geopolitical insecurity and severe resource constraints*" (ibid.).

The logic beyond the systemic vulnerability argument runs as follows: in any political system the leaders' political survival depends on the supporting coalition beyond him. Generally leaders would tend to keep this coalition as narrow as it is possible, however, if there is intense elite or social conflict, or a credible threat that the deterioration in the living standards of broader parts of the society could lead to unmanageable mass unrest, compromising at the end of the day the leader's political survival, ruling elites can be forced to enlarge their coalitions. This was in principle the basic logic beyond the autocratic bargains of the classic DS in East Asia. There is consensus regarding the East Asian experiments, that even though the broad sectors of the society (such as the working class) were politically excluded, and sometimes even brutally repressed (in these mostly authoritarian regimes), they have rarely been economically ignored. On the contrary, a growth-with-equity approach was not only an unintended side effect of some lucky initial conditions (such as the Japanese colonial heritage or Asian values), but was an essential part of these autocratic deals.

To keep such broad coalitions together and sustain these over time needs willingness and ability to cover extensive side payments to the different actors. Which in turn is however difficult to finance if due to geopolitical insecurity, the nation's survival depends on an increased defence spending, and at the same time the lack of easy revenues for the state make the budget constraint hard. Under these systemic vulnerability conditions the ruling elite's political survival depends on its success to continuously expand national production and thus the state resources available for redistribution, which means to sustain economic growth over substantial time period. And this is only viable through continuous economic upgrading, thus with a constant shift from lower value added (low-skill, low-wage) production towards higher value added activities, based on a higher-skill and quality-based production structure and export performance. The implementation of such upgrading policies has largely depended on the developmentalist institutional setting and its impressive capacities, as it has been highlighted and explained by the classic authors of the developmentalist school. The bottom line of the argumentation here is that these institutional arrangements and capacities are the result of broad coalitional pressures under external threat and severe resource constraints.

It is straightforward to see, that two of the three conditions are externally determined, the credible external threat (resulting in an extraordinary pressure on the budget in terms of heightened defence spending), and the scarcity of easy revenue sources (which would undermine the pressure towards economic upgrading). From the point of view of aspirational or to-be-DS governments, these two conditions can be taken as exogenous variables, while the existence of broad societal coalitions is rather an endogenous factor resulting from the domestic political situation, and this is to which we turn our attention in the final section of this paper.

Finally we highlight that in the original systemic vulnerability concept Doner and his coauthors have treated the institutional capacity as a dependent variable, while they aimed at explaining why the impressive institutional capacities of the classic DS only emerged in the classic DS cases (besides the archetypical case of Japan, in South Korea, Taiwan and Singapore). The authors come to the final conclusion that any explanation for the (rather rare) emergence of DS must be a political one, as (along the institutionalist argumentation, e.g. by Acemoglu and Robinson 2006, 2012) economic institutions ultimately arise from the political struggles of the elites in power, who are primarily motivated by maximizing their own political and economic benefits. Along with more recent lines of argumentation however we have to add here the other actors of the social arena, most importantly the working class (Fine 2013) and also broader parts of the society (see also, Acemoglu and Robinson 2019). All in all we argue throughout this paper in line with the above logic, that a political economy approach is needed, if we want to understand why there are so few, if any developmental states in the twenty-first century.

Our argumentation on the constraints regarding the emergence of DS in the twenty-first century will aim to follow a similar political economic logic, before this however we shortly present the new circumstances, which lead to newly emerging or intensifying challenges in the twenty-first century and determine the external and internal context (and the interdependencies of external and internal factors) in which the most recent statist experiments have to operate.

New Environment for Aspirational in the Twenty-First Century

As we have argued earlier in this paper at the latest by the end of the twentieth century changes in the external and internal context of classic (East Asian-type) developmental states has led to the fall of the classic DS paradigm. At the beginning of the twenty-first century all the "to-be-developmental states" face new challenges (constraints and potentially enabling factors), that significantly differ from circumstances and conditions given at the time of the emergence of classic developmental states by the mid of the last century.

The External Environment for Governments Aiming at Actively Promoting National Development in the Twenty-First Century

In recent development state literature four challenges are mostly highlighted, that represent a new environment for developmentalist states in the early twenty-first century. First, we recall these four challenges mainly relying on Williams (2014: 8–20), while we also revisiting and adapting these to the most recent changes over the last few years. In the following section we add four further aspects which inevitably shape the possibilities of current governments to implement their national development projects.

The first challenge is the *new economic re-structuring*, referring to the shift from manufacturing to the knowledge and service sectors, the so-called bit-driven or new economy based on knowledge and innovation. In this "new economic" setting beyond physical capital accumulation expanding human capabilities and the spread of information (like investments in education, health and the legal infrastructure) play an ever-larger role. Besides these changes, important changes also occurred in the organization of global production. The emergence of global value chains (GVCs) also poses new challenges (constraints but maybe also new opportunities) for governments with developmentalist aspirations (Gereffi 2014). Even though it is less feasible not to participate, still questions arise on how to access, how to connect local firms to GVCs, and how to "persuade" GVCs to contribute to the national development project, and the answers are not yet trivial. Under the new external and internal circumstances of the twenty-first century there is a need to redefine the roles and tools of the states in the context of "late-late developing" countries (Gerschenkron 1962), taking into account the role of GVCs, and also by adding science, technology and innovation (STI) policies to the traditional policy areas.

The second challenge relates to *changes in the political context* of the twenty-first century's developmental states. Changes in domestic politics in the early 2000s were thought to be moving from authoritarian regimes towards more democratic ones was (at least) going hand in hand with the above mentioned spread of new information and communication technologies. By now we know that these presumptions proved to be illusionary, and the retreat of democracy (Freedom House 2018[5]), also referred to as reverse wave of democratization in Huntingtonian sense (Huntington 1991) is the most recent dominant tendency (see also Rodrik 2011; Kurlantzick 2013; Kornai 2016; Bermeo 2016). Without doubts, the emergence of a new bit-driven economy has its direct and indirect consequences also for the society and politics. Due to the appreciation of knowledge and human capabilities, a new "enlightenment" might be taking place (with involving many, while also leaving out other parts of the societies and leading to new tensions and inequalities). These tendencies provoke changes in social needs, norms, values and perceptions. The specific context of classic DS was determined by the late development, the mobilization for war, the external threat of the Cold War and economic nationalism (and due to all these factors the societies of the classic DS were willing to undertake some sacrifices—such as accept repressive authoritarian regimes). In contrast today any "to-be-developmental

[5] https://freedomhouse.org/report/freedom-world/freedom-world-2018.

state" must create and build up a new legitimacy base according to the new circumstances of the twenty-first century. Within this new political context community priorities and the developmental agenda has to be set up based on a new alliance between the state and society, including broader parts of the society (such as the labour class, whoch used to be repressed—or at least co-opted by means of economic growth—in the early DS versions). According to the conventional expectations relying on the development as freedom approach related changes should imply the move from authoritarian regimes towards more democratic ones, where the embeddedness of the political subsystem into the society, political freedom, participation, the involvement of the civic society and the collective determination of the main priorities of the community. According to Amartya Sen (1999) a democratic political system based on representative, deliberative political participation is not just a mean for achieving widely defined development but is a goal in itself. However more recent political changes reveal a political-ideological turn globally with the rise and spread of illiberal or autocratic regimes, accompanied by populist, nationalist and patriotic tendencies. Recent illiberal tendencies have led to democratic backsliding, materializing in changes showing towards strengthened reliance on autocratic governance style, personalistic ruling, attacking checks and balances of political power and hurting independent agencies and institutions. While some authors tend to name these illiberal regimes as some kind of new developmentalist states (see e.g. Wilkin 2016; Scheiring 2020), we do not agree. According to our theoretical framework the starting point for a new developmental state shall be the capability approach to human development, and the main lesson from the classic DS experiences shall be the growth-with equity approach and the resulting inclusive development trajectory. Huge debates are surrounding the possibilities and challenges of the democratic developmental states (see e.g. Robinson and White 1998; Edigheji 2010; Tapscott et al. 2018), which we do not aim to resolve here, merely mention it as a relevant dimension of the currently ongoing developmental states debates.

Accordingly the third challenge is related to *epistemic changes in the meaning of development* and its interpretation (see also Williams 2014: 18). The expansion of the meaning of development is undoubtedly moving away from the'economic growth-centred' thinking of the last century, towards the "development as freedom" interpretation according to Sen (1999), also called human-capabilities approach. Thus the promotion of development does not equal any more with the "technical problematic" of economic growth that merely requires economic knowledge, but a development-oriented approach has to be considered more and more as a political problematic, as social welfare is a function of different non-economic factors (besides of course economic growth), such as social justice, poverty, inequalities or social participation and perception. These changes are however rather representing the changes in development economic thinking and academic debates, than in politician's rhetoric, which is still skewed towards economic growth obsessions, while at the same time (at least in new populist regimes) tends to shift towards emphasizing the need to secure stability and security (and not necessarily promising material or non-material improvements such as higher income-levels or better living conditions).

The last challenge to mention from the conventional list (Williams 2014: 20) is the *ecological* one: environmental limits, including the new challenges posed by the climate change and the aspects of environmental justice. By now it is beyond any doubt, that the resource-intensive development path of the last century based predominantly on fossil-fuels cannot be maintained globally in the twenty-first century. This inherently leads to inevitable changes in existing consumption and production patterns and habits, while existing structures and infrastructures also have to be revised and altered. In the light of market failures and externalities the state has to play a central role in the realization of a green development path. At the same time many authors tend to highlight (such as Mazzucato 2013) that environmental limits also offer the possibility for governments to revise their development strategies, and consider green technology developments as engines for economic growth, employment and innovation on the long run (and to realize an environmentally sustainable development trajectory) (see also Szalavetz this volume). Furthermore we add, that in the light of the past experiences of developmental states besides the environmental aspects greater attention to the spatial dimension of development, and consequently a larger focus on territorial imbalances, especially the development possibilities of rural areas (see Kollai this volume).

There are many further urging pressures (either long existing, intensifying or newly emerging) that might significantly alter possibilities and the room for manoeuvre of the twenty-first century's developmental states. We highlight four of these. First, the effects of intensifying *economic and financial globalization* and additionally the experiences and effects of recent financial and economic crises. Due to these the significance of efficient resource allocation is appreciating, while the financial viability of nation-based development interventions is deteriorating. In an increasingly open global economic system the role of foreign direct investments is appreciated, and leads to important changes in the organization of global production. First the organization into global value chains (GVCs), and more recently in the light of the COVID-19 crisis their reorganization (relocation or regionalization) also poses new challenges (constraints but maybe also new opportunities) for governments with developmentalist aspirations (Gereffi 2014). Even though it is less feasible not to participate, still questions arise on how to join, how to connect local firms to GVCs, and how to "persuade" GVCs to contribute to the national development project, and the answers are not yet trivial.

In order to understand the effects of financial globalization on the viability of development-oriented interventions in the twenty-first century, one has to distinguish between productive (real) and speculative (financial) investments. While in the case of the former it might be a plausible objective to support the generation of employment or the expansion of human capabilities, in the case of the latter state regulation might be needed to decrease the resulting financial vulnerability.[6]

Taking into account the current stage of financial globalization and most recent experiences of global financial (and economic) crises, we can state the DS in the twenty-first century have a much narrower room for manoeuvre to finance their (much broader) economic growth (development) agenda, as did their classic antecedents in the mid of the last century (Fine and Pollen 2017).

In our financially globalized world economy securing macroeconomic stability becomes central, as a solid macroeconomic position might build up good business confidence and thus encourage investors and attract foreign direct investments (FDI). Though in the short run and only temporarily today's developing countries also might rely on external sources (besides FDI, foreign aid and credit) during the implementation

[6] Fine and Pollen (2017) refer to this challenge as *financialization* ('the extraordinary growth of finance'), and highlight its wide-ranging consequences, such as the influence of finance regarding investments, value judgements, and more broadly extending over economic and social policy issues, and as a result constraining (or at least transforming and conditioning) the prospects for development, or even for developmental states to emerge.

of their development strategies, on the longer run a more balanced development budget is needed, and the role of domestic resources cannot be overrated. Incentives for domestic savings, rationalization of government expenditures, the system of national taxes as well as the government's abilities to collect those taxes become central issues to development.

As a second issue, we mention *high and rising inequalities* and its consequences both in terms of political consequences (rise of populism and illiberalism—see next section) and regarding the increased pressures towards active social policies in the short term, while on the longer-term posing inevitable burdens on the economic growth potential. There is emerging consensus that currently real or perceived economic inequality in several countries approaches or surpasses the highest levels of inequality ever recorded (see e.g. Milanovic 2012; Piketty 2014; Mihályi and Szelényi 2019). Even though there are also some success stories from countries that managed to decrease inequalities recently—even if only temporarily, such as in major Latin American countries (López-Calva and Lustig 2010; Cornia 2014—see also Riberio and Rodrigues M. da Silva this volume)—however these trends seem to be halted, and inequalities still remained at steadily high levels. High and/or increasing (real or perceived) levels of inequalities pose pressing challenges to governments with developmental aspirations, as social pressure towards redistribution increases and compete for scarce state revenues (also needed to finance developmentalist interventions). Current governments have to take into consideration, on the one hand, the effects of growing inequalities both on economic performance and on political legitimacy, while on the other hand also how increasing inequalities and social tensions might affect government revenues (via e.g. the ability to collect taxes).

As third we draw attention to *rising populism and illiberal tendencies* both in political and economic terms, emerging as a global trend mainly in the post 2014/16 period (Gerőcs and Szanyi 2019). Along with the rise of political populism, we can observe a tendency towards heterodox economic policy answers, revealing unique specificities and characteristics in different countries, demonstrating however a common tendency towards attacking institutional checks and balances, restraining the autonomy and independence of core agencies and institutions. In this vein we see a new ideational, ideological change towards a more permissive ambient for strong political leaders with developmentalist aspirations (at least in the rhetoric, as more often than not these populist, illiberal leaders aim to maximize their time in power at all costs and means, even if this might compromise economic growth and development on the longer term).

Last but not least we cannot leave out the *most recent effects of the COVD-19* pandemic, the global spread of the coronavirus and its severe social and economic consequences. Throughout the world (though to very different extent—see e.g. the International Monetary Fund's COVID policy tracker[7]) governments have enacted heavy lockdown strategies to slowdown the spread of the virus and introduced stimulus packages to minimalize the economic consequences. The role of the state has increased dramatically ranging from controlling social life to helping out some specific (strategic) sectors and providing social assistance to the most vulnerable groups. Though we consider this return of the interventionist state mostly as crisis-driven and anticyclical, it is yet to early to draw any conclusions regarding their longer-term impacts. However it is almost a commonplace to claim, that every crisis offers an opportunity, and the COVID-19 might have a longer lasting impact on the spreading use of IT-based solutions, resulting in the wider spread of distance working, learning (and to some extent even in medical or other services). All these changes might change the social and political setup (while the composition of winners and losers both in terms of social strata and economic sectors might differ from country to country), leading also to changes in the social and developmental agendas of states with developmentalist aspirations.

Finally we sum up by arguing that in the eve of the third decade of the twenty-first century, we are confronted with an ever changing global context providing new circumstances for statist experiments. Even in the post 2000 period substantial changes have taken place, which would require to differentiate between the period before and after the GFC, or probably to tackle the post 2014/16 (or even post COVID) period separately.

To provide a few examples, as long as the *„new normal"* in the world economy in the early 2000s (the so-called short Golden decade) has meant relatively high economic growth rates, in emerging economies mainly driven by the commodity boom (the rising demand for and increasing prices of primary products), which boosted export performance and incoming FDI. In the more recent 5–6 years however the "*post-new*

[7] https://www.imf.org/en/Topics/imf-and-covid19/Policy-Responses-to-COVID-19.

normal" has meant first sharply declining commodity prices and then remaining at relatively low levels, accompanied by the slowdown of the Chinese economy and one of the lowest interest rates ever recorded. All these represent a totally new external context for all actors in the world economy, but seem to be especially decisive in the global periphery, where externally dependent development and vulnerability are historically paved.

On a global level we can witness *the emergence of new economic powerhouses*, the rise of Asia (and China becoming a regional leading power), and this (along with some traditional economic powers struggling in the aftermath of the Global Financial Crisis to revive economic growth) might add up to the emergence of a new global economic order, with important potential consequences and threats to existing formal and informal international institutions and agreements determining the space for manoeuvre for national states.

More recently the *liberal world order has become under threat* both in political and economic term, which represents however that the pendulum might be swinging back in the Polanyian sense (Polányi 2001/1944; see also Nölke et al. 2019), and these changes might provide even more supportive or permissive conditions for strong leaders to pursue their nationalist development agendas in the twenty-first century. In a post Polanyian approach emancipatory movements might counterbalance these changes, nevertheless, how effectively these newly emerging social forces can alter domestic power dynamics, is yet to be seen (and differ from country to country).

The open global economic system, and increasing global trade volumes as a main source of economic growth might be threatened by *new protectionist* tendencies *(US—China trade war)*, impeding also mega-regional trade agreements. New initiatives might however offer new possibilities for trade and economic cooperation both between the Global North and South (such as the recent EU-Mercosur trade agreement, which still awaits ratification), but also within the group of emerging economies (South to South cooperation).

The *global governance and regulatory environment* has also been seen as significantly constraining the to-be-developmental states' room for manoeuvre in the twenty-first century, with the classic example of the WTO regulations impeding the use of industrial policies to promote national economic development. In this regard however we also have to point towards other possibilities, such as the more permissive regulations regarding STI policies and R&D promotion activities (Wade 2018).

To sum up, on the external front we see both new constraints and potentially enabling factors for to-be-DS in the first two decades of the twenty-first century, and it is very difficult to draw a balance at this general and high abstraction level. The room for manoeuvre for states to implement a developmentalist agenda differs from country to country, depending on the size and role in the world economy, economic structure and political/geopolitical stance. While it is worth to recall the logic of SV, and at least to note that permissive or even favourable conditions (such as those in the first decade of the 2000s—before the GFC) might act perversely. Windfall revenues can be easily spent and distributed without providing "external" pressure on governments to build developmentalist institutions and implement developmentalist policies (the Latin American cases, especially that of Brazil provide a good illustration for this—see Riberio and Rodrigues M. da Silva this volume).

More recently, since the GFC and even more so amidst the COVID-19 pandemic countries are confronted with an ever more urging external context (with serious economic and social consequences), which might effectively push governments towards formulating and implementing national developmentalist agendas. Yet, whether this opportunity will be seized, depends to a large extent on the domestic political circumstances, and the changes occurring in the domestic power relations.

Domestic Dynamics: A Political Economy Perspective on the Institutional Origins of Developmental States

Turning towards the domestic factors of building developmental states in the twenty-first century we aim to look at the domestic institutional and political origins of developmental states. That is, we ask, what factors play an essential role to motivate key actors of the domestic economy and society to coordinate their activities and act together towards building the unique institutional setting (along the required development capacities and autonomy) needed for implementing a developmentalist economic policy package. To put it differently which pressures might urge self-interested political and economic elites to concentrate scarce resources on upgrading developmentalist institutions and policies promoting long-term economic development, instead of just maximizing their own economic and/or political benefits.

Regarding potential domestic driving forces, first we highlight that due to the above presented economic and other changes upgrading in the twenty-first century is more difficult and more institution-intensive task, than it used to be in the mid of the last century. Thus new developmental alliances are needed to effectively push current governments to facilitate intertemporal bargains to cover the mainly short-term costs of investing in *institution-intensive* upgrading-related investments of today, which mostly result in their benefits on the medium or longer term. (Doner and Schneider 2016: 12). This leads to a more accentuated need for a broad coalition of social groups to pressure current state capitalist governments to enact and implement an inclusive developmentalist agenda.

It is straightforward to see, that even despite the most recent years' democratic backsliding, even in the so-called "electoral" democracies political horizons are much shorter, than in the classic developmentalist autocracies, and this weakens the incentives of current governments for long-term investments. Under these circumstances a sustained and accentuated political pressure from broad social coalitions with long-term commitment towards economic upgrading is appreciating (Doner and Schneider 2016: 12). We aim to emphasize that this insight remains relevant even in the light of the recent illiberal regimes with strong leaders ruling for a decade or more. On the one hand their time horizon remains still fairly short, on the other hand even if elections are not always fair and free, some political competition takes place and regular elections tend to shorten the time horizon of governing politicians. This might cause some cyclicality in policy making and implementation even in "quasi"-democratic settings.

If we recall once again the Latin American experiences of the 2000s (such as Argentina or Brazil) it is straightforward to see, that the new developmentalist governments were rather populist, redistributive and even though some partial (and transitional) success stories, these were mostly sinking into corruption (see also the chapters of Csaba and Szigetvári this volume). Doner and Schneider (2016) and Kurlantzick (2016) mention many other interesting examples ranging from Turkey, South Africa, Russia or Malaysia, but the bottom line here is that in these recent statist experiments, governments did not face strong bottom-up pressures from broad social coalitions to implement the necessary reforms for economic upgrading. Weak social demand for such institutions and policies can be explained with the high and rising fragmentation of the society in many emerging and developing economies (whereas the social arena includes not only different segments of the business sector—such as highlighted by the above cited authors, but also different fractions of the labour sector and civil society). In the case of these (late-)late-comers the historical growth paths have led to an overly fragmented social stratification, with many cleavages within and between sectors and classes. Looking at the business sector we see the divisions between domestic and foreign, big and small businesses, or even between those producing on the internal or external markets important, while also the rising tendencies of economic patriotism can be observed (Clift 2019, see also Gerőcs and Szanyi 2019). In the labour arena the interests of formal and informal, or of skilled and unskilled labour force might and more often than not do diverge. While looking in more general terms on the social classes, high and rising inequalities can be accounted for more and more diverging interests, while the move towards prebendalism, where social ranks are more importantly paving the way for upwards social mobility, than did social classes (Szelényi and Mihályi 2020) might also result in deepening social cleavages. To put it short in current emerging and developing countries it seems that it is more difficult to build broad coalitions (that could effectively push governments towards a growth-with-equity approach via building developmentalist institutions and policies) and it also seems less probable.

Conclusions

The aim of this chapter was to shed light on the political origins of developmental states of the twentieth century and try to look at the most recent statist experiments of the twenty-first century by applying a similar political economic approach used in the classic developmental state literature but adopted to the new global and domestic circumstances.

By looking back on the experiences of the classic developmental states, we have recalled the specific global and Northeast Asian context, which has resulted in a unique interplay of external and internal factors and has enabled a unique, impressive and inclusive catching up with the more developed part of the world. From the wide-ranging academic literature on the emergence, rise and fall of the classic DS, we have presented the political economy explanation of Doner et al. (2005), also called systemic vulnerability concept, and argued that its logic has still some relevance if looking at more recent statist experiments.

In the second section, we have presented recent and ongoing changes in the global scene, which provide very different circumstances for states with developmentalist aspirations in the twenty-first century compared to the classical period. We have looked at the global economic and political changes in a dynamic perspective, as even in the post 2000 era constant changes in the global arena have been under way. We have concluded that at this high abstraction level it is very difficult to make plausible predictions on the external factors and conditions, yet we might argue that the ideational context seems to be more permissive towards state-led developmental strategies (and according to McCloskey [2016] ideas do matter for long-term developmental perspectives—see also Csaba [2018] applying a similar approach on some European countries). The post-crisis world economy (which is currently ridden by the impacts of the COVID-19 pandemic and its severe social and economic consequences) might offer a more constrained external environment and thus to pressure domestic governments to look for domestic drivers of development. This would need the building of developmentalist institutions and the implementation of developmentalist policies (preconditioned upon state capacities and autonomy) which result in transformative changes and lead to sustained growth and development on the longer term.

Regarding the domestic political factors we were however more pessimistic and have rather provided a path-dependent story of catching up attempts. Basically many factors that have accompanied latecomer economies since the early stages of development, such as dualistic and fragmented economic and social structures, are still present, and have been even reinforced recently. These historical trajectories, and the resulting deep social cleavages still constrain the possibilities of building strong developmentalist coalitions (this is in line with the Doner and Schneider [2016] argumentation). Thus we have concluded that building successful DS is more difficult in the twenty-first century. Even though we have found that post crises changes on the global level might have led to a more constrained external environment which might push national governments towards opting for state-led development strategies, deep structural cleavages in the domestic arena among very diverse social groups impede building of broad and inclusive coalitions required for pushing economic and political elites towards building developmentalist institutions conducive to upgrading (meaning transformative changes both in the economy and in social terms).

Finally the bottom line is, that to understand the difficulties in terms of economic catching up in the twenty-first century, one has to combine economics with politics (and with sociology), as the reasons for failure (in terms of catching up) are multifaceted and require a wider international political economy perspective. Accepting that the main driving forces of long-term sustainable development are institutions and policies, we still have to ask, where these institutions and policies might come from. The more recent illiberal turn in many emerging and post socialist countries has resulted in the emergence of strong leaders, some even with explicit developmentalist rhetoric (and often with explicit reference to the classic developmental states of the twentieth century). Many tendencies might even resemble some features of the classic developmental states, such as the strengthening of the executive powers or the repression of civil society. However, the overall picture is rather different. In East Asia the economic and institutional system was given and predetermined by unique contextual factors, and the newly emerging national capitalist elite was a result of a competition-based market selection procedure. In contrast in the case of the more recent (illiberal) statist experiments, the logic of institutional changes is rather different. In most of these new cases institutions (and policies) are tailored to favour some pre-selected new national capitalists as the concept of Economic Patriotism in the Capitalist World-Systems thoroughly explains (Gerőcs and Szanyi, 2019), whereby the criteria for selection is political loyalty and personal ties. Thus the central governments of these (pseudo-) developmentalist regimes here are driving institutional change according to their own (more political than economic) priorities leading to higher levels of corruption and rent-seeking (Mihályi and Szelényi 2019; Szelényi and Mihályi 2020). The underlying reason according to our argumentation in this paper is the lack of systemic vulnerability conditions, in fact the lack of severe urging pressures, though more in the domestic arena, and less in the external context, where in the post-crises period (first following the GFC and amidst the most recent COVID-related crisis) urgency has re-gained ground. On the external front the conditions have been continuously changing during the first two decades of the new Millennium from a more favourable one to a more crisis-driven period in the post-GFC era (and even more so since the spread of the COVID-19 epidemic and the resulting lock down strategies). In contrast however in the domestic arena the changes have shown towards increasing fragmentation and deepening cleavages, which were in most cases historically present and rooted, but were also reinforced by recent populist policy making and rhetoric and "divide et impera" cooptation strategies. Rising inequalities and increasing stratification of societies by rank (Szelényi and Mihályi 2020) have hindered broad coalition building in emerging and developing countries, and this explains the lack of strong or "unified" domestic pressures on elites to pursue a growth-with-equity strategy, via building developmentalist institutions and implementing developmentalist policies, instead of just reaping the fruits of favourable external conditions (as it was the case before the GFC in Latin America) or to maximize their own economic and/or political benefits. Thus a rather "urging" global environment combined with the lack of (unified) domestic pressures might however re-open the way for the traditional agency views and shed light on the role of elites in promoting economic development under a basically (at least domestically) unconstrained conditions.

Finally, throughout in this chapter we have argued that the systemic vulnerability approach might be helpful even today if we want to better understand the statist experiments of the early twenty-first century, and even if we admit that it was exactly the lack of urgency (at least within the domestic arena) that has (re-)opened the way towards the emergence of strong leaders (and widened their policy space offering basically more room for maneuver). The statist experiments of the twenty-first century seem to differ not only in their strategies towards development, but also in their achievements both in economic and social terms from their classical counterparts—we leave this question however open for further research. What we claim is rather that the recent illiberal and statist turn has brought the agency views back into the post-crisis developmental state debates and has shed light on the need for a systemic approach, and the need for thoroughly analysing the domestic power dynamics and go beyond the focus on the role of elites in development, and by including all actors of the domestic social arena (representatives and associations of business, labour, civil society).

References

Acemoglu, D. – Robinson, J A. (2006): *Economic Origins of Dictatorship and Democracy.* Cambridge, UK: Cambridge University Press.

Acemoglu, D. – Robinson, J A. (2012): *Why Nations Fail: The Origins of Power, Prosperity and Poverty.* New York: Crown Publishers.

Acemoglu, D. – Robninson, J. A. (2019): *The Narrow Corridor: How Nations Struggle for Liberty.* London: Penguin Books.

Agénor, P. R. – Canuto, O. – Jelenic, M. (2012): Avoiding Middle-Income Growth Traps. *The World Bank, Economic Premise,* Nr. 98.

Amsden, A. (1989): *Asia's Next Giant: South Korea and Late Industrialization.* New York, NY: Oxford University Press.

Amsden, A. H. – Di Caprio – Robinson, J. A. (2012): *The Role of Elites in Economic Development.* Oxford: Oxford University Press.

Beeson, M. (2004): The Rise and Fall (?) of the Developmental State: The Vicissitudes and Implications of East Asian Interventionism. In: Low, L. ed.: *Developmental States: Relevancy, Redundancy or Re-configuration.* New York, NY: Nova Science Publisher. pp. 29–40.

Benczes I. (2000): Válság és átalakulás a Távol-Keleten. (Crisis and Tranformation in the Far East). *Külgazdaság*, 44(3): 56–75.

Benczes I. (2002): A fejlesztő állam válsága Ázsiában. (The Crisis of Developmental State in Asia). *Külgazdaság*, 46(5): 23–40.

Bermeo, N. (2016): On Democratic Backsliding. *Journal of Democracy*, 27(1): 5–19.

Boltho, A. – Weber, M. (2009): Did China Follow the East Asian Development Model? *The European Journal of Comparative Economics*, 6(2): 267–286.

Clift, B. (2019): Economic Patriotism, the Politics of Market-Making, and the Role of the State in Twenty-First-Century Capitalism. In: Gerőcs – Szanyi eds.: *Market Liberalism and Economic Patriotism in Capitalist Systems. The Role of State in Varieties of Capitalism (SVOC).* Cham: Palgrave Macmillan. pp. 9–21.

Cornia, G. A. ed. (2014): *Falling Inequality in Latin America: Policy Changes and Lessons.* Oxford: Oxford University Press.

Csaba L. (2018): *Válság–gazdaság–világ: Adalék Közép-Európa három évtizedes gazdaságtörténetéhez (1988–2018).* (Crisis–Economy–World: Addendum to the Three-Decade Economic History of Central Europe, 1988–2018). Budapest: Éghajlat Könyvkiadó.

Doner, R. F. – Ritchie, B. K. – Slater, D. (2005): Systemic Vulnerability and the Origins of Developmental States: Northeast and Southeast Asia in Comparative Perspective. *International Organization*, 59(2): 327–361.

Doner, R. F. – Schneider, B. R. (2016): The Middle-Income Trap: More Politics than Economics. *World Politics*, 68(4): 608–644. doi: https://doi.org/10.1017/S0043887116000095.

Edigheji, O. ed. (2010): *Constructing a Democratic Developmental State in South Africa: Potentials and Challenges.* Cape Town: HSRC Press.

Evans, P. B. (1995): *Embedded Autonomy: States and Industrial Transformation.* Princeton, NJ: Princeton University Press.

Fine, B. (2013): Beyond the Developmental State: An Introduction. In: Fine, B., Saraswati J. – Daniela, T. eds.: *Beyond the Developmental State: Industrial Policy into the Twenty-first Century.* London: Pluto. pp. 1–32.

Fine, B. – Pollen, G. (2017): The Developmental State Paradigm in the Age of Financialization. In: Munck, R. – Fagan, H. eds.: *Handbook of Development and Social Change*.

Gereffi, G. (2014): Global Value Chains in a Post-Washington Consensus World. *Review of International Political Economy*, 21:1, 9–37.

Gerőcs , T. – Szanyi, M. eds. (2019): *Market Liberalism and Economic Patriotism in Capitalist Systems*. Cham: Palgrave Macmillan.

Gerschenkron, A. (1962): *Economic Backwardness in Historical Perspective. A Book of Essays*. Cambridge, Mass.: The Belknap Press of Harvard University.

Haggard, S. (2018): *Developmental States*. Cambridge: Cambridge University Press.

Huntington, S. P. (1991): *The Third Wave: Democratization in the Late Twentieth Century*. University of Oklahoma Press, Norman.

Johnson, C. (1982): *MITI and the Japanese Miracle: The Growth of Industrial Policy, 1925–75*. Stanford, CA: Stanford University Press.

Johnson, C. (1999): The Developmental State: Odyssey of a concept. In: Woo-Cumings, M. ed.: *The Developmental State*. New York, NY: Cornell University Press. pp. 32–60.

Knight, J. B. (2014): China as a Developmental State. *The World Economy*, 37(10): 1335–1347.

Kornai, J. (2016): The System Paradigm Revisited. Clarification and Additions in the Light of Experiences in the Post-Socialist Region. *Acta Oeconomica*, 66(4): 547–596.

Kurlantzick, J. (2013): *Democracy in Retreat. The Revolt of the Middle Class and the Worldwide Decline of Representative Government*. Yale University Press, New Heaven – London.

Kurlantzick, J. (2016): *State Capitalism: How the Return of Statism is Transforming the World*. New York, NY: Oxford University Press.

López-Calva, L. F. – Lustig, N. C. (2010): *Declining Inequality in Latin America: A Decade of Progress?* Washington DC: Brookings Institution Press.

Low, L. ed. (2004): *Developmental States: Relevancy, Redundancy or Reconfiguration*. New York, NY: Nova Science Publisher.

Mazzucato, M. (2013): *The Entrepreneurial State: Debunking Public vs. Private Sector Myths*. London: Anthem Press.

McCloskey, D. N. (2016): *Bourgois Equality—How Ideas, not Capital or Institutions, Enriched the World*. Chicago, IL: University of Chicago Press.

Mihályi P. – Szelényi I. (2019): *Rent-Seekers, Profits, Wages and Inequality—The Top 20%*. Palgrave Pivot Series, Cham: Palgrave-Macmillan.

Milanovic, B, (2012): Global Income Inequality by the Numbers: In History and Now. *The World Bank, Policy Research Working Paper* 6259. pp. 1–28.

Naughton, B. (2017): Is China Socialist? *Journal of Economic Perspectives*, 31(1): 3–24.

Nölke, A., ten Brink, T., May, C. – Claar, S. (2019): *State-permeated Capitalism in Large Emerging Economies*. Routledge, New York.
Onis, Z. (1991): The Logic of the Developmental State. *Comparative Politics*, 24(1): 109–126.
Pempel, T. J. (1999): The Developmental Regime in a Changing World Economy. In: Woo-Cumings, M. ed.: *The Developmental State*. Ithaca, NY: Cornell University Press. pp. 137–181.
Piketty, T. (2014): *Capital in the Twenty-First Century*. Cambridge, MA: Belknap Press.
Polanyi, K. (2001/1944): *The Great Transformation: The Political and Economic Origins of Our Time*. Boston, MA: Beacon Press.
Pye, L. W. (1985): *Asian Power and Politics: The Cultural Dimensions of Authority*. Harvard University Press, Cambridge.
Ricz, J. (2016): *Developmental States in the 21st Century: Analytical Structure of a New Approach*. Working Paper Nr. 223, Institute of World Economics, Centre for Economic and Regional Studies Hungarian Academy of Sciences.
Ricz, J. (2019): The Changing Role of the State in Development in Emerging Economies: The Developmental State Perspective. In: Szanyi, M. eds.: *Seeking the Best Master: State Ownership in the Varieties of Capitalism*. Budapest—New York: Centre for Economic and Regional Studies, Hungarian Academy of Sciences, Central European University Press. pp. 237–273.
Robinson, M. – White, G. (1998): *The Democratic Developmental State: Politics and Institutional Design*. Oxford: Oxford University Press.
Rodrik, D. (2011): *The Globalization Paradox: Democracy and the Future of the World Economy*. W. W. Norton & Co., New York.
Scheiring, G. (2020): *The Retreat of Liberal Democracy: Authoritarian Capitalism and the Accumulative State in Hungary*. Palgrave Macmillan.
Sen, A. (1999): *Development as Freedom: Human Capability and Global Need*. New York: Alfred A. Knopf: Anchor Books.
Stubbs, R. (2005): *Rethinking Asia's Economic Miracle*. Palgrave Macmillan, New York.
Szanyi, M. ed. (2019): *Seeking the Best Master: State Ownership in the Varieties of Capitalism*. Budapest - New York: Center for Economic and Regional Studies, Hungarian Academy of Sciences, Central European University Press.
Székely-Doby A. (2020): The Chinese Developmental State: Threats, Challenges and Prospects. *Issues & Studies: A Social Science Quarterly on China, Taiwan, and East Asian Affairs*.
Szelényi I., & Mihályi P. (2020): *Varieties of Post-Communist Capitalism: A Comparative Analysis of Russia, Eastern Europe and China*. Series: Studies in Critical Social Sciences, volume 157, Brill.

Tapscott, C. — Halvorsen, T. — Cruz-Del Rosario, T. eds. (2018): *The Democratic Developmental State: North-South Perspectives. CROP International Poverty Studies*. Stuttgart: ibidem Verlag.

Wade, R. H. (1990): *Governing the Market: Economic Theory and the Role of Government in East Asian Industrialization*. Princeton, NJ: Princeton University Press.

Wade, R. (2018): The Developmental State: Dead or Alive? *Development and Change*, 49(2): 518–46.

Wilkin, P. (2016). *Hungary's Crisis of Democracy: The Road to Serfdom*. London: Lexington books.

Williams, M. ed. (2014): *The End of Developmental State*. New York, NY: Routledge.

Woo-Cumings, M. ed. (1999): *The Developmental State*. New York, NY: Cornell University Press.

CHAPTER 6

Green Industrial Policy and Development—Taking Advanced Economies Over?

Andrea Szalavetz

Introduction

There are two usual ways how papers discussing environmental economics issues are introduced. The first kind of introduction discusses the formidable threat the disregarded *environmental limits to growth* represent for humanity. Ironically, the second usual manner of leading in studies on greening is to allude to the beneficial impact of environmental investments on *growth* and competitiveness.

The second kind of introduction became increasingly common, once certain high-performing developmental states started to display phenomenal growth in installed renewable power generating capacity, and increased their export competitiveness in renewable energy technologies.

A. Szalavetz (✉)
Institute of World Economics, Centre for Economic and Regional Studies, Budapest, Hungary
e-mail: szalavetz.andrea@krtk.hu

T. Gerőcs and J. Ricz (eds.), *The Post-Crisis Developmental State*, International Political Economy Series,
https://doi.org/10.1007/978-3-030-71987-6_6

Indeed, the recognition that the promotion of green industries and technologies is an adequate industrial policy instrument for fostering economic development, innovation, and upgrading has added impetus to a phenomenon coined by Fankhauser et al. (2013) as a 'green race'. It is acknowledged that green industrial policy (GIP) may engender indigenous innovation, generate new market opportunities, contribute to the creation of high-paying (green-collar) jobs, foster the development of new industries and facilitate countries' shifting to a high-road growth trajectory (Mathews 2017; Mazzucato 2015; Rodrik 2014). Hence, similarly to traditional industrial policy, above certain development level, there are no 'why', only 'how' questions, also in the case of GIP.

As the recurrent trade disputes over renewable energy technologies demonstrate, selected developmental states (Jha 2017) have managed to achieve good position in the global green race. Their export competitiveness is increasingly perceived as a threat by developed economy Greentech actors (Knuth 2018; Lewis 2014).

Indeed, green sectors developmental states have undergone rapid technological and economic progress. China, for example, is increasing not only its non-fossil fuel energy generation capacity (Mathews and Reinert 2014) but also its technological and R&D capacities in the field of renewable energy (Gosens and Lu 2013; Huang et al. 2016). India's National Solar Mission is making progress in ramping up its indigenous solar energy industry (REN21 2018) By funding R&D programmes in the field of green technologies, clean energy and electric cars, Korean developmental policy kick-started new growth engines (Kim and Thurbon 2015).

In contrast to the staggering results of GIP in developmental states, observers of GIP in developed economies would come across a number of contributions reporting inferior-to-expectations environmental outcomes (Verzijlbergh et al. 2017), poor cost efficiency and questionable overall net welfare effects (Helm 2014), a wave of bankruptcies, and cases of outright policy failure (Gaddy et al. 2017; Knuth 2018).[1]

[1] Gaddy et al. (2017) demonstrate that the cleantech boom in the USA, in the mid-2000s ended up in a bust by the end of the decade with venture capital investments yielding prohibitively low returns, coupled with expensive failure cases (Rodrik 2014). Several German solar companies have also filed for bankruptcy in the 2010s. Further, Germany's decision to shut down profitable nuclear reactors and build expensive clean energy facilities was heavily criticised, causing huge financial difficulties, among others,

The above selection of cases is intended to suggest neither that GIP in developmental states is necessarily well-designed and effective, free from misallocation and political capture, nor that developing countries embracing developmental environmentalism could already significantly mitigate the serious environmental crisis in their economies.

Nevertheless, the above-sketched background provides strong motivation to explore what lies behind advanced economies' comparably great difficulties with achieving satisfactory performance of their GIPs. Do the observed phenomena refer to advanced economies' relinquishing their leadership position in green energy industries to developmental states?

This chapter employs appreciative theorising (Nelson and Winter 1982: 46) to provide an explanation. We propose that over the life cycle of green energy industries, the drivers of development in the beginning of the growth phase of the industry life cycle are different from those in the transition-to-maturity phase. Contrary to the beginning of the growth phase, when the development of green energy industries is driven by scale-up and progress along the learning curve, in the transition-to-maturity phase, further development is driven, rather, by complementarities and spillovers, that is, by the development of related technologies and by the integration of renewable energy into new sectors and applications.

Green energy industry actors in developmental states, in particular, in China, displayed spectacular catching up and were forging ahead during the beginning of the growth phase. Since the drivers of growth are bound to change in the coming transition-to-maturity phase, we conjecture that despite the enviable global market position of some developmental states, 'game is not over in the ongoing global green race'.

Note that the empirical context used to illustrate our arguments is narrower than what the title of this chapter suggests. The case of China—considered as a particular example of twenty-first century developmental states (e.g. Knight 2014)—will illustrate the experiences of developmental states, which immediately introduces an important caveat to be kept in mind: that of non-negligible differences across developmental states in terms of both environmental governance and the problems GIPs need to address.

for its largest utility company RWE, and making energy costs prohibitively expensive for German customers (Follett 2016).

As for advanced economies, the country cases that illustrate our arguments will be confined mainly to the US (and occasionally to Europe). Similar caveats apply.

Furthermore, the term of GIP will also be used in a narrow sense, referring to green (renewable) energy industrial policy. Over and above green energy industries, green industries encompass, among others, energy efficiency-related industries, pollution control industries, energy storage industries. The focus of this chapter is, however, limited to green energy industries, since performance differences in the GIPs of the two country groups are most conspicuous in this segment of green industries.

To set the context for developing our arguments, we first provide a brief summary of the literature on the main difficulties GIPs in developed countries currently need to cope with. Thereafter, we discuss two explanations of the apparent relative shortcomings of GIP in advanced economies, at least, if compared with the success accounts of developmental states' GIPs. Next, we elaborate on the factors shaping the prospects of green energy industries-driven competitiveness in developmental states (exemplified by China) and in advanced economies. Finally, some concluding remarks are provided.

Difficulties in the Process of Advanced Economies' Clean Energy Transition

Apart from coordination challenges, such as coping with the resistance of existing regimes, governing amidst political struggles, reconciling contradictory interests, and aligning the efforts of isolated agents (Geels 2014), the literature would point to three main types of difficulties to be overcome by the stakeholders of the green (energy) agenda in advanced economies.

The first and most conspicuous challenge is trade related. Green energy technology exporters from developmental states are effectively outcompeting advanced economy producers, who struggle with overcapacity. Consequently, neither public subsidies nor venture capital investments delivered on expectations in advanced economies (Gaddy et al. 2017; Lewis 2014; Knuth 2018). On top of that, a large share of the public subsidies invested by advanced economies with the aim of fostering the local deployment of renewable energy technologies has been captured by developmental state green technology exporters Karp and Stevenson (2012). By contrast, advanced economy exporters faced difficulties in penetrating the markets for renewable technology in developmental states because of protectionist local content regulations (Lewis 2014).

Another series of difficulties faced by advanced economies, in particular European countries, are cost related. Transition to clean energy imposes hardly affordable costs on energy users, particularly, if compared with the costs of competing cheap conventional energy sources and the newly emerging unconventional energy supplies, for example shale gas, (Helm 2014; Verzijlbergh et al. 2017). According to Follett (2016), despite substantial fiscal support to renewable energy, which in turn exacerbated budget deficit, the average German (private) customer pays more than 3.5 times as much for a unit of electricity than its American counterpart. Obviously, a system in which energy users finance the costs of transition has a detrimental impact on industrial competitiveness (Böhringer et al. 2017; Helm 2014).

Ironically, the rapidly declining price of clean energy technologies (Wesoff and Lacey 2017), that was achieved mainly because of developmental states' overwhelming price competitiveness, have also caused problems. The rapidly falling price of imported solar modules and components prevented incumbent clean energy manufacturers in advanced economies from investing in the further development of solar technologies and shifting to quality-based competition.

The third kind of challenge concerns technological, institutional and infrastructural constraints. Over and above the triple requirement of developing, producing, and deploying clean energy technologies, clean energy transition necessitates a bundle of complementary innovations (Markard and Hoffmann 2016). For example, breakthrough innovations in storage technology are regarded as the primary precondition of achieving a transformative change in the energy system. Equally important is clean energy *consumption*, calling, among others, for further innovations in the transport and buildings sectors, in industry and agriculture. Some of the additional necessary complementary innovations concern grid technology: the reorganisation and expansion of electricity distribution, and the enhancement of grid flexibility—indispensable for the integration of renewable energy.[2]

[2] Currently, the grid system is designed for steady electricity flows, which is hardly compatible with volatile renewables providing fluctuating energy inputs.

Altogether, this latter bundle of challenges is rooted in the systemic character of green energy-driven transition to sustainability. Consequently, scholars investigating the reasons of the slow progress of renewable energy-driven transition would point to lock-in problems and system failure (Seto et al. 2016).

Although the latter two kinds of challenges apply not only to advanced economies, our review of the literature identified hardly any papers *discussing difficulties* with respect to developmental states' GIPs (notable exceptions are Cai and Aoyama 2018; Hayashi et al. 2018). The above-listed challenges are usually elaborated upon in studies discussing the reasons why transition to green energy is progressing slowly in advanced economies.

In the following section we review and critically analyse two tentative explanations why GIPs in advanced economies seemingly face more-difficult-to-overcome challenges, compared with GIPs in developmental states.

More-Difficult-to-Overcome Challenges of Gips in Advanced Economies?

Differences in Policy Objectives

An intuitive explanation is that the objectives of GIP are different in the two country groups, hence, policy evaluations consider different proxies.

Developmental states consider investments in green energy transition primarily as an opportunity of creating new growth engines, building new industries, gaining new (export) market opportunities and accelerating technological learning (Kim and Thurbon 2015; Mathews 2014; Schmitz 2017).[3]

Although developmental motivations are also present in advanced economies' green growth strategies (Mazzucato 2015), studies discussing advanced economies' low-carbon energy transition would mainly consider

[3] A telling quote by Schmitz (2017: 521–522) is: "…key actors behind climate-relevant policies are not primarily concerned with environmental or climate issues. Their prime concerns are securing energy for the country, fostering new green industries and making them competitive, creating jobs and incomes in these industries, or laying the foundation for increasing public revenue. Mitigating climate change is not irrelevant, but it tends to be a co-benefit rather than driver."

environmental, i.e. planetary boundaries-related, (Rockström et al. 2009) *and not economic proxies.*[4]

Consider, for example the differences between the two country groups in their purview of renewable energy technology deployment. Advanced economy GIPs consider deployment in the sense of a broader process: uptake of low-carbon technologies across economy and society (Geels et al. 2017). Developmental states, instead, regard it mainly in terms of exporting to international markets (building an internationally competitive renewables sector) and capturing the domestic market by indigenous companies (Chen and Lees 2016).[5]

Altogether, intuition suggests that the developmental targeting of green industries is easier and the building up of domestic manufacturing capacity can be more effectively implemented, than achieving good performance in the highly complex field of renewable energy-driven environmental sustainability. Differences in policy objectives, design and implementation account for the relative inefficiency of GIP in developed countries, which is particularly annoying in the light of the trade-disputes-prompting expansion of industries producing renewable energy technologies in selected developmental states.[6]

[4]The claim that the scope of developmental states' GIPs is much narrower than that of advanced economies is of course exaggeration, valid only in relative terms, since developmental states have also been implementing more or less strict policies in the framework of their Nationally Determined Contributions to Paris Agreement targets (www.climateactiontracker.org).

[5]This is best illustrated by a quote from Knuth (2018: 223–224): "With strong state supports, including in some cases state ownership, Chinese companies rapidly scaled up production of both wind turbines and solar PV modules […] Chinese producers achieved significant economies of scale in their rapid ramp-up, and several quickly became globally ranked solar and wind companies […] new Chinese renewables manufacturers targeted both China's booming domestic market and international exports, they rewrote the rules of the global industry virtually overnight."

Further, according Lam et al.'s (2017) data, China's indigenous wind turbine manufacturing companies dominated the explosive growth of Chinese wind capacity after 2005. At the same time, Chinese wind producers became dominant players in global markets: in 2017, four of the top ten global original equipment manufacturers in the wind turbine industry were based in China, with a cumulative market share of 27.8% (author's calculations from REN21 2018 data).

[6]Besides China, major developmental state exporters of solar technology include Taiwan, Malaysia, Korea, Singapore, Philippines and Mexico. China, India, and to some extent Vietnam, Singapore and Mexico are major wind technology exporters. Note that Brazil is an important player in wind technology manufacturing but except for wind

While it is safe to argue for this proposition, it represents, at best, partial truth. The next section is concerned with another explanation of advanced economies' apparently greater difficulties, compared to developmental states, with achieving satisfactory performance of their GIPs. Its point of departure is that over time green energy industries have matured: they are no more in the emergence phase of their development trajectories. While the institutions and policies of advanced economies were well-aligned with the requirements of the emergence phase of green energy industries, those of developmental states display a better fit with the requirements of the growth phase.

New Challenges in the Growth Phase of Green Energy Industries—Institutional and Policy Alignment

Advanced by Abernathy and Utterback (1978) and further developed by Nelson (1994), the industry life cycle theory describes four phases of industry evolution (emergence, growth, maturity, and decline), explains the features of each phase, and analyses the factors driving transition from one phase to another.

A particularly important assertion of this scholarship, analysed among others in Mowery and Nelson (1999) and Von Tunzelmann (2003), is that institutions, public programmes and policies need to co-evolve with technologies and industries. As the patterns of growth, competition, and innovation differ in the individual stages of the life cycle, industrial policy needs to address different problems. Phase transitions require adjustments in institutions and policy design to maintain policy effectiveness.

Accordingly, as renewable energy industries have undergone phase transition from emergence to growth, industrial policy also needs to be accommodated to the changed context and the associated new types of challenges.

Although at first sight, policy exigencies in the growth phase of new industries are inferior to those in the emergence phase, as *developing* cutting-edge technologies is more challenging than *manufacturing* cutting-edge technologies—the case of GIP requires a more nuanced evaluation.

turbine generators, Brazilian companies produce mainly for the domestic market (Jha 2017). Over the period from 2006 to 2015, 45 trade remedy cases in the clean energy sector have been notified to the WTO (Kampel 2017, p. vii).

Contrary to the emergence phase of green energy industries, when industrial policy was concerned mainly with supporting R&D and new technology-oriented start-ups, the growth phase requires, among others, support to scale-up: to companies' overcoming poor initial economies of scale and bringing technologies down the learning curve. Support to scale-up necessitates increased emphasis on demand-pull instruments (compared with the predominantly technology-push ones in the emergence phase), which entails-related adjustments in fiscal and regulatory policies.

Additionally, since the diffusion of renewable energy technologies presupposes *structural change*, policy needs to concentrate also on combating lock-in, by addressing cultural, infrastructural, economic[7] and institutional barriers (Seto et al. 2016; Unruh 2000). This involves extensive coordination problems.

It should be noted that the financing requirements of GIP in the growth phase are much higher than the expenses of funding and nurturing emerging industries. Moreover, the time required for growth phase-specific interventions to deliver, may also exceed that of emergence phase-specific ones.

In many respects, institutions and policies in developmental states seem better fit to cope with these challenges.

Consider support to scale-up and market building. Achieving industrial leadership through development of industrial capacity, technological catch-up, and foreign market penetration has been a traditional industrial policy objective in developmental states.

In China, developmental interventions have consistently supported technology acquisition, local knowledge creation, and scale-up through exports to global markets/integration into global value chains.[8]

[7] An important economic barrier stems from the fact that competing 'dirty' technologies are usually more advanced than emerging green ones. Moreover, incumbent dirty technology providers usually invest in further developing their technologies.

[8] Note that there are non-negligible differences across developmental states with respect to export orientation: Brazilian wind industry actors, for example, have achieved scale-up and technological learning mainly through acquiring the domestic market (for further details of the Brazilian case see the chapter by Riberio Marques da Silva in this volume). Differences can be observed even within China: the spectacular growth of the wind power industry was driven mainly by the expansion of the domestic market that enjoyed substantial policy support funding the increase of domestic installed capacity. Conversely,

In a way, historical institutional contexts, firm strategies and patterns of state–economy interactions have predestined Chinese green energy industry actors' effective scale-up and global expansion (Chen and Lees 2016; Huang et al. 2016). By contrast, historical institutional contexts, firm strategies, and patterns of state–economy interactions are important explanatory factors of US firms' specialisation in clean energy technologies-related R&D (Knuth 2018; Mazzucato 2015).

Consider also the intensification of coordination challenges in the growth phase. Developmental states are adept at applying authoritarian environmentalism[9] (Beeson 2010). A top-down command and control mode of environmental governance can significantly mitigate structural change-related coordination challenges that prevail in advanced economies characterised by participatory modes of governance (Dent 2018). Developmental states are less subject to internal resistance by representatives of dirty incumbent industries (Dent 2018; Kim and Thurbon 2015) and needn't face such a powerful internal opposition because of the equity implications of low-carbon energy transition as policy-makers in advanced economies (Lauber and Jacobsson 2016). Hence, green industrial policy-makers in developmental states can more effectively steer the structural transformation related to the diffusion of renewable energy technologies.[10]

With regard to finance provision, again, developmental states are in a better position than advanced economies to fill the green investment gap and finance mission-oriented approaches, for example, through relying on state-owned development banks, and monetary policy innovations (Campiglio 2016; Mazzucato and Penna 2016).

Moreover, when it comes to mobilising resources for accelerating technology diffusion, developmental states, exercising executive power more autonomously than established advanced economies, face less

the Chinese solar industry was export-oriented from the outset (Lam et al. 2017; Zhang et al. 2013).

[9] In accordance with Beeson (2010) authoritarian environmentalism is defined here as policy model featuring a relatively autonomous central state, with experts and technocrats playing key role, while the power of business groups and social actors is limited.

[10] Geels (2014) and Johnstone et al. (2017), for example, offer detailed overview, how incumbent regime actors in the UK mobilised power to resist climate change-related pressures and prevent fundamental system change. Kungl (2015) provides a similar account for Germany.

internal resistance to employing vertical industrial policy instruments and resorting to direct subsidies—at least compared to the heated ideological debates on industrial and climate policy in selected advanced economies (MacNeil and Paterson 2012). Vertical policy instruments are expected to have swifter impact, hence, regarded more effective than horizontal, market-based instruments. Developmental states can apply dirigiste state planning and can directly promote strategic industries through establishing new state-owned enterprises and providing direct guidance to existing ones (cf. Ricz, this volume, introductory chapter).

Altogether, while the institutions and policies of advanced economies were well-aligned with the requirements of the emergence phase of green energy industries (effectively promoted R&D and new technology-oriented start-ups), those of developmental states display a seemingly better fit with the requirements of the growth phase. As mentioned earlier, this proposition relies on the established scholarship of coevolution of institutions, governance and technology.

Although these arguments seem well-substantiated, if we dig deeper into the GIP literature some ambiguities emerge, worth elaborating upon. The first, most conspicuous controversy is that several advanced economies (for example the USA, Germany, Denmark) are, themselves, large *producers* and exporters of renewable energy technologies (Jha 2017): they do not specialise exclusively in clean energy-related R&D. By contrast, Chinese solar industry actors have come to specialise also in research and development of next-generation technologies, and have non-negligible innovation achievements (Gosens and Lu 2013; Huang et al. 2016).

GIP literature is far from straightforward with respect to advanced economies' alleged refraining from vertical targeting and employing dominantly market-based, horizontal instruments. Consider the growing literature on the direct, entrepreneurial role of states in developed countries, among others, in the field of green (energy) technologies (Mazzucato 2015; Meckling 2018). As for par excellence vertical and direct policy instruments, such as investment subsidies, rebates or energy production payments, the comprehensive data published in REN21 (2018: 64) demonstrate that most high-income advanced economies resort to one or another form of these fiscal incentives. Another well-known feature of GIP in advanced economies, questioning a black-and-white differentiation, is that these latter countries also resort to state-owned development banks or to mission-oriented developmental institutions for funding green initiatives (Mazzucato and Penna 2016). Note that China is gradually employing also market-based instruments[11] such as carbon taxes and tradeable permits.

The argument that the top-down command and control mode of environmental governance in authoritarian developmental states grant them exceptional advantage over advanced economies in implementing GIP, also falls short of empirical evidence. On one hand, evidence is accumulating that the effectiveness of China's authoritarian environmentalism is undermined by energy-intensive firms' weak compliance and by the failure of the central government to control local governments (Cai and Aoyama 2018; Lo 2015). Moreover, Shen (2017) pointed out that influential corporations in the renewable energy industry or state-owned electricity utility companies have played active role in the design of China's renewable energy policy priorities, and have been able to constrain central and local governments' autonomy in policy design and occasionally, execution.

On the other hand, there are abundant examples of advanced economies' effectively implementing programmes that provoke controversies and are contested by various interest groups. The highly contested phase-out programmes in the field of nuclear energy, coal, petrol and diesel cars, and incandescent light bulbs are salient examples (Rogge and Johnstone 2017).

Prospects of Green Energy Industries-Driven Competitiveness

Our review of the literature indicates that the institutional and operational differences between developmental states and advanced economies in the design and implementation of GIP are less clear-cut than what is suggested by the better-institutional-and-policy-alignment proposition.

Moreover, neither advanced economies, nor developmental states can be unambiguously classified by the degree, methods and direction of state intervention in green industries. Even within China, there are important differences between the wind and the solar industries regarding the features of state intervention.

[11] For instance, China launched the world's largest emissions trading scheme in 2017 (REN21 2018).

An additional argument against hasty categorisation is that analyses of GIPs using an approach of *comparative statics* can only produce ephemeral results: in accordance with the accelerated development of green industries, the objectives and features of state intervention in green energy industries may undergo rapid changes.[12]

With this said, it is time to return to the question advanced in the title of this chapter. China's solar industry is described by Huang et al. (2016) as having been able to bring leading manufacturers from industrialised nations to their knees—this happened for the first time in an emerging, high-tech sector. Is China's renewable energy industrial policy capable to maintain the country's global leadership in the field of renewable energy technologies? What are the prospects of green energy industries-driven competitiveness in advanced economies, in particular in the US, in the context of their (its) current difficulties?

To answer these questions, the difference between renewable energy policy and renewable energy industrial policy seems a good point of departure (Pegels et al. 2018; Zhang et al. 2013). Renewable energy policy aims to promote transformative change in the energy sector. State intervention is motivated either by pure sustainability-oriented considerations or also by other purposes, such as energy security and electricity access of rural population. Renewable energy industrial policy targets renewable energy industries, and the main purpose of state intervention is to promote the competitiveness of these industries.

Obviously, these two policies are interconnected. Over the decade marked by the rapid rise of Chinese renewable energy industries, their interaction was synergistic[13] but renewable energy industrial policy was not contingent upon renewable energy policy. Consequently, Zhang

[12] While the traditional virtues of industrial policy in developmental states (flexibility, pragmatism and responsiveness) remain relevant under increased volatility, uncertainty, complexity and ambiguity (VUCA) characterising the context of today's industrial policy (cf. Petricevic and Teece 2019), these virtues need to be combined with agility. Agile industrial policy—similarly to the somewhat overused concept of enterprise agility—refers to policy-makers' capability to dynamically redirect priorities and resources in response to new requirements and/or opportunities, while still preserving structural stability.

[13] The synergistic interaction of the two kinds of policies refers to the fact that renewable energy industrial policies contributed to lowering the price of green technologies, and had, thus, beneficial impact also on sustainability-oriented transformative change in the energy sector. Similarly, renewable energy policies fostering the development and deployment of renewable energy technologies have also furthered competitiveness objectives.

et al.'s (2013) assertion that China placed priority mainly on developing its renewable energy manufacturing industry, whereas renewable energy-driven transition to sustainability was only of secondary importance, did not hamper the effectiveness of industrial policy for renewable energy.

However, above a threshold level in the development of green energy industries, referred to as transition-to-maturity phase in the industry life cycle, further improvements in the performance of renewable energy industrial policy *presuppose* improvements in the effectiveness of renewable energy policy. New end-use markets for renewable electricity need to be found, for example, through the transformation of energy-intensive industries (integration of renewable power into manufacturing processes), and transportation. Efforts need to be devoted to the modernisation and digitalisation of the grid in order to achieve effective integration of renewables into the power system. Most importantly, the development of related technologies needs to be promoted, for instance, that of ICT, energy storage and electric vehicles. These developments, depending on the effective implementation of renewable energy policy will gradually become indispensable for sustaining the momentum of growth in renewable energy industries.

Consequently, a novel combination of instruments of the two kinds of policies is required. GIPs—even the ones that used to be more or less limited to strengthening the competitiveness of green energy industries—will need to focus increasingly on energy transition-related issues, more specifically on *system failures* that hamper the further development and diffusion of green energy technologies.

Moreover, the required policy mix needs to be more diversified than either in the emergence phase of green energy industries, when a pure technological approach, combined with the protection of new industries seemed sufficient in selected advanced economies, or in the beginning of the growth phase, when policies targeting deployment and further technological improvement were appropriate. In the transition-to-maturity phase, GIP is also expected to orchestrate institutional and regulatory changes, manage structural change, and focus, in particular, on technological and infrastructural complementarities (Markard and Hoffmann 2016).

On the other hand, pure scientific and technological problems will also abound among the challenges GIPs need to cope with, since the evolution of green energy industries will be propelled mainly by the innovation-driven transformation of related technologies and by the integration of renewable power into new sectors and applications. Both developments require considerable investments in R&D supply and demand.

These arguments make it highly uncertain to predict who will 'lead the dance' in the coming, transition-to-maturity phase of the development of green energy industries.

There are signs supporting the proposition that advanced economies, in particular the US, whose industrial policy promotes specialisation in non-contestable, innovative activities (Leamer 2007), can maintain leadership—not in terms of manufacturing and exporting green energy technologies but rather in terms of green energy technologies-related value capture. Consider the effectiveness of the US innovation system at fostering the generation of scientific and technological solutions for the integration of renewable energy in adjacent industries (Knuth 2018; Meckling and Nahm 2018). Consider also the flexibility of the US innovation system, illustrated among others by the recent restructuring of the cleantech portfolios of US venture capital firms towards smart grid technologies, solar and wind forecasting technologies, electric vehicle and storage technologies, energy management platforms and energy analytics solutions (Day 2015).

By contrast, China needs to cope with still substantial 'teething' problems, stemming from the compressed development (Whittaker et al. 2010) of its green energy industries, for example, with grid connection problems and with a high (albeit gradually declining) rate of curtailment (REN21 2018).

Alternatively, consider China's efforts to develop its energy storage industry, in response to the recognition of the paramount importance of energy storage for the integration and consumption of renewable energy resources (Yu et al. 2017). Previously, over the past couples of decades, China demonstrated remarkable capabilities to bring about spectacular achievements in various industries and technologies its industrial policy decided to focus on. It has been particularly adept at leveraging its integration into global value chains to achieve technological learning. Currently, China is devoting immense efforts to build indigenous R&D capabilities. It is rightly depicted as a rapid innovation follower in the solar industry (Zhang and Gallagher 2016) albeit somewhat more of a laggard with respect to wind technology innovation (Lam et al. 2017). Altogether, although China still has a long way to go along the energy storage innovation cycle, these capabilities suggest that it may catch-up with currently more advanced competitors also in energy storage. At a later point along the cycle, it may even acquire industrial leadership in energy storage.

Nevertheless, there is more to addressing system failures in green energy-driven transitions than gaining control of the market in specific industries, however, high-tech they are.

In contrast to solving particular unitary problems or accomplishing discrete policy objectives (such as achieving technological breakthroughs and industrial leadership in energy storage industry), addressing system failures and promoting the transformation of energy-intensive industries requires the ability to resolve multi-dimensional and interconnected (trade-off laden) problems.

Consequently, the further development and diffusion of green energy technologies and thus, green energy industries-driven competitiveness will mainly depend on countries' ability to overcome system failures in the transition to green energy. More specifically, it will be influenced by countries' ability to promote and effectively orchestrate the renewables-driven transformation of related technologies and industries.

As the aforementioned difficulties of advanced economies' GIPs demonstrate, advanced economies are not necessarily better at resolving systemic problems. Nevertheless, intuition suggests that public policies in advanced economies have longer been exposed to addressing systemic problems (for example grand societal challenges) than those in developmental states, and have thus, accumulated more experience in adaptive governance, policy learning, collaboration, and institutional adjustment (Nelson 1974). Moreover, the institutional set-up, the policy-making mechanisms, and the governance modes of advanced economies, that is their adaptive, polycentric governance (Jordan et al. 2018) grant them better adaptation capability than what is the case in China, irrespective of the long-term development planning, resource mobilisation and effective plan implementation capabilities of the latter.

Concluding Remarks

The results of this chapter indicate that analysis of the practices of GIP, and/or the features of environmental governance is of little help to position countries in the 'global green race'—if Fankhauser et al.'s (2013) metaphor make any sense.

Instead of predicting the dynamics of comparative advantage and prospective leadership in green energy industries, this study contributes to the discussion on GIPs, and in a more general sense on the perspectives of developmental states, in three ways.

First, arguing for a nuanced evaluation of the differences between developmental states (exemplified by China) and advanced economies, the chapter highlights that the institutional, operational, and governance-related differences between these two country groups are less clear-cut than what is suggested in the literature.

Second, it draws attention to the evolutionary dynamics of the relation between green energy policy and green energy industrial policy. It shows that above a threshold level in the development of green energy industries, further diffusion and development of green energy technologies become contingent upon progress in low-carbon energy-driven transition, that is, upon the performance of renewable energy policy. Contrary to the beginning of the growth phase, when the development of green energy industries is driven by scale-up and progress along the learning curve, in the transition-to-maturity phase, further development in renewable energy technologies and industries is driven by the development of related technologies and by the integration of renewable energy into new sectors and applications.

Third, our study suggests that although there were notable differences between the two country groups in terms of the principal objectives of GIP, the above-outlined evolution of the relation between green energy policy and green energy industrial policy will start to revoke the resulting differences in the policy mixes, and will thus make the performance of GIPs easier to compare.

These results generate important implications for industrial policy in developmental states in general, and in China, in particular. An obvious implication is the imperative of reorganising industrial policy for green energy industries, fostering the transformation of related technologies and supporting the integration of renewables into new sectors and applications. Technology breakthroughs enabling the integration of renewables combined with an effective management of complementarities could create new end-use markets for renewable electricity. This could open up new synergies, necessary for the further development of renewable energy industries.

References

Abernathy, W. J. – Utterback, J. M. (1978): Patterns of industrial innovation. *Technology Review*, 80(7), 40–47.

Beeson, M. (2010): The coming of authoritarian environmentalism. *Environmental Politics*, 19(2), 276–294.

Böhringer, C. – Garcia-Muros, X. – Cazcarro, I. – Arto, I. (2017): The efficiency cost of protective measures in climate policy. *Energy Policy*, 104, 446–454.

Cai, Y. – Aoyama, Y. (2018): Fragmented authorities, institutional misalignments, and challenges to renewable energy transition: A case study of wind power curtailment in China. *Energy Research & Social Science*, 41, 71–79.

Campiglio, E. (2016): Beyond carbon pricing: The role of banking and monetary policy in financing the transition to a low-carbon economy. *Ecological Economics*, 121, 220–230.

Chen, G. C. – Lees, C. (2016): Growing China's renewables sector: A developmental state approach. *New Political Economy*, 21(6), 574–586.

Day, R. (2015): The next wave of green tech. CB Insights Research Briefs. https://www.cbinsights.com/research/greentech-next-wave (accessed on 21 September 2018).

Dent, C. M. (2018): East Asia's new developmentalism: State capacity, climate change and low-carbon development. *Third World Quarterly*, 39(6), 1191–1210.

Fankhauser, S. – Bowen, A. – Calel, R. – Dechezleprêtre, A. – Grover, D. – Rydge, J. – Sato, M. (2013): Who will win the green race? In search of environmental competitiveness and innovation. *Global Environmental Change*, 23(5), 902–913.

Follett, A. (2016): Green energy could cause the largest bankruptcy in German history. *The Daily Caller*. http://dailycaller.com/2016/07/06/green-energy-could-cause-the-largest-bankruptcy-in-german-history/ (accessed on 27 August 2018).

Gaddy, B. E. – Sivaram, V. – Jones, T. B. – Wayman, L. (2017): Venture capital and cleantech: The wrong model for energy innovation. *Energy Policy*, 102, 385–395.

Geels, F. W. (2014): Regime resistance against low-carbon transitions: Introducing politics and power into the multi-level perspective. *Theory, Culture and Society*, 31(5), 21–40.

Geels, F. W. – Sovacool, B. K. – Schwanen, T. – Sorrell, S. (2017): Sociotechnical transitions for deep decarbonization. *Science*, 357(6357), 1242–1244.

Gosens, J. – Lu, Y. (2013): From lagging to leading? Technological innovation systems in emerging economies and the case of Chinese wind power. *Energy Policy*, 60, 234–250.

Hayashi, D. – Huenteler, J. – Lewis, J. I. (2018): Gone with the wind: A learning curve analysis of China's wind power industry. *Energy Policy*, 120, 38–51.

Helm, D. (2014): The European framework for energy and climate policies. *Energy Policy*, 64, 29–35.

Huang, P. – Negro, S. O. – Hekkert, M. P. – Bi, K. (2016): How China became a leader in solar PV: An innovation system analysis. *Renewable and Sustainable Energy Reviews*, 64, 777–789.

Jha, V. (2017): Building supply chain efficiency in solar and wind energy: Trade and other policy considerations. ICTSD Issue Paper, International Centre for Trade and Sustainable Development, Geneva: https://www.ictsd.org/sites/default/files/research/building_supply_chain_efficiency_in_solar_and_wind_energy_digital.pdf (accessed on 17 August 2018).

Johnstone, P. – Stirling, A. – Sovacool, B. (2017): Policy mixes for incumbency: Exploring The destructive recreation of renewable energy, shale gas 'fracking and nuclear power in the United Kingdom. *Energy Research and Social Science*, 33, 147–162.

Jordan, A. – Huitema, D. – van Asselt, H. – Forster, J. (Eds.) (2018): *Governing climate change: Polycentricity in action?* Cambridge University Press, New York.

Kampel, K. (2017): Options for disciplining the use of trade remedies in clean energy technologies. ICTSD Issue Paper, Geneva: International Centre for Trade and Sustainable Development. https://www.ictsd.org/sites/default/files/research/options_for_discipling_trade_remedies_in_cets.pdf (accessed on 17 August 2018).

Karp, L. – Stevenson, M. (2012): Green industrial policy: Trade and theory. World Bank Policy Research Working Paper, No. 6238.

Kim, S. Y. – Thurbon, E. (2015): Developmental environmentalism: Explaining South Korea's ambitious pursuit of green growth. *Politics and Society*, 43(2), 213–240.

Knight, J. B. (2014): China as a developmental state. *The World Economy*, 37(10), 1335–1347.

Knuth, S. (2018): "Breakthroughs" for a green economy? Financialization and clean energy transition. *Energy Research and Social Science*, 41, 220–229.

Kungl, G. (2015): Stewards or sticklers for change? Incumbent energy providers and the politics of the German energy transition. *Energy Research & Social Science*, 8, 13–23.

Lam, L. T. – Branstetter, L. – Azevedo, I. M. (2017): China's wind industry: Leading in deployment, lagging in innovation. *Energy Policy*, 106, 588–599.

Lauber, V. – Jacobsson, S. (2016): The politics and economics of constructing, contesting and restricting socio-political space for renewables—The German renewable energy act. *Environmental Innovation and Societal Transitions*, 18, 147–163.

Leamer, E. E. (2007): A flat world, a level playing field, a small world after all, or none of the above? A review of Thomas L. Friedman's The World is Flat. *Journal of Economic Literature*, 45(1), 83–126.

Lewis, J. I. (2014): The rise of renewable energy protectionism: Emerging trade conflicts and implications for low carbon development. *Global Environmental Politics*, 14(4), 10–35.

Lo, K. (2015): How authoritarian is the environmental governance of China? *Environmental Science and Policy*, 54, 152–159.

MacNeil, R. – Paterson, M. (2012): Neoliberal climate policy: From market fetishism to the developmental state. *Environmental Politics*, 21(2), 230–247.

Markard, J. – Hoffmann, V. H. (2016): Analysis of complementarities: Framework and examples from the energy transition. *Technological Forecasting and Social Change*, 111, 63–75.

Mathews, J. A. (2014): *Greening of capitalism: How Asia is driving the next great transformation*. Stanford University Press, Stanford, CA.

Mathews, J. A. (2017): *Global green shift: When ceres meets Gaia*. Anthem Press, London.

Mathews, J. A. – Reinert, E. S. (2014): Renewables, manufacturing and green growth: Energy strategies based on capturing increasing returns. *Futures*, 61, 13–22.

Mazzucato, M. (2015): The green entrepreneurial state. In: Scoones, I. – Leach, M. – Newell, P. (Eds.) *The politics of green transformations*. Routledge, London.

Mazzucato, M. – Penna, C. C. (2016): Beyond market failures: The market creating and shaping roles of state investment banks. *Journal of Economic Policy Reform*, 19(4), 305–326.

Meckling, J. (2018): The developmental state in global regulation: Economic change and climate policy. *European Journal of International Relations*, 24(1), 58–81.

Meckling, J. – Nahm, J. (2018): When do states disrupt industries? Electric cars and the politics of innovation. *Review of International Political Economy*, 1–25.

Mowery, D. – Nelson, R. R. (Eds.) (1999): *The sources of industrial leadership*. Cambridge University Press, New York.

Nelson, R. R. (1974): Intellectualizing about the moon-ghetto metaphor: A study of the current malaise of rational analysis of social problems. *Policy Sciences*, 5(4), 375–414.

Nelson, R. R. (1994): The co-evolution of technology, industrial structure, and supporting institutions. *Industrial and Corporate Change*, 3(1), 47–63.

Nelson, R. R. – Winter, S. G. (1982): *An evolutionary theory of economic change*. Harvard University Press, Cambridge, MA.

Pegels, A. – Vidican-Auktor, G. – Lütkenhorst, W. – Altenburg, T. (2018): Politics of green energy policy. *The Journal of Environment and Development*, 27(1), 26–45.

Petricevic, O. – Teece, D. J. (2019): The structural reshaping of globalization: Implications for strategic sectors, profiting from innovation, and the multinational enterprise. *Journal of International Business Studies*, 50(9), 1487–1512.

REN21 (2018): *Renewables 2018 global status report.* Renewable Energy Policy Network for the 21st Century. http://www.ren21.net/wp-content/uploads/2018/06/17-8652_GSR2018_FullReport_web_final_.pdf (accessed on 17 September 2018).

Rockström, J. – Steffen, W. – Noone, K. – Persson, Å. – Chapin III, F. S. – Lambin, E., ... & Nykvist, B. (2009): Planetary boundaries: Exploring the safe operating space for humanity. *Ecology and Society*, 14(2).

Rodrik, D. (2014): Green industrial policy. *Oxford Review of Economic Policy*, 30(3), 469–491.

Rogge, K. S. – Johnstone, P. (2017): Exploring the role of phase-out policies for low-carbon energy transitions: The case of the German Energiewende. *Energy Research & Social Science*, 33, 128–137.

Schmitz, H. (2017): Who drives climate-relevant policies in the rising powers? *New Political Economy*, 22(5), 521–540.

Seto, K. C. – Davis, S. J. – Mitchell, R. B. – Stokes, E. C. – Unruh, G. – Ürge-Vorsatz, D. (2016): Carbon lock-in: Types, causes, and policy implications. *Annual Review of Environment and Resources*, 41, 425–452.

Shen, W. (2017): Who drives China's renewable energy policies? Understanding the role of industrial corporations. *Environmental Development*, 21, 87–97.

Unruh, G. C. (2000): Understanding carbon lock-in. *Energy Policy*, 28(12), 817–830.

Verzijlbergh, R. A. – De Vries, L. J. – Dijkema, G. P. J. – Herder, P. M. (2017): Institutional challenges caused by the integration of renewable energy sources in the European electricity sector. *Renewable and Sustainable Energy Reviews*, 75, 660–667.

Von Tunzelmann, N. (2003): Historical coevolution of governance and technology in the industrial revolutions. *Structural Change and Economic Dynamics*, 14(4), 365–384.

Wesoff, E. – Lacey, S. (2017): Solar costs are hitting jaw-dropping lows in every region of the world. https://www.greentechmedia.com/articles/read/solar-costs-are-hitting-jaw-dropping-lows-in-every-region-of-the-world#gs.ZfvU22M (accessed on 27 August 2018).

Whittaker, D. H. – Zhu, T. – Sturgeon, T. – Tsai, M. H. – Okita, T. (2010): Compressed development. *Studies in Comparative International Development*, 45(4), 439–467.

Yu, H. – Duan, J. – Du, W. – Xue, S. – Sun, J. (2017): China's energy storage industry: Develop status, existing problems and countermeasures. *Renewable and Sustainable Energy Reviews*, 71, 767–784.

Zhang, F. – Gallagher, K. S. (2016): Innovation and technology transfer through global value chains: Evidence from China's PV industry. *Energy Policy*, 94, 191–203.

Zhang, S. – Andrews-Speed, P. – Zhao, X. – He, Y. (2013): Interactions between renewable energy policy and renewable energy industrial policy: A critical analysis of China's policy approach to renewable energies. *Energy Policy*, 62, 342–353.

CHAPTER 7

Educational Developmentalism: The Case of Taiwan

György Csáki

Introduction

Taiwan has certainly been one of the greatest success stories of East Asian developmental state of the second half of the twentieth century.

Developmental states in East Asia in the 1950s–1970s were based upon export-led development in addition to strong market protection—that is *followed the Japanese neo-mercantilist model*. Domestic entrepreneurs were protected on the internal market and could rely on active state support on the world markets. In economic policy terms, the basis of this developmental state was a state *planning system* which articulated and validated *sound sectoral preferences*: these sectoral preferences were based upon the clear identification of the then world economic conditions, the main task of the state was to identify those sectors which provided the most favourable sales opportunities. In East Asia, permanent foreign exchange evaluations required permanent sectoral modernisation and technological development. High saving rates made it possible to

G. Csáki (✉)
Institute of Business, Metropolitan University, Budapest, Hungary

T. Gerőcs and J. Ricz (eds.), *The Post-Crisis Developmental State*, International Political Economy Series,
https://doi.org/10.1007/978-3-030-71987-6_7

finance with low interest rates. A further *requirement of this modernisation/industrialisation process was* the *great mass of labour force which was, at the same time, easily trainable/retrainable and ready to accept new labour opportunities*. South-East Asian developmental states realised the above characteristics of their labour forces required *effective education and training reforms* with special attention *to education in technical and natural sciences as well as technical training*.

According to *Amsden*'s major work "Taiwan distinguishes itself as one of the few non socialist economies since Japan to rise from the grossest poverty to the world of the developed. As if this were not enough (...) income distribution has also been far less inequitable in Taiwan as in other poor market economies" (Amsden 1979: 341), Taiwan's macroeconomic performance in the 1950s–1960s–1970s was unique among developing countries: per capita GDP grew 3.5 fold between 1953 and 1977, in the same period exports grew from 11 per cent to 58 (!) per cent of the net national product while the share of agriculture in GDP decreased from 34 to 12 per cent. A special characteristic of Taiwanese development that regardless of huge foreign capital inflows and high growth rates income inequalities decreased permanently: the Taiwanese Gini coefficient was 0.56 in 1953, 0.32–33 in 1963 and 1968 and decreased to 0.29 in 1973, while the income share of bottom 20 per cent of all population increased from 1.7 per cent in 1953, 7.7 per cent in 1963 to 8.9 per cent in 1973 (Barrett and Whyte 1982: 1069). This tendency of low-income inequality lasted till the mid-1990s (Bourguignon et al. 2001).

Middle-income trap has also been an extremely popular narrative in recent decade that was adequate to make difference between successful and non-successful attempts to exceed from the group of developing countries and to catch up with developed economies (see also Csaba this volume). "The "middle-income trap" is the phenomenon of hitherto rapidly growing economies stagnating at middle-income levels and failing to graduate into the ranks of high-income countries. (...) several East Asian economies have in recent decades provided a template for » success « : continuing to grow rapidly after attaining middle-income status, and thereby attaining per capita income levels comparable to advanced countries" (Aiyar et al. 2013). Empirical works suggest that the growth rate generally slows substantially at per capita GDP of 10–15 thousand USD. Growth slowdowns can often be attributed to the disappearance of factors that generate high growth during an initial phase of rapid development. The first stage of growth from low to middle income is based upon cheap labour force that had streamed from agriculture to industry (and, therefore, from the villages to the cities) and high rates of investment. Further growth towards the high-income level may only be based upon high-quality human capital and availability of technological and managerial resources. "*Middle-income countries are squeezed between the low-wage poor-country competitors that dominate in mature industries and the rich-country innovators that dominate in industries undergoing rapid technological change*" (GES 2014).

It is a common understanding, that some East Asian countries, so-called classic developmental states, notably Hong Kong, South Korea, Singapore and Taiwan have successfully exceeded this trap and have become developed economies and even *knowledge-based developed economies.* Obviously "*There is no uniform policy prescription for avoiding the middle-income trap. It is not a destiny but an obstacle to be overcome.* South Korea, Taiwan, Hong Kong and Singapore have made the transition to advanced economies. In each case, strong domestic political and bureaucratic forces had to be overcome to unleash a new wave of dynamism before these countries could move ahead. Their paths were different but they shared a willingness and ability to change course"[1] (Kharas 2013—display setting by Gy. Cs.).

It has been obvious, that there is *no outcome from the middle-income trap* without *strong macroeconomic stabilisation policies* (that is sound fiscal and monetary policies) as well as without stable institutions and rule of law, since effectively operating public sector, control of corruption and the enforcement of civil contracts are strongly correlated to the growth performance. "*Investment in education and human capital development are crucial to growth.* As the returns to physical capital accumulation diminish, the rate of productivity improvement and technological innovations depend largely on the presence of highly skilled human capital" (Larson et al. 2016—display setting by Gy. Cs.).

In Taiwan, demographic changes, that is the *population decrease*, put an important pressure towards *efficiency based growth and development*. External conditions, mainly the development of globalisation also require major economic policy changes and make the development of a

[1] Although Japan is frequently taken as the first East Asian country that stepped out the middle income trap, and is thus considered the archtype of classic developmental states, Japan had realised that a historical age earlier and was a developed country when the above mentioned four countries started to catch up.

knowledge-based economy as the one and only potential way of further development. It is an extremely hard job but "within Asia, experience suggests that there is not such a sharp distinction between the domination of low-income countries in manufacturing and the domination of rich countries in the knowledge economy. The newly industrializing economies remain successful manufacturers, even in quite mature industries, while China and India show that success in the knowledge economy is not reserved only for rich countries. For middle-income countries, it seems the trick is to straddle both strategies" (Gill and Kharas 2007).

The key importance of education is evident not simply to understand the sources of Taiwan's recent socio-economic successes but in order to explore the possibilities of future development. In Taiwan, there has been an almost seventy-years-long tradition of social equity and extended educational efforts: although Taiwan was quite poor in the early 1960s, the social indicators placed the country among the ranks of countries several times higher per capita GDP level (and the same was true for South Korea as well). The same may be said about educational attainments too: school enrolment and literacy rates in Taiwan were much higher even in the early 1960s than it would have expected on the basis of the actual level of per capita GDP (Rodrik 1994).

Education has obviously played a key role in Taiwanese developmental state and it makes it worth to be analysed a bit more profoundly in order to understand the secret (or, certainly more precisely: one of the secrets) of the Taiwanese "miracle".

In Singapore, just as in Taiwan and South Korea, the ruling elites faced a situation in which they had to break into world markets with little in the way of a competitive advantage apart from an abundance of unskilled labour. Unlike Japan they had low levels of education and very low levels of technological capability. However, perhaps the most important feature of the geo-political environment was the fact that they were all faced with continuing threats to their political independence (In line with the systemic vulnerability approach, Doner-Ritchie-Slater 2005, see also Ricz this volume). To guarantee the country's existence as an independent political entity, as a state, it had to industrialise extremely rapidly, and Taiwan could not afford to wait for market forces to deliver the necessary level of wealth to secure their independence. Meanwhile, Japan was demonstrating how an industrial policy could speed up the process of economic growth.[2] There was a relatively unique situation in Taiwan, again just as in South Korea and Singapore, which caused a strong pressure on the political elite to adopt Japanese type industrial policies which would have enabled them to speed up the process of economic growth. If the country wanted to maximise the benefits from its industrial and trade policy it had also to devise ways of upgrading the skills of the labour force and targeting them at the distinctive requirements of the companies and industries they sought to develop. Otherwise their overall strategy would be undermined by skill shortages. It is this combination of circumstances which led the country to develop innovative ways to manage the process of skill formation at a national level and that was *the developmental model of skill formation* (Ashton et al. 2002: 11).

This developmental model consists of *three main components*. The *first component* was a *clearly articulated industrial and trade policy* which was to drive the process of industrialisation and closely determined the required structure of the education system. The *second element* of this model was the *centralised control over the whole education systems*, that the state assumed, in order to provide the necessary skilled labour force, but at the same time, to develop a sense of nation-building. The *third component* was the *innovative mechanisms* they devised to ensure that the *skill requirements of the new industries informed the decisions made about the outputs of the education and training system* (op. cit.: 12).

The Formation and Development of the Taiwanese Educational System[3]

Modern education system in Taiwan (Formosa) may look back very long historical traditions: even Dutch colonisers established missionary schools in the seventeenth century which taught, beyond religious instructions, Dutch language and western literature as well. The basic language of these missionary schools was a local one.

During the Japanese colonial period, between 1895 and 1945, school attendance increased from 3.8% in 1904 to 71.3% in 1943 and literacy in Taiwan became common. Modern schools were formed with widespread

[2] See the seminal work by *Johnson, Chalmers 1982.*

[3] For reasons of largeness, in our study we address the issue of higher education only briefly.

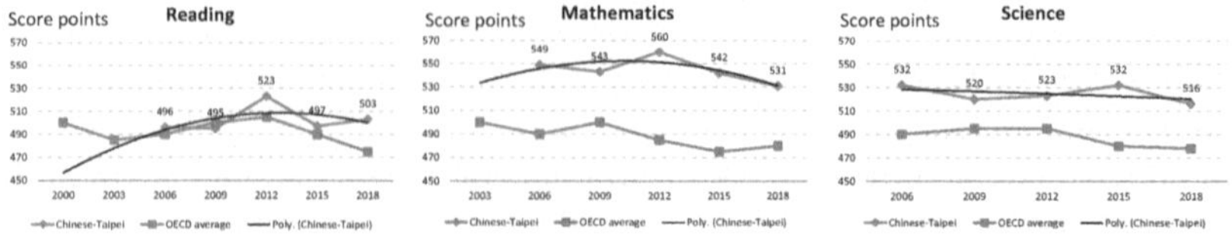

Fig. 7.1 Trends in recent performance in reading, mathematics and science in Taiwan (*Source* https://www.oecd.org/pisa/publications/PISA2018_CN_TAP.pdf)

establishment of primary schools while secondary schools and colleges were mostly for Japanese nationals. Literacy came to most of the school-aged populace by the end of the Japanese tenure on Taiwan. School attendance for Taiwanese children rose steadily throughout the Japanese era, from 3.8 per cent in 1904 to 13.1 per cent in 1917; 25.1 per cent in 1920; 41.5 per cent in 1935; 57.6 per cent in 1940; and 71.3 per cent in 1943 (Davison 2003: 64).

Six-year mandatory education was introduced by Japanese colonisers and this term prevailed after 1945 and 1949 as well. Nine-year-long education has been mandatory and free since 1968. Until the late 1980s, severe regulation prevailed in the Taiwanese education system—especially in the following four fields: *the establishment of new schools, teachers' licensure, the issuance of diplomas and school curricula*. Between 1945 and 1968 about *60 per cent of elementary school students* followed studies in *junior high school* (see: Fig. 7.1) after successfully passing the *joint entrance examination* (*JEE*) that consisted of standard written tests and those students who had achieved the highest scores were allowed to choose their junior high school. In 1968 *JEE* was eliminated between the primary school and the junior high school, elementary school graduates were assigned to the neighbouring junior high school and a very small minority was allowed (and able) to choose an extensive private school. This radical reform of the mandatory education system was quite surprising from a political point of view,[4] but *economic constraints* forced the comprehensive reform of education (see Chu and Yu 2010). Obviously, a centralised control system prevailed—especially through the formation and licensure of teachers (at every level of the education).

[4]This was introduced long before political liberalisation and took place in a highly centralised political trend system.

Table 7.1 Some general data of the Taiwanese educational system

School year	*No. of schools*	*No. of teachers*	*No. of students*	*No. of students per teacher*
1950	1504	29,020	1,054,927	36.35
1961	3095	71,098	2,540,665	35.73
1971	4115	126,454	4,130,691	32.67
1981	5241	170,347	4,641,975	27.25
1991	6787	219,788	5,323,715	24.22
2001	8158	271,625	5,354,091	33.30
2002	8222	273,391	5,376,947	33.25
2003	8252	274,847	5,385,135	33.31
2004	8184	274,251	5,372,346	33.51
2005	8287	275,743	5,319,364	33.27
2006	8254	273,978	5,286,885	33.19
2007	8202	275,524	5,243,062	33.59
2008	8097	275,308	5,165,817	34.00
2009	8060	274,007	5,065,962	34.00
2010	8196	273,189	4,965,690	33.33
2011	8100	271,523	4,860,022	33.52
2012*	11,496	301,911	5,007,275	26.26
2013	11,426	303,113	4,859,558	26.53
2014	11,078	303,078	4,729,465	15.60
2015	10,948	299,917	4,616,078	15.39
2016	10,881	294,932	4,504,331	15.27

Source MoE: http://english.moe.gov.tw/ct.asp?xItem=14504&CtNode=11430&mp=1
*Since 2012 preschool formation is included

The quantitative development of the Taiwanese education system has been constantly spectacular[5]: between 1950 and 2012 the number of students was multiplied by five, while the number of schools and the number of teachers have increased tenfold (see: Table 7.1). As a consequence the number of students per teacher decreased from 36.35 to 26.25 in the same period of time. The number of school was slightly decreased since 2012 (with about 15 per cent between 2012 and 2016), while the number of teachers peaked in 2014 and the number of students decreased 10 per cent since its peak in 2012: 5007275 students were

[5] In this paper, due to space constraints, we address higher education only tangentially.

Table 7.2 Educational expenditures in Taiwan, 1951–2016

	Expenditures as of the percentage of the GNI			*Percentage of government expenditures*
School year	*Total*	*Public*	*Private*	
1951	1.73	–	–	9.93
1961	2.49	2.19	0.30	13.32
1971	4.49	3.62	0.87	16.51
1981	4.44	3.61	0.83	14.71
1991	6.20	5.09	1.10	17.77
1993	6.64	5.50	1.14	18.43
2001	5.70	4.25	1.46	17.91
2002	5.63	4.18	1.45	19.72
2003	5.60	4.10	1.50	19.17
2004	5.47	4.02	1.46	19.65
2005	5.52	4.07	1.46	19.95
2006	5.42	3.99	1.43	21.20
2007	5.17	3.84	1.34	20.82
2008	5.43	3.97	1.46	20.53
2009	5.82	4.45	1.37	19.93
2010	5.26	4.02	1.24	20.13
2011	5.34	4.11	1.23	20.58
2012	5.40	4.11	1.29	20.49
2013	5.32	3.97	1.35	20.76
2014	5.09	3.82	1.28	21.32
2015	4.95	3.71	1.24	21.75
2016	4.87	3.65	1.22	20.47

Source MoE: http://english.moe.gov.tw/ct.asp?xItem=14504&CtNode=11430&mp=1

taught in 11496 schools by 301911 teachers in the school 2012. Interesting to realise, that the number of students per teacher declined sharply since 2013 and almost halved till 2016.[6]

While in 1951, education expenditures were equal to 1.73 of the then GNI and 9.93 per cent of total government expenditures, since the 1990s total educational expenditures were well over 5 per cent of the yearly GNI. In the same period of time, educational expenditures increased from less than 10 per cent to more than 20 per cent of total government expenditures (see: Table 7.2).

[6]One reason for the quantitative changes in 2012 lies in the fact that since then preschool playgroups and kindergartens are included legally and statistically into the overall education system.

Between 1961 and 2003 the part of private funding grew steadily, from the initial 0.30 per cent of the GNI to 1.5 per cent (in the school year 2003, public educational expenditures amounted 4.1 per cent of the GNI). Since then, educational expenditures slightly decreased till 2016 (from 6.64 per cent of the GNI) to 4.87 per cent of the GNI. In the latter figure public expenditures had a 3.65 per cent share compared to the 1.22 per cent share of private funding. In the meantime, the share of educational expenditures of total government expenditures persisted over 20 per cent (ibid.).

Public Education: One of the Foundations of Outstanding Economic Successes

It has been widely accepted for quite a while, that "the allocation of public resources to primary and secondary education was the major determining factor in East Asia's successful educational strategies" (World Bank 1993: 192). Taiwan has had certainly one of the greatest successes in this field.

The Taiwanese education system is well structured (see: Fig. 7.1): 6-year-long *primary school* and 3-year-long *junior high school* are mandatory and are followed by a diversified secondary education system. 9-year-long compulsory educational system was introduced in 1968. Children start their primary studies at the age of 6—after having spent 3 years in preschool playgroup and kindergarten. Students leaving junior high schools can choose either 3-year long *general* or *vocational schools* or 5-year long *junior college*. After these 12- or 14-year-long education processes, students from general or vocational schools are obliged to pass a *Joint University Entrance Examination* in order to follow their studies either in higher professional education (2 years) or in university education (4 years) in order to obtain a Bachelor‘s degree. Those who passed junior colleges may follow their studies in the university education. The "top" of the system follows international standards: after a successful entrance examination, students may follow their studies for a master's degree (in 1–2-year-long education) and best and most ambitious students can take part in 2–7-year-long advanced studies in order to obtain a Ph.D. degree. The *official language of instruction is Mandarin Chinese* and the academic year runs from September to June. *English* tuition is compulsory since the 5th school year of the elementary school. *Taiwanese* and *Hakka Chinese* as local languages are also widely taught. 9-year-long compulsory education has existed since 1968.[7] As of 2014, the literacy rate of Taiwanese population of 15 years of age and above was 98.5 per cent.

Preschool education is not part of Taiwan's mandatory education system; it is, however, strongly supported by the government by financial assistance to financially disadvantaged families to enrol their children in kindergartens. In 2012, the *Early Childhood Education and Care Act* consolidated the education and care of young children (between 2 and 6 years of ages) under a single administrative system. Since the early 2000s, 96 per cent of children aged 5 years or more are enrolled in education and "The government is currently promoting a program to help disadvantaged five years old children to receive early education as a preparatory step for compulsory education to begin earlier by one year".[8]

Major subjects of primary education include: Mandarin Chinese (as the official language), mathematics, science, English (typically beginning in grade 5), native languages, social studies, homeland education, music and arts. Students graduate from primary school with a *primary school diploma* and may follow their studies in *junior high schools*—without formal entrance examination. *Senior high schools* last for 3 years during which the goal of students is *to aspire to enter university*. In most junior high schools, there is a choice between science and liberal arts programs. University entrance is granted through entrance examinations, followed by lecturer recommendations regarding the best study course to follow.

Vocational training takes place in parallel also for 3 years. In vocational training, there is obviously a great emphasis on practical skills. Most students are specialised in a core subject, for example computer science, a particular engineering skill or business methods, etc. A part of students in vocational training become able to follow their studies on universities as well. The current law mandates *9 years of free and compulsory education* (between the age of 6 and 15), but a substantial reform is under way in order *to extend it to 12 years* (see later).

[7] Earlier, the compulsory learning period was 6 years—as it had been introduced under Japanese colonial rule.

[8] http://english.moe.gov.tw/ct.asp?xItem=7089&ctNode=502.

The country has three administrative levels: national, provincial and municipal (county). The Ministry of Education is responsible for the development and implementation of educational policy at all levels. The Taiwanese education system takes after the American system and is centralised in character. There is a strong emphasis on factual knowledge and rote learning, and the system is geared towards examinations. The Taiwanese education system constitutes of a significant number of private institutions. The Private School Law and the Standards For The Establishment Of Private Schools Of All Kinds And Levels outline the requirements that need to be met by private institutions founded in Taiwan.

Junior high school students may opt either an *academic or vocational track*. Upon graduation from grade 9, students may continue on to senior high school. Those on the academic track must take an exam to obtain placement in high school.

Subjects covered in the *academic track* are as follows: literature; mathematics; English; science & technology (biology, chemistry, physics & earth sciences and technology); social studies; home economics & crafts; art; physical education. At the end of junior high school, students are obliged to take part in a two-day exam in order to help to select their specialisation at high school.[9]

Subjects covered in the *vocational program* are decided by a technical curriculum called the *Practical Technical Program*. The curriculum aligns with the academic track until the third year of junior high school when a technical training is introduced. Students on the vocational track can attend senior vocational school without any additional entry requirements.[10]

[9] In 2015, the *MoE* began requiring senior high schools to admit at least 50 per cent of students based on results of the exam, which is called the Comprehensive Assessment Program.

[10] On the other hand, students of the vocational training programs are not required to study English, mathematics and science.

Taiwanese Public Education in International Comparison: Taiwan in PISA Ranking

PISA rankings have been published by OECD since 2000[11]—in the first assessments only OECD member-countries were involved but since 2006 and 2009 the number of assessed countries increased and nowadays almost every county being influential in the world economy is involved. Therefore, PISA rankings provide excellent opportunities to make international comparisons. If we assess PISA rankings country by country, we can make inquiries about the relation between economic growth, social development and the primary and secondary educational systems of the countries examined. It is certainly interesting and instructive to make this inquiry about the relationship of the extraordinary development performances of some South-East-Asian countries with the development of their public education system. *Singapore, South Korea and Taiwan* are *three successful developmental states*, their public education systems will be briefly presented in the following, with a demonstration of their positions in PISA rankings. The latter seems to be the most useful tool to position in international context the three educational systems.

Taiwan's educational outcomes have always been strong mostly in sciences and mathematics. But Taiwan got really the world's attention when its reading performance skyrocketed on the 2012 PISA tests, moving from 18th in the world in 2009 to 7th in 2012 in *reading*. What explained this dramatic improvement? The reason behind this extraordinary improvement seemed to be a very simple one: the *Ministry of Education (MoE)* realised that the country's "education system had historically been criticised for putting too much pressure on students and focusing too heavily on exams requiring rote memorisation rather than creative application of knowledge. The Ministry felt that this emphasis on cramming for fact-based exams hampered students' chances for success on the PISA test, which required substantial critical thinking skills, and handicapped the nation's international competitiveness. In response to

[11] OECD does manage the so-called PISA ranking: the Programme for International Student Assessment (PISA) is a triennial international survey which aims to evaluate education systems worldwide by testing the skills and knowledge of 15-year-old students. PISA rankings are internationally accepted as the best comprehensive measurement of students' competences in the fields of sciences, mathematics and reading.

this need, the Ministry has promoted changes to policy on teacher professional development, so that teachers are encouraged to teach reading and develop reading curriculum with more of a focus on critical thinking. It also improved teacher preparation programs and set the bar for entry into the teaching profession much higher. As a result of the poor results in reading on the 2006 PISA, the Ministry announced the Happy Reading 101 Initiative in 2008, which invested substantial funds in an effort to improve how reading is taught in schools. The reforms to teacher preparation, the new focus on reading professional development and the substantial investment in reading curriculum and instruction are all designed to ensure that students receive a more well-rounded education, are exposed more regularly to high-quality materials and are able to apply what they are learning to practical problems. In other words, they are intended to align Taiwan's system more intentionally with the critical thinking skills required on the PISA assessments (Driskell 2014).

Taking a historical view, Taiwan was considered in PISA ranking *in 2006 for the first time*. This "entrée" was especially successful since in *science* the country was ranked fourth with a score 532—following Finland (563), Hong Kong (542) and Canada (534).[12] Plus, the gender difference was no more than 7 points (in favour of male students) that is a mere difference of 1.34 per cent. The *reading* performance was much less outstanding: Taiwan figured in 17th place with a score of 496 while South Korea obtained 556 and Hong Kong 536. Taiwan's performance was very close to that of Japan which achieved a score of 498 (ibid.).

In the *PISA Ranking 2009,* Taiwan featured quite well again: in *mathematics,* its score of 543 (compared to the OECD average of 496) was enough for the *3rd place*, while in *sciences* Taiwanese students achieved a score of 520 (compared to the OECD average of 501) and figured in ranking on the *11–13th place*. There again, the performance in *reading* was the relatively poorest one: the 495 points achieved by Taiwanese students were only slightly over the OECD average of 493 and it was enough for the 18th place. In the *PISA Ranking 2012,* Taiwan performed even better: Taiwanese students performed "*statistically significantly above OECD average*" in all the three fields of competencies. In *mathematics,* the country's students achieved *4th place* with a score of 560 (compared to the OECD average of 494), in the field of *sciences* Taiwanese students

[12] See: http://www.oecd.org/pisa/pisaproducts/39725224.pdf. Downloaded: 15/05/2018.

performed a score of 523 (compared to the OECD average of 501) and achieved *8th place*. The performance in *reading* improved significantly since 2009: with a score of 523 (compared to the OECD average of 496) Taiwanese students obtained *7–8th place*.[13]

Taiwan's position in the PISA rankings improved until 2012—but since then there has been a slight decline in all areas.

According to PISA 2018, students in Chinese Taipei (that is the official name of the country in the use of OECD) scored higher than the OECD average in every three subjects. "Compared to the OECD average, a larger proportion of students in Chinese Taipei performed at the highest levels of proficiency (Level 5 or 6) in at least one subject; at the same time a larger proportion of students achieved a minimum level of proficiency (Level 2 or higher) in at least one subject".[14]

82% of Taiwanese students attained at least Level 2 proficiency in *reading* (OECD average: 77%) and 11% of students were top performers in reading, meaning that they attained Level 5 or 6 in the PISA reading test (OECD average: 9%). Taiwan outperformed the OECD average with 3.08% (503 score points compared to 487). 86% of students in Chinese Taipei attained Level 2 or higher in *mathematics* (OECD average: 76%) while 23% of students scored at Level 5 or higher in mathematics (OECD average: 11%). Taiwanese students outperformed the OECD average in this subject with 8.58% (531 score points compared to 489). *In science*, 85% of Taiwanese students attained Level 2 or higher in science (OECD average: 78%), 12% of the students were top performers in this subject, meaning that they were proficient at Level 5 or 6 (OECD average: 7%). The performance of Taiwanese students was higher than the OECD average with 5.52% (516 score points compared to 489) (ibid.). It is quite obvious that 15 years old Taiwanese students have the smallest advantage on the OECD average in reading (3% compared to 5.5 and 8.5%). [15]

There are interesting trends in the performances of the three subjects. As far as reading and mathematics are concerned, Taiwanese students

[13] See: http://www.oecd.org/pisa/keyfindings/pisa-2012-results-overview.pdf. Downloaded: 15/05/2018.

[14] *OECD (2019)*: Results from PISA 2018. Country note: Chinese Taipei. Source: http://www.oecd.org/pisa/publications/PISA2018_CN_TAP.pdf. Downloaded: 12/02/2020.

[15] It is well known than the PISA assessment of reading is focused on comprehension.

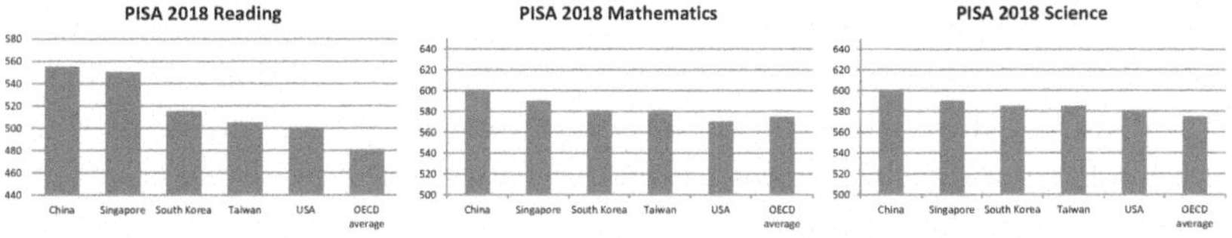

Fig. 7.2 Taiwanese performances in PISA 2018—an international comparison (*Source* http://www.oecd.org/pisa/Combined_Executive_Summaries_PISA_2018.pdf)

performed the best in 2012,[16] while in science the best performance occurred in 2015. The performance in 2018 was weaker in every subject. "The trajectory was more negative in mathematics, where PISA 2018 results were significantly lower than in any previous year, and particularly compared to 2012 results (a decline of 29 score points), the last time mathematics was the focus of the assessment. The highest-achieving students performed worse in mathematics over time, declining 5. Two score points every 3 years on average over the 2006 to 2018 period; and the proportion of top-performing students (scoring at Level 5 or 6) shrank by 14 percentage points between 2012 and 2018. Nevertheless, mean performance in mathematics remained well above the OECD average" (ibid.).

Socio-economically advantaged Taiwanese students outperformed disadvantaged students in reading by 89 score points in PISA 2018, that is approximately the same as the OECD average. About 23% of advantaged students in Taiwan and 4% of disadvantaged ones were top performers in reading (The OECD average is 17 and 3%.). Socio-economic status of Taiwanese students has the same predictive force in the performance differences in mathematics and science as elsewhere in the OECD. The same is true for chances of disadvantaged students to score in the top quarter of students (Fig. 7.2) (ibid.).

The performance of 15 years old Taiwanese students in the global competition of PISA ranking has been outstanding in recent two decades. Results reflect the successful pragmatism of Taiwanese educational strategy: for a contemporary knowledge-based economy, mathematics and sciences are of a predominant importance and the Taiwanese educational

[16] Taiwan was first assessed in 2006.

system has reflected it in the recent quarter of a century. Nevertheless, it is also obvious, that without improving reading performances,[17] that is without improving text comprehension among Taiwanese students there isn't any further development or even the preservation of global economic positions will be fairly difficult.

Taiwan's performance in the PISA survey in global comparison is really excellent. However, Taiwan compares itself and its performance primarily to Singapore and South Korea— and the country is only third in this comparison. This "relative failure" encourages Taiwan to pursue continuous self-correction and the development of its primary and secondary education.

Vocational Training System

After two-years of *preschool* education, students follow their studies in six years of *primary education* and the system follows with the education in a three-years long *junior high school*. Students opting for vocational education may choose vocational training in the third school year of the junior high school. Above the junior high school level, there are two possibilities for students: there are *senior high school* for those who intend to follow in the higher education and there are *senior vocational schools*. Senior vocational schools offer training in the following areas: agriculture, industry, business, maritime studies, marine products, medicine, nursing, home economics, drama and art. Vocational schools are not dead ends for students: after graduated from a senior vocational school, students can join the last two school years of junior high school which opens the way to higher education.

In 1968, when primary education was enlarged to 9 years of compulsory and free public education, a *Vocational Education Department* was set up in the *Ministry of Education*, in 1973 the department was renamed the *Department of Technological and Vocational Education*.

The development of *Taiwanese vocational education system has followed and served the overall economic development*, having pragmatically reformed itself according to the *changing structural needs of economic*

[17] It is a huge problem and the Taiwanese authorities are taking this issue very seriously—one possible explanation lies in the use of Mandarin Chinese (unlike the modernised language used in the People's Republic of China) that is very hard to learn and even to understand.

development. Even in the 1960s, 56 per cent of the labour force was employed in agriculture and only 17 per cent in industry, therefore, in the early period vocational training focused mainly on agriculture.[18] In order to provide the necessary amount of manpower for agriculture and basic manufacturing, the then Taiwanese government started to create an extensive *vocational training system* consisting mainly of *agricultural and industrial vocational schools*. After the evolution of manufacturing based export-led development, in the second half of the 1960s and in the 1970s, the *Ministry of Education* began dynamically developing vocational education in technics. After educating the necessary amount of basic and higher level technicians, *since the late 1970s* there was a constantly growing demand for commercial training, therefore, the number of *commercial vocational schools* expanded quickly and an important part of industrial vocational schools was transformed into *medium-level schools of business and technology*. In the 1980s, vocational educational system started to adapt to the growing demand of the service sector. In the 1990s, the emergence of informatics challenged very much the Taiwanese educational system: both in higher education and in vocational training, an immediate reaction became indispensable.

Since the very early 1990s, the structure of Taiwanese manufacturing shifted towards *information and communication technologies (ICT)* and the main economic policy goal was to provide interim goods for global ICT giants. This economic policy modification transformed the demand for labour force. Due to the development of the vocational training system, students demanded more higher education opportunities and the Ministry of Education accepted this demand by allowing technical colleges to become institutes of technology that provide higher education diplomas. At the same time, universities started to establish two-year technology programs based upon the tuition of technical colleges. In the mid-1990s, the government implemented an extended higher vocational education policy.[19]

Taiwanese political elite has always been aware of the importance of education and the same pragmatism that characterised the overall economic policy in Taiwan prevailed in educational policy as well. The

[18] See an informative paper of the *International Cooperation and Development Fund (ICDF)*: http://www.icdf.org.tw/web_pub/20020726112915centamspecial.pdf.

[19] www.icdf.org.tw/web_pub/20020726112915centamspecial.pdf.

planning of education has been an organic component of macroeconomic planning. Taiwanese vocational education system expressed the effective pragmatism in the overall development of the education system: legal and institutional framework of the vocational education system followed closely the qualitative and quantitative needs of the macroeconomic/structural policy. It made vocational education capable to provide the necessary workforce for social development. Therefore, the main goal of Taiwanese vocational training institution is obviously to meet the needs of labour market flexibility. Technical schools at all levels primarily seek to provide practical skills and knowledge, therefore the main consideration in the planning of vocational education is to adapt to the current needs of economic development (ibid.).

In 2008 a *Provisional Guidelines for New Curriculum for Vocational Schools* was issued in order to consolidate fields of studies in vocational schools and to emphasise the necessity of standard school curricula as well as the permanent need of meeting the changing industrial demand. In accordance with general liberalisation tendencies, since 2008 junior colleges and above institutions are authorised to prepare their own curriculum according to the spirit of *Junior College Act* and *University Act*.[20] The vocational education system has more and more independence but, at the same time, the Ministry of Education is making almost permanent reform efforts. The most important plans for vocational education reform have been implemented in about a decade. In 2004, almost 500 vocational high schools participated in the reformed training structures. 45 different campuses provided vocational higher education programs in a centrally planned manner concerning financial consolidation and curriculum improvement. At the same time, the individualised guidance system of the institutions as well as taking into account the labour needs of local communities lead to a much greater satisfaction of the communities and community residents alike (ibid.).

In Taiwan the co-ordination of economic and professional (vocational) formation policies is exercised by the *Council for Economic Planning and Development (CEPD)*, that is educational planning is an integral part of the overall macroeconomic planning.[21] *CEPD*'s main goal is that

[20] http://english.moe.gov.tw/fp-32-14631-7DF9C-1.html.

[21] There are similarities with *Singapore*'s *Ministry of Trade and Industry* and its *Economic Development Board*.

the education and training system should meet the requirements of the economy, especially that of the industrial policy as it is defined by the *Industrial Development Board*.

In Taiwan, the government faced for decades the problem of forming the education and training infrastructure for an economy that has been based mostly on SMEs.[22] State enterprises were used to demonstrate the need for in-plant training to supplement education provision in the early 1970s and as a source of skill formation in the larger enterprises. But the continued reliance on SMEs presented a problem because these companies did little training. The main means of addressing this problem were to use the education system to provide mostly vocational and technical-trained personnel and Taiwan was fairly successful in this respect. Although over half the age cohort receiving technical or vocational education, state measures in this field were evaluated as insufficient. The government has always been obliged to maintain a publicly funded system of training institutes and it has been coordinated and controlled by the *Employment and Vocational Training Administration (EVTA)*. Since the reliance of the Taiwanese economy on small firms prevails, the government play permanently an active role in order to establish the necessary conditions for providing adequately trained workforce for new high tech industries.

In Taiwan, the government has been successful in upgrading the educational levels of the labour force through the use of vocational schools. During the decade of the 1960s, while the period of compulsory education was extended to nine years, the proportions in vocational schools increased from 40% in 1960 to 57% in 1970 and by 1990 the proportion in vocational high schools had increased to 72%. This was achieved against a background of popular demand for academic education. However, as the economy was moving into higher value-added forms of production the government sought to increase the supply of those with more academically oriented, intellectual and problem-solving skills, and by 1995, it had reduced the proportion in vocational high schools to 70 with a further reduction to 60% planned for the year 2000. In the field of tertiary education the government remained in control through its "narrow gate"

[22]Taiwan has been in a totally different situation compared to South Korea, where a couple of Cheabols have always dominated the industry and these „mega firms" were able to articulate and support the education and training system that provided then the necessary labour force.

policy which restricted access to higher education, but over time this was relaxed although strict control was still exercised over the proportion of science and engineering/technically educated graduates it produced. As early as 1984, some 47% of undergraduates, 70% of masters students and 74% of Doctoral students were either scientists or engineers (Ashton et al. 2002: 17–18 and 19).

During the period from 1950 to the end of the 1970s, the government adopted a centralised mechanism for governing vocational education and training. The national economy prospered and the manufacturing industry developed especially dynamically. By the late 1970s, pressure was mounting to loosen central controls and move to a devolved system. In the 1980s, in line with general policy democratisation the government took a much more democratic approach in formulating rules and regulations for vocational education and training. Views and opinions from local government were considered and *CEPD* and the Ministry of Education formed partnership to draft policies for final approval by the *Executive Yuan*.[23] The *Legislative Yuan* fulfilled a different role in acting as a consulting body for the Executive Yuan on any decisions to be made. In the 1990s, as Taiwan's society has become more diversified than ever, therefore, education policies must have made through consultation among all levels of the central government and local governments. Under these circumstances, before any *MoE* decision making views and information are sought from the bottom levels of the government. At the same time, *CEPD* has become the consulting partner of *MoE*. The Executive Yuan examines the bills and regulations presented by *MoE*, makes necessary revisions, and submits them to the *Legislative Yuan* for approval. When a bill becomes law, it's the obligation of *MoE* to implement it (Rau 2005: 70–71).

[23] *Sun Yat-sen*, the founding father of the *state*, that is the post-War Taiwan, formulated a so-called *Five-Power Constitution*, according to which the *National Assembly* does exercise political power in the name of the people. The central government, at the same time, consists of five *Yuans (Yuan* means "*governmental organ.*"*)*: *Executive Yuan, Legislative Yuan, Judicial Yuan, Examination Yuan* and *Control Yuan—Legislative Yuan* is the equivalent to the Parliament that is the law-making body of the country.

The Development of Higher Education in Taiwan: Massification, Over-Capacity, and Contraction

Senior high schools last for 3 years during which the goal of students is *to enter university*. In most junior high schools, there is a choice between science and liberal arts programs. University entrance is granted through entrance examinations, followed by lecturer recommendations regarding the best study course to follow.

After having been graduated from *Senior high schools* or *Senior vocational school,* students can pass to *Junior College Institute of Technology* or—for a bachelor degree—to a four-year-long *University College Institute of Technology*. These *Junior College Institutes of Technology* may be achieved directly from the *Junior High Scholl* if students pass an entrance exam. Those who graduated from *Senior high schools* and *Senior vocational schools* are obliged to pass a *New System of Diversified University Admission (NSDUA)* which makes the selection of students between *Junior College Institutes of Technology* and *University College Institutes of Technology*. Master's degrees may be obtained after being graduated from *University Institutes of Technology* generally in four school years (the maximum is seven years) and passing a successful entrance exam. Those graduated from a *Junior College Institute of Technology* may also pass the same entrance exam after 2–3 years of working experience.[24]

In Taiwan, there are four types of universities. *Research Universities* are the few universities in the country that are responsible for conducting sophisticated research work. These universities seek to create new knowledge, invent new technologies and train the future technical/industrial leaders. Since these universities are expensive, the total number in this category is obviously small. These universities are selected with the help of a group of external independent scholars, in an open, transparent process based on a set of performance indicators (Liu 2004: 2–3).

The majority of Taiwanese universities may be classified as *Teaching Universities*. This group of universities forms the country's future merchants, managers, bankers, engineers, politicians, doctors, etc.

Special Purpose Universities generally are those former vocational schools that have been transformed into four-year colleges and poly-tech universities in order to form technicians, nurses and elementary school

[24] https://wenr.wes.org/wp-content/uploads/2016/06/WENR-0616-Country-Profile-Taiwan-new.png.

teachers. Colleges and universities of medical studies as well as those in fine and performing arts may also be included in this group.

Community Colleges are local colleges with a two-year-long education program replacing the old vocational schools to be set up by local governments, as part of the lifelong learning network in the country.

Till 2001 there used to be a *Joint University Entrance Examination (JUAA)* as an exclusive way of admittance for higher education either to colleges or/and universities. In 2001, reforms took place to transform higher education admittance system into a multi-channel process. There are two groups of exams—and students wishing to enter higher education (depending on the requirements of each university) must pass one or both exams. The two exams are as follows:

Subject Competency Test—the exam consists of a number of 100-minute tests that cover the most important general subjects of the curriculum, such as Chinese and English, mathematics and natural sciences, as well as social sciences. Subject competency tests must be completed in the final semester of senior school studies.

Designated Subject(s) Examination is based upon the former JUEEs and examines in-depth knowledge of two or three subjects. This exam is organised generally in early July (WENR 2016).

The multi-channel admission system provides different pathway for admission:

- *performance-based admission* is determined by a combination of both *Subject Competency Tests* and *Designated Subject(s) Examination.*
- in case of *recommendation- and performance-based admission* high schools recommend students to a given university faculty required by the students who are obliged to pass the *Subject Competency Test*. This is the Faculty that selects admitted students based upon the test results and interviews.
- students may also choose a *self-selection process* when they select the desires High School/College Faculty independently of the decision/proposal of their high school. In this case the above *recommendation-and performance-based* scenario does apply (WENR 2016).

As far as academic education is concerned, *undergraduate education typically lasts for 4 years and follows mostly the relevant education structure of the USA*. Bachelor's degrees are offered by *universities, four-year colleges, institutes of technology and universities of technologies* as well. A minimum of 128 credits are to be completed but most faculties require between 135 and 175 credits. Additional credits and study time are required in some specific areas of education: in the field of art education, in the training of medical doctors and veterinarians, as well as in the field of architectural studies, there are specific education structures and the training time differs from the general one (ibid.).

The *first massification of the Taiwanese higher education system* took place in the *1960s*. While in 1960 there were 15 universities and colleges and 12 junior colleges in Taiwan (out of which 6 + 7 were private ones), in 1965 the respective figures were equal to 21 plus 35 (out of which 12 + 20 were private institutions) and in 1969 there were 22 universities and colleges as well as 69 junior colleges in the country, while the number of private institutions grew to 12 plus 49. The number of university and college students was 26,735 in 1960 (27.7% of them were private institutions), while in 1969 the number of students in higher education was 86,233 and 52.0% of them studied in private institutions. At the same time, the number of students in junior colleges grew from 7 888 to 95,988 and the share of the students of private institutions grew from 36.2 to 73.1% (Wang 2003: 262).

Since the mid-1980s, Taiwan's higher education system has undergone a *second wave of massification*, transforming it into a universal system. Nowadays, about 5 million Taiwanese hold post-secondary degrees and about 1.3 million have graduate degrees. This figure increased from 570,000 in the recent ten years. Highly educated graduates have flooded the Taiwanese labour market that is not able to absorb them (despite an important population decline that is significant in the younger generations as well). Growth began in the mid-1980s, and accelerated since 1996, when the Taiwanese government allowed the creation of private higher education institutions and new players flooded the sector. In three decades, the number of institutions of higher education in Taiwan increased from 105 to 159. Because of the demographically based declining demand, Taiwan's *MoE* plans to *merge some universities*. According to some unofficial information, the ministry planned that 8 to 12 of the 51 public universities and 20 to 40 of the 101 private universities would merge or close by 2023. The plan is a response to the population decline, as well as to concerns about both the quality and international performance of the sector (WENR 2016).

Concluding Remarks

Taiwanese education system had three features which were instrumental to its spectacular economic success. *First*, it had an infrastructure already built up by 1950 for basic education that extended fairly broadly among the population—it was the positive legacy of the Japanese colonial rule. *Second*, a ready supply of highly educated labour force arrived in 1949–50 from the Mainland which was able to replace the Japanese and to begin the process to build up the local economy. *Third* and the *most important* factor was, that the education system was planned to grow in a manner that closely matched the changing requirements of the growing economy. The compulsory basic education was raised from six to nine years as early as in 1968, the secondary level curriculum was shifted towards vocational fields, the supply of university graduates was strictly limited, and the secondary and higher education curricula started to shift towards sciences and technical subjects. The levels above basic junior high level were expanded through the involvement of the private sector into the education system, so that transformation was not too costly for the budget (see: Chen et al. 2004).

The key to the seventy-years-long successful development of the Taiwanese education system certainly lies in the pragmatism of education strategies and the successful implementation of these strategies. Planning of the development of education became an integrant part of national economic planning, therefore the pragmatism[25] of the Taiwanese economic policy has always determined the fruitful pragmatism of education policies and administration. As a result of these pragmatist transformations of the Taiwanese education system, the country, similar to Singapore and South Korea, "managed a pace of skill formation that it achieved within the space of one generation something which it took the advanced industrial countries three generations to achieve" (Ashton et al. 2002: 6).

Strong central planning of the education system has ensured that the government has maintained effective control of the educational direction of the nation. In the 1970s, increasing emphasis was put on vocational education to meet the demands of a rapidly industrialising economy. Political reforms of 1986 ended 38 years of martial law in Taiwan

[25] See: Csáki (2016).

and culminated in the peaceful transfer of power from the Nationalist to the Democratic Progressive Party in 2000. Along with political reforms, many professors and students have been urging more academic freedom and institutional autonomy in recent years. In response, the government revised the University Act, allowing for greater academic self-determination and university independence in terms of both student enrolment and faculty appointments, previously tightly controlled by the Ministry of Education (Chen and Huang 2017).

Nowadays, both vocational training and higher education are facing new challenges: greater flexibility, strengthened cooperative education, narrowing gaps between public and private institutions, improvement of practical training—all of which are essential for the Taiwanese economy to have access to the manpower with which it can maintain its competitiveness in the knowledge-based economy as well. "One possible way to deal with the situation is to implement a lifelong learning system that can be freely accessed by all the people" (Rau 2005: 74). This would help labour force adjust to changing economic directions of the twenty-first century.

Higher education faces special challenges all over the world since competition is nowadays really global and knowledge-based economy also requires new skills and capabilities from graduated people. Therefore, higher education must adapt to these new challenges, that means, that policymakers have to be prepared to start thinking in a new way and to be willing to put taxpayers' money into the right places. By trying to push Taiwanese higher education system upward in global rankings and making it more attractive for international students and the best local students, to study here, Taiwan's economy could receive once again a new boost. Soft-diplomatic benefits that would ensue would be felt in time as well. It's a win-win situation.

All the above needs an adequate understanding of the world, the courage of policymakers, creativity in higher education, and, of course, adequate financial resources from both the budget and market sources.

References

Aiyar, Shekhar – Duval, Romain – Puy, Damien – Wu, Yiqun – Zhang, Longmei (2013): Growth Slowdowns and the Middle-Income Trap. IMF Working Paper WP13/71. March.

Amsden, Alice H. (1979): Taiwan's Economic History: A Case of Etatism and a Challenge to Dependency Theory. Modern China, Vol. 5, No 3. Source: http://www.jstor.org/stable/188839. Downloaded: 15/04/2018.

Ashton, D. – Green, F. – Sung, J. – James, D. (2002): The Evolution of Education and Training Strategies in Singapore, Taiwan and S. Korea: A Development Model of Skill Formation. Journal of Education and Work, Vol. 15, No. 1.

Barrett, Richard, E. – Whyte, Martin King (1982): Dependency Theory and Taiwan: Analysis of a Deviant Case. American Journal of Sociology, Vol. 87, No. 5 (March) pp. 1064–1089.

Bourguignon, F. – Fournier, N. – Gurgand, M. (2001): Fast Development with a Stable Income Distribution: Taiwan, 1979–1994. Review of Income and Wealth, Series 47, No. 2. June.

Chen, Hsiao-Lan Sharon – Huang, Yi (2017): Advancing 21st Century Competencies in Taiwan. Asia Society Center for Global Education. February. See: https://asiasociety.org/files/21st-century-competencies-taiwan.pdf. Downloaded: 24/04/2018.

Chen, Sheu Hua – Lin, Hung Tso – Lee, Hong Tau (2004): Enterprise Partner Selection for Vocational Education: Analytical Network Process Approach. International Journal of Manpower, Vol. 25, No. 7.

Chu, C. Y. Cyrus – Yu, Ruoh-Rong (2010): Understanding Chinese Families. A Comparative Study of Taiwan and South-East Chine. Oxford University Press.

Csáki, György (2016): Developmental State, Globalisation, Crisis – Taiwan's Macroeconomic Adjustment. *In:* Karalekas, Dean – Moldicz, Csaba (eds., 2016): Miracles Do Happen: Taiwan's Economic Development. Budapest Business School University of Applied Sciences.

Davison, Gary Marvin (2003): A Short History of Taiwan: the Case for Independence. Praeger Publishers.

Doner, Richard F. – Ritchie Bryan K. and Slater, Dan (2005): Systemic Vulnerability and the Origins of Developmental States: Northeast and Southeast Asia in Comparative Perspective. International Organization, Vol. 59, No. 2: pp. 327–361.

Driskell, Nathan (2014): Global perspectives: explaining Taiwan's dramatic improvement in Pisa reading. National Center on Education and the Economy. Oct 27. See: http://ncee.org/2014/10/global-perspectives-explaining-taiwans-dramatic-improvement-in-pisa-reading/. Downloaded: 10/04/2018.

Gill, Indermit – Kharas, Homi (2007): An East Asian Renaissance. Ideas for Economic Growth. The World Bank, Washington DC. See: https://openknowledge.worldbank.org/bitstream/handle/10986/6798/399860REPLACEM1601OFFICAL0USE0ONLY1.pdf?sequence=1&isAllowed=y. Downloaded: 12/04/2018.

Global Economic Symposium = GES (2014): Escaping the Middle Income Trap. See: http://www.global-economic-symposium.org/knowledgebase/escaping-the-middle-income-trap. Downloaded: 12/04/2018.

Kharas, Homi (2013): Developing Asia and the Middle-Income Trap. See: https://www.brookings.edu/opinions/developing-asia-and-the-middle-income-trap/. Downloaded: 12/04/2018.

Larson, Greg – Loayza, Norman – Woolcock, Michael (2016): The Middle-Income Trap. Myth or Reality? Research and Policy Briefs, No 1. World Bank Group. March. See: http://documents.worldbank.org/curated/en/965511468194956837/pdf/104230-BRI-Policy-1.pdf. Downloaded:12/04/2018.

Liu, Chao Hang (2004): Taiwan's Higher Education Reform towards Building a Knowledge-Based Economy. See: http://fsi.stanford.edu/sites/default/files/events/media/CLiu_Taiwans_Higher_Education_Reform.pdf. Downloaded: 25/05/2018.

Rau, Dar-chin (2005): Transformation and Reform of Vocational Education and Training in Taiwan, Republic of China. In: Finley, Ian – Niven, Stuart – Young, Stephanie (2005): Changing Vocational Education and Training. In international comparative perspective. Francis & Taylor.

Rodrik, Dani (1994): Getting Interventions Right: How South Korea and Taiwan grew rich. NBER Working Paper No 4964. December.

Wang, Ru-Jer (2003): From Elitism to Mass Higher Education in Taiwan: The Problem Faced. Higher Education, Vol. 46, No. 3. October.

World Bank (1993): The East Asean Miracle. Economic Growth and Public Policy. Published for the World Bank Oxford University Press.

World Education News + Reports (WENR) (2016): Education in Taiwan. June. See: https://wenr.wes.org/2016/06/education-in-taiwan. Downloaded: 30/04/2018.

CHAPTER 8

Easier Said Than Done: Namibia's "Declaratory" Developmental State and the Obstacles to Successful Industrial Policy

Christopher Hope

Introduction

Since independence in 1990 Namibian economic policy had been characterised as subscribing to "neoliberal fundamentals", focusing on ensuring macroeconomic stability and encouraging foreign direct investment via incentives and liberalisation (Winterfeldt 2007: 66). Industrial policy—the "range of implicit or explicit policy instruments selectively focused on specific industrial sectors for the purpose of shaping structural change in line with a broader national vision and strategy" (Oqubay 2015: 18)—was, for a long time, evidently not part of the Government's economic strategy. Whilst Ministers would frequently mention the desire to develop Namibia's manufacturing sector and diversify the economy, the approach

C. Hope (✉)
University of Cambridge, Cambridge, UK

T. Gerőcs and J. Ricz (eds.), *The Post-Crisis Developmental State*, International Political Economy Series,
https://doi.org/10.1007/978-3-030-71987-6_8

was to be non-interventionist. An early policy paper, for instance, set out that the Government's "primary commitment" was "to create an enabling environment within which the private sector can prosper" and that the "Government's overall policy is one of non-interference with market mechanisms" (Republic of Namibia 1992: i, 15).

Over the last decade, however, there has been a notable shift in the Government's rhetoric around industrial policy and state-led economic development. In 2012 the Ministry of Trade & Industry (MTI) published a new industrial policy, the first since 1992, which presented a far more interventionist framework than its predecessor As the press commented, "[a]fter 21 years Government has finally woken up to the need for an industrial policy in Namibia" (Duddy 2011). The Minister of Trade stated that, "we are convinced that government must accept a new role to unlock the industrial potential of different sectors and projects" (quoted in Insight Namibia 2013), later calling on the Namibian state to become one of "the best performing countries in the world" in industrial policy implementation (Schlettwein 2015: 2). The language of "developmental states" has increasingly appeared in Namibian press and discourse, to such an extent that SWAPO, the governing party, has been reported to be considering enshrining a commitment to a "developmental state" philosophy within its party constitution (Shikongo 2018).

But despite the clear shift in rhetoric around industrial policy and developmentalism, as well as examples of policy changes to reflect this new approach, the ambitions towards state-led development have remained relatively unfulfilled; certainly compared to the fanfare around the purported changed in approach. In this regard, it appears that for now, Namibia can be considered a *declaratory* developmental state, comparable to that identified in South Africa by Satgar (2012).

The question, then, is what has stopped Namibia's declaratory developmental state from becoming fully fledged?

There are various generic and typical factors that play their part in explaining the difficulties Namibia has faced in its industrial policy implementation. For industrial policy to work well requires a winning combination of vision, capacity, timing, and luck. That Namibia's decision to emphasise industrial policy as a viable tool has not automatically converted the state into the developmental kind is, in itself, not surprising. But it is of great importance that researchers try to understand the difficulties and processes at play when the state tries to pursue developmentalism. The more that we understand about successes and failures, the easier it should become for states to execute developmentalist principles.

In this chapter, I do not want to focus attention on state capacities for the implementation of industrial policy (e.g. coordination of the policy across Ministries, inefficiencies within relevant Ministries, the issue of limited budgets, etc.). Whilst these are certainly a part of this—and most—industrial policy stories, I want to concentrate attention on the role of power in affecting Namibia's industrial policy progress. As Whitfield and Buur (2014: 126) state, "we cannot understand why some governments pursue and implement industrial policy better than others without understanding its politics". Relatedly, Fine (2013: 26) highlights the importance of understanding countries' "systems of accumulation"; that is, "the underlying interests and the structure and dynamic of the economy through which these interests are formed and expressed".

With this in mind, this chapter will try to explore Namibia's "system of accumulation" and the way that the functioning of the national economy and national socio-political system has stood as structural hurdles to the implementation of industrial policy. Moreover, I draw attention to the interactions between the domestic political economy and the international variant, drawing on the observation of Wade (2018: 537) that "[t]he world economy seems to contain something analogous to a 'glass ceiling'".

There are four features of Namibia's system of accumulation to be discussed: the functioning of Namibia's political system; the interests of Namibia's economic elites; the actions of South Africa; and the role played by international bodies and globally predominant ideologies. Though discussed in the following discretely, it should be remembered that they are closely linked. What I want to build up is an understanding of the logics at play that contributes to the retainment of the status quo, and with it a limited industrial policy.

Namibia's Political System

A conceptualisation that I present in Hope (2020) of Namibia's political-economic system is one wherein SWAPO, the sole party to have governed Namibia since independence, has focused attention on ensuring that foreign investors stay in the country. These investors are taxed accordingly, and the state also derives significant revenue from the Southern African Customs Union (SACU). The state then distributes wealth to a sufficient extent to stop unrest, either from prospective additional political factions or from the public. The system works because of SWAPO's unchallenged dominance of Namibian politics. Indeed, SWAPO has near-absolute control over the Namibian political system. "It's cold outside of SWAPO" is a common refrain, and to date all attempts to form meaningful opposition parties have been unsuccessful.

Within and around SWAPO emerged a "post-colonial elite", centred on the President and some thirty leading figures in SWAPO and further made up of a "middle stratum of SWAPO politicians, senior civil servants, security chiefs and black empowerment entrepreneurs, [whose] personal affluence is derived from privileged access to power" (Cooper 2012: 193). Melber (2011, 2014) has criticised Namibia's governing elites, who have recreated colonial-era inequalities and appear "to be about self-enrichment within a given and unchallenged system of crude capitalism and class. In other words, it's business as usual" (Melber 2014: 143, 149). Jauch and Tjirera (2017: 182) have argued that the ideological orientation of the independent Namibian state has been "towards a system of patronage that is geared towards personal gratification rather than any higher ideal".

A powerful, centralised political elite has emerged in Namibia which, since independence, has proved successful in achieving political, economic and social stability—particularly through its effective distribution of patronage—but has failed to notably advance economic development. The point of relevance here is how the system described affects industrial policy.

The nature of SWAPO's political system has, at times, directly undermined industrial policy and development. A first example is the phenomenon of "tenderpreneurship", which became widespread in Namibia in the years following the global financial crisis. The term "tenderpreneur", a portmanteau of "tendering" and "entrepreneur", refers to individuals who make their money through the obtaining of government tenders (e.g. contracts to supply school textbooks). The archetypal tenderpreneur operates without any productive business in place (i.e. they do not produce the goods or provide a service) and sources the item which they have been contracted to supply from a third party. Tenderpreneurs are typically businesspersons intimately associated with SWAPO.

Concerning industrial development, the primary issue with the tenderpreneur system is that it makes it harder for manufacturing firms to secure government contracts. For example, the Managing Director of a printing and publishing firm told me in 2016 that until 2011 his firm would often win government tenders (or lose out to other printing press firms in Namibia). From then on, however, tenderpreneurs began winning *all* government contracts, with the middlemen then approaching the firm to actually conduct the work.[1] In the case of printing and publishing the practice tends not to negatively affect firms (because most often they still, eventually, get the business), but in most other manufacturing industries it is cheaper for tenderpreneurs to source the goods that they are supplying to Government from abroad, meaning that local firms lose contracts to foreign firms. This, for example, is the case of a successful pharmaceutical firm which relies on the Government for contracts. In 2015, when a new Minister of Health and Social Services was appointed, the firm suddenly lost some 70% of its government contracts.[2] A government source told me that the contracts were instead awarded to tenderpreneurs who were importing the products from other African countries.[3]

The tenderpreneur system is also part of the story of the failure of Namibia's Small and Medium Enterprise (SME) Bank to support industrial development. The SME Bank, it transpired, rather than financing the growth of productive enterprises, was effectively a conduit for the tenderpreneur system. Staff of the now defunct bank conceded that the majority of the loans that they gave out were to individuals seeking government tenders and that in most cases these individuals were importing the goods that were to be supplied to Government.[4] The Government was, essentially, via loans from the SME Bank, giving funds to well-connected individuals, then awarding these individuals tenders so that they could accrue massive profits. This was both a drain on state resources and a distortion of the developmental role that the SME Bank should have been playing.

Moreover, the system of elite individuals profiting from government projects can serve to dictate government investment policy, with recent proposed projects seemingly prestige projects linked to the kickbacks that

[1] Interview #001 19.4.2016.

[2] Interview #002 21.1.2016.

[3] The case of *Fabupharm* is particularly emblematic of industrial policy issues – *Fabupharm* had in fact received financial support from the Government as part of the Industrial Upgrading and Modernisation Programme in 2014, yet just one year later the Government cancelled the majority of the firm's contracts.

[4] Interview #003 29.4.2016.

certain parties would receive from their construction.[5] Consequently, government investments can often be driven principally by the aim of satisfying narrow interests. As Jauch and Tjirera (2017: 182) state, "[t]he awarding of tenders and scholarships to family members of the political elite… the continuous increase of politicians' earnings and benefits, the enormous amounts spent on civil servants' and politicians' travel and subsistence allowances… plans to build an even more luxurious new parliament, houses for regional governors and a N$450 million state of the art military hospital… are all elite projects that will have very little developmental impacts".

Moreover, in the face of persisting high levels of unemployment, public sector jobs and enterprises have served SWAPO as an essential way to generate employment and distribute wealth. The number of people working in the sector has grown gradually since independence, such that today nearly one in four employees in the country work for the Government or one of its SOEs, a ratio that puts Namibia amongst the most public-sector dominated economies in the world (Namibia Statistics Agency 2017). Throughout the independence era government expenditure as a percentage of GDP has been amongst the highest in sub-Saharan Africa (generally between 22 and 26%). The number of SOEs has also grown dramatically: whereas in 1990 there were some ten SOEs, by 2015 there were over seventy.

For industrial policy implementation the concern is not the presence of a large number of bureaucrats and SOEs, which *could* serve to make industrial policy more effective. Rather, the issue is that the presence of a large government sector in Namibia is mainly about employment creation. This has led to oversaturated ministries, including within the Ministry of Trade and Industry (MTI), with many staff idle. Overstaffed ministries can undermine effectiveness and efficiency. For example, I was told that a senior official in MTI is widely regarded as being corrupt and disruptive, but despite their reputation remain in their post, according to an anonymous source within MTI.

Meanwhile, SOEs, embedded in the are an "ever growing fiscal burden", plagued by "numerous high-profile instances of mismanagement and poor performance" (Sherbourne 2016: 420). Some SOEs have been referred to as having "become a black hole into which taxpayer

[5] Interview #004 14.12.2015.

funds are continuously poured" (Brown 2017: 10). Over the past ten years "mismanagement and outright fraud [within SOEs] have continued unabated and possibly even increased" (Sherbourne 2016: 417). Rather than serving as productive enterprises, SOEs have diverted government revenues, limiting the availability of funds for the pursuit of industrial policy and undermining the provision of productive services, such as water and electricity.

As the examples above indicate, the Namibian Government has acted in certain ways (e.g. handing out lucrative contracts to well-connected individuals, appointing unsuitable candidates for key positions) in order to maintain the stability of its power base, and these choices are frequently not conducive to industrial policy. The Government, pivotal to how money moves around Namibia, has been argued by commentators to have created "the environment for initiating and allowing private sector corruption to take place" (Coetzee 2018: 31). States always have competing priorities, groups to appease and budgets to balance. But as a backdrop to industrial policy implementation, the significant role that the state has to play in generating employment and distributing wealth in Namibia has undoubtedly made industrial policy implementation more difficult.

The Interests and Views of Namibia's Economic Elites

The presence of the "traditional class" of economic actors has long been identified as an impediment to structural transformation (Hirschman 1968; Cardoso and Faletto 1979). Thomas (1985: 6), writing of the Namibia's colonial economy, stated that "the mines, a large segment of the large scale farmers and probably a substantial segment of the... trading class only have a short to medium run time horizon with respect to their involvement in the local economy. This almost inevitably dampens efforts towards the steady, yet determined exploration and utilisation of industrial opportunities". Thomas's observations hold true today, where actors from the trading, mining and finance sectors, which dominate the economy, have continued to show aversion to industrial development and policy in influential ways.

Namibia's Minister of Finance, for example, described the challenges of industrial development in the following terms:

> The reason is also to be found in a certain extent in the fact that our business community is a bunch of agents. They are actually only trading. They are buying finished goods from South Africa and trading in the market. And they are doing fine with that... So the big players are trying very hard to maintain the status quo and not transform the economy.[6]

Indeed, trading and retail firms have shown resistance towards industrial development. Due to Namibia's colonial history retail firms in Namibia are mostly South African and have shown a reluctance to integrate Namibian firms into their supply chains. For example, the retail firms in Namibia were vocal in their disapproval of the onset of infant industry protection for dairy (2000), pasta (2002), and poultry (2013), lobbying strongly within the Namibia Chamber of Commerce and Industry for the organisation to oppose the protectionism so as to assure the retailers of continued access to South African dairy, pasta and poultry.[7]

Namibia's liberal attitude to foreign investment meant that there was no effort to induce the retailers to source more locally manufactured goods, until finally Namibia introduced its "Retail Charter" in March 2016. The charter is a voluntary agreement that retail firms can sign, pledging to source more locally. Even in its tame format, firms have proved slow to change their supply-chain practices and, moreover, the charter has effectively been at a standstill since March 2017, when the Namibian Competition Commission received a complaint (most likely from the South African retail firms) that the charter violates the Namibia's Competition Act of 2003 and consequently instructed the State to cease implementation. One of Namibia's flagship industrial policies was now dead in the water.

The mining companies, meanwhile, have resisted increased value-addition to Namibia's minerals. In 2011 the Government announced the establishment of an export levy tax of up to 5% on unprocessed mineral exports to increase its tax revenues and to encourage local processing (Sherbourne 2016). The industry, represented by the Chamber of Mines, was in uproar, arguing that the tax changes would "have led to mine closures and huge disinvestment", and the chamber lobbied strongly and effectively against the imposition of the levy (ibid.: 215). The

[6] Interview with Calle Schlettwein, Minister of Finance of Namibia. 23.3.2016.

[7] Interview with Tarah N. Shaanika, CEO, Namibia Chamber of Commerce and Industry. 31.3.2016.

export levy was eventually introduced in 2016 in a watered-down form, with individual levies for specific minerals as opposed to a blanket 5% rate, and no minerals receiving a levy greater than 2% (the Republic of Namibia 2016). Uranium oxide—one of Namibia's largest mineral exports—became subject to a levy of just 0.25%.

Namibia's important and relatively large financial sector—closely linked to the mining sector—shares an attitude that borders on disdain towards Government efforts to advance manufacturing. For example, the Managing Director of one of the largest banks in the country, reflecting on early ambitions towards industrial development in independent Namibia, remarked to me that "President Nujoma used to talk about manufacturing helicopters! [laughs] We laugh about it, but that is the level of political thinking... it's just crazy".[8]

Similarly, most major economists in independent Namibia have been ardent free-market enthusiasts. The think tank NEPRU was the country's leading economic research centre in the 1990s and 2000s, with its staff largely adhering to free-market principles and advocating "neoliberal" policies from the state (Jauch 2001; Hansohm 2007). NEPRU was often closely associated with Government and was one of the key authors of the non-interventionist industrial policy white paper of 1992 (Curry and Stoneman 1993).

The free-market view continues to be prominent amongst Namibia's leading economists today, with the likes of the Economic Association of Namibia (EAN) in 2012, particularly vociferous in his disapproval of government intervention and in his belief that Namibia's economy needs further liberalisation. A member of EAN was part of the small team that wrote Namibia's industrial policy white paper in 2012, and they stated in an interview that "we tried to push as much as we could to have a more free-market industrial policy".[9]

The anti-government intervention stance of most of the private sector and the economic policy-related civil society of Namibia was well-emblematised in the case of the Namibia Investment Promotion Act (NIPA). The Government attempted to replace the extremely liberal Foreign Investment Act (FIA) of 1990 with NIPA in 2016 to try to encourage foreign investors to contribute more to the Namibian

[8] Interview #005 15.12.2015.

[9] Interview #006 13.1.2016.

economy. Despite the minor differences between NIPA and FIA, the negative response to NIPA was enormous. For example, a law firm in Namibia who specialise in assisting private investors, wrote in their brief on NIPA that it "proposes [sic.] a very real threat to the current economic order in Namibia" (Cronjé & Co, n.d.). Amongst their grievances were that NIPA empowers the Minister to reserve economic sectors either solely for the state or for Namibians and that it grants the state-wide powers of expropriation, yet both provisions were actually already part of the FIA. Meanwhile, Brown (2017: 3) stated that NIPA contains "anti-business clauses" and that it has "led to a loss of investor confidence in the country". The strong campaign against NIPA was successful. Even though the Act was promulgated in August 2016 it has still not been officially implemented, with the Government having been forced to withdraw and fundamentally review it following the public outcry.

Much of the private sector in Namibia has been a stalwart of the status-quo, advocating effectively for the continuation of "business-as-usual" and for limited government intervention in the economy. Leading economists, too, have been highly critical of Government, contributing to a palpable atmosphere of disdain towards the state. There is a racial element to the tension between the private sector and the state, with most of the leading members of the private sector white and most government officials black. The tensions are also a question of class. Colonial Namibia was evidently a capitalist state ruled by white capitalists with a black working class. The end of the apartheid system in Namibia and South Africa can be interpreted as one of the only times in the twentieth century that the Western powers endorsed the overthrow of the capitalist governing class and its replacement by a previously working class. That the white capitalist class has lost its ability to direct policy appears to fuel resentment, contributing to the unwavering criticism from the private sector of government economic policy. This matters for industrial policy. NIPA, the Retail Charter, and the export levy tax have all been undermined or watered down due to the influence of Namibia's lead economic actors.

The Role of South Africa

Industrial development is often more difficult in countries with small populations, such as Namibia, with one of the major reasons being that it is harder for small countries to reach high economies of scale in manufacturing production merely through production for the domestic market. As such, on purely economic terms, it can be challenging for small countries to compete in the same market with larger ones. But the issue of large countries being able to outcompete smaller countries in their respective markets is not merely "economic". As this section demonstrates, in the case of the relationship between South Africa and Namibia, the former's political power has enabled it to limit Namibia's industrial development.

South Africa's economy dwarfs that of Namibia. Its GDP is nearly thirty times as large, and although South Africa's manufacturing sector has been declining markedly since the 1990s, its MVA is close to thirty times that of Namibia. Moreover, South African colonial rule and uninterrupted free trade between the countries since 1915 have left the economies extremely connected, with South Africa the largest export and import destination of Namibia. South African firms are prevalent throughout the Namibian economy, dominating the retail, banking and fishing sectors. Namibian manufacturing firms have been struggling in the face of South African manufacturing competition since at least the 1930s, and the negative effects of competition from South Africa have continued to be extremely important for manufacturers in the independence era, according to surveys of the sector (Kadhikwa and Ndalikokule 2007).

South Africa is most effectively able to exercise power in Namibia (and Southern Africa more broadly) through SACU, an organisation which South Africa has politically dominated since its creation in 1910. Apartheid-era South Africa jealously guarded the SACU market for its own manufactured goods and undermined industrial development efforts in Botswana, Lesotho, Swaziland and Namibia (Hope 2020). As apartheid ended in Namibia and South Africa, the future of SACU was ambiguous, with Nelson Mandela having referred to the organisation as a "reflection of the colonial oppressor's mentality" (quoted in Gibb 2006: 595). Nevertheless, efforts towards reform in the 1990s were painfully slow, and the familiar power dynamics of the region's economies continued, with South African firms, for example, obstructing efforts towards the establishment of car assembly plants in Botswana (Good and Hughes 2002).

In Namibia, there are clear examples of the power of South African firms to undermine industrial development. The tendency during the colonial era of South African firms to undercut prices when Namibian firms attempted to produce a new product continued in the 1990s, with numerous instances of local firms being forced to close following the dumping in the Namibian market by South African firms (Lee 2003).

Large-scale investments also failed to get off the ground because of South Africa's influence. For example, in the early 1990s *Citroen* was close to setting up a car assembly plant in Namibia. As soon as plans for the plant emerged in 1990 the National Association of Automobile Manufacturers of South Africa began lobbying against its establishment, fearful of the competition that it would pose (Minney 1991). SACU (whose external tariff rates are set by South Africa) already had a tariff of 110% on the import of cars not produced within the union, and in response to the prospect of the Gobabis plant being established SACU altered the definition of "manufactured within SACU" in 1991 such that at least 75% of the car had to be made within the region for it to avoid paying the 110% duty (Minney 1992). Consequently, it was reported that *Citroen* was left with little choice but to pull out, telling Namibia's MTI that "they could not see any way to come to Namibia under customs union regulations recently imposed by South Africa" (ibid.).

In view of the disparities in power within SACU, the union was finally reworked in 2002, with parties seeking to make it more democratic and equitable (Gibb 2006). Nevertheless, there remains a "profoundly unequal" relationship between South Africa and the other members (ibid.: 584). Tellingly, sixteen years later the SACU tariff board has still yet to be established, with a Namibian trade expert arguing that "certain of the structurers being provided for in the [2002] agreement are not yet set up because South Africa do not want them to be set up".[10] Tariffs in SACU continue to be largely dictated by South Africa, meaning that, just as in the 1990s, "Namibian firms in all sectors therefore suffer from a double disadvantage in that they get no protection from South African firms, but have to pay high tariffs on their extra-regional inputs (or above world prices for South African inputs) so as to protect South African firms" (Curry and Stoneman 1993: 51). SACU is currently in

[10] Interview #007 21.1.2016.

a state of limbo, with South Africa unwilling or unable to change its structure.

As well as dominating the Namibian market, South Africa has also proved wary of Namibian firms penetrating its domestic market. For example, a Namibian pharmaceuticals firm has been unable to export its products to South Africa because South African regulation—despite purported free trade between Namibia and South Africa—stipulates that medical goods can only be imported through certain airports and harbours. The firm's trucks have therefore been turned around at the South African-Namibian border.[11] Other firms, too, have complained of cumbersome regulations serving to effectively cordon off the South Africa market. A Windhoek-based machinery firm told me: "South Africa are very smart and crafty in finding loopholes within the Customs Union", explaining that "it's just not cost-effective to get there [South Africa] because there is a lot of hidden detail... South Africans have designed [their regulations] in a way where it would almost take twenty-four months to get approval [to export]".[12]

Moreover, established institutions concerning the relationship between Namibia and South Africa are helping to sustain Namibia's system of accumulation. The most fascinating element of the impact of SACU on Namibian industrialisation, for example, is how, via the "revenue-sharing formula" of the Union, South Africa is effectively paying the other SACU members *not* to develop industry and to accept the disparities between their economic structures and that of South Africa. It would take an incredibly bold leader to decide to walk away from SACU, and thereby forego the valuable additional revenue that it brings the state. The price to pay is unwavering competition from South African firms and the acceptance that trade policy is largely dictated by South Africa.

The actions of South African firms (and firms of other countries) can also have a direct impact on industrial policy implementation in Namibia. For example, Namibia has used infant industry protection (IIP) four times since independence (commencing in 2000 for milk, 2002 for pasta, 2012 for cement, and 2013 for poultry). However, on three of these occasions the Namibian State has been taken to court—twice by groups of South African firms, once by a Chinese firm. In milk, once tariff protection had

[11] Interview #002 21.1.2016.

[12] Interview #008 16.2.2016.

expired in 2012 the Namibian Government sought to impose a quota restriction on its import. In response, two South African dairy producers who export to Namibia appealed to the Namibian High Court, and in 2014 the court ruled in the firms' favour, on what appeared to be largely arbitrary grounds.

In cement, it was a Chinese cement importer that took the Government to court when it introduced a tariff on cement, arguing that the Government had violated the Customs and Excise Act of 1998 (Sherbourne 2016). This was indeed the case, but again on largely spurious grounds.[13] The Judge ruled in favour of the company, and the tariff protection of the industry was revoked, with the Chinese import company able to import duty free (Menges 2012). Meanwhile, in poultry, the South African Poultry Association took the Namibian Government to court over its decision to impose a quota on the import of poultry, arguing that this "violated the Protocol to the SADC Agreement and also the SACU Agreement" (High Court of Namibia 2016: 7).

The consequence of these time-consuming and costly court cases has been that the Government's willingness to use IIP—a device that featured notably in its recent industrial policy documents—has visibly cooled. As one Namibian trade expert put it, because of the court cases "the Government has lost its appetite for infant industry protection".[14] In an interview, the Minister of Finance expressed his frustrations:

> We assisted the poultry industry, we assisted the dairy industry, we assisted the cement industry, all of them ended up in court. So there is strong resistance, and that's the establishment that kicks back, that doesn't like what we aim at with transforming the economy.[15]

In this regard the actions of foreign firms have directly led to curtailed industrial policy in Namibia, and it is unlikely that IIP will be used to any significant degree in Namibia again in the near future. Here again, we see

[13] The company argued that when a tariff is introduced it must be promulgated in the Government Gazette by Government first, and then be tabled in the National Assembly, whereas in this case the Government first tabled the bill at the National Assembly (Menges 2012).

[14] Interview #007 21.1.2016.

[15] Interview with Calle Schlettwein, Minister of Finance of Namibia. 23.3.2016.

how the likelihood of active industrial policy emerging being thwarted by the actions and interests of foreign actors.

The International Political Economy of Industrial Policy and Development in Namibia

The preceding sections of this chapter have shown the ways that Namibia's system of accumulation contains an assortment of elements—be it the way in which SWAPO seeks to maintain its position of power, the resistance of the influential mining sector to increased value addition, or the power that South African firms (both based in Namibia and in South Africa) exert over Namibian policy—that stand as significant obstacles to the successful implementation of industrial policy and help to quell any motivation to pursue industrial policy to begin with. In this section I will point to the way that international ideologies and bodies have shaped and often further thwarted Namibia's efforts towards industrial development.

Firstly, on ideology. Governments' approaches to economic policy are affected by the prevailing ideological frameworks of the time. The 1990s was a perfect example, a decade which saw "the forging and embedding of an ideological, political and technical consensus both globally and with governing regimes in key developing countries" (Craig and Porter 2006: 63). This consensus was around what Craig & Porter term "embedded neoliberalism", wherein to foster development states should create an enabling environment (through, e.g. practices of good governance) within which markets can flourish, but do little more. In Namibia, the Government's approach to industrial policy in the 1990s and 2000s was strongly shaped by this predominant discourse on developmental policy, most notoriously in the case of Namibia's Export Processing Zone (EPZ) scheme, with the Government's focus time and time again on the provision of an "enabling environment".

It does not even matter whether these policies were "right" or not. What matters is that the direction of industrial policy in Namibia, and with it the direction of industrial development, was being importantly influenced by global developments. In the 1990s the likes of the IMF and World Bank, despite Namibia having never received a SAP, became "regular visitors to Namibia and 'assisted' with the country's public expenditure review and with 'training' high-ranking staff members of government economic institutions" (Jauch 2007: 60). The Governor of the Bank of Namibia from 1997 to 2010 recalled in an interview how high-income nations and international organisations would advise against industrial policy:

> There are people who say governments should not even bother to try and have industrial policy because it does not work, and that is the view you normally hear from the developed countries. When I was at the Bank of Namibia that argument would always be brought up by the IMF. People would boast 'we don't have those industrial policies and things are working for us, so why do you have them?'[16]

The great body of counsel being afforded to the newly independent Namibian state was advocating a free-market, business-enabling approach to economic development. Particularly in the 1990s and 2000s, it is reasonable to conclude that the scope for Namibian industrial policy was constrained by the recommendations emanating from the rich countries of the world. As Jauch (2007: 60) argues, deviation from the neoliberal policy framework was "extremely difficult in the face of an onslaught by the neoliberal ideology that was usually portrayed as the only practical policy option for Namibia".

In reflecting on the importance of the diffusion of ideologies on industrial policy, it is pertinent to examine the change in Namibia's approach to industrial policy that occurred in the early 2010s. The emergence of purported active industrial policy was not solely occurring in Namibia. Rather, in the late 2000s and early 2010s industrial policy was experiencing a "renaissance" (Wade 2014: 2). Just as the absence of industrial policy in Namibia in the 1990s and 2000s coincided with an era of the "ideologically-motivated wilful neglect" of industrial policy (Chang and Andreoni 2016: 3), so too did the return of the subject in the 2010s reflect international changes. Clearly, the Namibian Government's approach to industrial policy was being influenced by external forces.

But, importantly, even if a country changes its attitude to industrial policy, institutional legacies can thwart actual change. The case of Namibia shows that once a free-market framework had been established, its institutional structure can become an impediment to industrial policy, even when the policy ambitions of the Government have changed. Constitutional acts designed to foster foreign investment and propagate the

[16] Interview with Tom Alweendo, Director-General of the National Planning Commission and former Governor of the Bank of Namibia. 27.1.2016.

primacy of private sector privilege, such as Namibia's Foreign Investment Act of 1990 and the Competition Act of 2003, can continue to be used to defend the rights of investors and curtail the actions of the state. The example above, of how implementation of Namibia's "Retail Charter" has been halted due to suspected violation of the Competition Act, is a case in point.

A further example is an attempt in early 2018 by the Government to repeal the EPZ Act of 1995. Following an outcry from the two major mining operations benefiting from the act—a copper smelter and a zinc refinery—the Government was forced to backtrack just one week after the announcement, stating that EPZ companies would be able to retain their status. As written in a national newspaper, the CEO of the Chamber of Mines stated that, "the EPZ regime is a contractual document between government and the players which cannot be cancelled without the other party's consent" (quoted in Windhoek Observer 2018). Namibia, it seems, had institutionally painted itself into a free-market corner due to the dictates of neoliberal development theory.

Moreover, during the recent era of marginally increased industrial policy efforts from the Namibian state, international institutions and agencies have proven obstacles to its implementation. An example is the international credit rating agencies, which have been highly influential in shaping countries' economic policies, because a downgrade from one of the three major credit rating agencies can have serious effects on the finances of a government by increasing the interest rate that they pay to borrow money (Hanusch et al. 2016).

The influence of the credit rating agencies over economic policy in Namibia has been clear, with the agencies contributing to heavily reduced government spending in recent years, including on industrial policy. Namibia, as part of a trend in low-income countries globally, saw its public debt-to-GDP ratio grow greatly in the years after the global financial crisis due to countercyclical government spending.[17] In their roles as "guardians of public fiscal discipline", the rating agencies loomed ominously over the spending habits of Namibia. In 2015 Moody's warned that a downgrade could occur where Namibia's debt-to-GDP continues to increase (Moody's 2015), and in 2016 the firm changed Namibia's rating outlook to "negative"—a step away from downgrading a rating

[17] Namibia's public debt-to-GDP ratio increased from 16% in 2010 to 45% in 2018 (so admittedly from a very low starting base).

(Moody's 2016). Partially in response to these pressures (similar concerns were being voiced by Namibia's economists and financial sector), the Namibian government launched massive budget cuts in 2016, but nevertheless in 2017 both Moody's and Fitch downgraded Namibia from "investment grade" to "non-investment grade" status (also known as "junk" status). Following the verdict, a team of Namibian Government Ministers flew to London to meet with the agencies to contest the decision, but their efforts were futile (Namibian Broadcasting Corporation 2017).

It is not just over the question of managing Namibia's debt-to-GDP ratio that the agencies sought to counsel. Like Namibia's private sector, Fitch was also critical of the Namibia Investment Promotion Act (NIPA, discussed above). In explaining Namibia's downgrade, the firm cited the "controversial provisions" within NIPA as "underscore[ing] the lingering policy risks" in the country, noting approvingly that the Act was likely to be significantly reworked and that this could have a favourable effect on Namibia's credit rating (quoted in Reuters 2017).

Globally credit rating agencies are playing an important part in shaping the policy choices of states, advocating a conservative approach to economic policy. In the case of Namibia, we can see their interventions to have contributed to the massive budget cuts that have left most of the industrial policy recent initiatives to be on hold, as well as to add further weight to calls for NIPA—a minor effort to increase the contribution of foreign investment to the national economy—to be fundamentally reformed.

A further example is the role that the EU has played in shaping Namibian industrial policy. Relations between the EU and Namibia over the past fifteen years have been centred around the free trade deals known as "Economic Partnership Agreements" (EPAs) between the EU and African, Caribbean, and Pacific (ACP) countries. EPA negotiations were undertaken at the regional bloc level, with Namibia part of the long-winded negotiations between the EU and the Southern African Development Community (SADC) which eventually led to the signing of an EU-SADC EPA in 2016. Whilst it has been claimed by the EU that EPAs will encourage industrialisation amongst ACP countries (European Commission 2016), critics argue that EPAs will likely make industrial development much more challenging for these countries (Sanders 2015).

In the late 2000s and early 2010s Namibia proved, despite pressure from its export industries such as meat, fish and grapes (which rely on access to the EU markets), reluctant to sign the EPA. The Minister of Trade and Industry stated that the agreement would forfeit Namibia's right to use export taxes on raw materials to incentivise value addition and force the country to abandon infant industry protection and the country's horticultural marketing scheme (Melber 2016). In response to Namibia's hesitance, the EU trade negotiators "increased pressure on Namibia" by, for example, announcing in 2011 that if the SADC-EPA was not signed by 2014 then all preferential market access for SADC goods into the EU would come to an end, effectively crippling Namibia's food export industries (ibid.: 143).

Namibia, along with the rest of the SADC bloc, did eventually agree to sign the EPA. SADC had, however, successfully negotiated some policy space within the EPA, with SADC states permitted to deploy quantitative restrictions on EU imports, tariff protection (for eight years, with the possibility of extension), and the ability to apply export taxes (European Union 2016). In the case of the EU-SADC EPA, Namibia was able to defend its right to deploy industrial policy, though not for want of trying, and manufacturing firms in Namibia will nevertheless likely struggle in the face of increased EU competition.

The EU has recently and in quite extraordinary ways exerted its authority over Namibian industrial policy by other means too. In December 2017, the EU published a list of "non-cooperative jurisdictions for tax purposes" ("tax havens") as part of a bid to stamp down on the practice of firms offshoring profits. The original list comprised fifteen countries, most of which were those commonly cited as suspected tax havens. But a curious inclusion on the list was Namibia, a country which has never been accused of being a tax haven and which, by an understanding of a tax haven as being a jurisdiction that is purposefully used by international corporations to avoid paying taxes, is *not* a tax haven. In 2018, the list of non-cooperative jurisdictions has been reduced to seven, with Namibia still amongst its ranks (Council of the European Union, n.d.).

The reasons cited by the EU as to why Namibia was included on the list were that it is not signed up to certain international bodies that aim to maintain standards of tax regulation and that Namibia has "harmful preferential tax regimes and did not commit to amending or abolishing them by 31 December 2018" (Council of the European Union 2017: 10).[18] It transpired that the "harmful preferential tax regimes" in question were Namibia's EPZ programme and its tax incentives for manufacturing firms. In response, the Minister of Finance initially suggested that Namibia would not give up its support for manufacturing firms just to be removed from the EU's list, stating that "it's wrong for Namibia as a sovereign state to be expected to make changes to its laws without taking its own interest into consideration" (quoted in Kaira 2017).

However, the perceived damage to Namibia's reputation was it to remain on the EU's list, coupled with revenue constraints in Namibia, meant that the Minister, "bowing to pressure from the European Union", announced the termination of manufacturing incentives and the EPZ programme (Kahiurika 2018). Namibia may avoid a damaging reputation if it can successfully remove itself from the EU's list, but in return Namibia's ability to support manufacturing firms has been deeply eroded.

Conclusion: The Absence of Developmentalism in Namibia

For industrial policy to be successful requires high levels of commitment from the state to the goal of structural transformation. In other words, states need to be developmental. Countries without high levels of commitment—without a "developmental mindset" (Thurbon 2016)—struggle to implement industrial policy because the pressures embedded within the country's system of accumulation often prove too great to overcome.

This chapter has shown some of the workings of independent Namibia's system of accumulation and the manifold ways in which industrial policy and developmentalism have been thwarted by the distribution of power in Namibia and globally.

These challenges are extremely difficult to overcome. The obstacles to industrial policy and development—be they the functioning of SWAPO's political system, the interests of Namibia's most influential economic

[18] The international bodies are: the Global Forum on Transparency and Exchange of Information for Tax Purposes, the OECD Multilateral Convention on Mutual Administrative Assistance, and the anti-Base Erosion and Profit Shifting's minimum standards.

actors, the actions of foreign firms, or the pressures exerted from international bodies—are multifaceted and interlinked, creating and recreating a social order that it is difficult to rupture. To overcome "the mountains of routine and prejudice" present in a given system (Gerschenkron 1962: 24) and successfully "generating and energizing human action" (Hirschman 1958: 25) in the direction of development it is crucial to have a state really needing or wanting successful industrial policy to occur. In the case of Namibia, this commitment from the state is absent, and it is absent in large part because of how the system of accumulation in Namibia works.

Moreover, the emergence of developmentalism is dependent in part on the very likelihood of developmental success (in a "virtuous circle"). In my view, many of the obstacles identified above (such as the constant court cases against the use of IIP, the pressures from international credit rating agencies, or the consistent pantomime-uproar from the domestic private sector following more-or-less any policy action from the state) have crucially thwarted the emergence of increased developmentalism from the Namibian governing elites. Almost every direction that the state turns it faces organised resistance.

It is true that a more committed state would be able to push back harder and more successfully override these conservative interests. But commitment in the first place becomes less likely to manifest itself because of how perilous the road to successful industrial policy and development is in Namibia. Amsden (1992: 72) wrote "the lower the probability of industrial success as a result of [a] set of objective conditions, the greater the likelihood that governments will become or remain nondevelopmental, in a vicious circle" (ibid.: 72). In Namibia, the lower probability of industrial *policy* success owing to its political economy context seems to curtail developmentalist tendencies.

In this regard, the experience of Namibia can be seen to closely reflect that of South Africa. Here, since the mid-2000s the South African state has frequently self-identified as a developmental state—in what has been called by Satgar (2012: 39) a "declaratory developmental-state"—but has failed to follow its rhetoric with action, and accordingly "the general contours of neoliberal macro-economic management have not shifted" (ibid.: 38). Satgar's account stresses the influence of international bodies and contestation amongst the economic groups of South Africa in shaping and curtailing its forlorn commitment to state-led development, concluding that "[i]n short, the forces shaping the post-Apartheid state are not pushing it toward being a developmental state, despite the state's discourse" (ibid.: 39). Somewhat similar experiences have been identified in other countries, with Ban (2013: 298), for example, arguing that in Brazil the Government has "institutionalized a hybrid regime that layers economically liberal priorities originating in the Washington Consensus and more interventionist ones associated with neo-developmentalist thinking" (see also Riberio and da Silva this volume). Across the world, the emergence of developmentalist tendencies must overcome a national and international status quo. The obstacles are manifold and to overcome them, as noted above, requires vision, capacity, timing and, perhaps above all, luck.

Bibliography

Amsden, A. 1992. "A Theory of Government Intervention in Late Industrialization." In L. Putterman & D. Rueschemeyer (eds.), *The State and Market: Synergy or Rivalry?* Boulder, CO: Lynne Rienner.

Ban, C. 2013. "Brazil's Liberal Neo-Developmentalism: New Paradigm or Edited Orthodoxy?" *Review of International Political Economy* 20(2): 298–331.

Brown, R. 2017. "The National Budget 2017–18: Prioritising Personnel." IPPR Democracy Report, Special Briefing No. 19, May 2017.

Cardoso, F. & Faletto, E. 1979. *Dependency and Development in Latin America.* Berkeley: University of California Press.

Chang, H-J. & Andreoni, A. 2016. "Industrial Policy in a Changing World: Basic Principles, Neglected Issues and New Challenges." *Cambridge Journal of Economics* 40 Years Conference.

Coetzee, J.J. 2018. "The Role of the Private Sector in Tackling Corruption." IPPR Briefing Paper. April 2018.

Cooper, I. 2012. *Parties, Factions and Votes: A Comparative Study of Electoral Politics in Post-Colonial Namibia.* University of Oxford: PhD thesis.

Council of the European Union. 2017. "The EU List of Non-Cooperative Jurisdictions for Tax Purposes." Outcome of Proceedings from General Secretariat of the Council. 15429/17. Brussels, 5 December 2017.

Council of the European Union. n.d. "Taxation: EU List of Non-Cooperative Jurisdictions." Available at: http://www.consilium.europa.eu/en/policies/eu-list-of-non-cooperative-jurisdictions/ [accessed 16.8.2018].

Craig, D. & Porter, D. 2006. *Development Beyond Neoliberalism? Governance, Poverty Reduction and Political Economy.* London: Routledge.

Cronjé & Co. n.d. "Namibian Law." Available at: http://www.cronjelaw.com/namibian-law [accessed 16.8.2018].

Curry, S. & Stoneman, C. 1993. "Problems of Industrial Development and Market Integration in Namibia." *Journal of Southern African Studies* 19(1): 40–59.

Duddy, J-M. 2011. "Industrial Policy Wake-Up Call." *The Namibian*, 22.11.2011.

European Commission. 2016. "10 Benefits of Economic Partnership Agreements (EPAs)." Directorate-General for Trade (European Commission). 28.11.2016.

European Union. 2016. "Economic Partnership Agreement between the European Union and its Members States, of the one part, and the SADC EPA States, of the other part." Official Journal of the European Union L 250/3. 16.9.2016.

Fine, B. 2013. "Beyond the Developmental State: An Introduction." In B. Fine, J. Saraswati, & D. Tavasci (eds.), *Beyond the Developmental State: Industrial Policy in the Twenty-First Century*. London: Pluto Press.

Gerschenkron, A. 1962. *Economic Backwardness in Historical Perspective: A Book of Essays*. Cambridge, Mass: Belknap Press of Harvard University Press.

Gibb, R. 2006. "The New Southern African Customs Union Agreement: Dependence with Democracy." *Journal of Southern African Studies* 32(3): 582–603.

Good, K. & Hughes, S. 2002. "Globalization and Diversification: Two Case Studies in Southern Africa." *African Affairs* 101(402): 39–59.

Hansohm, D. 2007. "Research and Policy-Making: The Unique Experience of NEPRU in Namibia." In E.T. Ayuk & M.A. Marouani (eds.) *The Policy Paradox in Africa: Strengthening Links between Economic Research and Policymaking*. African World Press.

Hanusch, M., Hassan, S., Algu, Y., Soobyah, L., & Kranz, A. 2016. "The Ghost of a Rating Downgrade: What Happens to Borrowing Costs When a Government Loses its Investment Grade Credit Rating?" World Bank Group MFM Global Practice, Discussion Paper No. 13. June 2016.

High Court of Namibia. 2016. "South African Poultry Association & 5 others v The Minister of Trade and Industry and 3 Others." NAHCMD 199 (A 325/2015). 8 July 2016.

Hirschman, A.O. 1958. *The Strategy of Economic Development*. New Haven: Yale University Press.

Hirschman, A.O. 1968. "The Political Economy of Import-Substituting Industrialization in Latin America." *The Quarterly Journal of Economics* 82(1): 1–32.

Hope, C. 2020. *Developmentalism, Dependency, and the State: Industrial Development and Economic Change in Namibia since 1900*. Basel: Basler Afrika Bibliographien.

Insight Namibia. 2013. "Kicking Over the Traces." Available at: http://www.insight.com.na/kicking-over-the-traces/ [accessed 16.8.2018].

Jauch, H. 2001. "Playing the Globalisation Game: The Implications of Economic Liberalisation for Namibia." Research Report prepared by the Labour Resource and Research Institute (LaRRI). July 2001.

Jauch, H. 2007. "Between Politics and the Shop Floor: Which Way for Namibia's Labour Movement?" In H. Melber (ed.), *Transitions in Namibia: Which Changes for Whom?* Stockholm: Elanders Gotab AB.

Jauch, H. & Tjirera, E. 2017. "The Need for a Developmental State Intervention in Namibia." In G. Kanyenze et al. (eds.) *Towards Democratic Developmental States in Southern Africa.* Harare: Weaver Press.

Kadhikwa, G. & V. Ndalikokule. 2007. "Assessing the Potential of the Manufacturing Sector in Namibia." *Bank of Namibia* Occasional Paper – 1/2007.

Kahiurika, N. 2018. "Namibia to Scrap Preferential Tax." *The Namibian*, 8.3.2018.

Kaira, C. 2017. "Namibia Resists EU Manufacturing Incentives Calls." *Windhoek Observer*, 8.12.2017.

Lee, M. 2003. *The Political Economy of Regionalism in Southern Africa.* Cape Town: University of Cape Town Press.

Melber, H. 2011. "Namibia: A Trust Betrayed—Again?" *Review of African Political Economy* 38(127): 103–111.

Melber, H. 2014. *Understanding Namibia: The Trials of Independence.* UK: C.Hurst & Co. Publishers Ltd.

Melber, H. 2016. *A Decade of Namibia: Politics, Economy and Society, The Era Pohamba, 2004–2015.* Leiden; Boston: Brill.

Menges, W. 2012. "Setback for Govt on Cement Import Tariffs." *The Namibian*, 3.9.2012.

Minney, T. 1991. "Major Battle for Citroen Hits Top Gear." *The Namibian*, 8.7.1991.

Minney, T. 1992. "Citroen Deal OFF." *The Namibian*, 24.3.1992.

Moody's. 2015. "Moody's Affirms Namibia's Baa3 Government Bond Rating; Outlook Stable." Available at: https://www.moodys.com/research/Moodys-affirms-Namibias-Baa3-government-bond-rating-outlook-stable–PR_341556 [accessed 16.8.2018].

Moody's. 2016. "Moody's Changes Outlook on Namibia's Baa3 Rating to Negative, Affirms Rating." Available at: https://www.moodys.com/research/Moodys-changes-outlook-on-Namibias-Baa3-rating-to-negative-affirms–PR_357255 [accessed 16.8.2018].

Namibia Statistics Agency. 2017. "The Namibia Labour Force Survey Report 2016." Windhoek: Namibia Statistics Agency.

Namibian Broadcasting Corporation. 2017. "Sparks Fly as Moody's Meet Namibian Ministers in London." 9.8.2017. Available at: http://www.nbc.

na/news/sparks-fly-moody%E2%80%99s-meet-namibian-ministers-london.12911 [accessed 16.8.2018].

Oqubay, A. 2015. *Made in Africa. Industrial Policy in Ethiopia.* Oxford: Oxford University Press.

Republic of Namibia. 1992. "White Paper on Industrial Development." Ministry of Trade and Industry.

Republic of Namibia. 2016. "Export Levy Act 2 of 2016." Government Gazette 20 June 2016, No. 6042.

Reuters. 2017. "Fitch Downgrades Namibia to 'BB+'; Outlook Stable." 20.11.2017. Available at: https://www.reuters.com/article/fitch-downgrades-namibia-to-bb-outlook-s-idAFFit7CcD1f [accessed 16.8.2018].

Sanders, R. 2015. "The EU, Economic Partnership Agreements and Africa." *The Round Table: The Commonwealth Journal of International Affairs* 104(5): 563–571.

Satgar, V. 2012. "Beyond Marikana: The Post-Apartheid South African State." *African Spectrum* 47(2–3): 33-62.

Schlettwein, C. 2015. "Statement by Hon. Calle Schlettwein, Minister of Trade and Industry, on the Growth at Home Strategy, Namibia's Execution Strategy for Industrialisation in the National Assembly, on Tuesday 17 February 2015." Republic of Namibia.

Sherbourne, R. 2016. *Guide to the Namibian Economy 2017*. Windhoek: IPPR.

Shikongo, A. 2018. "Will Swapo's Socialism Come to 'Mixed Economy' Namibia?" *The Namibian*, 21.8.2018.

Thomas, W. 1985. "Prospects for Industrial Development in Namibia." In *RP Congress 1985, SWA Economy.*

Thurbon, E. 2016. *Developmental Mindset: The Revival of Financial Activism in South Korea*. Cornell University Press.

Wade, R. 2014. "Industrial Policy – Better, Not Less." *UNCTAD Trade and Development Board Sixty-first session*. Geneva, 15–26 September 2016.

Wade, R. 2018. "The Developmental State: Dead or Alive?" *Development and Change* 49(2): 518–546.

Whitfield, L. & Buur, L. 2014. "The Politics of Industrial Policy: Ruling Elites and Their Alliances." *Third World Quarterly* 35, 1: 126–144.

Windhoek Observer. "Relief for Manufacturers." 16.3.2018.

Winterfeldt, V. 2007. "Liberated Economy? A Case Study of Ramatex Textiles in Namibia." In H. Melber (ed.), *Transitions in Namibia: Which Changes for Whom?* Stockholm: Elanders Gotab AB.

CHAPTER 9

Bringing the 'International' into Discourses on Developmental Statehood in Ethiopia

Ekaette Ikpe

Introduction

Ethiopia is posited as an African exemplar of developmental statehood. Its extensive interaction with China offers a context within which to examine the influence of international dynamics on developmental statehood. Ethiopia stands out as a net resource importer that attained the highest growth globally in 2017 as well as an average of 10.3% growth from 2006 to 2017 that has been linked to declines in poverty (World Bank 2020; UNDP 2018). Ethiopia's performance has been defined by key factors including government investment and consumption and efforts towards industrial development described as modelling East Asian economies including China and South Korea (Bezawagaw et al. 2018; World Bank 2020; Vaughan 2011). The narrative on success is not without critique on the reliability of the data as well as contentions about the state's scant regard for populations in the peripheries (Feyissa 2011).

E. Ikpe (✉)
King's College London, London, UK
e-mail: ekaette.ikpe@kcl.ac.uk

T. Gerőcs and J. Ricz (eds.), *The Post-Crisis Developmental State*, International Political Economy Series,
https://doi.org/10.1007/978-3-030-71987-6_9

In this chapter, I discuss an international political economy (IPE)-enhancement of the developmental state paradigm (DSP) that is based on Hirschman's linkages thesis. It examines fiscal, production and consumption linkages with attention to industrial policy and intersectoral resource transfers. The IPE-enhanced DSP highlights two sets of dynamics: synergies, that is, fiscal, production and consumption linkages and how they do (not) address savings, raw materials and industrial demand constraints on industrialisation and; lines of influence, that is, economic, social and political factors including international capital dynamics that influence the state's actions (Ikpe Forthcoming).

This chapter analyses the Ethiopian state's interactions with industrial development and links with the agricultural sector as with the Agricultural Development Led Industrialisation Strategy and how these are impinged upon by foreign and in particular Chinese capital. It responds to a gap in the literature on developmental statehood on the analysis of the interrelatedness between the state and foreign capital in developmental processes. It enables us to examine developmental statehood in Ethiopia at a key moment. This is in the wake of Prime Minister Abiy Ahmed's proposal for innovating away from a traditional sense of developmental statehood towards Medemer-led development (Mariam 2019). The chapter speaks also to the recent intensity in the mobilisation of industrial policy to support domestic manufacturing across the Global North and South in addressing the 2020 COVID-19 pandemic. There are emerging calls for these dynamics to energise state support to manufacturing sectors across Africa (Mwambari 2020). These important arguments need to be located within understandings of the complex relations between manufacturing on the continent and the dominance of international capital and finance (Ikpe 2020).

The rest of the chapter is divided into three sections. First, it discusses developmental statehood in relation to IPE dynamics as well as the literature on developmentalism in Ethiopia. Second, it examines the analytical value of the IPE-enhanced DSP in Ethiopia with a focus on ADLI. Third, the chapter concludes with reflection on the utility of an expanded DSP for understanding development trajectories.

The International Dynamics and Developmental Statehood: Considering Ethiopia

Analyses of the first-tier developmental states conclude that the state is essential to socio-economic transition anchored on manufacturing and industrialisation (Amsden 1989; Wade 1990). This draws on classical development economics theories that locate economic transformation in industrial development (Lewis 1954; Nurkse 1953; Hirschman 1958). Fine (2007) has presented the DSP as comprising two schools that are distinct but interlinked. The economic school is concerned with economic policies, including the control of finance, industrial and trade policy and the political school is focused on the nature and construct of the state. This distinction rests on the basis of the DSP in the state-market dichotomy. Connecting to this, Radice (2010) has argued that such an approach fails to acknowledge the immense power of global market forces in relation to states even in domestic spheres.

The DSP provides the opportunity for greater depth and breadth because it has its conceptual roots in empiricism as a foundation for theorising. This allows for the (re)introduction of significant issues including agriculture and resource wealth, conflict as well as complex state–market interlinkages and IPE dynamics that may otherwise have been neglected, as long as they have been relevant in the DSP's own empirical underpinning (Ikpe Forthcoming; Ikpe, 2020; 2018).

In reality, the economic successes of first-tier developmental states depended on engagement with the global economy. International trade has been central to the defining characteristics of developmental statehood. In fact, high levels of growth due to increasing exports of agricultural and later manufacturing exports in developmental states has been a pivotal challenge to classical development thought on dependency theory. The role of international trade in developmental states' economic success is well documented and credited as a core contributory factor to their experiences. In developmental states, the exports of manufactured and industrial goods, facilitated by protectionist trade policies, have been strong drivers of phenomenal economic growth levels (Wade 1990; Amsden 1989). Agricultural exports have also been especially important for generating savings for capital investments in earlier stages in the industrialisation cycle in first-tier developmental states (Akyüz et al. 1998).

In addition, the concerns around the post-second world war global influence of communist regimes drove untied aid transfers from the US to Taiwan and South Korea (Thorbecke 1979; Tsai 2002: 138). In essence, developmental states pursued developmental agendas that were shaped by powerful global interests.

Contemporary discussions on global production networks and global value chains (GVC) engage the significance of international dynamics in industrial production. However, these have tended to challenge the focus of developmental statehood on states' agency in industrial development processes and outcomes (Gereffi 2014). Horner and Alford (2019) attempt to redress this tendency with a useful re-examination of the role of the state in relation to GVCs as facilitator, regulator, producer and buyer. While this is a helpful contribution to the literature it reinforces the analytical challenge of the state–market dichotomy in the treatment of the state and market as devoid of their intrinsic interrelatedness.

Another factor that is significant for the wider applicability of the DSP is the need for a broadened engagement with industrial transformation beyond a focus on the late industrialisation phase. Linkages between agricultural and industrial sectors even within the developmental states, have been little considered within the framework. Both Francks et al. (1999) and Karshenas (1995) show that the agricultural sector was fundamental to the structural transformation processes in the first-tier developmental states, through intersectoral resource transfers of savings, labour and food and raw material supply and industrial demand.

Against this background, Ikpe (2013, 2018) uses Hirschman's linkages thesis, to propose a framework for broadening analysis of industrialisation to include the primary sector. This explains how the developmental state influences structural transformation by managing fiscal, consumption and production linkages across sectors to address classical constraints on industrialisation and the underlying economic, social and political interests that influence the state's actions. Building on this Ikpe (Forthcoming) contributes the IPE-enhanced DSP that reflects how international political economy dynamics can impinge on underlying economic, political and social interests that underpin the actions of the state as shown in Fig. 9.1. This IPE-enhanced DSP highlights two sets of dynamics as a basis for conceptualising: synergies, that is, fiscal, production and consumption linkages and how they do (not) address savings, raw materials, and industrial demand constraints on industrialisation and; lines of influence, that

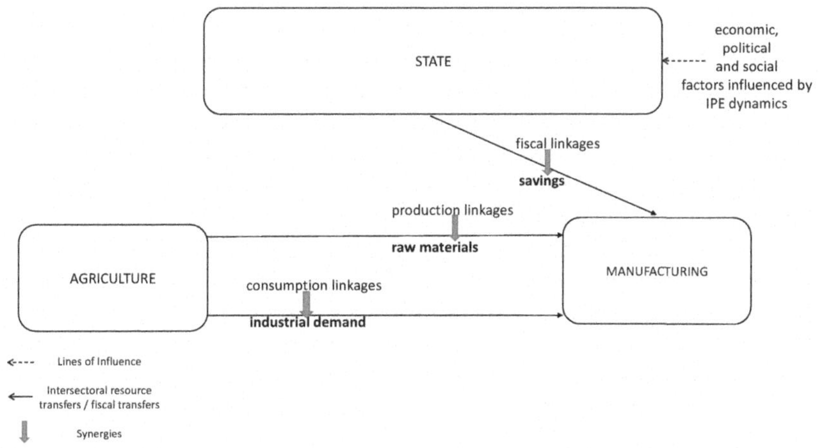

Fig. 9.1 IPE-Enhanced DSP (From Ikpe Forthcoming)

is, economic, social and political factors including international capital dynamics that underscore the state's actions.

The literature on developmental statehood in Africa, has roots in the studies on archetypes, Botswana and Mauritius (Taylor 2005; Meisenhelder 1997). Significantly the place of industrial development and structural transformation within developmental statehood is engaged in Mkandawire's (2001) conceptual contribution in his reflection on African contexts. Ethiopia is a case of growing significance in the gradual expansion of this body of work on developmental statehood (Zenawi 2012; Lefort 2012; Clapham 2018; Hailu Woldegebrael 2018; Planel 2014; Di Nunzio 2015; Gagliardone 2014; Fantini 2013; Brown and Fisher 2019; Pellerin 2019). While much of this literature falls within the political school, there is evidence of some progression beyond the traditional static distinctions across economic and political schools with some contributions transcending this divide. Lefort (2012), Planel (2014) and Chinigò (2015) complicate the divide in analyses of the complex economic and political factors underpinning development processes in the dominant agricultural sector. These discussions do not consider agriculture within structural transformation processes and therein along an industrialisation trajectory in line with the DSP logic.

Debates on Ethiopia's developmental statehood remain confined to the domestic sphere across history, politics, elites and class dynamics alongside economics with limited reference to the complex ways through which extranational factors are intertwined with the Ethiopian state's actions in developmental pursuits. Understanding these interactions are especially important given the substantial role of foreign capital in Ethiopia's growth trajectory. Exceptions are Feyissa (2011), Gagliardone (2014) and Clapham (2018) that reflect on IPE dynamics in relation to the Ethiopian state's developmental pursuits. Though engaging elements of IPE dynamics Brown and Fisher (2019) do not address the real sectors of the economy as they focus on Western donors' engagement with the notion of developmental statehood. The focus on domestic contexts is very much in line with the lack of conceptual engagement with IPE dynamics within the DSP.

Ethiopia evidences the importance of the agricultural and industrial sectors to its economic progress within a developmentalist agenda. Manufacturing value added as a percentage of GDP, increased from 9.4% in 2010 to 24.6% in 2017 vis-à-vis 10% for Sub-Saharan Africa over this period (World Bank 2020). Manufacturing progress has also been linked intrinsically to the agricultural sector also through spillover effects and industrial upgrading in the latter (World Bank 2018; UNDP 2018). To be sure, it is premature to speak of structural transformation in Ethiopia. Nonetheless, agricultural employment as a proportion of total employment has been on a slow and steady downward trend from 76% in 2000 to 65% in 2019 with employment in industry trending upwards from 7% to 13% over the same period (World Bank 2020). However, it is vital to note also that employment in services has been on the increase from 15% in 2005 to 22% in 2019 (World Bank 2020).

Industrial policy in Ethiopia has also been organised around the link between agriculture and manufacturing as with the 1994 Agricultural Development Led Industrialisation (ADLI) strategy with emphasis on intersectoral resource transfers. Within the Growth and Transformation Plan (GTP) attention to industrialisation has singled out sectors including leather, food processing-sugar and textiles with strong agriculture and manufacturing sector links (Shifweraw 2017). On the leather sector specifically, hides and skin are an agricultural by-product of the livestock sector (Leach and Wilson 2009). Ethiopian leather production is presented as attractive to foreign capital because of access to raw materials (KIDI 2013: 4470). Cramer et al. (2018) highlight that success in the leather sector in other parts of the Global South as reliant on sound intersectoral linkages.

The Utility of the IPE-Enhanced DSP: Interactions Across the Agricultural and Industrial Sectors in Ethiopia

Using the lens of the IPE-enhanced DSP, drawing on Fig. 9.1, we consider interactions across agriculture and industry, with some attention to the ADLI agenda, in Ethiopia in terms of synergies, that is, fiscal, production and consumption linkages and interactions with savings, raw materials, and industrial demand constraints on industrialisation and; lines of influence, that is, economic, social and political factors including international capital dynamics that underscore the state's actions.

On Fiscal Linkages and the Savings Constraint

In Ethiopia gross domestic savings and gross capital formation have been on the rise albeit with a substantial gap, going from 17% to 22% and 32% to 38% over 2011–2017 respectively (World Bank 2020). Public investment has been volatile but on a rising trend from 5% of GDP in 1992–93 to 16% in 2014 and private investment has similarly been on an increasing trend from 17% in 2000 to 24% in 2014 (Shifweraw 2017). Savings for investment in manufacturing have come largely from the state; these are state-manufacturing savings transfers in Fig. 9.1. In fact, Ethiopia's consistent economic growth performance has been linked to the public sector as investor (UNDP 2018). Investment in infrastructure has been driven by the state in transport over 1997–2007, power and telecommunications through the 2000s with the state expending about 10% of GDP on infrastructure, one of the highest levels on the continent (Gebreeyesus 2013).

Public revenue in Ethiopia is mainly reliant on tax revenue from direct and indirect sources. In 2016–2017 it constituted 80% of total public revenue (NBE 2017). The most directly delineable elements of agriculture's contribution to fiscal revenue are land use taxes and agricultural income taxes; agricultural taxes are reported as constituting less than 1% of total tax revenue (Hassen 2016). However, this does not account for indirect contributions such as value-added tax, which is generally a higher contribution to total tax revenue in African contexts. Nonetheless tax revenue from the sector makes a minimal contribution to state finance in spite of its significance as the largest employment sector and the second largest share of GDP at 34% (World Bank 2020; UNDP 2018). This is explained partly by limited export trade taxes in contrast to the general pattern in Sub-Saharan Africa (NBE 2017). Agriculture as a whole continues to play a dominant role in export earnings (Shifweraw 2017; UNDP 2018). But the sector appears to have made limited contribution towards addressing investment needs. Clapham (2018) argues that the agricultural sector was never able to generate the necessary surplus to support industrialisation.

UNDP (2018) has shown that Ethiopia suffers a substantial savings–investment gap. Minister of Finance Ahmed described this gap as a structural factor of the Ethiopian economy (Tadesse 2019). This has accounted for emerging concerns around Ethiopia's rising debt-GDP ratio that is seen as resulting chiefly from a robust public sector-driven infrastructural investment agenda (World Bank 2019). The savings–investment gap has consistently been met through foreign capital flows. In a review of the investment and innovation policy regime in Ethiopia, UNCTAD (2002) reflects on how the Ethiopian state has targeted and relied traditionally on foreign investment and capital flows and the role of Chinese finance emerges as significant. Ethiopia was the largest African recipient of Chinese loans at 13.7 bn USD over 2000–2017 (CARI 2018). It was also the highest recipient of Chinese investment flows in the Horn at a total of 1.6 billion USD.

In particular, Fitawek and Kalaba (2016) document huge increases of Chinese investment in the leather sector from less than about 400, 000 USD to 58.5 million USD in 2004–2010. As noted, this is an important sector in the drive to strengthen industrial production through linkages with agriculture. In 2011 foreign-owned firms accounted for 25% of ownership but 55% of leather goods exports (Oqubay 2016: 209). We see foreign capital play a significant role in industrial development within the sector.

Against this background Ikpe (Forthcoming) identifies synergies between addressing the savings constraint and indirect fiscal transfers within the Ethiopian leather sector in line with Fig. 9.1. The influx of Chinese capital has been influenced by an industrial policy direction that prioritises a focus on exports in the leather subsector. Abebe and Schaefer (2014) reflect on the sector as linked to industrial policy efforts to generate foreign exchange through exports to be invested more widely. It is to this end that the Ethiopian state has foregone fiscal revenue by offering investors tax holidays on profits and preferential treatment for export-oriented sectors (Gebreeyesus 2013).

Regarding the lines of influence, underlying economic dynamics that have influenced the state's interactions with foreign capital emerge in the tendency to prioritise this constituency over the domestic private sector in its export promotion agenda (Ikpe Forthcoming). Significantly, in political terms, foreign capital is depicted as more malleable than domestic private capital by the Ethiopian state (Clapham 2018).

On Production Linkages and Food Supply as Well as Raw Material Constraints

The ADLI agenda has had some success in improving food production and strengthening food supply. This has taken Ethiopia very close to food self-sufficiency in staple grains at a ratio of about 90% (Van Ittersum et al. 2016). Yield increases across the key grains of maize, sorghum and wheat, and nitrogen and phosphate fertiliser use have been on a rising trend since 2006 (Van Ittersum et al. 2016). It is against this background that food imports as a proportion of merchandise imports have been on a declining trend from 24% in 2003 to 7% in 2015 although fluctuating upwards to 15% in 2018, these levels of decline are higher than the African average (World Bank 2020). This shows some potential for intersectoral resource transfer in offering production linkages and addressing food supply constraints on industrialisation.

Consumption patterns and tastes of industrial often urban-based labour are key determinants of food self-sufficiency for industrial workers. This is an important consideration for the way that intersectoral resource transfer can support the manufacturing sector. Abraham (2015) reports periodic export bans on core food groups aimed at satisfying domestic and especially urban demand. Mottaleb and Rahut (2018) agree that this approach can bring some benefits to domestic producers. This evidences how the state steers market dynamics to enable intersectoral resource transfers between agriculture and industry to address input and food constraints on industrialisation.

Production linkages can be important for the provision of raw materials for the industrial sector. Diao et al. (2007) argue that Ethiopia's manufacturing sector is import-dependent with poor levels of demand for domestic inputs. Geebreyesus (2013) shows that higher technology manufacturing sectors such as chemicals, plastic, rubber, iron and engineering present high levels of import dependence at 70–98% of imported raw materials relative to total raw materials costs. However, agro-industrial sectors, such as leather, exhibit far lower levels of import dependence at 5–35% of imported raw materials as a proportion of total raw materials costs. This has been an important factor in the prioritisation of the leather sector within the industrial development agenda.

Considering the leather sub sector, Ikpe (Forthcoming) shows synergies between the raw material supply and production linkages in line with Fig. 9.1. These are linked to the Ethiopian state's imposition of 150% export taxes on agricultural by-products that constitute the raw materials from the agricultural sector, hides and skin, in order to channel them to domestic manufacturing of leather and leather products with emphasis on exports (Fitawek and Talaba 2016). We see the state's efforts to mitigate raw material constraints and drive forward production linkages. These efforts steered an inflow of foreign capital into activities that served to mitigate raw material supply constraints and improved leather production and exports (Ikpe, Forthcoming; Fitawek and Talaba 2016).

On the lines of influence, underlying dynamics emerge in the social concerns about the pervasiveness of foreign capital and the impact of that on domestic private capital (Ikpe Forthcoming). Local tanners and leather goods producers have actively lobbied the state to limit foreign entry into tanning activities to maintain their dominance (Oqubay 2016: 214–215). This is linked also to a path dependence for domestic tanneries from the central planning period. Nonetheless, the economic need for addressing raw material constraints and support industrial upgrading for exports influenced the state's eventual abolishment of the ban.

On Consumption Linkages and Constraints on Domestic Industrial Demand

The ADLI is clear on the centrality of the agricultural sector to energising the industrial sector through domestic demand of manufactured outputs. For one thing the largest share of the population is employed in agriculture. Block (1999) and Altenburg (2010) have argued that the Ethiopian rural agricultural sector plays a limited role in contributing to effective demand of industrial goods. This suggests poor consumption linkages from agriculture to the manufacturing sector that would mitigate the domestic demand constraints on industrialisation. In general, this linkage is strengthened by rising income levels (Dorosh and Mellor 2013). In fact, Diao et al. (2007) demonstrate that increases in agricultural income are disproportionately expended on consumer industrial goods due to low levels of disposable income. Meaza (2011: 33) shows this to be the case with primary research into consumption patterns of rural agricultural households in Tigray. In considering pluriactivity and rural manufacturing, McCullough (2015) and Rijkers et al. (2010: 1282–1291) highlight opportunities for fuller employment and improved productivity levels that could potentially raise incomes and therein domestic demand.

Turning attention to the leather sector Ikpe (Forthcoming) finds that the synergies between consumption linkages and industrial demand are not a strategic concern for the Ethiopian state. This is in spite of evidence that with rising demand of footwear and higher prices of imported footwear as well as the devaluation of the Birr, local demand has at times been met by domestic production (Oqubay 2016: 215). This signals the potential synergies between industrial demand and consumption linkages. Rather the state describes the domestic leather market as 'insignificant' (GRM International 2007: 41). Yet the leather sector was historically located in areas that were deemed the most important domestic markets (Oqubay 2016: 207). As production and exports of leather footwear have increased with the entry of major foreign and Chinese producers so too have imports with implications for domestic producers (Tsefaye 2020: 64–65; Fitawek and Talaba 2016).

In terms of the lines of influence, Ikpe (Forthcoming) reflects on underlying economic and socio-political dynamics that have been at play with little effort to address industrial upgrading domestically given both the domestic private sector's interests in providing inputs but also the state's prioritisation of exports as an element of industrial policy. These are influenced by the economic need for foreign exchange as savings and the political reticence to rely on the domestic private sector as earlier noted. In a sense, domestic private capital has tended to be more attentive to the upstream activities such as tanning, in attempting to protect that from foreign participation by lobbying the state. Oqubay (2016: 215) argues that, as part of the Ethiopian Leather Industries Association, domestic tanning firms lobbied to prevent foreign capital investment in the sector to retain a structure with limited competition. This has coexisted with the state's attention to and prioritisation of leather goods exports with a focus on strengthening foreign capital participation through the incentive structures already discussed.

Conclusions

The rooting of the DSP in empiricism has foregrounded the possibility of considering the interplay between the state and other milieus, such as the domestic and foreign private capital and an extended understanding of industrialisation with the case of Ethiopia. The IPE-enhanced DSP has highlighted two sets of dynamics namely: synergies, that is, fiscal, production and consumption linkages and how they do (not) mitigate savings, raw materials and industrial demand constraints on industrialisation; and lines of influence, that is, economic, social and political factors including international capital dynamics that underscore the state's actions (Ikpe Forthcoming).

In Ethiopia foreign capital has been important for building synergies between savings and fiscal linkages as well as between raw materials and production linkages. This can be seen as being linked to the limited contributions from the agricultural sector to savings. The state's role has been clear in an incentive structure that has built in fiscal linkages in foregone tax revenues as well as tariff structures that have facilitated raw material supply for enabling forward production linkages. Yet the synergies between consumption linkages and domestic industrial demand have been poor, influenced in part by the state's attention to exports as a priority element of industrial policy (in support of savings generation) and greater attention to domestic capital as input suppliers than in industrial upgrading for the domestic market. This is in spite of the possibilities of connections between improved rural and agricultural incomes and demand for consumer industrial goods. Certain lines of influence underpin this in the state's prioritisation of foreign capital due to a political reticence to engage domestic private capital and economic prioritisation of exports to generate savings.

This attention to export markets resonates with the emphasis of GVCs on insertion into global production systems. This shows the potential challenge this poses for developing industrial upgrading that is focused on domestic markets and therein the significance of domestic industrial demand as part of industrial policy. Ghosh (2019) speaks of how the exploitation of national production conditions due to the immense power of international capital in relation to the state undermines socio-economic transformation. For Ethiopia, some domestic producers appear to have a more limited role in industrial upgrading vis-a-vis their foreign counterparts with the potential outcome of a digression from the significance of domestic industrial demand in this ADLI trajectory.

Bibliography

Abebe, G., and Schaefer, F. 2014. High Hopes and Limited Successes: Experimenting with Industrial Polices in the Leather Industry in Ethiopia Working Paper No. 011. Ethiopian Development Research Institute.

Abraham, R. 2015. Achieving Food Security in Ethiopia by Promoting Productivity of Future World Food Tef: A Review. Advances in Plants and Agriculture Research 2(2).

Akyüz, Y., Chang, H-J., and Kozul Wright, R.S. 1998. New Perspectives on East Asian Development. Journal of Development Studies, 34(6), pp. 4–36.

Alden, C. 2012. China and Africa: The Relationship Matures. Strategic Analysis, 36(5), pp. 701–707.

Altenburg, T. 2010. Industrial Policy in Ethiopia. Discussion Paper/Deutsches Institut für Entwicklungspolitik. Bonn: DIE.

Amsden, A.H. 1989. Asia's Next Giant: South Korea and Late Industrialization. New York: Oxford University Press.

Bezawagaw, M., Dihel, N., Geiger, M.T., and Getachew, K.Z. 2018. Ethiopia Economic Update: The Inescapable Manufacturing Services Nexus: Exploring the Potential of Distribution Services (English). Washington, DC: World Bank Group. http://documents.worldbank.org/curated/en/811791526447120021/The-inescapable-manufacturing-services-nexus-exploring-the-potentialof-distribution-services.

Block, S.A. 1999. Agriculture and Economic Growth in Ethiopia: Growth Multipliers from a Four-Sector Simulation Model. Agricultural Economics, 20(3), pp. 241–252.

Brown, S., and Fisher, J. 2019. Aid Donors, Democracy and the Developmental State in Ethiopia. Democratization, 27(2), pp. 1–19.

China-Africa Research Initiative Database (CARI). 2018. Data on Chinese Loans and Foreign Direct Investment Data. Johns Hopkins University. http://www.sais-cari.org/data.

Chinigò, D. 2015. Historicising Agrarian Transformation: Agricultural Commercialisation and Social Differentiation in Wolaita, Southern Ethiopia. Journal of Eastern African Studies, 9(2), pp. 193–211.

Clapham, C. 2018. The Ethiopian Developmental State. Third World Quarterly, 39(6), pp. 1151–1165.

Cramer, C., Di John, J., and Sender, J. 2018. Poinsettia Assembly and Selling Emotion: High Value Agricultural Exports in Ethiopia, AFD Research Papers Series, No. 2018–78, August.

Diao, X., Fekadu, B., Haggblade, S., Taffesse, A.S., Wamisho, K., and Yu, B. 2007. Agricultural Growth Linkages in Ethiopia: Estimates Using Fixed and Flexible Price Models. Washington, DC: International Food Policy Research Institute.

Di Nunzio, M. 2015. What is the Alternative? Youth, Entrepreneurship and the Developmental State in Urban Ethiopia. Development and Change, 46(5), pp. 1179–1200.

Dorosh, P.A., and Mellor, J.W. 2013. Why Agriculture Remains a Viable Means of Poverty Reduction in Sub Saharan Africa: The Case of Ethiopia. Development Policy Review, 31(4), pp. 419–441.

Fantini, E. 2013. Developmental State, Economic Transformation and Social Diversification in Ethiopia. ISPI Analysis, 163(7).

Federal Republic of Ethiopia (FRE). 2019. A Homegrown Economic Reform Agenda: A Pathway to Prosperity. Office of the Prime Minister. Addis Ababa.

Feyissa, D. 2011. Aid Negotiation: The Uneasy "Partnership" Between EPRDF and the Donors. Journal of Eastern African Studies, 5(4), pp. 788–817.

Fine, B. 2007. State, Development and Inequality: The Curious Incidence of the Developmental State in the Night- Time. In Sanpad Conference, Durban, June 26–30, 2007. Durban, South Africa.

Fitawek, W.B., and Kalaba, M. 2016. The Role of Trade Policy on Ethiopia's Leather Industry: Effect of Export Tax on Competitiveness. Presented at the 5th International Conference of the African Association of Agricultural Economists, September 23–26, 2016, Addis Ababa, Ethiopia.

Francks, P., with Boestel, J., and Kim, C.H. 1999. Agriculture and Economic Development in East Asia: From Growth to Protectionism in Japan, Korea, and Taiwan. London: Routledge.

Gagliardone, I. 2014. New Media and the Developmental State in Ethiopia. African Affairs, 113(451), pp. 279–299.

Gebreeyesus, M. 2013. Industrial policy and development in Ethiopia: Evolution and present experimentation (No. 2013/125). WIDER working paper.

Gelan, A. 2019. Ethiopia's 'Homegrown' Economic Reform: An Afterthought, Addis Fortune. October 12, 2019. https://addisfortune.com/ethiopias-homegrown-economic-reform-an-afterthought/.

Gereffi, G. 2014. Global Value Chains in a Post-Washington Consensus World. Review of International Political Economy, 21(1), pp. 9–37.

Ghosh, J. 2019. A Brave New World, or the Same Old Story with New Characters? Development and Change, 50(2), pp. 379–393.

Giannecchini, P., and Taylor, I. 2018. The Eastern Industrial Zone in Ethiopia: Catalyst for Development? Geoforum, 88, pp. 28–35.

GRM International. 2007. Livestock Development Master Plan Study for Government of Ethiopia- Ministry of Agriculture and Rural Development and African Development Bank. http://www.igadhost.com/igaddata/docs/LDMPS_Phase%20I_Vol.K_Hides%20&%20Skins.pdf.

Hailu Woldegebrael, E. 2018. The Materialization of "Developmental State" in Ethiopia: Insights from the Gibe III Hydroelectric Development Project Regime, Omo Valley. L'Espace Politique. Revue en ligne de géographie politique et de géopolitique (35).

Hassen, A.A. 2016. Agricultural Taxation and Economic Growth in Ethiopia. In 2016 AAAE Fifth International Conference. https://ageconsearch.umn.edu/bitstream/246395/2/129.%20Agricultural%20tax%20in%20Ethiopia.pdf.

Hirschman, A.O. 1958. The Strategy of Economic Development, CT: Yale University Press.

Hirschman, A.O. 1981. A Generalized Linkage Approach to Development, with Special Reference to Staples. In Essays in Trespassing: Economics to Politics and Beyond. Cambridge: Cambridge University Press.

Horner, R., and Alford, M. 2019. The Roles of the State in Global Value Chains: An Update and Emerging Agenda (No. 362019). GDI, The University of Manchester.

Ikpe, E. 2013. Lessons for Nigeria from Developmental States: The Role of Agriculture in Structural Transformation. In Fine, B., Saraswati, J., and Tavasci, D., eds. Beyond the Developmental State: Industrial Policy into the 21st Century, pp. 187–215. London: Pluto Press.

Ikpe, E. 2018. The Enduring Relevance of the Developmental State Paradigm Across Space and Time: Lessons for Africa on Structural Transformation and Agriculture in Oil-Rich Contexts. Journal of Asian and African Studies, 53(5), pp. 764–781.

Ikpe, E. 2020. Covid-19 and Manufacturing in Africa: Reflections on Syringe Manufacturing in Nigeria ALC Op-ED Series 5(4). https://www.africanleadershipcentre.org/index.php/covid-19-research/669-covid-19-and-manufacturing-in-africa-reflections-on-syringe-manufacturing-in-nigeria.

Ikpe, E. Forthcoming. Thinking About Developmental Statehood, Manufacturing and International Capital: The Case of Ethiopia.

Karshenas, M. 1995. Industrialization and Agricultural Surplus: A Comparative Study of Economic Development in Asia. New York: Oxford University Press.

Korea International Development Institute (KIDI). 2013. GTP and Sector Analysis, Business Cases and Policy, Recommendations Based on the Korean Experiences. Korea International Cooperation Agency.

Leach, I., and Wilson, R.T. 2009. Higher Value Addition Through Hides and Skins. FAO Diversification Booklet Number 8. Rome: FAO. http://www.fao.org/3/a-i0523e.pdf.

Lefort, R. 2012. Free Market Economy, 'Developmental State' and Party-state hegemony in Ethiopia: The Case of the 'Model Farmers'. The Journal of Modern African Studies, 681–706.

Lewis, W.A. 1954. Economic Development with Unlimited Supplies of Labour. The Manchester School, 22(2), pp. 139–191.

Mariam, A. 2019. Innovating the Developmental State Through Homegrown Economic Reform? Addis Fortune. October 12, 2019. https://addisfortune.com/innovating-the-developmental-state-through-homegrown-economic-reform/.

McCullough, E.B. 2015. Labor Productivity and Employment Gaps in Sub-Saharan Africa. Food Policy Volume 67, February 2017, pp. 133–152.

Meaza, K.A. 2011. Is Industrialisation Possible Through Agricultural Development Led Industrialization? A Micro Based Study in Tigray, Ethiopia. Masters Thesis. Department of Economics and Resources. Norwegian University of Life Sciences.

Meisenhelder, T. 1997. The Developmental State in Mauritius. The Journal of Modern African Studies, 35(2), pp. 279–297.

Mkandawire, T. 2001. Thinking About Developmental States in Africa. Cambridge Journal of Economics, 25(3), pp. 289–314.

Mottaleb, K.A., and Rahut, D.B. 2018. Household Production and Consumption Patterns of Teff in Ethiopia. Agribusiness, 34(3), pp. 668–684.

Mwambari, D. 2020. The Pandemic Can Be a Catalyst for Decolonisation in Africa Al Jazeera Opinion. April 15, 2020. https://www.aljazeera.com/indepth/opinion/pandemic-catalyst-decolonisation-africa-200415150535786.html.

National Bank of Ethiopia (NBE). 2017. Annual Report 2016–17 Addis Ababa: National Bank of Ethiopia. http://www.nbebank.com/pdf/annualbulletin/NBE%20Annual%20report%202016-2017/NBE%20Annual%20Report%202016-2017.pdf.

Nurkse, R. 1953. Problems of Capital Formation. New York: Oxford University Press.

Oqubay, A. 2016. Made in Africa: Industrial Policy in Ethiopia. African Development Bank Working Paper Series, No. 299. Abidjan: African Development Bank.

Oqubay, A. 2018. The Structure and Performance of the Ethiopian Manufacturing Sector. In The Oxford Handbook of the Ethiopian Economy. Oxford: Oxford University Press.

Pellerin, C.L. 2019. The Aspiring Developmental State and Business Associations in Ethiopia–(dis-) Embedded Autonomy? The Journal of Modern African Studies, 57(4), pp. 589–612.

Planel, S. 2014. A View of a Bureaucratic Developmental State: Local Governance and Agricultural Extension in Rural Ethiopia. Journal of Eastern African Studies, 8(3), pp. 420–437.

Radice, H. 2010. Book Review: Capital, Class and Crisis: The False Dichotomy of Market and State: An Extended Book Review. Capital & Class, 34(1), pp. 137–142.

Rijkers, B., Söderbom, M., and Loening, J.L. 2010. A Rural–Urban Comparison of Manufacturing Enterprise Performance in Ethiopia. World Development, 38(9), pp. 1278–1296.

Samaro, Z. 2019. Reform Agenda Neither Homegrown Nor Pathway to Prosperity, Addis Fortune, Addis Ababa, September 21, 2019. https://addisfortune.news/reform-agenda-neither-homegrown-nor-pathway-to-prosperity/.

Shifweraw, A. 2017. Productive Capacity and Economic Growth in Ethiopia. CDP Background Paper No. 34 ST/ESA/2017/CDP/34 United Nations, Department of Economics and Social Affairs. https://www.un.org/development/desa/dpad/wp-content/uploads/sites/45/publication/CDP-bp-2017-34.pdf.

Tadesse, F. 2019. Ethiopia: A $10 Billion Economic Reform Package, Addis Fortune, Addis Ababa September 14, 2019. https://allafrica.com/stories/201909170544.html.

Taylor, I. 2005. The Developmental State in Africa: The Case of Botswana. The Potentiality of 'Developmental States' in Africa. Dakar: CODESRIA.

Thorbecke, E. 1979. Agricultural Development. In W. Galenson, ed. Economic Growth and Structural Change in Taiwan: The Postwar Experience of the Republic of China. Ithaca: Cornell University Press.

Tsai, M.C. 2002. Taming a Leviathan: Geopolitics, State Power and the Making of a Development Regime in Taiwan. Canadian Journal of Development Studies/Revue canadienne d'études du développement, 23(1), pp. 127–153.

Tsefaye, A. 2020. China in Ethiopia: The Long-term Perspective. Albany: SUNY Press.

UNCTAD. 2002. Investment and Innovation Policy Review Ethiopia Geneva: UNCTAD. https://unctad.org/en/docs/poiteipcm4.en.pdf.

UNDP. 2018. Ethiopia's Progress Towards Eradicating Poverty. Paper to Be Presented to the Inter-Agency Group Meeting On the "Implementation of the Third United Nations Decade for the Eradication of Poverty (2018–2027)" UNDP: Addis Ababa. https://www.un.org/development/desa/dspd/wp-content/uploads/sites/22/2018/04/Ethiopia%E2%80%99s-Progress-Towards-Eradicating-Poverty.pdf.

Van Ittersum, M.K., Van Bussel, L.G., Wolf, J., Grassini, P., Van Wart, J., Guilpart, N., Claessens, L., de Groot, H., Wiebe, K., Mason-D'Croz, D., and Yang, H. 2016. Can Sub-Saharan Africa Feed Itself? Proceedings of the National Academy of Sciences, 113(52), pp. 14964–14969.

Vaughan, S. 2011. Revolutionary Democratic State-Building: Party, State and People in the EPRDF's Ethiopia. Journal of Eastern African Studies, 5(4), pp. 619–640.

Wade, R. 1990. Governing the Market: Economic Theory and the Role of Government in East Asian industrialization. Princeton: Princeton University Press.

World Bank. 2014. 3rd Ethiopia Economic Update Strengthening Export Performance Through Improved Competitiveness. Washington, DC: World Bank. http://documents.worldbank.org/curated/en/560521468028152818/pdf/895480REVISED00c0Update0v0final0web.pdf.

World Bank. 2018. Ethiopia Economic Update- the Inescapable Manufacturing Services Nexus: Exploring the Potential of Distribution Services. Washington, DC: World Bank.

World Bank. 2019. Global Economic Prospects January 2019- Sub-Saharan Africa Chapter. Washington, DC: World Bank.

World Bank. 2020. World Development Indicators. Washington, DC: World Bank.

Zenawi, M. 2012. States and Markets: Neoliberal Limitations and the Case for a Developmental State. In Akbar, N. ed. Good Growth and Governance in Africa: Rethinking Development Strategies. Oxford: Oxford University Press.

CHAPTER 10

Developmental or Impoverishing Urban Cores? The Case of Slovakia

István Kollai

Introduction

However decade-long developmental programmes and 'miracles' of convergence are primarily attached to South-East Asian region, some traditionally underdeveloped CEE countries could also significantly change their ranks and positions comparing with Western Europe, but within the whole CEE region as well. For instance, there is a relatively widely spread narrative within the academic and public discourse about Slovakia, pointing out the successfulness of the small and semi-peripheral post-Communist country, as having emerged from the political and economic invisibility. This narrative has been more forceful when recalling the uneasy birth of the new sovereign state. When Czechoslovakia ceased to exist on 1 January 1993, the world-renowned Czech culture, the

I. Kollai (✉)
Department of World Economy, Institute of International, Political, and Regional Studies, Corvinus University of Budapest, Budapest, Hungary
e-mail: istvan.kollai@uni-corvinus.hu

T. Gerőcs and J. Ricz (eds.), *The Post-Crisis Developmental State*, International Political Economy Series,
https://doi.org/10.1007/978-3-030-71987-6_10

strong Czech industry, the well-developed urban area of Prague and the centuries-old tradition of Czech statehood became detached from Slovakia, and the Slovaks were left to their own devices. Slovakia had to establish its political, economic and cultural relations from a nullity. It was no coincidence that the independence of the country was not decided in a referendum but by the resolution of the Prague and Bratislava Parliaments, since Slovak citizens did not seem to opt for the dissolution, and most of them had reservations about or serious doubts as to the separation on the basis of the then surveys. As a matter of fact, only a part of the Slovak political elite had the creation of a sovereign state at heart (Vodička 2003).

What happened after the independence of Slovakia appeared to confirm the above fears: Vladimir Mečiar's government regarded Slovakia as its own and exclusive domain and ushered in a new era of a pro-Russian and anti-EU policy, rampant clientelism and war against the media and culture instead of Euro-Atlantic integration (Samuel 1994). Only barely formed internal structures could counterbalance the aggressive building up of his political power. Finally, in 1998, it took the joining of four political forces from different parts of the ideological spectrum, the so-called 'Rainbow Coalition', to set Slovakia on a path to Euro-Atlantic integration (Samuel 2001).

What happened afterwards is regarded by the academic and public discourse as a successful integration struggle of late-comers: the accession to NATO, the EU and eurozone was conducted, economic growth resumed and growth rates remained persistently high. It is well known in this regard that the impressive economic boom was based on the automotive industry and the introduction of a basic tax rate of 19 per cent, in addition to some strong neoliberal economic policy measures in the country. The excessively rapid expansion ended only in 2008 when the economic downturn erupted; there had been years when annual GDP growth of a world record 8–10 per cent had been recorded. The automotive industry has indeed become a key pillar of Slovakia: Slovakia has become the world leader in car production per capita, and 45 per cent of the Slovak industrial production is being owned by automotive manufacturers employing over 80,000 people. The number of produced cars has passed for many years now the one-million mark on an annual basis (Luptáčik et al. 2013; Slušná and Balog 2015). Slovakia was then given the nickname 'Tatra Tiger', as a clear reference of Asian Tigers; its economic development brought the interest of the spheres of academics and politics, starting to call Slovakia as a 'role model country' where transitions reforms happened to be successful.

However, the country-wide data on economic growth hides its interesting spatial pattern, i.e. that economic growth is concentrated primarily in Bratislava and its Western Slovakian environs. The regional distribution of GDP highlights it clearly. As an urban region, Bratislava became the sixth richest region of the European Union in 2018 in terms of GDP per capita, soaring to 184.02 per cent of the EU average, exceeding Paris, Stockholm, Rome, Berlin and all capital regions in Central Europe (Kotzeva et al. 2018). Meanwhile the Eastern regions of Slovakia are among the poorest ones within the EU, and there is no region in Slovakia, with the exception of the Bratislava Region, where the level of development exceeds 75 per cent of the EU average in terms of GDP per capita. The excessive differences within the country are reflected in the OECD data according to which Slovakia was one of the countries where inequality increased the most between 2000 and 2013 (OECD 2016). Vast territorial disparities therefore make national statistics somewhat unreliable, which is intended to indicate the development of Slovakia with a single figure, while at least two distinct realities exist: the urban areas of Western Slovakia around Bratislava and the remaining parts of the country.

The list of data relating to the distorted territorial structure is extensive. Regional disparities are also large in terms of innovation potential, and of unemployment: while the unemployment rate has been mostly above 10 per cent in Eastern Slovakia, it has been below 5 per cent in Western Slovakia. Moreover, the proportion of the long-term unemployed has been very high in the Eastern part of Slovakia, while the long-term unemployment rate has been negligible in the western part of the country. The unemployment rate has been in the range of 10–11 per cent nationally, which, in this regard, can only be regarded as a misleading statistical figure (Kotzeva et al. 2018, 82). The distribution of automotive manufacturers recognized as the engine of economic progress also reflects territorial imbalances within the country: none of the global motor vehicle manufacturing groups is established more than 80 kilometres from the western border of the country in Slovakia, and, as reported in the Pravda database, four-fifths of all automotive suppliers operate in the western part of the country that is reached by motorways running out from Bratislava.[1] The list of 54 first-tier suppliers established by the Automotive Industry Association of the Slovak Republic (ZAP SR) also shows a steep west-east slope. Accordingly, at NUTS 2 level, 68.5 per cent of the suppliers operated in Western Slovakia, 27.8 per cent in Central Slovakia, while only 3.8 per cent in Eastern Slovakia.[2]

In the next chapters, these developmental biases and problems of Slovakia will be placed within various theoretical strands on territorial disparities, debating on how *path-dependency*—originating from past economic structures—and how *post-Fordism*—present structures of IT-adaptive globalized economy—can constrain the developmental path of monocentric small states. Are such spatial inequalities encoded in the emergence process, thanks to historically inherited economic structures? And could be such core–periphery imbalances bridged or at least reach an equilibrium position in the twenty-first century when post-Fordist networks of global cities decisively influence the growth capacities of national economies? In the next chapters, these questions will be scrutinized from a rather theoretical perspective, meanwhile Slovakian country data will be shown as a case study highlighting the above-mentioned dilemmas. Embedding these data within European databases, Slovakia seems to be an extreme but not sole example for such national economies in which global economic performance relies on a single highly developed core area, from which not just the international competitiveness of the entire country derives, but several policy results (e.g. OECD, EU and Eurozone memberships) have been achievable solely thanks to this urban core.

How Can Core-Hinterland Disparity Be Measured?

Despite constant alternative attempts, GDP figures continue to sustain its primacy in policy papers as the main indicator of development, despite that GDP does not necessarily indicate changes in future competitiveness, in human capital or in general living conditions. However these shortcomings are acknowledged by EU experts and politicians (see documents

[1] Branislav Toma: Piata automobilka na Slovensku má vyrábať nákladiaky. *Pravda*, accessed 21 April 2016. Online: https://spravy.pravda.sk/ekonomika/clanok/390668-piata-automobilka-ma-vyrabat-nakladiaky.

[2] Own calculation based on the database of the Automotive Industry Association of the Slovak Republic (ZAP SR). Available at: www.zapsr.sk.

of the initiative 'Beyond GDP', inter alia COM[2009]433), this indicator continues to be the key measure in official policy reports, fuelling a resilient optimism about the convergence process of CEE countries. According to country-level GDP data, catch-up process is progressing gradually but permanently (Kotzeva et al. 2018; COM[2017]583).

Similarly, widely used variation data also divert attention from the special patterns of spatial inequality, identifying great interregional gaps but not alarming outliers. There is no significant difference in development between the seven hinterland regions behind Bratislava Region; the variation from the national average is therefore not very high, since only capital city region is far above the average. Indeed, Slovakia can be included among the most equal countries of the EU on the basis of the variation data, as do analyses for the European Commission (Filauro 2018, 13). The issue of methodology can no longer be evaded: if the situation in Slovakia is declared to be 'extreme', the claim needs to be substantiated. As pointed out above, the mere variation data is not necessarily suitable for this purpose.

In addition to variation, there are, of course, several other widely used measures, such as the Gini coefficient or the Herfindahl index, which are also not suitable for measuring excessive development concentration or for cross-country comparisons, as they could only be applied to countries with the same number of regions (Tvrdon and Skokan 2011). Spatial statistics recommends the use of the Theil index measuring entropy for special distributions, or the so-called *decomposition indices* (Nemes Nagy 2005), when extreme outliers are removed from the original data series, providing a new variation data, thus the impact of outliers can be detected. It is therefore advisable to create a decomposition index that specifies the impact of a capital city region on spatial inequality. That is, the official national-level variation data should be compared (divided) by the variation *without* the capital region. The latter is a figure that refers to a fictitious country (Slovakia without the Bratislava Region) and indicates what the degree of territorial inequality would be if Bratislava Region was not part of the country. Slovakia without Bratislava is rather homogeneous and hardly produces territorial inequality, the latter fictitious variation data is therefore very low, while the national variation data—due to the inclusion of Bratislava—takes a much higher value. The decomposition index created from the ratio of the two figures reveals how much of the heterogeneity of the country's territorial development is attributable to

Table 10.1 Decomposition index indicating capital city-centred development in the European Union

	2005	*2013*
SK	4.54	5.48
EE	4.45	4.71
BG	3.55	4.01
HU	3.9	3.97
LV	4.17	3.66
SF	3.21	3.62
RO	3.13	3.28
IRL	3.03	3.22
HR	2.96	3
SL	2.46	2.56
PT	n/a	2.52
PL	2.34	2.4
LT	1.97	2.05
CZ	2.09	1.97
SE	1.76	1.87
GR	1.88	1.85
UK	1.72	1.8
ES	1.47	1.55
BE	1.53	1.51
FR	1.35	1.33
NL	1.27	1.31
IT	1.27	1.24
DK	1.14	1.19
AT	1.01	1

the core capital areas. As can be seen in Table 10.1, Bratislava increases more than five times the degree of territorial inequality in Slovakia.[3]

When calculating decomposition indices for all member states of the European Union, the highest value is obtained for Slovakia. Thus, our decomposition indicator provides us with a statistically verifiable outcome that the gap between the capital core and the rural periphery is widest in Slovakia within the EU (while it is clear that the phenomenon itself is not a country-specific issue, since many CEE countries are also top-ranked in terms of capital-countryside disparities). It makes Slovakia a great example to scrutinize from a theoretical perspective of spatial inequality.

[3] Source: Eurostat, Database of Regional Statistics. https://ec.europa.eu/eurostat/web/regions/data/database.

Theories on Spatial Inequality: 'Optimistic' and 'Pessimistic' Views

The increasing difference in development between metropolitan core and rural periphery has long been a matter of preoccupation of social sciences, even when optimistic theories dominated these fields of study. Such theories say that social and territorial disparities temporarily—which can mean several decades from a *longue durée* perspective—increase as a natural side-effect of convergence, and, after the period of robust growth has ended, these disparities diminish again. Such theories can be regarded as optimistic as they consider intra-regional disparities merely a temporary (and later spontaneously disappearing) phenomenon. The Kuznets theory (1955) created one of the first high-impact and optimistic models for social inequality, suggesting that once a new wave of industrial revolution or transition is sparked off, an uneven development process is also triggered: the productivity of new industrial branches will increase faster than the average, offering a higher level of income as well within these sectors. If power engines of economic convergence form territorial clusters, this temporary social inequality will reshape territorial disparities as well. Thus, modern-day urban areas—providing home for innovative clusters and hubs—are liable to widen the income gap between urban and rural residents and increases income stratification within a country. In Kuznets's opinion, the completion of urbanization turns these trends around, for instance through internal migration, when employees move from hinterland regions to jobs-rich cities (Kuznets 1955). The internal transformation of the society thus erodes temporary income disparities.

Political doctrines and policy analyses have transformed the Kuznets theory—originally a strongly dilemmatic paper—into a prophecy as the evidence of the temporary character of all kinds of internal inequalities (Moran 2005; Nemes Nagy 2005). It is also important to see that the theory under discussion does not put energy into modelling the catching-up of *hinterland* and only provides an explanation of the catching-up of *underclass*, for instance through internal migration. Kuznets neglected to consider thoroughly spatial inequalities. Jeffrey G. Williamson furthered the theory towards such a direction by arguing that developed core areas ultimately have spin-off growth effects on peripheries through *technology spreading*, resulting higher degree of human capital and infrastructure. He sought to prove his theory with the economic history of Great Britain (Williamson 1985; Feinstein 1988).

Similarly, optimistic theories include the 'growth pole' theory developed by François Perroux after the Second World War, which considers large urban areas as growth poles whose spread effects 'trickle down' slowly to towns and villages at lower levels of the settlement hierarchy, mostly through *corporate links*. While the French economist considered core-hinterland relationship as the embodiment of dominance of core areas in economic space (Perroux 1950; Meardon 2001), various experts and policy papers reframed the originally dilemmatic idea as an uncritically optimistic political strategy (Parr 1999). Neoliberal theories originating from neoclassical economics should also be included among optimistic approaches. They argue that the free movement of financial capital and labour force ultimately leads to a more balanced distribution of factors determining future competitiveness and development (Barro and Sala-i-Martin 1991).

In contrast, pessimistic theories emphasize that internal inequality may become self-sustaining or self-reinforcing. It is uncertain whether technology and knowledge flow out of urban cores, as concluded by Williamson (1985); it is not at all certain that development of metropolitan areas simply 'trickles down' to lower levels along the urban hierarchy, like Perroux (1950) argued; and it is also questionable that financial capital moves towards under-capitalized regions, as neo-liberals believe. Moreover, empirical studies also confirm the ambiguities around optimistic views. For instance, an increasing number of studies has disproved the existence of the Kuznets curve, i.e. decreasing territorial convergence after reaching a peak (Moran 2005). Gunnar Myrdal developed one of the most influential pessimistic theories, arguing that asymmetrical relations can maintain or exacerbate disparities between advanced cores and less developed peripheries, both in terms of inter-country and interregional relationships (Myrdal 1957). The literature refers to these mechanisms as backwash effects, pointing out primarily the migration of well-educated labour force from hinterland to core areas (Meardon 2001; Hall and Ludwig 2009). The same backwash effect can be detected in capital flows, when financial surplus of hinterland's entrepreneurs are rather invested in developed core regions, or when companies operating in peripheral areas relocate their headquarters to developed cores, transferring their profits towards the core areas as well (Gaile 1979, 278–279). Lastly, asymmetry can also be assumed in trade of goods, when developed cores provide high value-added products to the populations of peripheries, who can mostly offer lower value-added products with reduced profit margins. However, the flow of skilled workers from rural to urban areas can be regarded as being most important (and most measurable) among all the presumed asymmetries, which could fatally undermine the long-term development perspectives of a region (Hall and Ludwig 2009).

It is finally worth mentioning the views of 'new economic geography' (NEG), and the works of Paul Krugman, which does not start to take an optimistic or pessimistic stance but attempts to conceptualize a dynamic model that implies the importance of *initial* conditions. As Krugman himself emphasized, NEG seeks to merge the hypotheses and outcomes of 'text-based' analyses of sociologists into econometric tools of economics, trying to remove the barriers between human and social sciences (Krugman 1991, 2011).

Contradiction between diametrically opposed optimistic and pessimistic theories might be partially resolved by case study and analyses that critically examine both strands and seek to determine under what *proper situations* trigger mechanisms of enrichment or impoverishment. Such empirical analyses proved to be extremely useful since they highlight factors bolstering backwash or spread effects (Gaile 1979; Barkley et al. 1996; Partridge et al. 2007; Khan et al. 2001). According to empirical outcomes, both optimistic and pessimistic views might be confirmed from Simon Kuznets to Gunnar Myrdal, depending on current particular circumstances. So, rather than divinize certain theories or reject others, it seems to be worth examining which circumstances trigger spread or backwash effects and could decisively influence the evolvement of core-hinterland relations. In the next subchapter, the influence of past economic structures and present economic mechanisms will be scrutinized, on the example of Slovakia.

'History Matters': The Role of the Socialist Past in the Capital-Countryside Dichotomy

'History matters', a study on territorial development concludes, referring to the fact that inherited structures can determine the future capability of certain regions to develop (Gill and Goh 2010, 249). All coincidences and legacy of the past affect the evolution of the urban structure and urban–rural relations, which then largely determines territorial development by virtue of its gravity. Even the closing section of Simon Kuznets' 1955 study addresses the issue of whether the increase in inequality leads to the same result in Africa and in North America, having regard to their different historical backgrounds (Kuznets 1955). Or Paul Krugman can be also quoted: 'the idea that an economy's form is largely shaped by historical contingency is not a metaphysical hypothesis; it is simply the obvious truth' (Krugman 1991, 100).

The previous semi-peripheral status of the area of Slovakia also entailed the development of dispersed urban areas and spatially scattered city networks with 'incomplete' urban hierarchy in the nineteenth and twentieth centuries. It is noted in the literature that for encountering spread effects from the core, a basic human and built infrastructure is needed even in the hinterland (Partridge et al. 2007, 139). Besides, a complex urban hierarchy as well as local nodes can also bolster spread effect, being capable of reacting with the core and allowing to 'trickle down' the wealth from the core (see e.g. 'nodal response', Hughes and Holland 1994, 365). It indicates that an *initial* urban hierarchy and a basic degree of hinterland development is crucial for utilizing the positive effects exerted by a rapidly developing core, in order to prevail spread effects. Some kind of 'division of labour' and cooperation can be created when the leading role of central metropolises can interplay with the capabilities of secondary urban centres, being significantly but not critically legging behind them. Thus, less innovation-intensive but labour-intensive production capacity can be 'outsourced' at the lower levels of urban hierarchy, i.e. production (and, to some degree, innovation) capacity spreads from metropolitan cores.

Accordingly, the spread effect can be received and facilitated by rural hinterland when a certain level of basic development and absorptive capacity is already given. This initial criterion was critically weakened in most Central and Eastern European countries right after the fall of Communism, due to the collapse of socialist socio-economic order on rural countryside. The purposeful levelling efforts—to maintain the development of metropolitan and rural areas at the same level—of socialism suddenly and abruptly ceased, which resulted in the decline of the rural-based processing industry and the disappearance of the economic infrastructure maintaining the peasant's and rural way of life. As a result, the post-socialist crisis dragging down the rural regions—transforming them apparently into a hinterland—meanwhile the robust inflow of new technology and capital emerged simultaneously in metropolitan areas (primarily in capital city regions). The unfortunate coincidence has been noted several times in the Slovak literature (Matlovič and Matlovičová 2011), which then has reduced the magnitude of possible spread effects. Since Bratislava and its agglomeration have been quickly set on a robust developmental path as an emerging link in the network of global cities, rural hinterland suffering from declining quality of public services and poor corporate portfolio did not prove to be a suitable structure for enjoying positive trickle down effect. It is worth stressing once again that Simon Kuznets foresaw precisely the possibility of such contradictory tendencies in semi-peripheries, suggesting that it would lead to hardly manageable social and spatial tensions (Kuznets 1955, 20–26).

Beside socialist past, present economic mechanisms—called post-Fordist mode of production—can also dampen the unravelling of spread effects within Slovakia. Post-Fordist IT-adaptive industrial and service branches are already technologically distant from a simple assembly line technology; an increasing share of industrial production and service sector has become outsourced, giant factories are replaced by elastic chains of smaller manufacturing and supply units. It results that the relational network among companies needs an increasingly intensive communication, motivating the business actors to be concentrated in hubs, i.e. urban centres. Many interesting analyses show that specialized and personalized services need face-to-face management, personalized client contacts and the physical proximity of skilled workforce gains importance again (Barkley et al. 1996; Polèse and Shearmur 2004; Partridge et al. 2007; Gill and Goh 2010). The profiles of companies have also become fluid: unlike large Fordist fixed-profile factories, IT-adaptive companies can alter their profiles easily. It makes their interrelationship more complex: many business actors compete with one another for customers, while participating in tenders through forming joint consortia, moreover one might become a supplier or sub-contractor to the others. Such plasticity also requires people-to-people contacts. In addition, the increasingly sensitive and creative job tasks—such as product testing, legal and other professional advice—all require intensive personal communication, which can be hardly substituted by information communication techniques (Gaspar and Glaeser 1998).

Meanwhile these urban hubs form a network of global cities among each other, their relationships with their geographically close hinterlands gradually wane. The transport infrastructure—shifting from railways towards the primacy of air transport—anticipates the further emergence of interlinked hubs and global cities, disconnected from their own hinterland. While the railway network contributed to a emergence of complex urban hierarchies, air transport has led to the selection of a very few irrevocably dominant nodes (Barabási, James 2001).

Dissimilarities between Fordism and post-Fordism lead to the conclusion that territorial inequality as a side-effect of convergence can be utterly different between the emerging economies of twentieth century and the late-late developing countries of twenty-first century. Meanwhile Fordist economic networks served as a possible platform of trickle down mechanism, post-Fordism does not offer such a clear chance for it. As IT-adaptive technologies begun to rise, there is little evidence that positive effect of the impressive metropolitan growth—typical of Bratislava—could easily 'trickle down' to rural areas through a natural outflow of technology or human capital (Casetti 1984).

Changing patterns of economic networks can alter the patterns of internal migration as well. Positive developmental effects of migration were observed in the post-WWII Western Europe and North America when de-urbanization coinciding with the golden age of development in the 1950s and 1960s: urban population moved not only to suburbs but also to distant rural areas and small towns. Similar trends can be hardly detected in late-late developing countries of the twenty-first century, including Slovakia; conversely, the move of population towards capital city region of Bratislava has become predominant. Similarly, the concentrated nature of post-Fordist knowledge-based development is reflected in the entrapment of innovative capacity in the capital city regions. This is reflected in the Innovation Sub-Index—a region-specific sub-index of the Regional Competitiveness Index developed by the European Commission—measuring the innovative capacity of NUTS 2 regions within the EU. While Bratislava is well above the EU average as regards this indicator, all other Slovak regions fall far behind this average.[4] The same is shown by the difference in the proportions of workers concerned with research and development, which reached 2 per cent (in relation to the employed) only in 11 regions in the EU, and only Prague and Bratislava

[4] Source: Data tables available on the European Commission's website dedicated to the Regional Competitiveness Index (Scorecard, pp. 226–229). https://ec.europa.eu/regional_policy/en/information/maps/regional_competitiveness/ [Last accessed 22 January 2019].

attained this level in Central Europe; while the other regions of Slovakia did not even reach 0.75 per cent (Kotzeva et al. 2018, 121).

Future Competitiveness: Urban–Rural Differences in Attractiveness for Human Capital

Emergence of post-Fordist network of global cities elucidates the importance of attractiveness for human capital, as a vital prerequisite for long-term competitiveness. To what extent urban and rural areas attract high-skilled workers says a lot about the evolution of long-term urban–rural disparity. The literature endeavours to define this attractiveness as the coefficient of 'push' and 'pull' factors: e.g. the expected income after moving to a city can serve as one—but not the only one—pull factor, meanwhile the expected risk of joblessness after moving to a city as an important push factor (Hautzinger et al. 2014).

In this last subchapter, two possible indicators are chosen from the plethora of possible measurement methods regarding push-pull factors: these are the unemployment ratio and the 'Well-Being Index' from the OECD. These data do not attempt to provide a structured picture of push-pull factors as a whole, just to elucidate some apparent differences between the Western and Eastern parts of the EU in the dynamics of territorial disparities. As it will be shown, there are such tendencies in Slovakia—and in the CEE region as a whole—which can hinder the autocatalytic elimination of core-hinterland inequalities.

Taking regional unemployment data, a comparison can be made between the ratio of unemployment in urban as well as in rural regions. As Table 10.2 shows, urban unemployment in many old EU member states is significantly or slightly higher than rural unemployment. In contrast, rural unemployment is higher in most CEE countries than in the urban areas; the gap is strikingly great in the case of Bulgaria, Slovakia, Croatia.

Without reaching a complex conclusion about the balance of push-pull factors in CEE region, unemployment ratios highlight the possibility of different balances between their interplays than in the Western part of the EU. A similar difference can be highlighted by the Well-Being Index constructed under the programme 'Better Life Initiative' launched by the OECD. The Index assesses living conditions in OECD member states in 11 categories, collecting the data from NUTS 2 regional level as

Table 10.2 Differences between urban and rural unemployment (expressed in percentage points)

	Urban unemployment minus rural unemployment %
AT	4.3
PT	3.4
SP	2.7
GR	2.5
IT	1.8
NL	1.7
B	1.3
DK	1.3
D	0.9
UK	0.8
FR	0.6
S	0.5
EE	−1
CZ	−1.1
RO	−1.5
SF	−1.9
LT	−2.3
IRL	−3
PL	−3
HU	−4
LV	−4.4
BG	−8.2
SK	−8.9
CR	−10.8

well.[5] As it can be seen from Table 10.3, capital city regions of the old member states are positioned as last ones in several categories relating to the quality of life. Meanwhile, capital city regions are ranked much better in peripheral regions, thus in Central and Eastern Europe as well. Moreover, the capital cities of Slovakia and the Czech Republic achieve several number one positions in these ranks: Bratislava and Prague offer higher well-being index than the hinterland in eight out of eleven categories.

[5] Source: https://www.oecdregionalwellbeing.org, database available on the website of the OECD dedicated to regional well-being [Last accessed 22 January 2019].

Table 10.3 Ranks of capital regions in 11 categories of the OECD Well-Being Index

	Categories in which the capital region is the lowest ranked	*Categories in which the capital region ranks first*
Austria	6	0
Belgium	5	1
Germany	4	0
Great Britain	3	3
Finland	3	4
Greece	3	2
France	2	3
The Netherlands	1	2
Sweden	1	2
Denmark	1	6
Hungary	1	6
Italy	0	0
Spain	0	2
Latvia	0	3
Lithuania	0	4
Poland	0	4
Portugal	0	5
Estonia	0	6
The Czech Republic	0	8
Slovakia	0	8

These two capital city regions therefore outstrip to the greatest extent their own hinterlands in terms of liveability.

Data comparisons above partially confirm the hypothesis which can be drawn from theoretical framework and from globally relevant empirical studies: weaker balancing mechanisms can be detected between metropolitan *wealth* and rural *well-being* more in the developed than in the emerging economies of the EU. Among the old member states, highly developed metropolitan cores tend to offer greater income at the expenses of somewhat poorer quality of life than rural areas and small towns (Behrens et al. 2014, 509), whereas it is not the case for Central and Eastern Europe. CEE data show that post-Socialist post-Fordist economies can encounter a coincidence of urban wealth with urban well-being. The differences between Western European and CEE spatial patterns are also reflected in the *Urban Agenda* supported by the European Commission, associating the problems of 'poverty and social exclusion' with metropolitan areas; whereas the same problems, e.g. higher unemployment or deteriorating living standards, are rather specific to rural areas in Central and Eastern Europe (Urban Agenda for the EU 2016).

Conclusions

Indeed, while the share of the population at risk of poverty or social exclusion is greater in urban areas in the western part of the EU—with the exceptions of Spain and Greece—urban residents have lower risk of poverty in CEE, with the exceptions of the Czech Republic and Slovenia (Kotzeva et al. 2018, 187). This all implies the possibility that skilled workforce in CEE can be attracted by a stronger pull effect towards urban cores. As a result, the inflow of human capital, as a cumulative and autocatalytic process, may maintain the attractiveness of urban areas and widen the capital-countryside gap.

In urban studies, disadvantages stemming from high population density, urban ghettoization, environmental pollution and, in general, stressed urban lifestyle are reflected by data relating to the remarkably low average speed of urban transport, urban air pollution levels, crime statistics or the creation of no-go zones (World Bank 2002, as cited in Gill and Goh, 251). It can be contrasted with 'small town values' beyond the realm of city centres and commuter towns, such as natural amenities, stronger social and cultural relations in small communities and opportunities for other non-market-based activities that are becoming increasingly important for masses of modern people dependent on recreation (Deller et al. 2001; Barkley et al. 1996; Behrens et al. 2014). According to above-presented data, such a contrast between urban wealth and rural well-being seems to be not so sharp in Central and Eastern Europe.

Basically, the decoupling of global cities and their peripheries in economic and mental terms seems to be one of the consequences of technological development and the fourth industrial revolution (Sassia 2002; Ricz 2007). When scrutinizing the worldwide phenomenon of core-hinterland imbalances, Slovakia has proved to be a classic—but not isolated example—for urban–rural dichotomy, having followed one of the most impressive convergence path over the last two decades. Although the geographical scope of positive spread effects may continuously expand in Slovakia due to infrastructural improvements (one-hour travel time distance is suggested in the literature as the boundary of such agglomeration effects, see Fox and Kumar 1965), an open question both for policymakers and academics is, what socio-economic mechanisms will prove to prevail beyond Bratislava conurbation and Western Slovakia in the long run.

References

Barkley, David L., Mark S. Henry, Shuming Bao, 1996. Identifying "Spread" versus "Backwash" Effects in Regional Economic Areas: A Density Functions Approach. *Land Economics*, Vol. 72, No. 3, 336–357.

Barro, Robert J., Xavier Sala-I-Martin, 1991. Convergence across States and Regions. *Brookings Papers on Economic Activity*, Vol. 22, No. 1, 107–182.

Behrens, Kristian, Gilles Duranton, Frédéric Robert-Nicoud, 2014. Productive Cities: Sorting, Selection, and Agglomeration. *Journal of Political Economy*, Vol. 122, No. 3, 507–553.

Casetti, Emilio, 1984. Peripheral Growth in Mature Economies. *Economic Geography*, Vol. 60, No. 2, 122–131.

COM(2009)433. Communication from the Commission to the Council and the European Parliament "GDP and Beyond. Measuring Progress in a Changing World".

COM(2017)583. Report from the Commission to the European Parliament, the Council, the European Economic and Social Committee and the Committee of the Regions. My Region, My Europe, Our Future: The 7th Report on Economic, Social and Territorial Cohesion.

Deller, Steven C, Tsung-Hsiu Tsai, David W. Marcouiller, Donald B. K, 2001. English: The Role of Amenities and Quality of Life in Rural Economic Growth. *American Journal of Agricultural Economics*, Vol. 83, No. 2, 352–265.

Dudaš, Tomáš, 2012. National Competitiveness of Slovakia in the Context of Global Competitiveness Indexes. *Gazdaság és Társadalom*, Vol. 4, No. 1–2, 74–87.

Feinstein, Charles, 1988. The Rise and Fall of the Williamson Curve. *The Journal of Economic History*, Vol. 48, No. 3, 699–729.

Filauro, Stefano, 2018. *The EU-Wide Income Distribution: Inequality Levels and Decompositions*. https://doi.org/10.2767/388578.

Florida, Richard, 2017. *The New Urban Crisis: How Our Cities are Increasing Inequality, Deepening Segregation, and Failing the Middle Class—And What We Can Do About It*. Basic Books, New York.

Fox, Karl A., T. Krishna Kumar, 1965. The Functional Economic Area: Delineation and Implications for Economic Analysis and Policy. *Papers in Regional Science*, Vol. 15, No. 1, 57–85.

Gaile, Gary L, 1979. Spatial Models of Spread-Backwash Processes. *Geographical Analysis*, Vol. 11, No. 3, 273–288.

Gaspar, Jess, Edward L. Glaeser, 1998. Information Technology and the Future of Cities. *Journal of Urban Economics*, Vol. 43 No. 1, 136–156.

Gill, Indermit S., Chor-Ching Goh, 2010. Scale Economies and Cities, 2010. *The World Bank Research Observer*, Vol. 25, No. 2, 235–262.

Hall, John, Udo Ludwig, 2009. Gunnar Myrdal and the Persistence of Germany's Regional Inequality. *Journal of Economic Issues*, Vol. 43, No. 2, 345–352.

Hautzinger, Zoltán, Hegedűs Judit, Klenner Zoltán, 2014. *A migráció elmélete.* Nemzeti Közszolgálati Egyetem, Budapest.

Hughes, David W., David W. Holland, 1994. Core-Periphery Economic Linkage: A Measure of Spread and Possible Backwash Effects for the Washington Economy. *Land Economics*, Vol. 70, No. 3, 364–377.

James, Jeffrey, 2001. Information Technology, Cumulative Causation and Patterns of Globalization in the Third World. *Review of International Political Economy*, Vol. 8, No. 1, 147–162.

Khan, Romana, Peter F. Orazem, Daniel M. Otto, 2001. Deriving Empirical Definitions of Spatial Labor Markets: The Roles of Competing Versus Complementary Growth. *Journal of Regional Science*, Vol. 41, No. 4, 735–756.

Kotzeva, Mariana (editor-in-chief), Teodóra Brandmüller, Åsa Önnerfors and Petronela Reinecke, 2018. *European regional yearbook. 2018 edition.*

Krugman, Paul, 1991. *Geography and Trade.* The MIT Press, Cambridge.

Krugman, Paul, 2011. The New Economic Geography, Now Middle-Aged. *Regional Studies*, Vol. 45, No. 1, 1–7.

Kuznets, Simon, 1955. Economic Growth and Income Inequality. *American Economic Review*, Vol. 45, No. 1, 1–28.

Luptáčik, Mikuláš, Michal Habrman, Martin Lábaj, Štefan Rehák, 2013. *The Importance of Automotive Industry for the Slovak Economy: Empirical Results.* University of Economics in Bratislava, Bratislava.

Massey, Douglas S, 1990. Social Structure, Household Strategies, and the Cumulative Causation of Migration. *Population Index*, Vol. 56, No. 1, 3–26.

Massey, Douglas S., Joaquin Arango, Graeme Hugo, Ali Kouaouci, Adela Pellegrino, J. Edward Taylor, 2012. A nemzetközi migráció elméletei: áttekintés és értékelés. In: *A migráció szociológiája 1.* Válogatta és szerkesztette Sik Endre. ELTE TáTK, Budapest, 7–29.

Matlovič, René, Kvetoslava Matlovičová, 2011. Regionálne Disparity a ich riešenie na Slovensku v rozličných kontextoch. *Folia Geographica*, Vol. 53, No. 18, 8–87.

Meardon, Stephen J, 2001. Modeling Agglomeration and Dispersion in City and Country: Gunnar Myrdal, François Perroux, and the New Economic Geography. *American Journal of Economics and Sociology*, Vol. 60, No. 1, 25–57.

Moran, Timothy Patrcik, 2005. Kuznets's Inverted U-Curve Hypothesis: The Rise, Demise, and Continued Relevance of a Socioeconomic Law. *Sociological Forum*, Vol. 20, No. 2, 209–244.

Myrdal, Gunnar, 1957. *Economic Theory and Under-Developed Regions*. G. Duckworth, London.

Nemes Nagy, József (szerk), 2005. *Regionális elemzési módszerek*. ELTE Regionális Földrajzi Tanszék, MTA-ELTE Regionális Tudományi Kutatócsoport, Budapest.

OECD, 2016. *Regions at a Glance 2016*. OECD Publishing, Paris.

Parr, John B, 1999. Growth-Pole Strategies in Regional Planning: A Retrospective View. *Urban Studies*, Vol. 36, No. 7, 1195–1215.

Partridge, Mark, Ray D. Bollman, M. Rose Olfert, Alessandro Alasia, 2007. Riding the Wave of Urban Growth in the Countryside: Spread, Backwash, or Stagnation? *Land Economics*, Vol. 83, No. 2, 128–152.

Perroux, François, 1950. Economic Space: Theory and Applications. *Quarterly Journal of Economics*, Vol. 64, No. 1, 89–104.

Polèse, Mario, Richard Shearmur, 2004. Is Distance Really Dead? Comparing Industrial Location Patterns Over Time in Canada. *International Regional Science Review*, Vol. 27, No. 4, 431–457.

Ricz, Judit, 2007. Az agglomerálódás klasszikus és új logikája. *Külgazdaság*, Vol. 51 No. 7–8, 83–102.

Samuel, Abraham, 1994. The Break-Up of Czechoslovakia: A Threat to Democratization in Slovakia? In: Soňa Szomolányi and Grigorij Mesežnikov (eds.): *The Slovak Path of Transition to Democracy?* Slovak Political Science Association, Bratislava, 13–44.

Samuel, Abraham, 2001. 1998 Elections: End of Illiberal Democracy in Slovakia. *Slovak Foreign Policy Affairs: Review for International Politics, Security and Integration*, Vol. 2, No. 1, 85–96.

Sassia, Sasken, 2002. Locating Cities on Global Circuits. *Environment & Urbanization*, Vol. 14, No. 1, 13–30.

Slušná, Ľubica, Miroslav Balog, 2015. *Automobilový priemysel na Slovensku a globálne hodnotové reťazce*. Slovenská inovačná a energetická agentúra, Bratislava.

Tvrdon, Michal, Karel Skokan, 2011. Regional Disparities and the Ways of Their Measurement: The Case of the Visegrad Four Countries. *Technological and Economic Development of Economy*, Vol. 17, No. 3, 501–518.

Urban Agenda for the EU. Pact of Amsterdam. Agreed at the Informal Meeting of EU Ministers Responsible for Urban Matters on 30 May 2016 in Amsterdam, The Netherlands.

Vodička, Karel, 2003. Příčiny rozdělení Československa: analýza po 10 letech. *Politologický časopis*, Vol. 10, No. 1, 55–64.

Williamson, Jeffrey G, 1985. *Did British Capitalism Feed Inequality?* Allen and Unwin, Boston.

World Bank, 2002. *Cities on the Move: A World Bank Urban Transport Strategy Review*. Washington, DC: World Bank.

CHAPTER 11

The Underperforming State of Zimbabwe—A Case Study on Tobacco Contract Farming

Ruvarashe Masocha

Introduction

For any form of economic development to occur in a country, there must be a guaranteed coherent flow between capital and resources. Capital comes in the form of domestic investors or foreign investors, but there is a need to attract foreign investments for many developing countries because domestic capital will be low. It is the duty of the developmental state to create institutions and state policies that ensure that they attract foreign capital, and policies that enable the easy connection to investment opportunities within the country and that resource exploitation is environmentally friendly and safe, which encourages the cycle to continue. In this case, the role of the developmental state is an essential one. It becomes the state's task to develop balanced policies that can lure suitable investments and benefit the state and the citizens. Some of these

R. Masocha (✉)
University of Iowa, Iowa, USA

T. Gerőcs and J. Ricz (eds.), *The Post-Crisis Developmental State*, International Political Economy Series,
https://doi.org/10.1007/978-3-030-71987-6_11

policies may include input subsidies, low-interest agricultural loans, and marketing initiatives that ensure that farmers can profit. The theorist Poulantzas propagates that "the nature of the state (cannot) be separated from ongoing conflicts, contradictions, and compromises of the struggles that permeate capitalist society."[1] Relating to the assertion by Poulantzas, I can say the state policies have the potential to propel the tobacco industry in the case of Zimbabwe. The laws that govern business engagement in Zimbabwe are the "economic infrastructure."[2]

In sub-Saharan Africa, the Zimbabwean state has been underperforming in its role as a regulator of institutional policy that shapes the relationship between local and international investors and local small-scale tobacco farmers. The tobacco industry is export-driven and one of the critical earners of foreign currency revenue; Zimbabwe is the sixth-largest tobacco producer globally and the largest in Africa.[3] In 2017, the Zimbabwean state made nearly 30 percent of its export revenue from tobacco dollars in tobacco export.[4] Historically tobacco has been considered a leaf of gold in the country (Fig. 11.1).[5]

Because it is an important foreign currency earner, the state highly monitors the tobacco sales markets and usually disadvantages the farmers by cutting their benefits and heavy taxation. During the hyperinflation of 2019, the state threatened to cut the earnings of tobacco farmers by half through its regulation policy that unfairly rated the US$ value at 1:1 with Zimbabwean bond note currency.[6] The state planned to take the US dollar earnings from farmers and pay the farmers in the bond note they pro-rated. This was because the state was facing massive foreign currency shortages and needed to preserve the US dollar in its reserves. The regulation caused resistance in the form of demonstrations and boycotts among the enraged farmers.[7] This example demonstrates that the state

[1] Martin, J. (ed) (2008): *The Poulantzas Reader: Marxism, Law and the State*, Verso, London, p. 1.

[2] Ibid., p. 4.

[3] Seminar presentation, FAO, "Tobacco in Zimbabwe," *Corporate Document Repository*, Economic and Social Development Department, 2000.

[4] Ibid.

[5] Rubert, S. C. (1998): *A Most Promising Weed, A History of Tobacco Farming and Labor in Colonial Zimbabwe 1890–1945*, Ohio University Press, Ohio.

[6] *News Day*, March 21, 2019, RBZ reneges on US$ payments to tobacco farmers.

[7] *News Day*, June 14, 2019, Mvurwi tobacco farmers protest against the buyer.

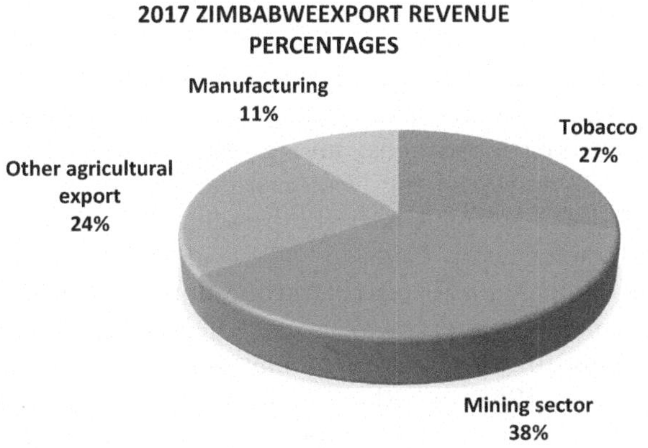

Fig. 11.1 2017 Zimbabwe's export revenue in percentages (*Source* WTO files Zimbabwe)

in its urgent need for foreign currency is compelled to subjugate farmers whose economic capacity is fundamental in producing that cash reserve via export.

The condition of a state that acts in an authoritarian nature is not unique to Zimbabwe. In many economically underdeveloped countries, many of which still bear the legacy of colonialism, the relationship between the postcolonial state, local marketable resources, and international capital coexist in haphazard conditions and coupled with numerous regulatory contradictions. In these scenarios, the state misses the opportunity/cannot competently execute the essential role of mediating via regulation between capital, labor, and farmers' competing interests. Due to this bureaucratic incompetency, the state fails to recognize the interests of the otherwise highly fragmented peasant class. Hence, it is alienated from the fragile urban middle classes in service industries and developed contradictions even to capital's needs. In short, this overall disconnection in the class relations and the bureaucratic contradictions that stem from this historical legacy cripple the state's capacity, which is behind the failure of a developmental model in Zimbabwe.

Why Is the State Underperforming?

The haphazard condition in state institutions for Zimbabwe and other underperforming states in Africa traces back to the colonial legacy of these states and their institutions, among other reasons. The state institutions were inherited from the "Colonial modernity" system described by Tani E. Barlow (1997). Under the paradigm of colonial modernity, the state and capital work hand and glove in squeezing out as much profit and investing the least possible in the human or otherwise infrastructure for colonized peoples to amass the benefits of capital in the metropolis.[8] Zimbabwe was a British colony known as Southern Rhodesia between 1900 and 1965 and Rhodesia from 1965–1980. The Zimbabwean postcolonial state was beginning in 1980 inherited institutions developed under "colonial modernity."[9] These colonial state institutions were designed to serve the interests of the state and capitalists, including exploiting resources to benefit mostly a small percentage of the population who were commercial farmers. The numerous state institutions such as banking and the state regulations were tailored to support and ensure a smooth flow of the connecting relationship between the labor market, foreign investments, and the small-scale farmers. Unfortunately, when the independent state inherited these institutions, such as the Agricultural Development Bank and the Marketing Boards, little was done to revamp and implement institutional reform to serve the needs of many small-scale farmers and entrepreneurs adequately. For example, the Agricultural Development Bank of Zimbabwe, which has the mandate to assist farmers with loans, only had policy provisions that most of the small-scale farmers could not meet.[10] This bank was an institution inherited from the colonial government. For this reason, small-scale farmers who were the most in need could not access the necessary farming loans from the bank. The state did not put emphasis on designing policies that would support

[8] Barlow, T. E. (ed) (1997): *Formations of Colonial Modernity in East Asia*, Duke University Press, London.

[9] Ibid.

[10] Alfred Bimha, Restructuring of the Agricultural Development Bank into a Land Bank, Implications and Repurcations, Dissertation submitted in partial fulfillment of the Master of Science in Banking and Financial, 2016. Services, Supervised by M. W. Ndlovu at the National University of Science Education, Bulawayo, Zimbabwe.

small-scale farmers; instead, they continued to rely heavily on large-scale farm production.

Many scholars in Zimbabwe have termed the period 1980–1990 a "socialist decade" in which the newly independent state of Zimbabwe adopted a welfare approach. The welfare approach involved the state dedicating more funding toward redressing inequalities in the health and educational systems of the country.[11] The postcolonial state reallocated resources for public investment, mainly focusing on human development; hence it wanted to make sure most of the population get access to public services, such as healthcare (hospitals and clinics), etc. However, the state was not able to adequately restructure all the competing policies needed for the middle and lower classes that would have also been compatible with the need of the dominant capitalist enterprises.[12] The state could not delink from the inherited status quo of the colonial past, which cushioned the large-scale capitalists and protected them from outside markets while ensuring their domestic circuits of capital.[13] The state offered more funding in state subsidies, tax credits, subsidized loans to large businesses, and it disinvested from a smaller domestic entrepreneurial class, which exhausted the country's long-term developmental prospect. The numerous upcoming small-scale start-up businesses suffered the most. Consequently, this hostile environment for domestic capital's internal accumulation prospect was very limited in the postcolonial era.

The political reason for this limitation on domestic accumulation is claimed to be the fact that there is no proper separation between the state and the ruling political party (Zanu PF) in Zimbabwe. The interests of the ruling party since independence in 1980 mirrors much of the state's economic intervention in the policy terrain.[14] For an extended period, Zimbabwe remained a one-party state. Toward the end of the 1990s,

[11] See Lloyd Sachikonya (2012): *Zimbabwe's Lost Decade, Politics, Development and Society*, Weaver Press, Harare.

[12] The middle class in Zimbabwe comprises the highly educated Africans who take white color occupations, and the low class consists of those involved in many informal activities and the rural dwellers. The distinction is no longer clear beginning after 2000 because of the economic meltdown and currency devaluation.

[13] Moyo, S. (1995): The Land Question in Zimbabwe: Research, Perspectives, and Questions.

[14] Mhandara, L., Hamauswa, S., and Nyemba (2013): "A Review of the Doctrine of Separation of Powers in Zimbabwe 1979–2013," *Southern Peace Review-Journal* 2 (2), 68–85.

opposition organizations, such as the Movement for Democratic Change (MDC) party, were permitted due to political liberalization. Despite the pressure for political liberalization, successive Zimbabwe African National Union-Patriotic Front (ZANU PF) governments responded to establishing the new opposition parties as a threat to their own power, and since then, successive governments have attempted to control state organs in order to make them operate in favor of the incumbent government.

The decade between 1990 and 2000 was challenging for the state as the welfare approach had drained most of its resources, and it was losing grip in controlling the political pact with capital. The state of Zimbabwe was assigned for the IMF Structural Adjustment Programme to salvage the situation of an urgent need of foreign currency.[15] The welfare state was forced to cut back on spending and adopt a more neoliberal developmental strategy that entailed a new balance between the major economic actors and the state.[16] Such a strategy was coupled with droughts causing distress and hunger in Zimbabwe in 1992. Following the continued distress, the state abandoned the structural adjustment program in 1996. However, it could not re-establish the former class compromise between peasants, middle classes, and the dominant fractions of the capitalist class, which are the large agro- and mining-business; therefore, its popular support quickly evaporated.

Essentially the relationship between the state and domestic capital soured in the 1990s decade as foreign investors and businesses, in general, were calling for a more democratized political system, and they threatened to overpower the state. The political system becoming more autocratic and limiting the rule of law created conditions for an unstable business environment. The contestation of power between the state and capital in Zimbabwe culminated in the abrupt land reform program of 2000.[17] In 2000, large capitalist classes did not devote their electoral support

[15] Raftoupoulous, B., and Mlambo. A. (eds) (2009): *Becoming Zimbabwe, A History from the Precolonial Period to 2008*, Weaver Press, Harare, 2009–p.10.

[16] Lloyd Sachikonye (2012): *Zimbabwe's Lost Decade, Politics, Development and Society*, Weaver Press, Harare.

[17] The land reform occurred very quickly when random Zanu Pf youths stormed into commercial farms during the night and demanded the farmers to leave. The party sanctioned these reports; thus, the police could not protect the white farmers. These events continued until lots of White farmers had left the country.

to the incumbent government but favored the presumably more democratic opposition party.[18] In response, the state took over most of the land the capitalist owned and expelled many commercial farmers out of the country. Taking over land and redistributing it to smaller peasants promised the necessary votes from the peasant class that helped to secure the political win for the government. Such an act became a turning point in the Zimbabwean developmental trajectory to the condition of crisis.[19] The land reform caused serious disturbances in almost the entire agricultural industry in Zimbabwe, and as a consequence, access to international markets was curtailed. With the loss of the international market and steep decline in exports, the government had to devalue the Zimbabwean dollar, which has triggered hyperinflation. The following crisis of the Zimbabwean economy has been slowly cascading from the 2000s up to the present.

The Tobacco Industry and Its Relevance in the Zimbabwean Economy

Since the early years of establishing a formal colonial economy in Zimbabwe, Tobacco was an important cash crop leading in commercial farming. Zimbabwean tobacco production began early in the precolonial period. African producers concentrated on sun-air cured tobacco (Chikwarimba). During the colonial period, Tobacco production was commercialized. According to Steven C. Rubert (1998), tobacco became the gold leaf in Zimbabwe with the increased demand for flue-cured Virginia tobacco on the international market.[20] Large-scale white commercial farms dominated the tobacco industry during the entire colonial period and the first decade of the postcolonial period. During this time, the state acted to protect the needs of the commercial farmers, and the institutions worked adequately in making farmers' well-being guaranteed.

[18] Lloyd Sachikonya (2012): *Zimbabwe's Lost Decade, Politics, Development and Society*, Weaver Press, Harare.

[19] Ibid.

[20] The beneficiaries of the Land reform included politicians and people politically affiliated with ZANU PF, (but other non-partisan people also benefited).

As mentioned before, the relationship between the commercial farmers and the postcolonial state soured in the year 2000 when the commercial farmers were not promising to continue with their support for the ruling party.[21] The commercial farmers favored the MDC, the new party which promised democracy and more benefits for the farmers. What followed was a very hurried fast-track land reform program in which large-scale commercial farms were disbanded into numerous smaller farms distributed to ordinary citizens unqualified for farming, and many of the commercial farmers were removed from the land.[22] Such a process harmed many international commercial agreements that the white farmers used to have and, as a consequence, negatively impacted tobacco production in Zimbabwe. However, the international demand for tobacco was still present, and so was the need for the country to continue with tobacco export as the primary source of foreign currency.

The period 2007–2014 represents those years in which small-scale tobacco farmers were trying to revive the tobacco industry from scratch.[23] This new small-scale peasant class replaced the former postcolonial large-scale export cash-crop farming that was largely dominated by white-settler farmers before the land reform. The small-scale farmers had their problems engaging in tobacco production; apart from the fact they acquired land by the fast-track land reform program, they were underskilled for professional farming, did not have proper access to capital (such as loans of equipment), and could not rely on labor other than their own power. Due to the fact the form of their land had no title deeds, they could not access loans, and except for some donations with inputs, the government made no significant effort to bolster these new farmers for production (Fig. 11.2).[24]

Tobacco contract farming had to be rejuvenated at the beginning of 2003 as part of the reorganization effort in the entire farming industry. Under the contract farming system in Zimbabwe, international investors

[21] Lloyd Sachikonya (2012): *Zimbabwe's Lost Decade, Politics, Development and Society*, Weaver Press, Harare.

[22] Moyo, S. (1995). The Land Question in Zimbabwe: Research, Perspectives, and Questions.

[23] Ibid.

[24] In the land-redistribution process, people were given the right to use the land but they were not given any ownership right. As a result, redistributed land cannot be sold, and there is always a lurking fear among farmers that the government might repossess those land in their use.

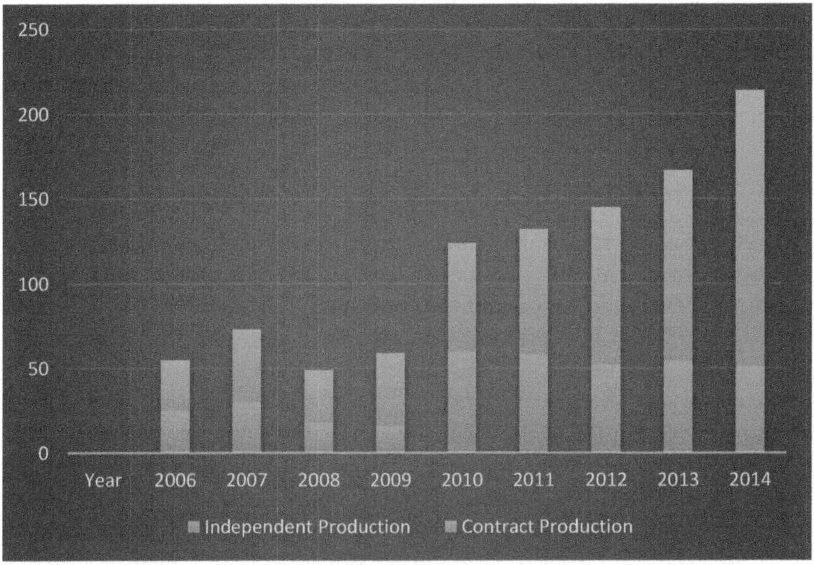

Fig. 11.2 Tobacco contract hectares versus independent farming hectares (*Source* Zimbabwe Tobacco Trends Publication, 2014)

could establish companies in the country to provide funding and training workshops to small-scale farmers who still had the land to produce tobacco but needed capital investments for sustaining production. The small-scale and communal farmers who entered into a contract agreement were in charge of providing the land and labor required to grow the crop until harvest. Many farmers chose to enter such contracts for two reasons: lack of funding and/or limited know-how in tobacco production. These contracts tended to solve many of the inherent problems that the farmers faced. The contract farming initiative has caused a very positive result in the Zimbabwean tobacco farming industry. There has been an increase in tobacco production in the country, and the tobacco revenues account for a significant amount of foreign currency income in the ailing Zimbabwean economy.[25] However, conditions could still be better, and

[25] Tobacco Industry and Marketing Board 2014–17 statistics show that in 2001, tobacco production dwindled to 48 million kgs, and in 2014 production improved to 200 million; in 2019, it is now at 252 million kgs.

the Zimbabwean farmers could make better deals if the state effectively executed its regulatory role in a more proactive fashion. The lack of sufficient regulatory support from the government makes the engagement between small-scale farmers and big capital not as smooth as it should be.

How Is the State Underperforming?

The Zimbabwean state takes much pride in showing improved tobacco farming in the country as evidence that the land reform program has been bearing successes and that farming is booming. The government-affiliated newspaper called "The Herald" and the state news station ZBC makes the point as a showcase for the statistics of increased tobacco production among the small-scale farmers as the success of the land reform program.[26] The improvements achieved in the tobacco industry show that the country is doing well in its path to indigenization.[27] However, despite all the positive remarks that the state wants to use to bolster its image, it provides inadequate support and protection in the form of policy intervention either to large businesses or to the small-scale farmers. I argue that more interventionist state support would achieve even better performances of the Zimbabwean tobacco industry. The Zimbabwean state institutions have been underperforming on at least two levels. The first major weakness of the state policies is that it is not very attentive to the needs of small-scale farmers. For any government policy to be sustainable, it has to be well researched and tailored in order to meet the need of the recipient population; such is not the case in Zimbabwe. The help that the state can provide is often inadequate or does not resolve the issues which are addressed by the farmers. Underperformance means that the state fails to service the needs of those basic producers who are the most important pillar in any large-scale developmental projects, let it be industry or agriculture (Fig. 11.3).

The second weakness is presented by the fact that a stable investment environment is missing. The investment climate in Zimbabwe is

[26] Tawanda Musarurwa, Zimbabwe's Tobacco Industry 40 years on, *The Herald*, November 10, 2020.

[27] Zimbabwe's indigenization program is an agenda toward protecting ownership of national assets by the indigenous Zimbabweans, including land and mining rights. It ensures the transfer of property in Zimbabwe from majority ownership by foreign capital to domestic people fostering domestic capital accumulation.

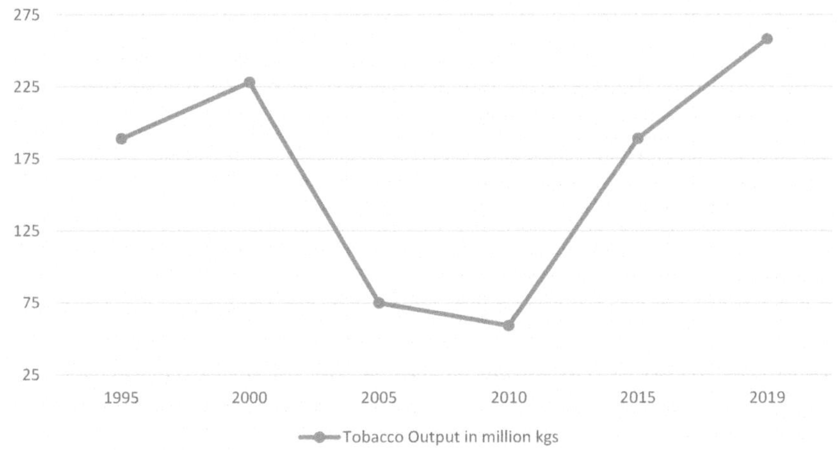

Fig. 11.3 Tobacco output before and after the 2000 land reform (*Source* Tobacco industry and marketing board statistics records)

very hectic and does not encourage long-term investments in business activities; in fact, it has discouraged international capital away from agriculture since the fast-track land reform program. The state makes erratic modifications and sometimes ad hoc legislation in the field of investment policies. Coupled with the hectic changes, the unpredictable exchange rate policy and the subsequent hyperinflation make Zimbabwe an unpredictable place to invest, even though it is a rich country of material resources. It takes much effort for investors to be able to make profits in an otherwise very lucrative industry because investments can easily be eradicated through hyperinflation, and lousy business conditions do not help either. The land reform tarnished the Zimbabwean credibility to foreign investors, and as a result, the contract farming terms tend to be more stringent, and it is the farmers who bear this burnt.

The small-scale farmers in Zimbabwe are made up of the resettled peasants who got small portions of land under the fast-track land reform program and the communal farmers who engage in larger farming businesses. These farmers require essential know-how, which would help them understand business-cycles in the international market, conduct market research, understand environmental issues, and be more informed when they go into the harvest season to put the foot forward in farming for the outside world. The farmers lack such necessary provisions, which should be the role of the state for guaranteeing a nationwide developmental agenda. Arguing that the state has been absent in this case would be false, but the point is that the state has implemented limited measures in this regard. The state runs a program in which the authorities install farmers' educators in each district. These farmer educators provide farmers with education about all types of crop and animal farming in that district. Any educator's actual task is huge and impractical because they will be 5 in a district and expected to offer guidance to farmers on all forms of agriculture the farmers practice in the district. At the end of the day, the guidance these government instructors provide would be general and basic; farmers would need to go the extra mile to achieve any form of excellence. Thus, in spite of providing the necessary general education, it is still not enough to assist the farmers.

One of the reasons companies develop the motivation to enter contracts is that the contracting companies provide educators who specialize in tobacco productions for the tobacco contract farmers.[28] They set up workshops and pay visits to the farmers to assist them throughout the tobacco season. Such help is significant to the farmers as they can produce quality crops by having access to the specialized knowledge of the educators. Let us suppose that the government had been more proactive in installing specialized tobacco training programs to better educate farmers in the areas such as where tobacco farming concentrates. These farmers would not have been compelled to enter some unfair and often exploitative contracts that they often end up in. The kind of farmer educational systems provided by the government is the same systems they used to provide before the land reform, which offered inadequate training and engagement for the farmers. In my interviews, farmers have revealed that tobacco farming is a scientific crop that requires specific skills and much attention.[29] Lack of proper knowledge of tobacco farming can easily result in a low-grade product, which, if unmarketable, can turn into a financial loss. All in all, tobacco production is a very risky business.

It is the responsibility of the state to put in place institutions that bring the possibility for small-scale producers to access funding for tobacco

[28] Moyo, S. (1995): The Land Question in Zimbabwe: Research, Perspectives, and Questions.

[29] Seminar presentation, FAO, "Tobacco in Zimbabwe," *Corporate Document Repository*, Economic and Social Development Department, 2000.

cash-crop production so that they can minimize those risks associated with tobacco farming. The state still uses the same regulatory framework that they used to have during the commercial farming era in which white farmers had to provide collaterals in order to be eligible for bank loans and state loans for their investments. However, the land that the farmers were distributed to does not have any form of title deeds that farmers could use as collateral.[30] Thus, the farmers are left to find alternative solutions to enhance the productivity of the land under their cultivation, which puts them at a disadvantageous bargaining position when they negotiate with larger international businesses in order to get funding.

Developmental state policies are supposed to execute a more regulated relationship between the business contractor and the small-scale farmers. However, in the case of Zimbabwe, contract farming is solely negotiated between the small-scale farmers and foreign investors in an almost "laissez-faire-like" situation. Liberal commentators tend to argue that the conditions for doing business are good in light of a non-interference of the state, but that situation leaves many small-scale farmers vulnerable as they cannot negotiate the deals that the businesses offer them. One factor that works to the advantage of the small-scale farmers is that there is a competition between the contractors who fund similar cash crops in some areas. Such competitions allow the farmers to weigh options between growing tobacco versus other cash crops like cotton and coffee. The competition incentivizes farmers' leverage to bargain for improved contract conditions.

Imbalances in the power relations between the small-scale farmers and the business contractors are most evident in the form of many of the contracts, which small-scale farmers without alternative options are compelled to engage with. Under those contractual circumstances, some clauses protect large capital from risks or losses stemming from the hectic business environment, making risk management one-sidedly available for them. In contrast, small farmers must bear the brunt of the associated risks making their situation more vulnerable. The small-scale farmers commit themselves to conditions in which they are liable to pay back all the funding they receive with usually high-interest rates at the market value

[30] Moyo, S. (1995): The Land Question in Zimbabwe: Research, Perspectives, and Questions. The farmers hold the land in the form of a lease; they are not able to sell the land or claim ownership to it. Many fear that, at any point, the government might reclaim the land from them.

charged by the business contractors regardless of whether the crop yield they end up producing can or cannot cover the cost. It is up to the farmer to produce crops that would cover all the funding he receives and leave him with some excess money to pay labor and any extra expenses. To make the matter worse, recent climatic changes increased the vulnerability of farmers; in an interview with the *Financial Gazette*, the agronomist T Mutenga explained that "The Zimbabwean rainfall pattern is now very erratic, and although tobacco is a resilient crop to mild droughts, it does affect the quality and crop output."[31] If the state had the capacity to develop an environmental alarm system in combination with seasonal assistance, it would better equip the farmers in planning for the harvest season. Under the contracts, it is up to the farmer to provide all the necessary labor, infrastructure for crop production, and pay for crop insurance in case of natural disasters like hail and droughts. Nevertheless, because these farmers already lack capital, most of them cannot afford the insurance and the adequate labor supply that would be needed; therefore, the state's intervention would probably be one of the most crucial contributions from a developmental perspective.

Furthermore, practices of many insurance companies, which typically search for legal loopholes to avoid possible compensation in the case of disasters, contribute to farmers' lack of trust and reluctance to get insured. One farmer complained in the interview that he suffered a hailstorm disaster in the 2013 crop season, but even though he had a valid hailstorm insurance cover, his claim was never satisfied. The insurance company never paid for his loss, and efforts to hold the company accountable did not pay off.[32] The interviewees explained that the loopholes in the state regulation weaken state capacity to bring financial tools those farmers could use to mitigate the hectic nature of the tobacco market in Zimbabwe. Farmers are often forced to mortgage their infrastructure as the contractors inspect that as an asset before making funding available. Such conditions put the farmers at risk of indebtedness or insolvency when the crop does not provide sufficient income. The contractors do not take collateral, but they assess the value of property or form of property the farmers may own, such as cattle and other infrastructure that the

[31] Mutenga, T. 2013–14 Agric Season Uncertain, *The Financial Gazette*, January 9, 2014.

[32] Interview with K. Mutengwa, Chisuvi Village, July 30, 2015.

farmers possess; as far as my research is concerned, no case of confiscation of the farmland has ever happened in any case of a default, but once the farmer becomes insolvent, he would never be able to secure funding from creditors again.

Crop prices are never fixed before the harvest season; therefore, farmers must engage in a contract without being aware of the possible yield return they could make from the harvest, especially in bad years when tobacco prices would be low. Despite the fact they provide the necessary labor, infrastructure, and land for the business, farmers in concern might still end up owing money to the contractor from whom they borrowed. Such a contract is unfair in the eyes of many farmers; hence they expressed their preference for the state to provide more protective interventions in safeguarding the interests of small-scale farmers vis-á-vis the larger agro-business. Some interviews shared their skepticism that they would ever opt for a contract again after their yield failed to cover the input costs, and they lost what they invested. Since all the responsibility for guaranteeing that crop yields would bring enough profit is on the farmers' shoulders, most of them find it necessary to supplement more inputs in order to achieve high-quality crops that they need for guaranteeing the minimum surplus. Thus, the farmers end up subsidizing inputs even though the contractors promised to provide all other needed inputs in the contract. According to many farmers' experiences, in order to get an A-grade tobacco leaf, they needed to add more fertilizers and charcoal bags for curing the tobacco.[33]

Under the framework of those contracts, farmers are left with no options but to accept unfavorable conditions for accessing inputs directly from the contractors. The negative effect is that they are charged above the market price by the contractors, which makes their debt bigger, and it becomes easy to end up in a debt-spiral or at least in a situation of financial dependence on the contractor. Such a situation could even lead to losing one's land.

As a result of the unfavorable conditions, the artificially extended price margin eats into their anticipated profits. Had they had the option to buy the products cheaper from other suppliers in the market, they would

[33] Masocha, R. (2016): "Tobacco Contract Framing in Zimbabwe Communal Areas of Nyakudya 2009–2014, A Necessary Evil?", Dissertation Submitted in Partial Fulfilment of the Bachelor of Arts Honors Degree in Economic History, University of Zimbabwe, Department of Economic History, Supervised by Dr. J. P. Mtisi, June 2016, p. 12.

have spent less money on investment inputs. Even the contractors could make more money from providing extra inputs at pre-rated prices in such a scenario. To illustrate the problem, let me give a concrete example: in the 2013–14 season, the contractor gave farmers Ammonium nitrate pegged at 39 USD each, yet the bags were valued at 32–35 USD in the market, and even cheaper when selling in wholesale-bulk.[34] The irony is that many farmers were unaware of this trend because very few of them had the opportunity to make a thorough market research before signing their contracts, and they were directly charged above the market price by the respective contractors. On the other hand, most of them were also grateful for having access to the inputs they needed. In sum, the contractors are often able to take advantage of the non-inquisitiveness of the farmers, which allows the former to extend the profit-margin in the contracted transactions. Interestingly, even though the contracts are legal liabilities, and most of the farmers are fully aware of what they are engaging with, many farmers still do businesses according to verbal agreements and operate on interpersonal trust. During the farmers' workshop, one of the spokespersons represents their wishes, and most of the farmers follow instructions with complete trust. This is still part of the business culture in many African societies. According to my observations, this way of doing business can make contradictions when it interferes with formalized business transactions characteristic of the international market system.

[34] Interview with A. Feso, Nyakudya Village, July 28, 2015.

Conclusion

This chapter discussed those historical circumstances in which the Zimbabwean state fostered development for the sake of agricultural advancement but to the detriment of many small farmers. State policies often contradicted even to the needs of big capital, which made the business environment very hectic for all producers in Zimbabwe. Simultaneously, state policies have been inadequate in providing support and protection for farmers. According to my conducted interviews, I learned from small farmers that many state policies appear very antagonistic and discouraging for sustaining farming activity in the country.

As a conclusion, I must stress that the tobacco industry could serve the purpose of a developmental model for Zimbabwe, including benefits for both small farmers and large capital, if economic policies could be enhanced and better coordinated for the sake of balancing the needs of competing actors. However, for that purpose, the state would need to step up to activate its role as a regulator. Such a regulatory responsibility would entail that the state authorities understand the unique needs that farmers have and design policies and programs according to institutionalized consultation with farmers' representatives. The state also needs to engage with international and domestic investors, ensuring much-criticized currency stability and coherent policy framework such that investors will not risk having all their money wiped out by hectic policy shifts. Thus, such a developmental model needs to be based on an institutional reform of representation and consultation on behalf of business actors. By becoming more open and geared in delivering on its institutional settings more transparently, the state would also become more accountable, hence democratic, which is another important feature of the developmental paradigm. All in all, such an institutional reform is the only path that can lead to the foundations for a new, more inclusive developmental model in the twenty-first century by allowing the current businesses and farmers to operate in Zimbabwe to benefit from the participation in international markets.

References

Secondary Sources

Arrighi, G. (1967). *The Political Economy of Rhodesia*, Mouton: The Hague.

Barlow, T E. (ed) (1997). *Formations of Colonial Modernity in East Asia*, Duke University Press, London.

Bimha, A. (2016). Restructuring of the Agricultural Development Bank into a Land Bank, Implications and Repurcations, Dissertation submitted in partial fulfillment of the Master of Science in Banking and Financial. Services, Supervised by M. W. Ndlovu at the National University of Science Education, Bulawayo, Zimbabwe.

Martin, J. (ed) (2008). *The Poulantzas Reader: Marxism, Law and the State*, Verso, London.

Masocha, R. (2016). "Tobacco Contract Framing in Zimbabwe Communal Areas of Nyakudya 2009–2014, A Necessary Evil?" Dissertation Submitted in Partial Fulfilment of the Bachelor of Arts Honors Degree in Economic History, University of Zimbabwe, Department of Economic History, Supervised by Dr, J. P. Mtisi, June 2016.

Mhandara, L., Hamauswa, S., and Nyemba, (2013). "A Review of the Doctrine of Separation of Powers in Zimbabwe 1979–2013," *Southern Peace Review-Journal* 2(2), 68–85.

Moyo, S. (1995). The Land Question in Zimbabwe: Research, Perspectives, and Questions, Paper presented at Codersria Conference on Land reform, Gaborone Botswana 18–19 October 2003 and Dakar Senegal 8–11 December 2003.

Raftoupoulous, B., and Mlambo, A. (eds) (2009). *Becoming Zimbabwe, A History from the Precolonial Period to 2008*, Weaver Press, Harare, 2009.

Rubert, S. C. (1998). *A Most Promising Weed, A History of Tobacco Farming and Labor in Colonial Zimbabwe 1890–1945*, Ohio University Press, Ohio.

Sachikonye, L. (2012). *Zimbabwe's Lost Decade, Politics, Development and Society*, Weaver Press, Harare.

Seminar presentation, FAO, "Tobacco in Zimbabwe," *Corporate Document Repository*, Economic and Social Development Department, 2000.s

Newspaper Articles

Financial Gazette, December 12, 2013.

Financial Gazette, January 9, 2014.

Financial Gazette, May 1, 2014.

Financial Gazette, August 20, 2015.

News Day, March 25, 2014.

The Chronicle, January 7, 2014.

The Chronicle, February 13, 2014.
The Herald, October 5, 2007.
The Herald, 16 May 2013.
The *Sunday Mail*, February 22, 2014.
Zimbabwe's Situation, July 16, 2014.

Interviews

Chisuvi, L., Chisuvi Village, July 28, 2015.
Chisuvi, N., Chisuvi Village, July 30, 2015.
Deve, N., Chisuvi Village, July 28, 2015.
Feso, A., Nyakudya Village, July 28, 2015.
Gudu, N., Masango Village, July 28, 2015.
Kamudyariwa, T., Mutyambizi Village, July 29, 2015.
Kapawo, S. (Agritex Officer Nyakudya station), Nyakudya Village, July 27, 2015.
Muragu, V. (Agritex officer Nyakudya), Nyakudya Village, July 29, 2015.
Marimo, A., Chisuvi Village, July 28, 2015.
Mufandaedza, R., Masango Village, July 29, 2015.
Musonza, F. (Agritex Officer Nyakudya), Nyakudya Village, July 30, 2015.
Mutengwa, K., Chisuvi Village, July 30, 2015.
Oholman, O. (Tribac Company Tobacco Contractor), August 20, 2015.
Zvomuya, K., Masango Village, July 30, 2015.

Magazines

Zimbabwe Tobacco Association, "Tobacco Trends," Harare, September 2001.
Zimbabwe Tobacco Association, "Tobacco Trends," Harare, September 2003.
ZimbabweTobacco Today: Magazine of The Zimbabwe Tobacco Association, December 2013/February 2014.

Annual Reports

Tobacco Industry and Marketing board statistical data.
Tobacco Industry and Marketing Board, "2014 Zimbabwe Tobacco statistics," 2014.

CHAPTER 12

State-Led Development in the Global Trading System—A Real Threat to Stability?

Gábor Vigvári

Introduction—The Developmental State and Trade

The concept of the developmental state is full of debates. Perhaps, the biggest cleavage is related to the issue of the role of the state: were East Asian countries successful because of the massive interventions of the government into free markets or despite that? (see i.e., World Bank 1993) This, obviously relates to question of trade and trade policies.

The role of trade in development, in general, is an already highly contested issue, and the debate has been largely shaped by the changing global economic environment. Until the 1980s and 1990s, there was a strong current in policy making, that highlighted market failures related to international trade, thus, favorizing, at least, temporary restrictive trade policy solutions, in line with the import substitution industrialization (Rodrik 2004). This interventionalist approach was, at least, partially

G. Vigvári (✉)
Department of World Economy, Institute of International, Political, and Regional Studies, Corvinus University of Budapest, Budapest, Hungary
e-mail: gabor.vigvari@uni-corvinus.hu

T. Gerőcs and J. Ricz (eds.), *The Post-Crisis Developmental State*, International Political Economy Series,
https://doi.org/10.1007/978-3-030-71987-6_12

overwritten by the emergence of global supply chains, that brought industrialization and modernization to many developing nation in a completely different way (Baldwin 2016 and Chang and Andreoni 2020).

Nevertheless, the traditional development state literature (Johnson 1982; Amsden 1989; Wade 1990; Leftwich 1995; Evans 1995) puts a significant emphasis on the role of international trade, and trade policy. This approach mostly focuses on how emerging nations of East and South East Asia used export-led growth models, and how the government helped in the creation of competitive industries throughout the region. This line of literature focuses on trade and trade policy from an internal perspective. The main focus is on the policies themselves, as well as the enablers of good policy choices, especially those institutional enablers that made it possible for governments to "pick the winners" (Rodrik 2004).

Another, though less significant branch of literature focuses on the external enablers of the success stories of developmental states. Stubbs (2005), in example, focuses on the importance of the external security regime, and our earlier research focused on the importance of international economic regimes, including international trade (Vigvári, 2012). From that perspective the importance of certain qualities of the Bretton Woods (from the perspective of international trade, the General Agreement on Tariffs and Trade—GATT) regimes, called "embedded liberalism" (Ruggie 1982) seemed to matter. This framework created "policy space" for developmental states to intervene into markets, and to use restrictive (or from an export perspective supportive) trade policy solutions.

After the creation of the World Trade Organization (WTO), but especially after the launch of the Doha Development Round,[1] several attempts were made to evaluate the new WTO trade regime from the perspective of this "policy space." And although the results of the literature are mixed (Gallagher et al. 2005; Newfarmer et al. 2006; Stiglitz and Charlton 2005; Hoekman—Mattoo—English 2002), the failure of the Doha Development Round, and evaluations of the results of the Uruguay

[1] The predecessor of WTO, the General Agreement on Tariffs and Trade worked using negotiation rounds around specific topics. Though, the WTO holds every other year ministerial conferences, talks still organized around negotiation rounds. The latest, still unfinished, round has started in 2001 at the Doha Ministerial Conference, and the main agenda of it initially was to help developing countries.

Round (see Gallagher 2008) seems to signal some issues with the role of the WTO regarding development policies.

As we can see from this short summary, the role of international trade dominated the developmental state literature from these two, internalist and externalist perspective. However, these two branches eventually try to put together the same puzzle: how trade affects development, so in this sense, international trade is an explanatory, or at least an intervening variable.

This chapter tries to take a look on this issue from a different perspective. If, there was a significant shift in the global norms and rules of international trade (the transformation of the GATT regime into the WTO regime), is it possible, that certain countries, that used restrictive trade policies in the past, still use some of these policies, that are against globally agreed rules? The chapter tries to answer this question by using the Global Antidumping Database (GAD), the Global Countervailing Duties Database (GCVD), and the China-Specific Safeguards Database (CSGD) (Bown 2016a, b, c).

This question is quite useful to be asked, especially nowadays. In the Fall of 2017 President Trump approved global safeguard tariffs on \$8.5 billion in imports of solar panels and \$1.8 billion of washing machines in January, 2018 (Bown—Kolb 2020). This was a starting point, of what we call today the trade war between the United States and China. However, this interpretation is misleading, as these tariffs didn't target exclusively China only (mostly because against China and Taiwan some special tariffs were already implemented), but other, mostly East and South East Asian countries (Bown 2018).

The escalation of this trade war highlighted many weaknesses of the global trading system. Until recently, the majority of research regarding the WTO highlighted three main problems:

1. The above mentioned issues of the lack of "policy space" within the WTO.
2. The issue of the lack of capabilities of the WTO to adopt itself to the new needs of the global trading system dominated by globalized supply chains and multinational corporations, the so called WTO + and WTO X[2] issues (see i.e., Ruta 2017).

[2] WTO+ (plus), and WTO X (extra) issues are trade related policies, regulations. Though WTO+ issues are regulated in the WTO, but bilateral and regional trade agreements

3. The problems of the dispute settlement mechanism, related to the lack of power of some member states to use the mechanism properly (Bown 2005).

In a later phase, the Trump administration invoked section 301 of the US Trade act of 1974, and the accusations of unfair trade practices mostly against China (Bown, 2017). This argument, widely used in the 1980s mostly against Japan, but other emerging, mostly East Asian countries, too, suggest, that the underlying cause of American protective actions are those policies, and their underlying institutional causes, that are mostly present there.

Hence, the trade war highlighted another major problem, that has been observable almost since the creation of the organization, but for some reason, was not paid much attention until recently. And that is the problem of lack of transparency in case of some policy practices,[3] and more precisely in case of highly interventionist institutional setup of various member countries (mostly in case of countries, we might call developmental states or state capitalist countries [Nölke 2014]). The goal of this chapter is to address this issue, and to illustrate, that this problem has existed for a while now. The main research question is therefore, if East Asian, and South East Asian institutional models (developmental states) are compatible with the current multilateral trading system? We selected 8 countries Japan, Korea, Taiwan, Hong Kong, Singapore, Malaysia, Thailand, and China.

This selection reflects the countries of the traditional developmental state literature, and is augmented with China.

The chapter justifies this solution using the varieties of capitalism literature. According to this we either can differentiate among Anglo-American, German and Japanese models (Zysman 1983 and Gilpin 2001), or liberal and coordinated market economies (Hall and Soskice 2001). What is common in both approaches, that Asia is mainly left out, or is reduced to the analysis of Japan.

achieved much more results (i.e. trade in services). WTO X issues are not within the mandate of the organization, but are regulated by other trade agreements (i.e. labor standards) (see i.e. Horn et al. 2009).

[3] The most notable example would be the problem of unclear boundaries between the public and private sector, where state support and subsidies are not clearly visible for outside observers.

One can argue therefore, and so does Hundt and Uttam (2017), that Asian developmental states can be considered as a separate model of capitalism. And in this model, one can fit not only the classical developmental states, but also China. This is in line with defining all these countries as representatives of state capitalism, although, of different generations (see Nölke 2014). In this way, developmental states, and also China can and should be understood as examples of state-led development.[4] In this sense, the state in these Asian countries is an activist agent: "[t]he key quality that made the state developmental was that it planned the development process rather than relied on market forces to determine the optimal allocation of resources." (Beeson 2009: 9).

This is useful from the chapter's perspective, because from the perspective of international trade and the international trading system, the behavior of the government, its trade policy-related decisions are of key importance. And it seems, that this happens quite similarly in these countries.

The Role and Design of the International Trading System

In this chapter, however, the main focus is not on the developmental state, but the international trading system. We will define the trading system, as an international regime, a concept widely used in the field of international political economy (IPE). According to Krasner's (1982: 186) definition regimes are, "implicit or explicit principles, norms, rules, and decision making procedures around which actors' expectations converge in a given area of international relations."

In the above mentioned approach international regimes are examined as intervening variables. This means, regimes are seen as institutions, that modify states' behavior. In a very simple model, this behavior is the dependent variable, that can be explained by independent variables, such as the structure of the international system, the relative power structure and the interest of the country.

We accept, that regimes, as intervening variables can actually modify the outcomes from this model. However, there is also a feedback loop, that is important to be mentioned. In case of regimes, the modified

[4] Or state-permeated market economies, to apply the term of Nölke et al. (2019).

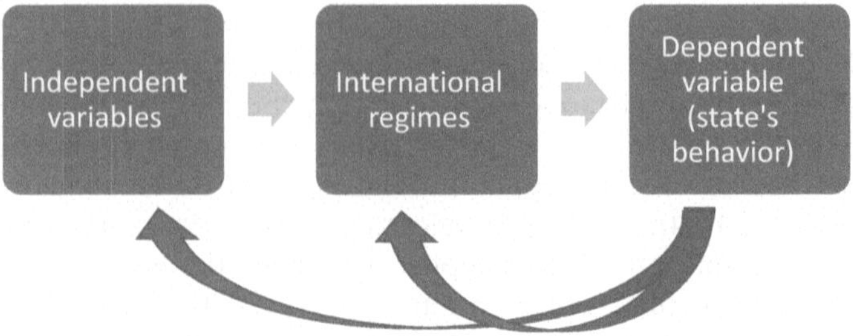

Fig. 12.1 The traditional regime theory augmented with the feedback loop (*Source* Based on Krasner [1982: 189], modified by the author)

behavior would mean, that governments actually do comply with the rules prescribed by the regime. However, if countries do not comply (and as regimes usually lack of enforcement power, this might happen very easily), that may weaken the regime, or even change independent variables in the model (see Fig. 12.1, where these feedback loops are shown).

If, as an example, a country does not comply with WTO rules, that might change the strength of the system, even making other countries not to comply with the regime's rules (the shorter feedback loop). Or, in some cases, not complying countries might become stronger and more powerful, changing the original independent variables, as well (the longer feedback loop). Therefore it is worth investigating these feedback loops as well. However, in this chapter, we will limit ourselves to the question of compliance, and its effect on the regime itself.

The global trading system can be described as a sum of all principles, norms, rules, and decision making procedures, that govern international trade. Using this definition, the global trading system can be understood in a broad and narrow way. In the broad definition, we shall include all the multilateral and bilateral trade-related agreements. In the narrow definition, we can translate the international trading regime as the multilateral trading system under the World Trade Organization (WTO). This approach is used by Hoekman and Kostecki (2001), and we will use this definition, as well.

The WTO has essentially two functions. The first one is to create new norms and rules governing international trade. In this sense, as Hoekman and Kostecki (2001: 25) put it, it serves as a market for the exchange of liberalization commitments. From the perspective of our chapter, this function is of lesser importance. The second function of the WTO is to provide the framework of cooperation and communication in relation to complying with existing rules. Obviously, this second function roots in the first one, as existing rules create a code of conduct of trade policy making. In case of international regimes in general, a part of this second function is rule enforcement. In case of the WTO the Dispute Settlement Mechanism was implemented to increase complying through negotiation, providing legal aid and, at the end, through enforcing WTO rules.

But what makes states to comply with existing international regimes, if regimes lack real enforcement power? As regimes, even if they are institutionalized in an international organization lack sovereign power, their enforcement possibility is zero. In case of the WTO, the dispute settlement mechanism, to put it very simple,[5] entitles member countries to force non-complying members using retaliation in the form of various trade barriers. Although, the WTO's enforcement mechanism is possibly one of the strongest among international regimes (Hoekman and Kostecki 2001), it still lacks proper mechanisms to reveal and remedy all non-compliance-related issues (see Bown 2005). However, compliance is not an exception, and, during the GATT years, when enforcement rules were much weaker, the situation was the same. According to Hoekman and Kostecki (2001) the reason of this was self-interest. As the WTO is a repeated game, meaning, that a non-complying country can find itself soon in trouble because of non-compliance of others, this created an incentive for compliance in case of simpler GATT rules. This argument is in line with the general theories of international regimes (Krasner 1982).

Another possible cause of the relative strength of the WTO regime, that is a great example, of what Keohane and Nye (2001) describes as the "club model" of international cooperation. This means, that, under other international regimes and institutions, in the WTO "cabinet ministers or the equivalent, working in the same issue-area, initially from a relatively small number of relatively rich countries, got together to make rules [...] to govern >>issue-areas<< defined in terms of clusters of issues" (Keohane and Nye 2001: 220) This resulted in a very supportive negotiating environment, where opponents of liberalization were only influential and that led to progression regarding the first function, and stability in the second function of the system.

[5] A very detailed legal and political economic analysis can be found in Van den Bossche and Zdouc (2017) and Hoekman and Kostecki (2001).

According to Keohane and Nye (2001), in case of the WTO, the "club model" is applicable to the Uruguay Round negotiations and the establishment of the organization. According to them, there has been three challenges present in the international trading system, that have questioned the "club model," and therefore the stability of the system: the increasing number of members, the increasing number and influence of non-governmental organizations, and the increasing spread of democratic norms.

From our perspective, the first argument is important. However, only two of the examined countries (China and Taiwan) are not founding members of the WTO, one might argue, that their institutional distance from other founding members might have caused some deviation of the club model. Our goal is to test, if this might be the case, and also, if the accession of China and Taiwan have had the same effect on the regime. In the next section we will explain the methodology we apply.

Non-compliance in the Trading System—The Explanation of Our Methodology

In the literature, there has been two historical waves of articles, mostly focusing on China in this matter. The first wave of articles dealt with the Chinese accession, either from an economic growth, or from a sectoral point of view.[6] The second wave of literature tries to evaluate the experiences gathered about the Chinese membership. As time progresses, and the closer we are to the outbreak of the trade war, the more critical these articles become. A reason for this might be, that since the early twenty-first century (parallel with the Chinese membership), the WTO failed to deliver results regarding its first function (creating new rules), and that with the trade war, and its successful blocking of the Appellate Body[7] of the WTO's dispute settlement mechanism, one of the strongest members of the organization, the United States signaled, that the second function (enforcement) has serious flaws as well. Besides this, Mavroidis and

[6] For a detailed list of authors, see (Ianchovichina and Walmsley 2003: 3).

[7] The Appellate Body (AB) is a group of elected judges, who (in case of an appeal) make the final decision on a trade dispute among WTO members. In the last couple of years, the US has blocked the election of new members of the Appellate Body, and because of this, the number of AB members fell below the required minimum in December, 2019. That means, currently all Dispute Settlement cases with an appeal are halted.

Sapir (2019) emphasize the declining economic performance and power of developed countries, as potential cause.

The common point of the existing literature on this, that they usually take a legal standpoint, and also seek for legal answers to the problem. The literature generally agrees on the source of troubles with China. They highlight its unique economic structure, the importance of state owned enterprises, but also the blurry relationship between the private and public sectors. This creates a "subsidy problem" as Bown and Hillman (2019) refer to it. The second important issue to be mentioned is the problem of forced technology transfer. Both of these are generally the reason, that is usually referred to by the Trump administration justifying the sanctions against China. The last common ground of the literature is, that the WTO with its current rules and mechanisms is not capable to contain these problems, which means, that in order to solve them, member states should change the WTO's regulation. Obviously, the question remains there quite open in an organization of unanimous decision making procedures: would China agree to this?

In a legal analysis of WTO Dispute Settlement cases Toohey (2011) splits Chinese behavior into three periods, highlighting that after 5 years of observation and adaptation, after 2009 China became not just the target of many investigation, but became active user of the Dispute Settlement Mechanisms (DSM).

In a rather political-economic analysis of the same topic Jain (2016) concludes, that China behaves in the WTO more like a realist player, focusing mostly on its own interest, though it is rather frequently packaged into a seemingly constructive "responsible stakeholder approach." In his very detailed analysis, Wu (2016) highlights, that the problems of Chinese membership are unique. He does not agree with Keohane and Nye (2001), and argues that institutional diversity has been always present in the GATT/WTO system. Traditional Asian developmental states were members in the system, but he also points out that the GATT had socialist members in the 1970s and 1980s. His argument is, that the Chinese case is so unique, that the WTO's institutional setup cannot handle it. However, Wu (2016) highlights the fact, that the root of the problem is not the Chinese accession, since many disputed policies with Chinese membership have emerged since only after the accession. Du (2014) agrees with this diagnosis, however, highlights, that in relations to state-owned enterprises, there has been a significant improvement in WTO compliance since the Chinese accession.

Mavroidis and Sapir (2019) have a different opinion on the question whether the case of China is unique. Though, their argument is not much different, on why Chinese membership might cause problems in the WTO, nevertheless, they do not believe, that this is a unique issue. They also emphasize, that there were other cases, where member countries' institutional setup was different from the "club model's" ideal structure. They even compare the current situation of China, with Japan's in the 1980s and 1990s.[8] Though, they also highlight the fact, that there are important differences in the size of these two economies (China being larger), in development level (Japan being more developed), the role of the state (Japan being acknowledged as a market economy), and their geopolitical position (Japan being an important US ally during the Cold War).

While the above-mentioned sources try to argue using mostly qualitative approaches, we will try to quantify these institutional differences. In order to do this, we will focus mostly on one single issue, the subsidy problem. In order to understand the subsidy problem, one needs to take a closer look at the WTO's regulation on the issue. Within the organization, the so-called SCM (Subsidies and Countervailing Measures) Agreement deals with this problem. In the WTO law, there are three categories of subsidies: prohibited (export and local content subsidies), actionable subsidies (that are not prohibited per se, but are actionable by countervailing measures and can be challenged under the Dispute Settlement Mechanism, in case of adverse effects), and allowed (i.e., agricultural subsidies) (Van den Bossche and Zdouc 2017)[9] The agreement does not take into consideration the problems of state-owned enterprises, and deals only with state trading enterprises. Should a member state believe, that any other member uses prohibited subsidies, or a subsidy that is

[8] This is not unique, in case of a similar comparison on monetary relations see Eichengreen (2011).

[9] According the WTO website "there are three types of adverse effects. First, there is injury to a domestic industry caused by subsidized imports in the territory of the complaining Member. This is the sole basis for countervailing action. Second, there is serious prejudice. Serious prejudice usually arises as a result of adverse effects (e.g., export displacement) in the market of the subsidizing Member or in a third country market. Thus, unlike injury, it can serve as the basis for a complaint related to harm to a Member's export interests. Finally, there is nullification or impairment of benefits accruing under the GATT 1994." (WTO website on the SCM Agreement).

actionable, they can use countervailing measures, mostly in the form of countervailing duties (CVD) if certain conditions are met.

Another important regulation, that has something to do with subsidies is the regulation of anti-dumping (AD) policies, that is part of the GATT (Hoekman and Kostecki 2001). "WTO Members can impose anti-dumping measures, if, [...] a determination is made (a) that dumping is occurring,[10] (b) that the domestic industry producing the like product in the importing country is suffering material injury, and (c) that there is a causal link between the two." (WTO Anti-Dumping Gateway 2020) Though this definition of dumping may not be understandable from an economic perspective, the formulation of the rule allows member states to use it flexible, usually, if they believe, that their trading partner conducts unfair trading practices (usually subsidies, but in case of Japan in the 1980s and 1990s the lack of anti-trust regulation) (Hoekman and Kostecki 2001).

Both AD measures and CVDs are part of what we may call safety valves in WTO law (Hoekman and Kostecki 2001 and Blonigen—Prusa 2015). Safety valves in general are used in regimes to increase compliance. As Kucik and Reinhardt (2008) emphasize it there is an uncertainty states face about the future costs of compliance. "Such uncertainty creates a 'time inconsistency' problem that endangers the prospects for a cooperative agreement in the present. The opportunity to temporarily escape from contractual obligations—without incurring excessive retaliation from other partners—may encourage states to enter into deeper cooperative agreements and sustain those commitments over time" (page 477–78). They call it the "flexibility hypothesis." The WTO includes various safeguard mechanisms, out of which the AD and SCM regulations are probably the most important and widely known, and are those, that can be invoked against countries, and not particular products or industries.[11]

However, as one can see from above definitions, these agreements do relate to the behavior of trading partners. That means, while in case of

[10] Dumping is defined as a situation if a company sets a lower export price in a foreign market, than in the home market (Hoekman and Kostecki 2001).

[11] In case of AD and CVD specific product coming from specific countries are targeted. But there are other examples of safeguards, where only production sectors are protected against import, regardless the import's country of origin. For our purpose, these are useless, as our goal is to measure countries non-compliance.

other safety valves (i.e., the national security argument,[12] or the infant industry case), the above-mentioned uncertainty is about the development of the domestic economy, in case of the AD and CVDs, the uncertainty is about the behavior of the trading partner. That means, that the use of any AD or CVDs policy methods may signal, that the other member country targeted by these, does not comply with WTO rules.

If we accept this line of argument, we can argue, that the implementation of AD and CVD measures may be understood as perceived non-compliance of the targeted country. Therefore a large number of such cases might signal problems in the compliance of a member state. This should be treated, however, on a relative basis: countries have different size and importance in the global trading system. Countries, that trade less, will have a lower absolute amount of cases, but also, their non-compliance might have a smaller effect on the stability of the whole system, if we think back on the feedback loops, we identified before.

Based on these we can introduce a very simple methodology for our investigation. Using the Temporary Trade Barriers website we identified three databases: the Global Antidumping Database (GAD), the Global Countervailing Duties Database (GCVD), and the China-Specific Safeguards Database (CSGD) (Bown 2016a, b, c). From these resources we established a database consisting of AD and SCM policies introduced against the countries of our investigation. Then we will calculate the share of the countries under investigation in the total sample.

We will then check if classical developmental states and China are overrepresented in the sample, where as a basis for comparison, we will use their contribution share to the WTO's budget. These are determined according to each member's share of international trade (in percentage), based on trade in goods, services, and intellectual property rights for the last five years for which data is available (WTO website on the budget). This comparison is justifiable, as according to the organization itself, this indicator shows the relative importance of a nation in international trade. A potential overrepresentation (a larger share in total cases, than the share in total trade) can be interpreted, that this particular country is less than average compliant with WTO rules. As the WTO provides data only for

[12] In the WTO there are various safety valves allowing countries to temporarily not complying with the agreed rules. One of them is the "national security argument". In case of this, exemptions are based on the claim, that trade hurts a member's national security.

the time period 2001 and 2019, for the time period before 2001, we will use as substitute UNCTAD's statistics on each countries' export's share in global exports (UNCTAD trade statistics).

There are, of course certain limitations of this approach. First of all, the time span of the database is limited. While there is data available for pre-WTO years, the time series ends at 2015, therefore we will use data available for the 1995–2015 period. Second of all, there might be cases, where an AD or CVD measure is used due to domestic political reasons, or, where eventually the implementation of the policy was not justifiable.[13] Blonigen and Prusa (2015) show, that especially in case of AD measures, that is quite frequently the case. This usually happens either because of successful group of lobbyist, or due to economic reasons, i.e., during recessions AD measures are more frequently used. To control for these cases might be the direction of further research. The database doesn't cover all measures, that were implemented during this period, however, according to the database, for the given time period, approximately 95% of all AD and CVD cases are covered. Last, but not least, not only these two mechanisms can signal non-compliance with WTO regulations. Therefore, we will also analyze DSM cases, using the WTO's dispute settlement gateway to augment the results.

Results

In the Antidumping Database we analyzed more than 5000 entries, while the Counterveiling Duties Database consist 415 entries for the time period 1995–2015. Because of this, percentage values show less variation in case of AD than in case of CVDs. This makes it also harder to compare countries in case of the latter. Our results are summarized in Fig. 12.2 and Table 12.1.

If we take a look at the following table and graphs, we can see, that our results are mixed. We can see, that there are three countries, that seem to fit quite well into the world trading system: Japan, Singapore and Hong Kong. The last two cases are less surprising: as Hundt and Uttam (2017) put it in their description of "entrepôt capitalism," their situation can be described as the "small country syndrome" (page 103), which led to less direct influence of the state into the market economy. Shin (2005)

[13] These policy measures can be implemented unilaterally, and can be challenged by the target country in front of the DSM.

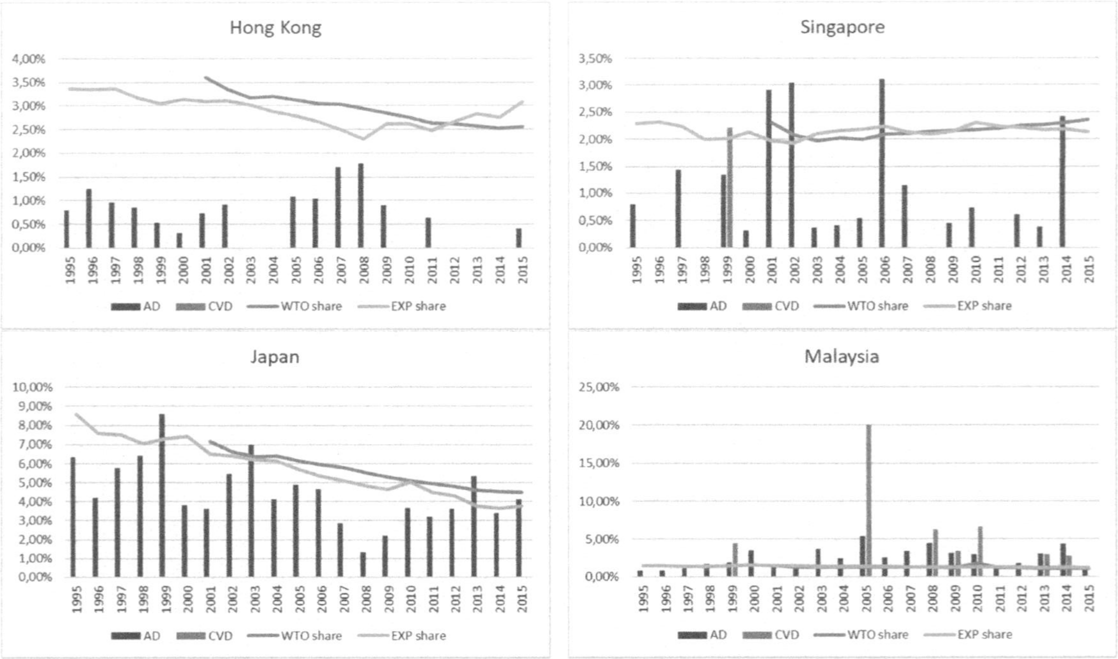

Fig. 12.2 Antidumping (AD) and countervailing duties cases against selected Asian economies as a percentage of total cases in a year (columns) compared to their importance in the global trading system measured as their contribution to the WTO budget (WTO share) in percentage, and the share of their total merchandised exports in global exports (EXP share) in percentage (lines) (*Source* Based on Bown [2016a] and [b], UNCTAD website, and WTO website on budget, the author's calculation)

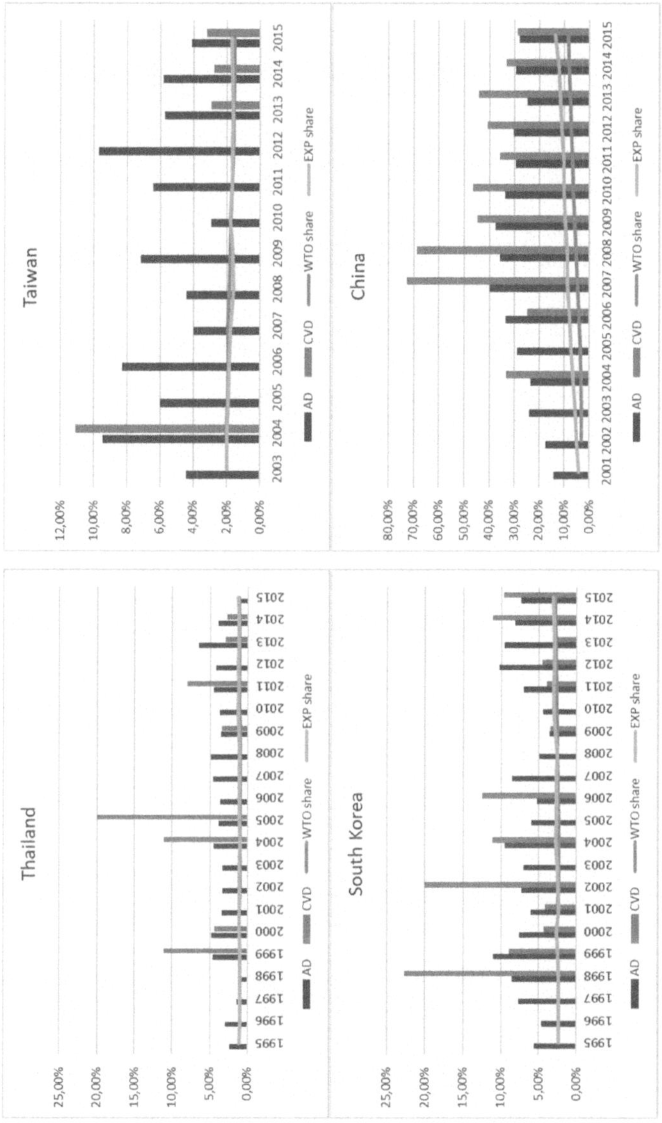

Fig. 12.2 (continued)

Table 12.1 Antidumping (AD) and countervailing duties cases against selected Asian economies as a percentage of total cases in a year compared to their importance in the global trading system measured as their contribution to the WTO budget (WTO share) in percentage, and the share of their total merchandised exports in global exports (EXP share) in percentage (*Source* Based on Bown [2016a] and [b], UNCTAD website, and WTO website on budget, the author's calculation)

Country		*1995*	*1996*	*1997*	*1998*	*1999*	*2000*	*2001*	*2002*	*2003*	*2004*	*2005*	*2006*	*2007*
CHN	*AD*	13.49%	27.20%	10.58%	7.26%	12.10%	13.65%	14.04%	17.33%	23.90%	23.46%	28.80%	33.68%	40.00%
	CVD	0.00%	0.00%	0.00%	0.00%	0.00%	0.00%	0.00%	0.00%	0.00%	33.33%	0.00%	25.00%	72.73%
	WTO share	NA	NA	NA	NA	NA	NA	NA	2.97%	3.16%	3.26%	3.60%	4.09%	4.73%
	EXP share	2.8742%	2.7915%	3.2643%	3.3342%	3.4060%	3.8620%	4.2952%	5.0092%	5.7736%	6.4324%	7.2548%	7.9896%	8.7044%
MYS	*AD*	0.79%	0.84%	1.44%	1.71%	1.88%	3.49%	1.69%	1.22%	3.68%	2.47%	5.43%	2.59%	3.43%
	CVD	0.00%	0.00%	0.00%	0.00%	4.44%	0.00%	0.00%	0.00%	0.00%	0.00%	20.00%	0.00%	0.00%
	WTO share	NA	NA	NA	NA	NA	NA	1.47%	1.31%	1.27%	1.30%	1.28%	1.27%	1.26%
	EXP share	1.4279%	1.4475%	1.4061%	1.3295%	1.4786%	1.5223%	1.4199%	1.4471%	1.3795%	1.3730%	1.3485%	1.3254%	1.2550%
THA	*AD*	2.38%	2.93%	1.44%	1.28%	4.57%	4.76%	3.39%	3.34%	3.31%	4.53%	3.80%	3.63%	4.57%
	CVD	0.00%	0.00%	0.00%	0.00%	11.11%	4.35%	0.00%	0.00%	0.00%	11.11%	20.00%	0.00%	0.00%
	WTO share	NA	NA	NA	NA	NA	NA	1.13%	1.00%	0.95%	0.99%	0.97%	0.99%	1.01%
	EXP share	1.0903%	1.0298%	1.0241%	0.9887%	1.0217%	1.0688%	1.0487%	1.0478%	1.0583%	1.0435%	1.0563%	1.0696%	1.0974%

Country		*1995*	*1996*	*1997*	*1998*	*1999*	*2000*	*2001*	*2002*	*2003*	*2004*	*2005*	*2006*	*2007*
TWN	*AD*	4.76%	4.60%	6.73%	5.98%	5.91%	4.13%	5.33%	4.86%	4.41%	9.47%	5.98%	8.29%	4.00%
	CVD	0.00%	0.00%	6.67%	0.00%	11.11%	0.00%	0.00%	0.00%	0.00%	11.11%	0.00%	0.00%	0.00%
	WTO share	NA	NA	NA	NA	NA	NA	NA	NA	NA	2.00%	1.95%	1.89%	1.93%
	EXP share	2.1839%	2.1684%	2.1994%	2.0412%	2.1601%	2.3457%	2.0322%	2.0782%	1.9802%	1.9778%	1.8893%	1.8471%	1.7593%
SGP	*AD*	0.79%	0.00%	1.44%	0.00%	1.34%	0.32%	2.91%	3.04%	0.37%	0.41%	0.54%	3.11%	1.14%
	CVD	0.00%	0.00%	0.00%	0.00%	2.22%	0.00%	0.00%	0.00%	0.00%	0.00%	0.00%	0.00%	0.00%
	WTO share	NA	NA	NA	NA	NA	NA	2.30%	2.08%	1.97%	2.02%	2.00%	2.09%	2.10%
	EXP share	2.2848%	2.3104%	2.2320%	1.9945%	2.0038%	2.1356%	1.9652%	1.9258%	2.1067%	2.1535%	2.1866%	2.2411%	2.1347%
HKG	*AD*	0.79%	1.26%	0.96%	0.85%	0.54%	0.32%	0.73%	0.91%	0.00%	0.00%	1.09%	1.04%	1.71%
	CVD	0.00%	0.00%	0.00%	0.00%	0.00%	0.00%	0.00%	0.00%	0.00%	0.00%	0.00%	0.00%	0.00%
	WTO share	NA	NA	NA	NA	NA	NA	3.61%	3.35%	3.17%	3.19%	3.12%	3.05%	3.03%
	EXP share	3.3589%	3.3434%	3.3608%	3.1736%	3.0473%	3.1411%	3.0840%	3.1066%	3.0132%	2.8788%	2.7814%	2.6605%	2.4918%
KOR	*AD*	5.56%	4.60%	7.69%	8.55%	11.02%	7.62%	6.05%	7.29%	6.99%	9.47%	5.98%	5.18%	8.57%

(continued)

Table 12.1 (continued)

Country		*1995*	*1996*	*1997*	*1998*	*1999*	*2000*	*2001*	*2002*	*2003*	*2004*	*2005*	*2006*	*2007*
	CVD	0.00%	0.00%	0.00%	22.73%	8.89%	4.35%	4.17%	20.00%	0.00%	11.11%	0.00%	12.50%	0.00%
	WTO share	NA	NA	NA	NA	NA	NA	2.55%	2.38%	2.37%	2.41%	2.39%	2.46%	2.53%
	EXP share	2.4159%	2.3972%	2.4316%	2.4014%	2.5106%	2.6697%	2.4283%	2.4996%	2.5535%	2.7520%	2.7080%	2.6836%	2.6495%
JPN	*AD*	6.35%	4.18%	5.77%	6.41%	8.60%	3.81%	3.63%	5.47%	6.99%	4.12%	4.89%	4.66%	2.86%
	CVD	0.00%	0.00%	0.00%	0.00%	0.00%	0.00%	0.00%	0.00%	0.00%	0.00%	0.00%	0.00%	0.00%
	WTO share	NA	NA	NA	NA	NA	NA	7.16%	6.63%	6.36%	6.40%	6.13%	5.95%	5.78%
	EXP share	8.5604%	7.5942%	7.5174%	7.0407%	7.3274%	7.4279%	6.5129%	6.4112%	6.2162%	6.1327%	5.6646%	5.3325%	5.0946%

Country		*2008*	*2009*	*2010*	*2011*	*2012*	*2013*	*2014*	*2015*	*2016*	*2017*	*2018*	*2019*
CHN	*AD*	36.00%	37.50%	33.82%	29.49%	30.30%	24.90%	29.47%	28.10%	NA	NA	NA	NA
	CVD	68.75%	44.83%	46.67%	36.00%	40.91%	44.12%	33.33%	29.03%	NA	NA	NA	NA
	WTO share	5.39%	5.90%	6.45%	6.88%	7.29%	7.70%	8.14%	8.62%	9.17%	9.59%	9.84%	10.10%
	EXP share	8.8592%	9.5699%	10.3103%	10.3512%	11.0662%	11.6566%	12.3232%	13.7322%	13.0749%	12.7601%	12.7732%	13.2302%
MYS	*AD*	4.44%	3.13%	2.94%	1.28%	1.82%	3.07%	4.35%	1.24%	NA	NA	NA	NA
	CVD	6.25%	3.45%	6.67%	0.00%	0.00%	2.94%	2.78%	0.00%	NA	NA	NA	NA
	WTO share	1.23%	1.20%	1.79%	1.15%	1.14%	1.04%	1.12%	1.12%	1.12%	1.07%	1.03%	1.01%
	EXP share	1.2348%	1.2523%	1.2979%	1.2437%	1.2291%	1.2049%	1.2307%	1.2078%	1.1827%	1.2298%	1.2711%	1.2610%
THA	*AD*	4.89%	3.57%	3.68%	4.49%	4.24%	6.51%	3.86%	1.24%	NA	NA	NA	NA
	CVD	0.00%	3.45%	0.00%	8.00%	0.00%	2.94%	2.78%	0.00%	NA	NA	NA	NA

Country		2008	2009	2010	2011	2012	2013	2014	2015	2016	2017	2018	2019
	WTO share	1.03%	1.04%	1.05%	1.07%	1.09%	1.10%	1.13%	1.18%	1.21%	1.21%	1.22%	1.23%
	EXP share	1.1008%	1.2139%	1.2632%	1.2136%	1.2375%	1.2058%	1.1967%	1.2945%	1.3425%	1.3341%	1.2993%	1.3037%
TWN	*AD*	4.44%	7.14%	2.94%	6.41%	9.70%	5.75%	5.80%	4.13%	NA	NA	NA	NA
	CVD	0.00%	0.00%	0.00%	0.00%	0.00%	2.94%	2.78%	3.23%	NA	NA	NA	NA
	WTO share	1.85%	1.80%	1.75%	1.67%	1.61%	1.57%	1.55%	1.54%	1.53%	1.54%	1.73%	1.73%
	EXP share	1.5829%	1.6221%	1.7945%	1.6808%	1.6551%	1.6434%	1.6841%	1.7235%	1.7473%	1.7886%	1.7254%	1.7504%
SGP	*AD*	0.00%	0.45%	0.74%	0.00%	0.61%	0.38%	2.42%	0.00%	NA	NA	NA	NA
	CVD	0.00%	0.00%	0.00%	0.00%	0.00%	0.00%	0.00%	0.00%	NA	NA	NA	NA
	WTO share	2.14%	2.16%	2.17%	2.20%	2.25%	2.27%	2.31%	2.36%	2.41%	2.42%	2.44%	2.44%
	EXP share	2.0941%	2.1490%	2.2994%	2.2329%	2.2060%	2.1648%	2.1854%	2.1237%	2.0599%	2.1054%	2.1212%	2.0688%
HKG	*AD*	1.78%	0.89%	0.00%	0.64%	0.00%	0.00%	0.00%	0.41%	NA	NA	NA	NA
	CVD	0.00%	0.00%	0.00%	0.00%	0.00%	0.00%	0.00%	0.00%	NA	NA	NA	NA
	WTO share	2.94%	2.85%	2.75%	2.63%	2.61%	2.57%	2.53%	2.55%	2.62%	2.64%	2.68%	2.78%

(continued)

Table 12.1 (continued)

Country		*2008*	*2009*	*2010*	*2011*	*2012*	*2013*	*2014*	*2015*	*2016*	*2017*	*2018*	*2019*
	EXP share	2.2926%	2.6236%	2.6184%	2.4841%	2.6625%	2.8260%	2.7575%	3.0834%	3.2203%	3.1000%	2.9199%	2.8318%
KOR	*AD*	4.89%	3.57%	4.41%	7.05%	10.30%	9.58%	8.21%	7.44%	NA	NA	NA	NA
	CVD	0.00%	3.45%	0.00%	4.00%	4.55%	2.94%	11.11%	9.68%	NA	NA	NA	NA
	WTO share	2.54%	2.59%	2.64%	2.69%	2.73%	2.77%	2.83%	2.88%	3.01%	3.04%	3.03%	2.96%
	EXP share	2.6132%	2.8953%	3.0477%	3.0274%	2.9593%	2.9531%	3.0151%	3.1817%	3.0881%	3.2343%	3.1069%	2.8707%
JPN	*AD*	1.33%	2.23%	3.68%	3.21%	3.64%	5.36%	3.38%	4.13%	NA	NA	NA	NA
	CVD	0.00%	0.00%	0.00%	0.00%	0.00%	0.00%	0.00%	0.00%	NA	NA	NA	NA
	WTO share	5.52%	5.30%	5.11%	4.96%	4.79%	4.61%	4.53%	4.49%	4.34%	4.27%	4.14%	4.04%
	EXP share	4.8387%	4.6250%	5.0303%	4.4885%	4.3135%	3.7709%	3.6313%	3.7747%	4.0207%	3.9370%	3.7915%	3.7352%

also highlight similar differences between Singapore and Korea. In case of Japan, there have been significant changes in its industrial policy since the 1990s crisis years. Firms rely less on the government (Callon 1995), and the Japanese economy have become more open (Ozawa 2007). These changes might be responsible for the fact, that in case of these countries, both AD and CVD case percentage values are less, than their share in global trade most of the time.

In case of all the other countries, the situation is different. In case of countries, where the AD and CVD values are quite a lot higher, than their share in global trade, that suggest, they do not fit that well into the world trading system. This is somewhat in line with the intuition based on the traditional role of industrial and trade policy in the developmental state model, and also, based on some issues with intellectual property right enforcement. The case of Thailand and Malaysia is a little bit surprising, as, especially the former, is well embedded into global supply chains (see Baldwin 2016 on the case on the automotive sector). However, state-owned enterprises, and the role of the elite working together with the government, is very important in the local economy, just as the developmental state model suggests (Hundt and Uttam 2017).

We can see, that in case of Taiwan and Korea the situation is very similar, though, in case of Korea the case of countervailing duties is more frequent. This is in line with the traditional developmental state narrative. However, the most striking numbers can be found in the case of China. And though, in 2015 a small improvement is visible from our graph, the situation is more complex, than this.

In case of China, another, specific safety valve could be used in the past, called "Transitional Product-Specific Safeguard Mechanism." Safeguards are generally to be used sectoral, should there be any unforeseen large increase in imports of a specific product. Hence, for us, they are not useful, as no countries, but products are addressed by them. However, during the Chinese accession, as China was not (and still isn't) considered as a market economy, after accession there was a 13-year-long transition period introduced, during which special safeguard could be used against it. Interestingly, not many safeguards were invoked (32 cases altogether) under this possibility, mostly Latin-American countries and the US used this possibility (Bown 2016c). This is maybe because, as Cai and Kim (2016) show, Chinese non-market economy status automatically caused a higher number of AD and CVD measures. Prusa and Vermlust (2013) even highlight through a case study, that, especially the US used AD and CVD measures parallel in the same industry, that the WTO ruled against.

Regarding dispute settlement, the picture is also worrying. As Wu (2016: 263) puts this analyzing statistics of WTO Dispute Settlement Mechanism's cases: "since the Great Recession, the pattern of WTO cases among the major trading powers—the United States, the European Union, Japan, and China—has shifted dramatically. Until the mid-2000s, the three major advanced economies (the United States, the EU, and Japan) regularly brought cases against one another. But since 2009, disputes among these established powers have virtually come to a halt. Only three such complaints have been filed, and only one has proceeded to requiring that a WTO Panel be constituted." And that "WTO disputes among major powers almost exclusively involve China. Between 2009 and 2015, China-related cases accounted for 90% of the cases brought by the 4 largest economies against each other. China's rise is thus reconfiguring WTO dispute settlement in a potentially worrying manner." In the WTO's database, there are 44 cases listed, with China as a respondent, while 16 cases are listed where Japan; 19, where Korea; 1, where Malaysia; 4, where Thailand is respondent. No other countries investigated by this chapter have had any DSM cases launched against (WTO Dispute Settlement Gateway) (Table 12.1).

Conclusion

In this chapter, we tried to show, whether East and South East Asian developmental states fit the global multilateral trading regime. We defined this as compliance with the WTO rules, and tried to measure it using anti-dumping and countervailing duties databases. We found that most previously defined developmental states seem not to comply with WTO rules as strong as others. The largest outlier from the system seems to be China. Based on these results, we might conclude, that the global trading system could not accommodate this type of institutional setup, and therefore, changes in this relationship might be required. In his analysis Bown (2007) also concludes, that while China had faced large discrimination before its WTO membership, this did not change significantly after the membership.

However, one must acknowledge, that while these problems might undermine the global trading system, there are other distortions too.

In example, especially developed countries cause trouble with their agricultural subsidies, that are also heavily disputed by developing countries, including many Asian economies (Hopewell 2019).

For further research there are two possible directions: one, immediate follow up may be a deeper investigation of the AD and CVD cases, in order to understand the motivation behind them: are they really invoked because of "unfair trade practices," or rather because of domestic political causes? This can be further continued by analyzing the outcome and further history of these measure. Our result can be also interpreted within the "club model" debate. According to this, the trading system (at least, as it is designed), should lead to convergence of various institutional models, or within varieties of capitalisms. Therefore, an interesting line of research can be continued, if there is a further need for institutional convergence (Hoekman and Kostecki [2001] discuss this in details, mostly focusing on non-tariff barriers), or whether it is the trading system, that should be re-designed to incorporate these differences (Rodrik 2017). We do not want to take sides on this matter, but it seems, a decision has to be made.

References

Amsden, Alice (1989): *Asia's Next Giant. South Korea and Late Industrialization*. Oxford University Press, New York

Baldwin, Richard (2016): *The Great Convergence. Information Technology and the New Globalization*. Harvard University Press, Cambridge

Beeson, Mark (2009): "Developmental States in East Asia: A Comparison of the Japanese and Chinese Experiences." *Asian Perspective* 33 (2): 5–39

Blonigen, Bruce A., and Prusa, Thomas J. (2015): "Dumping and Antidumping Duties." *NBER Working Paper* 21573

Bown, Chad P. (2005): "Participation in WTO Dispute Settlement: Complainants, Interested Parties, and Free Riders." *The World Bank Economic Review* 19 (2): 287–310

Bown, Chad P. (2007): "China's WTO Entry: Antidumping, Safeguards, and Dispute Settlement." *NBER Working Paper* 13349

Bown, Chad P. (2016a): "Global Antidumping Database." The World Bank

Bown, Chad P. (2016b): "Global Countervailing Duties Database." The World Bank

Bown, Chad P. (2016c): "China-Specific Safeguards Database." The World Bank

Bown, Chad P. (2017): "Rogue 301: Trump to Dust Off another Outdated US Trade Law?" Peterson Institute for International Economics, Trade and Investment Watch https://www.piie.com/blogs/trade-investment-policy-watch/rogue-301-trump-dust-another-outdated-us-trade-law Last access: July 28th, 2020

Bown, Chad P. (2018): "Donald Trump's Solar and Washer Tariffs May Have Now Opened the Floodgates of Protectionism." *The Washington Post*, January 23, 2018

Bown, Chad P., and Hillman, Jennifer A. (2019): "WTO'ing a Resulotion to the China Subsidy Problem." *Peterson Institute for International Economics Working Paper* 19–17

Bown, Chad P., and Kolb, Melinda (2020): *Trump's Trade War Timeline: An Up-to-Date Guide*. Peterson Institute for International Economics https://www.piie.com/sites/default/files/documents/trump-trade-war-timeline.pdf Last access: July 28th, 2020

Cai, Yan and Kim, Eun-Mi (2016): "Analyzing China's Non-market Economy Status: A Focus on Anti-dumping Measures." *Journal of International Trade & Commerce* 12 (4): 131–150

Callon, Scott (1995): *Divided Sun: MITI and the Breakdown of Japanese High-Tech Industrial Policy*. Stanford University Press, Stanford

Chang, Ha-Joon and Andreoni, Antonio (2020): "Industrial Policy in the 21st Century." *Development and Change* 51 (2): 324–351 https://doi.org/10.1111/dech.12570

Du, Ming (2014): "China's State Capitalism and World Trade Law." *The International and Comparative Law Quarterly* 63 (2): 409–448

Eichengreen, Barry (2011): *Exorbitant Privilege: The Rise and Fall of the Dollar and the Future of the International Monetary System*. Oxford University Press, Oxford

Evans, Peter (1995.): *Embedded Autonomy. States & Industrial Transformation*. Princeton University Press, Princeton

Gallagher, Kevin P. (ed) (2005): *Putting Development First. The Importance of Policy Space in the WTO and International Financial Institutions*. Zed Books, London and New York

Gallagher, Kevin P. (2008): "Understanding Developing Country Resistance to the Doha Round." *Review of International Political Economy* 15 (1): 62–85

Gilpin, Robert (2001): *Global Political Economy: Understanding the International Economic Order*. Princeton University Press, Princeton

Hall, P and Soskice, D (2001): *Varieties of Capitalism: The Institutional Foundations of Comparative Advantage*. Oxford University Press, Oxford

Hoekman, Bernard M., and Kostecki, Michel M. (2001): *The Political Economy of the World Trading System* Oxford University Press, Oxford

Hoekman, B., Mattoo, A., and English, P. (2002): *Development, Trade and the WTO*. The World Bank, Washington DC

Hopewell, Kristen (2019): "US-China Conflict in Global Trade Governance: The New Politics of Agricultural Subsidies at the WTO." *Review of International Political Economy* 26 (2): 207–231

Horn, Henrik, Mavroidis, Petros C., and Sapir, Andre (2009): "Beyond the WTO? An Anatomy of EU and US Preferential Trade Agreements." *Bruegel Blueprint Series, Volume VII.* https://www.bruegel.org/wp-content/uploads/imported/publications/bp_trade_jan09.pdf Last access: November 8th, 2020

Hundt, D., and Uttam, J. (2017): *Varieties of Capitalism in Asia: Beyond the Developmental State.* Palgrave Macmillan, London

Ianchovichina, Elena and Walmsley, Terrie (2003): "Impact of China's WTO Accession on East Asia." *World Bank Policy Research Working Paper* 3109

Jain, Romi (2016): "China's Compliance with the WTO: A Critical Examination." *Indian Journal of Asian Affairs* 29 (1/2) 57–84

Johnson, Chalmers (1982): *MITI and the Japanese Miracle.* Stanford University Press, Stanford

Keohane, Robert O., and Nye, Joseph S. Jr. (2001): "The Club Model of Multilateral Cooperation and Problems of Democratic Legitimacy." In: Keohane, R. O. (eds.) (2002): *Power and Governance in a Partially Globalized World.* Routledge, London and New York

Krasner, Stephen D. (1982): "Structural Causes and Regime Consequences: Regimes as Intervening Variables." *International Organization* 36 (2): 185–205

Kucik, Jeffrey and Reinhardt, Eric (2008): "Does Flexibility Promotes Cooperation? An Application to the Global Trade Regime." *International Organization* 62 (3): 477–505

Leftwich, A. (1995): "Bringing Politics Back In: Towards a Model of the Developmental State." *Journal of Development Studies* 31(3): 400–427

Mavroidis, Petros C., and Sapir, Andre (2019): "China and the World Trade Organization: Towards a Better Fit." *Bruegel Working Paper*, Issue 06

Newfarmer, Richard (ed) (2006): *Trade, Doha, and Development.* The World Bank, Washington DC

Nölke, Andreas (2014): *Multinational Corporations from Emerging Markets: State Capitalism 3.0.* Palgrave Macmillan, Hamphire

Nölke, Andreas, Ten Brink, Tobias, May, Christian, and Claar, Simone (2019): *State-Permeated Capitalism in Large Emerging Economies.* Routledge, New York.

Ozawa, Terutomo (2007): "Institutionally Driven Growth and Stagnation—and Struggle for Reform." In: Bailey, David, Coffey, David, and Tomlinson, Phil (eds.) (2007): *Crisis or Recovery in Japan.* Edward Elgar, Cheltenham

Prusa, Thomas J., and Vermulst, Edwin (2013): "United States—Definitive Anti-Dumping and Countervailing Duties on Certain Products from China: Passing the Buck on Pass-Through." *World Trade Review* 12 (2): 197–234
Rodrik, Dani (2004): *Industrial Policy for the Twenty-First Century*. https://drodrik.scholar.harvard.edu/publications/industrial-policy-twenty-first-century Last access: July 28th, 2020
Rodrik, Dani (2017): *Straight Talk on Trade: Ideas for a Sane World Economy*. Princeton University Press, Princeton
Ruggie, John G. (1982): "International Regimes, Transactions, and Change: Embedded Liberalism in the Postwar Economic Order." *International Organization* 36 (2): 379–415.
Ruta, Michele (2017): "Preferential Trade Agreements and Global Value Chains. Theory, Evidence, and Open Questions." *Policy Research Working Paper* 8190, World Bank, Washington DC
Shin, Jang-Sup (2005): "Globalization and Challenges to the Developmental State: A Comparison Between South Korea and Singapore." *Global Economic Review* 34 (4) 379–395
Stiglitz, Joseph E., and Charlton, Andrew (2005): *Fair Trade for All. How Trade Can Promote Development*. Oxford University Press, New York
Stubbs, Richard (2005): *Rethinking Asia's Economic Miracle*. Palgrave, New York
Toohey, Lisa (2011): "China and the World Trade Organization: The First Decade." *The International and Comparative Law Quarterly* 60 (3): 788–798
UNCTAD website: https://unctadstat.unctad.org/wds/ReportFolders/reportFolders.aspx
Van den Bossche, Peter, and Zdouc, Werner (2017): *The Law and Policy of the World Trade Organization. Text, Cases and Materials*. 4th Edition. Cambridge University Press, Cambridge
Vigvári, Gábor (2012): *Globalizáció és a fejlesztő állam. A nemzetközi regimek változásának hatása a fejlesztő államra. (Globalization and the Developmental State. The Effects of Changing International Regimes on the Developmental State)* Ph.D. dissertation, Corvinus University of Budapest
Wade, Robert (1990): *Governing the Market: Economic Theory and the Role of Government in East Asian Industrialization*. Princeton University Press, Princeton
World Bank (1993): *The East Asian Miracle: Economic Growth and Public Policy*. Oxford University Press, Oxford
WTO Dispute Settlement Gateway: https://www.wto.org/english/tratop_e/dispu_e/dispu_e.htm
WTO website on the budget: https://www.wto.org/english/thewto_e/secre_e/budget_e.htm
WTO website on the SCM Agreement: https://www.wto.org/english/tratop_e/scm_e/subs_e.htm

Wu, Mark (2016): "The "China, Inc." Challenge to Global Trade Governance." *Harvard International Law Journal* 57 (2) 261–324

Zysman, John (1983): *Governments, Markets and Growth: Financial Systems and the Politics of Industrial Change*. Cornell University Press, Ithaca

CHAPTER 13

Development and Trade Policy in North Africa

Tamás Szigetvári

Introduction

Since the 1980s, many developing countries started economic restructuring and an opening up towards global markets, following partly the receipt of the ruling neoliberal economic theory. Export-orientation and gradual trade opening, however, have also been a core element of East Asian success stories. In these classical Developmental State (DS) models, an active state involvement has supported the trade opening. In case of North African countries (Morocco, Tunisia and Egypt) the results of this process were mostly ambiguous, however, especially regarding the social consequences. Being strongly connected to the EU economy, these countries have signed free trade agreements to create better access to

T. Szigetvári (✉)
Institute of International and Political Studies, Pázmány Péter Catholic University, Budapest, Hungary
e-mail: szigetvari.tamas@krtk.hu

Centre for Economic and Regional Studies, Institute of World Economics, Budapest, Hungary

T. Gerőcs and J. Ricz (eds.), *The Post-Crisis Developmental State*, International Political Economy Series,
https://doi.org/10.1007/978-3-030-71987-6_13

the European Single Market, but they were gradually opening up their economies to a growing competition as well.

The chapter examines trade opening in North Africa and presents the impacts of these agreements on North African economies and societies. It puts the trade opening in its domestic political economic environment: why governing elites and insiders were interested in the liberalisation process, and how they were able to transform trade policy reforms in their own interest. The chapter is structured as follows. In the first part we look at North Africa's position in the global economy, and the restructuring efforts of the last several decades. Then we discuss the role of trade opening in development, and the specificities and impacts of the process in North Africa. Finally, we investigate the institutional set-up of development and trade opening, based on a DS and VoC approach.

North Africa in the Global Periphery

While up to the fourteenth–fifteenth centuries the Mediterranean was one of the core economic poles of the world economy, North Africa, and the entire Mediterranean region was gradually pushed from its central position to the periphery (Findlay and O'Rourke 2007: 132). First it became the South Western periphery of the Ottoman Empire, then, from the nineteenth century onwards the European colonizers—Britain, France, Italy—took over the rule over the region. The countries that gradually became independent during the twentieth century (Egypt, Tunisia, Morocco, Algeria and Libya) tried to establish functioning economic structures similarly to other developing countries, with more or less success. Similarly to Latin American countries, they adopted import-substitution industrialization mostly accompanied by high tariffs and other protectionist measures, and a dominant state ownership.

From the 1960s most countries of North Africa experienced robust economic growth. The oil price explosion in the early 1970s brought with it the beginning of a new golden decade for the entire Arab world. Even countries that did not have significant exploitable oil resources could benefit indirectly (inter-Arab aid, remittances from guest workers). It is not surprising, then, that between 1960 and 1980, the countries of the region came to the forefront of the world in terms of economic growth: the pace of economic growth was at the same level or even higher than in East Asia. High levels of investment in physical capital that facilitated substantial increases in per capita income (Yousef 2004: 91). The states of the region were burning in the fever of modernisation: they began with huge infrastructure investments, creating industries from scratch in most places.

For countries with large populations, industrial development was a necessity, but compared to other developing countries, there was ample funding for the programme due to oil-related revenues. While without windfall revenues Latin American and Asian countries were forced to undergo fundamental structural reforms in the mid-to-late 1970s, Arab countries were still able to weave ambitious plans for their economies to flourish. Authoritarian regimes were more durable due to massive exogenous revenues (Glasser 1995: 49).

When the price of crude oil began to fall sharply in the mid-1980s, the source of income previously thought indelible had disappeared at once. Most Middle East And North African (MENA) states were forced into economic reforms in the mid- and late 1980s (Yousef 2004: 98). Economic growth has been dampened by several factors. Although the decline in external income inflows was more pronounced for oil-producing countries, it affected all countries in the region: remittances from Arab guest workers employed in oil-producing countries have declined, together with inter-Arab aid flows. In contrast to Asian developmental states, in Arab countries the level of domestic savings has traditionally been low, and investment has been hampered by a lack of resources: due to the uncertain economic situation and the lack of a proper domestic financial system, a significant part of these savings has flowed abroad (Richards and Waterbury 2007). At the same time, the region has never been particularly attractive to foreign capital (excluding oil and gas production), most countries have been dominated by state ownership and overly bureaucratic procedures, privatisation has been delayed, and investors have seen high political risk high in many places. The products of the Arab economies were not competitive on the international market. As a result of the Dutch disease, despite unemployment, the cost of factors of production was relatively high. The production structure was not diversified, the internal market was artificially closed to the world market. Showing a high similarity to Latin American models, Arab countries were generally characterised by an opaque customs structure, high tariffs and other protectionist measures. The system was also a breeding ground for corruption due to the uncertainties it contained. Moreover, all this has not only affected importers and those wishing to invest, but also severely reduced the international competitiveness of domestic producers who used imported products in production.

Since the 1980s growth rates in the region have been volatile and low relative to other developing countries (Abed and Davoudi 2003). With a high population growth rate in the region, per capita national income has stagnated or barely increased in many countries. The rapid growth of the population and the economy has increased the demand for food and other imports, necessitating the construction of health and other infrastructures, the maintenance of which has encountered serious difficulties with the depletion of the source of income. In addition to declining living standards, rising unemployment created further problems, the economy was unable to provide employment to the large number of young people entering the labour market year after year, which resulted in growing social tensions. Due to growing fiscal imbalances most countries of the region had to start with fundamental economic restructuring programmes after the 1980s, mostly based on a neoliberal recipe.

Economic Reforms

States without rents such as Morocco and Tunisia were forced to start reforms and restructure their economies earlier (in 1983 and 1986, respectively), than Egypt (1991) (Glasser 1995: 60). In the case of Morocco, economic reforms have sought to develop knowledge-based sectors and to create jobs. The reforms resulted in a growth of 4–5% in the 2000s that was not only higher than the average of previous years, but also much more balanced, less and less dependent on fluctuations in agricultural production (see Table 13.1). By Tunisia, we can speak of similarly successful years of reforms, mostly after the Millennium. Economic restructuring has more or less taken place, productivity growth (TFP) has improved the country's competitiveness and the amount of foreign capital investment in the country has increased. However, the good economic results (here as well) have also been overshadowed by growing social tensions and persistent unemployment (especially among young people).

In Egypt, reform efforts, accompanied by economic restructuring, began in the 1990s, and were given a new impetus in 2004. As a result, significant liberalisation has been implemented in the economy, the general tariff level has been reduced, the business environment has been

Table 13.1 Some development indicators in North African countries

	Average annual GDP growth 2000–2009	*Average annual GDP growth 2010–2019*	*GDP per capita 2000*	*GDP per capita 2019*	*HDI 2000*	*HDI 2018*	*Trade, in percentage of GDP 2000*	*Trade, in percentage of GDP 2019*
Algeria	3.9	2.7	3558	4710	0.65	0.76	62	52
Egypt	5.0	3.6	1980	3009	0.61	0.70	39	52
Libya	4.6	6.2*	8964	8122	0.73	0.71	45	118
Morocco	4.8	3.4	1976	3396	0.53	0.68	59	87
Tunisia	4.3	1.9	3001	4405	0.66	0.81	82	110

Source World bank dataset, own calculations

*Due to an abnormal volatility of the annual growth rate (e.g. −62% in 2011, +123% in 2012) the data is not relevant

improved and corporate tax has been reduced from 40 to 20%. In addition, many state-owned companies have been privatised. The reforms have had economic results, and Egypt has been one of the best-performing Arab states after 2005. Confidence in the country has increased, and the inflow of foreign capital has picked up. Economic growth increased from 3–4% in the early 2000s to 6–7% after 2005 (World Bank dataset).

Algeria and Libya had much larger oil-revenues, but the "reverse" oil shock of the mid-1980s affected the two countries even more dramatically. While Algeria has started with ambitious political and economic reforms, it has turned backward due to unexpected consequences of the opening (Akacem 2004: 120), Qaddafi's Libya offered an even more specific case in the region, it started gradual economic opening and reforms only after 1999, when the UN suspended its decade-long sanctions against the country (St. John 2008: 75).

All in all, we can say that promising reform processes have begun in most North African countries, which, although extremely slow in the 1990s, has gained new momentum since the 2000s and allowed for a relatively significant rate of economic growth in those countries. However, the macroeconomic indicators and external account balances may have improved, this has not been the case as far as microeconomic circumstances are concerned (Joffé 2011: 508). In almost all countries, serious social tensions have arisen, which have become an increasingly difficult task for the political leaders to deal with. Although the growth rate of economic output has barely slowed in the years of the global crisis, growing political, social and economic tensions have become increasingly apparent in the background.

Though indirectly, the global financial crisis in 2008 played a fundamental role in the outburst and spreading of protests across the region (Talani 2014: 14). The previously functioning system collapsed unexpectedly in early 2011. At the start of the riots, the first reaction from all governments was as usual: an increase in wages, social benefits and price subsidies. Algeria, which had significant resources to mobilise, was able to prevent major social discontent. In the case of Morocco, it was not so much economic as political concessions that dominated. Egypt and Tunisia, however, have sought to apply a mixture of repression, economic instruments and political concessions, without success. The previously proven authoritarian bargain worked no longer. Partly because the governments could not provide the masses with a decent livelihood (work, a decent income, or, in their absence, low prices for necessities). On the other hand, because the bargain was unacceptable to the younger (more informed) generations anyway, and it was incompatible with their ideas of freedom, dignity, and social justice. Authoritarian regimes could not maintain their legitimacy, and they failed. However, this did not result in a process of democratisation, as many in the Western world expected, rather in a rise of Islamic movements (Egypt, partly Tunisia and Libya), anarchy and civil war (Libya), or a return to the authoritarian bargain (Egypt, Algeria, Morocco).

Today North Africa's economic outlooks are not bright. Unemployment has barely declined in recent years, youth employment is still among the highest in the world. The participation of women in the labour market is historically low. The income difference compared to EU countries is increasing, especially since the Arab Spring (Dadush and Myachenkova 2018). The HDI indicator, which reflects changes in living standards better than GDP, has remained low and barely improved.

North Africa was, and still is relatively weakly integrated to the world economy. The region receives much lower amounts of FDI expected for a developing country of comparable size, and most is concentrated in a handful of countries. Portfolio investment is virtually nonexistent because of the poor state of development of equity markets.

While in East Asian models, export-orientation and a gradual trade opening was able to integrate these countries to the world economy, North Africa (and the whole Middle Eastern region) was experiencing a growing peripheralization from the global political economy (Talani 2014: 235). Indicators of integration, such as the level and share of global FDIs, the number and values of mergers and acquisitions, or the performance of exports and trade openness, all indicate a growing peripheralization of the area. The latter is all the more interesting since trade opening was one of the core elements of neoliberal reforms in these countries. What happened then?

Trade Opening and Its Consequences

Concerning the role of international trade in economic development, there are two fundamentally different approaches. While mainstream economics considers trade openness as a fundamental element of a successful economic catch-up process, critics reflect on the risks and negative consequences of the process.

The importance of international trade as a catalyst for economic growth and national development is widely recognised today. However, as Rodrik (1999) states, openness by itself is not a reliable mechanism to generate sustained economic growth, it will likely exert pressures that widen income and wealth disparities within countries, and openness will leave countries vulnerable to external shocks that can trigger domestic conflicts and political upheavals (Rodrik 1999: 13–14). Furthermore, in recent years it has become increasingly clear that many developing and least developed countries face significant supply-side constraints that prevent them from participating effectively in the international trading system (Grainger and McLinden 2013: 877).

With the slow-down of multilateral trade negotiations under WTO-umbrella, there is a growing popularity of bilateral and regional FTAs. Advanced economies such as the EU, the US, Japan, or Canada started to negotiate free trade agreements with each other (TTIP, CETA, EU-Japan EPA, TPP), and with emerging and developing economies. The global FTA network was not only extended but so was the agenda of the agreements, with an ever-growing appetite for complexity and regulatory issues beyond tariffs for trade in goods (Meissner 2018). Recent agreements often include services, and FTAs across rather than within world regions are on the rise. Despite decreasing average global tariff rates, tariffs still matters: many countries have high tariffs, and countries with low tariff averages often have "sensitive" sectors with high tariffs (ibid.: 12). Still, regional agreements are today less about preferential tariffs than they used to be and more about other market access tools, economic cooperation, and even non-economic dimensions (Maur 2013: 537). The EU and the US aim to establish the core for future global standards which will spill over to other trade relations due to the economic pull of these mega-regional trade agreements, and the negotiating leverage of the EU and the US (Griller et al. 2017: 8).

Although the trade regimes of North African countries continue to be ranked among the most protective, they are more liberal than in the past. Trade liberalisation has progressed, trade reforms following WTO membership, as well as bilateral and regional trade agreements have cut tariff rates significantly (Dadush and Myachenkova 2018). While for the export oriented East Asian countries the US market has provided a good opportunity, the EU as an economic pole and as a dominant trade partner for the North African region might have paly a similar role (Mevel et al. 2016: 597).

A massive wave of trade liberalisations in North Africa started with the initiation of the EU's new Mediterranean policy in the 1990s. Created in 1995, the Euro-Mediterranean Partnership (EMP) provides a framework for the EU to conclude Association Agreements (AAs) with the Southern Mediterranean countries. The EMP was built upon three pillars: political, economic, and cultural cooperation. The economic pillar of the association agreements gave rise to FTAs with the individual countries rather than the region, so the originally envisioned Euro-Mediterranean Free Trade Area has never actually been created. Tunisia (1995), Morocco (1996), Egypt (2001), and Algeria (2002) signed Association Agreements with the EU.

The European Union (EU) is a pivotal player in international trade relations, holding formidable power in trade but also capable of exercising substantial power through trade. Trade policy therefore represents a strategic field for the EU to shape its image as a healthy economy and an ethical trade power. As Poletti and Sicurelli (2018) put it, the EU is an actor committed to using trade agreements in order to promote norms such as economic liberalism, sustainable development, and human rights on a global level (Poletti and Sicurelli 2018: 2).

A closer look at the trade relations of the North African countries and the EU over the past period reveals that the high expectations of FTAs' positive impacts have not been fulfilled. The region's position in bilateral trade has markedly deteriorated (see Table 13.2). While up to 2007, the region had a positive trade balance overall, mostly due to fossil

Table 13.2 Goods trade between the EU-28 and North African countries, in 2007 and in 2018

	Imports from the EU-28 million euro		*Exports to the EU-28 million euro*		*Trade balance million euro*	
	2007	*2018*	*2007*	*2018*	*2007*	*2018*
Algeria	11,270	18,911	20,585	20,990	9315	2079
Egypt	10,343	19,210	7039	8502	−3304	−10,708
Libya	4228	4521	27,401	16,785	23,173	12,264
Morocco	12,380	23,250	8115	16,071	−4265	−7179
Tunisia	9552	11,634	8991	10,139	−561	−1495

Source Eurostat

export in Libya and Algeria. After 2008, however, the North African positions in bilateral trade balance started to worsen. While the EU's export towards the region almost doubled, North African export developments were less convincing: the Arab Spring and subsequent political events slashed exports in Tunisia, Egypt, and Libya, with improvements starting only in recent years.

Trading in services generates a positive balance for the Southern Mediterranean countries primarily thanks to tourism, but the surplus is way below the deficit in the trading of goods and does little to offset the deficit in overall trade with the EU. In addition, in recent years the Mediterranean surplus in the trade of services has shrunk as tourism has been declining as a result of the political instability of the region. It seems evident that trading with the European Union is vital for the Mediterranean states, primarily the North African countries. It is also beyond doubt that these countries would be unable to develop without strengthening their relations with the EU.

FTAs generated no breakthrough in the main export areas where the Southern Mediterranean countries would be competitive; in fact, changes in the multilateral regulation actually made their opportunities worse (De Ville and Reynaert 2010: 5).

Despite their favourable geographic location, the Southern Mediterranean businesses have not managed to become integrated into the global value chains of multinational companies, and are hardly successful on their own. The missing internal conditions (poor infrastructure, widespread but low level education) made firm-level competitiveness also hard to achieve. Still, there are a few positive examples in Tunisia, Morocco, or even Egypt, but they are rather exceptions than the general rule (Del Prete et al. 2016: 265).

Tunisia's economy was best prepared for the trade liberalisation, still, even in Tunisia the impacts were not entirely positive. Complicated administrative processes, the lack of foreign and domestic capital investments, poor economic policies were all among the causes. The international organisations and the EU—instead of strengthening competitiveness and the potential for economic growth—endorsed the enforcement of strict fiscal and exchange rate policy (Chemingui and Bchir 2012: 113). The lack of success of the European model of economic cooperation built on free trade in the Southern Mediterranean countries has other reasons as well. They include the political instability of the Mediterranean region, the EU's weaker commitment due to internal crises, absence of the liberalisation of services, and non-harmonisation of regulations (Borrell-Porta 2012: 15). These factors gave rise to the idea that renewing and deepening the agreements could enhance the positive impacts of free trade.

The so-called Deep and Comprehensive Free Trade Agreement (DCFTA) is similar to comprehensive free trade agreements but creates deeper relations with the EU. DCFTAs cover industry, agriculture, and services, and also include extensive convergence towards EU standards in areas related to trade. Offered to neighbouring countries, DCFTAs practically make the countries concerned part of the single European market, as the neighbouring state is required to enshrine the EU's market regulations (regulation of competition, standards, trade regulations, etc.) in its own legislation.

The preliminary sustainability impact assessments (SIA) prepared for the European commission in 2013 and 2014 (Ecorys 2013a, b, 2014) analysed in detail the expectable economic, social, and environmental impacts of a DCFTA in the countries concerned. For example, the scenario developed for the DCFTA assumes that tariffs reduction on agricultural products between the EU and Tunisia will be 95% for Tunisian products entering the EU market and 80% for EU products entering the Tunisian market. As regards non-tariff measures, the potential impacts are assessed on a sectoral basis, and spill-over effects are also taken into account. The SIA concluded that a DCFTA could be successfully implemented with each of the four countries while also mentioned existing risks.

Comparing the four countries, it appears that Tunisia can realise the greatest economic benefit with a long-term GDP growth of over 7%. Interestingly, the expected economic benefit of Morocco, the other economy with close ties to the EU, is far below the envisioned Tunisian figure. The SIAs also conducted sector-specific analyses and highlighted which sectors would benefit and which would lose out as a result of the DCFTA. Although the impacts are different in the individual countries, the food industry generally appears to be a loser. While for grain and corps, and for animal products it may be true, conversely, the vegetables and the fruits sector as well as vegetable oils would be high-flying winners of the DCFTA in both Tunisia and Morocco. The textile and leather industries would generally fare poorly, but the Agreement would have highly positive impacts on the machine industry and some other manufacturing and processing industries.

As regards the social pillar, the impacts are expected to be multifarious. In general, the beneficial effect on the GDP and national income would entail wage increases. In Egypt the SIA prognosticates increase for only the higher and medium income groups, and the effect of the DCFTA on the lower income population would be rather negative. The costs of regulatory approximation required by the DCFTAs are extremely high and could only be offset by surplus income of an economy that has become competitive and is able to fully exploit the benefit of access to the single European market.

Based on past experience, the dynamic driver effect of free trade is highly questionable in regard to North African countries. This casts doubts as to whether the new model of deepening free trade is the best way to further develop relations between the EU and the North African countries.

EU officials maintain that the implementation of DCFTAs, in particular, will result in "win-win" outcomes for all concerned. Still, increased trade between the blocs upon tariff liberalisation, services liberalisation, and regulatory convergence, will mean more jobs and greater prosperity for peoples on either side of the Mediterranean Sea (Langan 2015: 1839).

Across various regional free trade area agreements concluded between the EU and its global partners, a common critique stresses upon the inability of these specific reforms in achieving equitable and sustainable growth, let alone improvement in sensitive social areas such as health, education, and broader developmental goals. On the contrary, they are perceived to be reinforcing the Union's hegemonic economic position in the world masked with a discourse built around the concepts of ownership, partnership, and cooperation (Knio 2013: 100). As Dreyer (2012: 52) notes, the EU is seeking to impose significant adjustment costs and higher prices on these economies, without obvious benefit for them. Still, from a theoretical approach the EU approach towards the region cannot be characterised as a purely neoliberal one. As Knio (2013) points out, there are several elements of the European policy that go well beyond a neoliberal market-oriented liberalisation receipt. It not only contains political and social baskets, but it delivers aid and other types of financial assistance as well, it allows protectionism in several sectors, and finally, it advocates a redefined role for the state where it intervenes in certain key areas (education, health, transport, and so on) to complement and strengthen market dynamics (Knio 2013: 105).

On the other hand, the normative drivers which ostensibly stand at the heart of European policy not only burden SMEs with costly criteria but in many cases dilute their comparative advantage vis-à-vis European counterparts (Langan 2015: 1839). And, more important from our aspect, the technocratic engineering of the EE has not yielded the results that policymakers expected due to the unchanged configuration of power in the domestic environment of both regions (Kourtelis 2015: 3). In the next part, we analyse this domestic environment in case of the North African countries, to see, how trade policy and the liberalisation process was influenced by the institutional setting and by the interests of local stakeholders.

Development and Trade Policy in the Arab VoC

After gaining independence, most Arab countries started ambitious state-building projects (Hertog 2019: 44). With underdeveloped infrastructures, and a low level of social and economic development, there was an urgent need for an active state involvement. While nationalist states pursued populist economic programmes with extensive nationalisation and subsidy regimes, in monarchies—formally following a different path—state-led development programmes with a high level of patronage were also common. Finally, however, Arab countries that initially adopted distinct economic strategies and political regimes ended up with variants of the same crony capitalist systems (Cammett and Diwan 2018: 24). The "Varieties of Capitalism" literature, inspired by the original ideas of Hall and Soskice (2001), tries to detect similarities of the coordination and of transactions of actors and institutions in the different economic systems (see also Yakovlev this volume). Based on several similarities among the institutional systems of Arab countries, the literature distinguishes a specific Arab variety of capitalism (Arab VoC) as well (e.g. Hertog 2019; Benner 2020).

The basic components of the Arab VoC consist of the following elements (based on Brenner 2020): (1) The government is the largest employer, and there are strong labour market regulations, (2) a widespread distribution of resources by state, (3) private sector is mostly dependent on government support and protection, (4) strong interest of insiders (cronies) resisting reform and change, (5) low cooperation and trust, (6) low-investment—low-skills equilibrium.

Insiders (cronies) are one of the most important common elements of Arab regimes. The uneven intervention of the government creates rents for insiders, who, on the other hand, are interested in regime stability. The tiny groups of cronies were the real winners of neoliberal restructuring in each countries. They have got ownership by most important industrial and service enterprises after privatisation that offered them further rents. These cronies were not only in a close connection with the ruling elites, but they had also played a primary role in foreign economic relations, and were partly interested in the trade opening process as well (see later). Foreign ownership remained low in most countries, and limited mostly to politically and economically less daunting sectors.

Concerning middle classes, though a new, market-oriented middle class rose in response to economic liberalisation (mostly small merchants and industrialists), who benefited from the pro-market reforms, but their importance and influence remained limited. Another, more influential group of middle classes were public servants. In most North African regimes, public servants compose the largest group of the middle class. Public servants, on the other hand, would have been the main losers of a radical neoliberal restructuring with a much smaller state bureaucracy.

In politics, the ferment of the ancient regimes became more and more noticeable. Although most regimes were able to hold executive power in their hands, they were forced to open up in more and more areas. The performance indicators of the government systems have clearly deteriorated, and corruption has become one of the most rejected elements of the political system for the North African population. The gap between the pro-power economic elites, enriched by privatisations, and the masses, losers of the reforms, has widened. The regimes struggled to maintain the old social contract, which had been built on the paternalistic promise (or autocratic bargain), in which large social-welfare expenditures and extensive public employment schemes served as compensation for limited political rights (Ricz 2019: 190).

Developmental State in North Africa?

In East Asia state-led development strategies resulted in a success, since these economies were able to develop mostly indigenously owned firms across a broad range of major global industries, and later integrate them to major GVCs, providing thus the base of a fast catching-up process. As Wade (2018) sums it up, the successful developmental state (DS) uses its powers to push production into sectors with increasing returns, keeping a large measure of ownership in private (national) hands and looking all the time for opportunities to replace sophisticated imports with domestic production. It deploys a wide range of instruments, including directed credit, fiscal investment incentives, or trade protection. Close state-business relations or even cronyism may also be part of this type of DS systems, as the case of South Korean chaebols illustrates it well. To the extent that they provide the right incentives to perform, close state-business relations can form the basis for a dynamic economic development.

Tight state-business relations within a supposedly "liberal" economic environment and political repression, however, did not translate into a successful industrial policy (Cammett and Diwan 2018: 24) Due mainly to institutional weaknesses and deep-rooting structural differences, an East-Asian-type developmental state is currently an unreasonable goal in North African countries (Cammett and Diwan 2018: 28).

Maybe Tunisia provided a case, where the state and bureaucracy was able to intervene in the economy to direct the reform efforts. It has displayed several elements of state-led development, where the centralised state was able to interact successfully with the private sector, and to intervene within the economic structure to promote development (Harrigen and El-Said 2009: 194). The state had an active industrial policy which involved picking and cultivating winning industries and then selling them off to the private sector (Harrigen and El-Said 2009: 192). As later analyses revealed, however, Tunisia's industrial policy was used mostly as a vehicle for rent creation for the president and his family (Rijkers et al. 2014).

But not only industrial policies were diverted in the sake of crony interests. In the following part we investigate how trade liberalisation was influenced in the Arab variety of capitalism by interest-groups, and what are the results.

Trade Policy and the Cronies

In authoritarian systems, trade policy is also an important element contributing to the logic of regime preservation (Malik and Eibl 2019: 232). While trade protection is an important source of rents for connected elites, tariff liberalisation may erode these rents, which means cronies could be the natural enemies of this liberalisation. On the other hand, cronies are also interested in global integration. In most countries in North Africa, foreign economic relations are mostly run by these elites, local small and medium enterprises had almost no connection to international businesses (Kourtelis 2015: 88).

In most North African countries, trade agreements became a source of reformist legitimacy. International commitments for tariff reduction have also improved the government's bargaining position. With partial liberalisation, the state was able to generate additional rents, thus offering substitutes for cronies, and strengthening regime stability. Falling tariff barriers were replaced by a wave of protective non-tariff measures (NTMs). Malik and Eibl (2019) offer clear empirical evidence from Egypt, Morocco, and Tunisia on how falling tariff barriers were substituted by much stronger NTM protection for cronies then before. Politically connected sectors were able to afford greater trade protection, but not all politically connected entrepreneurs benefited equally from trade protection. Regulatory standards have crucial importance. With a selective enforcement of trade regulations compliance to NTMs can be more costly for not- or less connected firms (Malik and Eibl 2019: 231). As it was analysed already in an earlier World Bank report in detail, in Tunisia NTMs were used for rent creation for the president and his family, by protecting certain subsectors insulated Ben Ali's firms from external competition (Rijkers et al. 2014). In Egypt, NTMs were tailored to individual products in such a way that only connected firms benefited from the narrowly targeted measures (Diwan et al. 2019: 73). Moroccan trade policy also offers ideal opportunities for business insiders to push their interests (Saadi 2019: 158). As data reveals, in case of not connected sectors the tariff rate has decreased to a lower level, than in connected ones: to 5–8% by not connected sectors, and 8–15% by connected ones (ibid.: 159).

Kourtelis (2015) analyses in detail how the unchanged power structures in the domestic environment of North African countries have reduced the expected efficiency of Euro-Med economic cooperation. As he argues, North African state elites were not only negotiators but also actors with interests in the (partial) implementation of the reforms (Kourtelis 2015: 24). North African businesses are heavily affected by the openness of the markets and under these circumstances the main factor that determines the win-sets and the position of the domestic actors is the orientation of the businesses. Lobbying on a collective basis, however, is not the safest way for industrialists to promote their interests. It is much more effective to let their interests be represented by the public officials. Especially, in Morocco and in Tunisia this sort of activity is easier, due to the small size of the country and of the business elite (Kourtelis 2015: 38).

After the Arab Spring, Tunisia, Egypt, and Libya went through more radical political transformations, while in the case of Morocco and Algeria remained almost intact from deep-rooted changes. Concerning connected elites of the earlier regimes, the stories are also diverse. In Tunisia, most of the firms connected to Ben Ali's associates were expropriated, and a new network of connected firms emerged, associated with the newly emerged parties. (Diwan 2019: 403). In Egypt, the situation was more complicated: with a military-led political turn after 2014, most Mubarak cronies were rehabilitated, but they retained much less influence, with the rise of a new network of state-favoured, army-associated groups of cronies (ibid.).

Overall, new regimes have only attempted to recalibrate the elites, thus leaving the configuration of power and the win-sets unchanged, sometimes even offering them new special privileges.

Conclusion

Being close to one of the global core economies, the European Union, North Africa's marginalisation and ongoing peripheralization was even more visible. Economic restructuring induced by the globalisation process has generated some positive macroeconomic changes in the region, but the social consequences, growing inequality, and corruption undermined the legitimacy of most of the regimes. Past experiences, and especially the failures of both socialism and earlier forms of state capitalism has limited policy choices for the Arab region. As an alternative to any Western-type modernisation ideas an Islamic view of society and of the state has been strengthened throughout the region (Talani 2014: 231). Globalisation empowered civil society, but in a very distinctive and maybe unexpected way by strengthening an Islamic alternative.

The European Union, interested in the stability of the region, promoted a closer integration of North African economies, by offering comprehensive trade liberalisation. Trade opening, however, had limited success, with a mostly deteriorating trade balance of North African economies towards the EU. The European side considers further trade liberalisation with a deeper regulatory harmonisation as a potential solution to the previous weaker results. Beside questionable consequences of the costly harmonisation process, the impacts of domestic factors in North African countries should also be taken into account.

The political economic system of most Arab regimes can be characterised as crony capitalists, where, in order to maintain the regime stability, the ruling elite offer rents for connected businesses. Trade liberalisation, non-trade measures and a differentiated use of regulatory power provide a substitute for the losses of tariff cuts, but in a selective manner, mostly for insiders. Despite strong presence of the state in these economies, and a selective, protectionist support for domestic businesses, the North African regimes are far from being considered as developmental states in the twenty-first century.

References

Abed, G. T. – Davoudi, H. R. (2003): *Challenges of Growth and Globalization in the Middle East and North Africa*. International Monetary Fund, Washington, DC.

Akacem, Kada. (2004): Economic Reforms in Algeria: An Overview and Assessment. *The Journal of North African Studies*, 9(2), 115–125.

Benner, M. (2020): *A New Arab Social Contract? Institutional Perspectives for Economic Reform in Arab Countries*. Springer, Cham.

Borrell-Porta, M. (2012): The Importance of Institution-Building in Free Trade Agreements. In: Costa-Font, J. (ed.): *Europe and the Mediterranean Economy*. Routledge, Abingdon – New York, 3–23.

Cammett, M. – Diwan, I. (2018): *The Political Economy of the Arab Uprising*. Routledge, New York – London.

Chemingui, M. A. – Bchir, H. (2012): Have the Promises Used to Sell the Euro-Mediterranean Partnership Come True? Illustration from the Tunisian Experience. In: Costa-Font, J. (ed.): *Europe and the Mediterranean Economy*. Routledge, Abingdon – New York, 93–115.

Dadush, U. – Myachenkova, Y. (2018): *Assessing the European Union's North Africa Trade Agreements*. Policy Contributions No. 22, Bruegel, November.
De Ville, F. – Reynaert, V. (2010): The Euro-Mediterranean Free Trade Area: An Evaluation on the Eve of the (Missed) Deadline. *L'Europe en Formation*, 2(356), 193–206.
Del Prete, D. – Giovannetti, G. – Marvasi, E. (2016): Small and Medium Enterprises' Competitiveness Through Global Value Chains. *IEMed Mediterranean Yearbook 2016*. European Institute of the Mediterranean, Barcelona, 263–268.
Diwan, I. (2019): The Future of the Private Sector in an Age of Uncertainty. In: Diwan, I. – Malik, A. – Atiyas, I. (eds.): *Crony Capitalism in the Middle East: Business and Politics from Liberalization to the Arab Spring*. Oxford University Press, Oxford, 400–432.
Diwan, I. – Keefer, P. – Schiffbauer, M. (2019): The Mechanics, Growth, and Political Economy of Crony Capitalism in Egypt. In: Diwan, I. – Malik, A. – Atiyas, I. (eds.): *Crony Capitalism in the Middle East: Business and Politics from Liberalization to the Arab Spring*. Oxford University Press, Oxford, 67–89.
Dreyer, I. (2012): *Trade Policy in the EU's Neighbourhood: Ways Forward for the Deep and Comprehensive Free Trade Agreements*. Studies & Research 90. Notre Europe.
Ecorys. (2013a): Trade Sustainability Impact Assessment in Support of Negotiations of a DCFTA Between the EU and Tunisia. Final Report. Rotterdam, 25 November. https://trade.ec.europa.eu/doclib/docs/2013/november/tradoc_151923.pdf.
Ecorys. (2013b): Trade Sustainability Impact Assessment in Support of Negotiations of a DCFTA Between the EU and Morocco. Final Report. Rotterdam, 25 November. https://trade.ec.europa.eu/doclib/docs/2013/november/tradoc_151926.pdf.
Ecorys. (2014): Trade Sustainability Impact Assessment in Support of Negotiations of a DCFTA Between the EU and Egypt. Final Report. Rotterdam, 3 November. https://trade.ec.europa.eu/doclib/docs/2013/november/tradoc_153139.pdf.
Findlay, R. – O'Rourke, K. (2007): *Power and Plenty: Trade, War, and the World Economy in the Second Millennium*. Princeton University Press, Princeton.
Glasser, B. L. (1995): External Capital and Political Liberalizations: A Typology of Middle Eastern Development in the 1980s and 1990s. *Journal of International Affairs*, 49(1), 45–73.
Grainger, A. – McLinden, G. (2013): Trade Facilitation and Development. In: Lukauskas et al. (eds.): *Handbook of Trade Policy for Development*. Oxford University Press, Oxford, 893–921.

Griller, S. – Obwexer, W. – Vranes, E. (2017): *Mega-Regional Trade Agreements: CETA, TTIP, and TiSA: New Orientations for EU External Economic Relations*. Oxford University Press, Oxford.

Hall, P. A. – Soskice, D. W. (eds.). (2001): *Varieties of Capitalism: The Institutional Foundations of Comparative Advantages*. Oxford University Press, Oxford.

Harrigen, J. – El-Said, H. (2009): *Aid and Power in the Arab World. IMF and World Bank Policy-Based Lending in the Middle East and North Africa*. Palgrave Macmillan, Basingstoke – New York.

Hertog, S. (2019): The Role of Cronyism in Arab Capitalism. In: Diwan, I. – Malik, A. – Atiyas, I. (eds.): *Crony Capitalism in the Middle East: Business and Politics from Liberalization to the Arab Spring*. Oxford University Press, Oxford, 39–63.

Joffé, George. (2011): The Arab Spring in North Africa: Origins and Prospects. *The Journal of North African Studies*, 16(4), 507–532.

Knio, Karim. (2013): *The European Union's Mediterranean Policy: Model or Muddle? A New Institutionalist Approach*. Palgrave Macmillan, Basingstoke – New York.

Kourtelis, C. (2015): *The Political Economy of Euro-Mediterranean Relations: European Neighbourhood Policy in North Africa*. Palgrave Macmillan, Basingstoke – New York.

Langan, Mark. (2015): The Moral Economy of EU Relations with North African States: DCFTAs Under the European Neighbourhood Policy. *Third World Quarterly*, 36(10), 1827–1844.

Malik, A. – Eibl, F. (2019): The Politics of Trade Protection in North Africa. In: Diwan, I. – Malik, A. – Atiyas, I. (eds.): *Crony Capitalism in the Middle East: Business and Politics from Liberalization to the Arab Spring*. Oxford University Press, Oxford, 205–235.

Maur, J. (2013): Deep Integration in Preferen'tial Trade Agreements. In: Lukauskas et al. (eds.): *Handbook of Trade Policy for Development*. Oxford University Press, Oxford, 537–568.

Meissner, K. L. (2018): *Commercial Realism and EU Trade Policy: Competing for Economic Power in Asia and the Americas*. Routledge, London – New York.

Mevel, S. – de Alba, J. M. – Oulmane, N. (2016): Optimal Regional Trade-Integration Schemes in North Africa: Toward a Pro-Industrialization Policy. *Journal of Economic Integration*, 31(3), 569–608.

Poletti, A. – Sicurelli, D. (2018): *The Political Economy of Normative Trade Power Europe*. Palgrave Macmillan, Basingstoke – New York.

Richards, A. – Waterbury, J. (2007): *The Political Economy of the Middle East*. Westview Press, Boulder.

Ricz, J. (2019): New Developmental Experiments in Two Emerging Economies: Lessons from Brazil and Egypt. In: Gerőcs, T. – Szanyi, M. (eds.): *Market Liberalism and Economic Patriotism in the Capitalist World-System*. Palgrave Macmillan, Cham.

Rijkers, B. – Freund, C. – Nucifora, A. (2014): *All in the Family: State Capture in Tunisia*. Policy Research Working Paper; No. 6810. World Bank, Washington, DC.

Rodrik, D. (1999): *Making Openness Work: The New Global Economy and the Developing Countries*. The Overseas Development Council, Washington, DC.

Saadi, M. S. (2019): Moroccan Cronyism: Facts, Mechanisms, and Impact. In: Diwan, I. – Malik, A. – Atiyas, I. (eds.): *Crony Capitalism in the Middle East. Business and Politics from Liberalization to the Arab Spring*. Oxford University Press, Oxford, 146–169.

St John, R. B. (2008): The Changing Libyan Economy: Causes and Consequences. *Middle East Journal*, 62(1), 75–91.

Talani, S. L. (2014): *The Arab Spring in the Global Political Economy*. Palgrave Macmillan, Basingstoke – New York.

Wade, R. H. (2018): The Developmental State: Dead or Alive? *Development and Change*, 49(2), 518–546.

Yousef, T. M. (2004): Development, Growth and Policy Reform in the Middle East and North Africa since 1950. *Journal of Economic Perspectives*, 18(3), 91–116.

CHAPTER 14

The Demise of Brazilian Developmental State: Political Constraints and the Role of Finance

Andrea Oliveira Ribeiro and Roberta Rodrigues M. da Silva

Introduction

As we finish revising this text, the Covid-19 pandemic transforms the world we live in, politically, culturally and economically. At first glance, this fact would be irrelevant for the purposes of this chapter, if it did not deeply touch the dilemma between capitalist forms of production and the institutions developed to allow for economic and social development.

The pandemic crisis has renewed the debate on the state and public management capacity to mitigate the effects of economic stagnation. The lack of long-term investments in infrastructure and human resources

A. O. Ribeiro (✉)
Department of Management, Universidade Federal Fluminense,
Niterói, RJ, Brazil
e-mail: aoribeiro@id.uff.br

R. R. M. da Silva
Department of Political Science, Universidade Federal Fluminense, Niterói, RJ, Brazil
e-mail: robertarodrigues@id.uff.br

T. Gerőcs and J. Ricz (eds.), *The Post-Crisis Developmental State*, International Political Economy Series,
https://doi.org/10.1007/978-3-030-71987-6_14

within the social protection systems raised unsatisfactory responses and exposed the importance of political coordination to deal with world epidemic risks. Although it is a global problem, solutions can only be provided by nation states, which have the power and the responsibility to offer assistance to their citizens.

Around the world, the pandemic has affected over 200 countries. Millions have been infected and hundreds of thousands of deaths have been registered, and numbers are still rising. Brazil is top among those with the highest number of cases and deaths worldwide, second only to the United States. The Brazilian government drew alarmed attention for its sluggish responses and for denying the risk of contagion by focusing its discourse on economic normalization. President Jair Bolsonaro's denialist attitude ("it's just a little flu") has escalated the conflict between the executive, legislative and judicial branches and the local governments. The lack of political coordination has delayed the approval of measures to alleviate the plunge in revenues and the effects of the decline in economic activity, such as the $25.3 billion emergency package for self-employed workers, small and medium-sized entrepreneurs and aid to states.

Those anti-examples are seemingly far removed from the purposes of this text. But that is not the case. In the previous version of this text, presented at the SVOC Conference 2018,[1] we argue that the ousting of President Dilma Rousseff should be understood as a consequence of the shattering of the broad political coalition that had brought her to power as legitimate heir to former President Luiz Inácio Lula da Silva. During that disruptive process, the financial sector would occupy a prominent place.

The year of 2016 was a watershed period for Brazil. Following the parliamentary coup (Santos 2017) against Rousseff, a regressive political, social and economic agenda was implemented, described in the document *Uma Ponte para o Futuro* ("A Bridge To the Future", PMDB 2015). The interim government strived to bury the dream of a new Brazilian developmental state that began in 2003. The persecution campaign against

[1] The 4th International conference on The Role of State in Varieties of Capitalism (SVOC) entitled "Uneven Development, Inequalities and the State" was organized by the Institute of World Economics of the Centre for Economic and Regional Studies (IWE CERS—belonging back then to the Hungarian Academy of Sciences) and the Center for European Neighborhood Studies (CENS) Central European University on 29–30 November 2018 in Budapest.

progressive and democratic forces under the banner of *antipetismo*[2] tore apart traditional political institutions and paved the way to the election, in 2018, of an authoritarian conservative president.

As part of the coalition supportive of Rousseff, the financial sector played a crucial though quite overlooked role (Minella 2003), as if the financial actors had been driven by a strictly rational logic of maximizing profits and, therefore, uninterested in the palatial infighting.[3] According to this perspective, such actors would be merely reactive to the movements of institutionalized political actors, but we argue that this fraction was essential to the balance of the governing coalition.

With that being said, we now proceed to analyse Rousseff's downfall as a result of the financial sector and the bulk of finance dropping out of the coalition that had promoted such a U-turn in Brazilian politics and then proceeding to consolidate a project for economic austerity and paving the way for Bolsonaro's election. In addition, we associate this phenomenon with the rise of multiple anti-democratic forces which exhibit traits that are specific to the Brazilian case, although not exclusive.

The construction of the Brazilian democracy can be described as a pendular movement (Avritzer 2019) in which democratic moments alternate with anti-democratic periods. During the latter, political divisions, economic crisis and disagreement on political projects become evident, provoking the realignment of political and social groups. By recognizing the trajectory of dependence of Brazilian institutions and the resilience of historical traits connected to slavery, patrimonialism and corporatism, we are then prompted to consider the profound dilemmas that have been demolishing governments elected based on inclusive economic and social development projects.

In order to understand the collapse of the coalition that had supported Rousseff's government and the emergence of a far-right government decisively backed by the financial capital fraction, it becomes necessary to first elucidate the process of structural change that led the financialization logic to filter into the Brazilian economy, with decisive consequences on the influence of the banking and finance sector on the country's politics. We do not overlook the fact that banks or financial agents are central

[2] Meaning "anti-PT"; political stance contrary to the Partido dos Trabalhadores, or PT, the Brazilian Workers' Party; Translator's note.

[3] It should be noted that the Executive Branch in Brazil is in fact located in a palace, the *Palácio do Planalto*.

to capitalism at any given historic period. But we must highlight that a structural change is going on within global capitalism, with its particular expression in Brazil, which led to the entrenchment of financial interests and the shift of the political pendulum in their favour, excusing the banking and finance sector from observing the rules of the democratic game.

Considerations About Financialization in Brazil—Structural Change and Tensions Within the Developmental State

The economic and political prevalence of the financial sector around the world has increased since the 1970s, with the rise of the so-called "financial globalization" (Chesnais 2016), which lead to financialization[4] (Epstein 2005). In Brazil, an increasing proportion of corporate profits come from investments in the financial market, instead of revenues from their industrial and commercial activities. Companies have been increasingly operating in the credit and banking market. Such change in the profile of the productive sector agents, coupled with the growing banking concentration experienced in recent years, have placed the banking and finance sector in the centre of the country's political game.

The increasing financialization of economies and the centrality acquired by the banking and finance sector, with its transnational nature, have imposed theoretical and empirical challenges to the Developmental State. Economic policies, previously focused on the real side of the economy, have been shifted away to provide a "sound economics" to corporation profit and maximization of shareholder value (Fine and Pollen 2018).

Financialization also calls into question the central assumptions to the literature on Varieties of Capitalism (Hall and Soskice 2001), as it highlights aspects that unify—rather than divide—different countries into the same globalized (and financialized) world economy (Streeck 2018). The VoC literature seeks to elucidate institutional complementarities within

[4] According to Epstein (2005: 3), "financialization means the increasing role of financial motives, financial markets, financial actors and financial institutions in the operation of the domestic and international economies".

political economies, which produce different forms of capitalist organization and expression. In the case of Western countries—the core countries in the world economy—institutions produce positive complementarities that allow for the establishment of different comparative institutional advantages. Successful economic development strategies are produced as a consequence (Jackson and Deeg 2006), which manifest either as liberal varieties of capitalism or as coordinated varieties of capitalism.[5]

In peripheral countries, the efficiency of such institutional complementarities is not given. In the case of Latin American countries, Schneider (2009) claims hierarchical varieties of capitalism have been established, centred on coordination mechanisms that produce negative complementarities that generate a favourable environment to the proliferation of "diversified business groups, MNCs, atomistic labour and employee relations, and low-skilled labor" (Schneider 2009: 555). On the other hand, Boschi (2011) highlights the central role of the state in the coordination of actors and in the articulation of pro-developmental coalitions in Brazil and other Latin American countries. He criticizes the prevailing literature, which depoliticizes the institutional processes that lay behind the different types of capitalism. In the same vein, Gerőcs and Szanyi (2019) have expanded the VoC analytical framework, pointing to the state's pivotal role in the economy, by investigating the role of economic patriotism in both advanced and developing countries.

Establishing a compatibility between the structural change brought about by the consolidation of financial capitalism and the variety of its manifestations at the domestic level is a challenge to be faced by both the Developmental State and VoC literature (Streeck 2018). In our perspective, it becomes necessary, to paraphrase Skocpol (1985), to bring politics back into analysis. In this sense, we are in line with Boschi's criticism (2011), arguing that it is only possible to understand capitalism in Brazil in recent years by analysing the ties between the state and coalitions, whether they are for the construction of a development strategy (Lula and Dilma governments), or for the dismantling of the New Developmental State (Temer and Bolsonaro governments).

[5] Following the analytical framework proposed by Hall and Soskice (2001), many other attempts to build a typology were made, in order to encompass either core countries whose economic institutions is not in accordance to the LME/CME duality, or peripheral economies, whose model of development is not considered efficient.

While assessing the Brazilian case, Bresser-Pereira et al. (2019: 13) argue that the maintenance of high interest rates in Brazil has led to the formation of a "coalition of rentiers and financiers' interests", which, in turn, reinforces the pattern of high interest rates in Brazil. This pattern of financial accumulation is different from the one observed in core economies, where revenues come from dividend payment, not interests. Paula et al. (2020: 20) argue that financialization in Brazil imposes limits to the adoption of pro-growth policies by the state, favouring financial or rentier interests. This is also the hypothesis defended by Ianoni (2017: 324), who, in his analysis of the relationship between financial groups and the investor relations agencies of the Central Bank and the National Treasury Secretariat, highlights that the "coalition of rentier and financial interests" influences public policy formulation. Singer (2018) claims that the rentier coalition was responsible for the articulations that led to the coup against Rousseff in 2016. Lavinas et al. (2017) argue that there is a loss of state autonomy in face of the banking and finance sector's hegemony. In their assessment, the state has become unable to conduct macroeconomic and other relevant public policies.

During the 1980s and 1990s, the expansion of neoliberalism in the world political economy—led by the governments of Ronald Reagan in the USA and Margareth Thatcher in the UK—placed peripheral countries under pressure: in the face of the Washington Consensus, they were pressured to adopt financial deregulation policies favouring banks. While in core economies market deregulation and free capital mobility derived from pressure from private agents, such reforms were incorporated into government agendas in peripheral economies due to the coercion from external sources, stemming from multilateral organizations such as the World Bank and the IMF (Freitas and Prates apud Camargo 2009). Such pressure was particularly relevant in Brazil, which was then negotiating a debt restructuring arrangement with these international organizations (Chesnais 2016).

Although there are common external pressures, the impacts of financial globalization are dealt with differently by each country, according to their previous institutional trajectories. In Brazil, the financialization of the economy occurred prematurely, within the scenario of foreign debt crisis and hyperinflation of the 1980s. Banks and companies established in the country reached the 1990s already with a known preference for the "accumulation of financial assets", to the detriment of productive investments that present low liquidity (Lavinas et al. 2017). As time went by, the rentier logic filtered into other sectors, including non-financial companies and wealthier classes.

The centrality of the banking and finance sector in Brazil was consolidated after price stabilization, with the emergence of the Real Plan (Plano Real) in 1994, which created a new currency and controlled inflation by exchange rate anchoring. With the Plano Real, the basic interest rate (Selic) began to reach extremely high levels, among the highest around the globe,[6] allowing for banks to migrate their investment portfolios to government bonds purchasing (Paula 1998) while increasing their gains from bank spreads (Minella 2007). Thus, "a new pattern of financialization has emerged, in which inflation gains are replaced by high interest income" (Lavinas et al. 2017: 11).

The exchange rate anchoring brought by the Real Plan made the Brazilian economy vulnerable to exogenous shocks, such as the financial crises in Mexico (1994), Asia (1997) and Russia (1998). In 1999, it was Brazil's turn to face the currency crisis. In the midst of the Mexican crisis, three large private banks were liquidated—Nacional, Econômico and Bamerindus. In response, the Fernando Henrique Cardoso (FHC) administration laid out a series of measures to aid banks, such as the Program of Incentives for Restructuring and Strengthening the National Financial System (PROER) and the Credit Guarantee Fund (FGC) (Paula 1998). In 1996, the FHC government also launched the Program of Incentives for the Reduction of the State's Participation in Banking Activities (PROES), which paved the way for privatizing most state public banks and some federal public banks (Paula et al. 2013). Two years later, foreign capital entry into the Brazilian banking sector was regulated.

As a result, the country's banking sector became more concentrated, with the formation of an oligopoly between large public and private national banks and foreign banks (Chesnais 2016: 191), which then strongly influenced the business segment as a whole and also the government decisions (Minella 2003). After new entry and exit of foreign banks and mergers between national banks, the Brazilian banking market is now concentrated in the hands of three state-owned banks—Banco do Brasil, Banco Nacional de Desenvolvimento Econômico e Social (BNDES) and Caixa Econômica Federal—, two national banks—Itaú and

[6] On the wake of the Brazilian exchange rate crisis in 1999, at some point Brazil's Central Bank fixed the Selic rate in 40%.

Bradesco—and a foreign bank—Santander—, in addition to others of lesser magnitude.

The strength of the banking and finance sector and the advance of financialization were stable throughout the 2000s, despite the election of Lula in 2003. Although Lula sought to articulate a developmental coalition, he also tried to accommodate the interests of the rentier coalition, given the centrality it acquired in the context of the structural changes observed in Brazilian capitalism. As pointed up by Ricz (2017), Lula aimed to articulate a new social contract between business, labour movements and the civil society, fundamental to sustaining a New Developmental State. However, tensions between the developmental and rentier coalitions, whose projects were fundamentally different, remained latent during the Lula government, while the distributive conflict was neutralized by economic prosperity. During the Rousseff administration, given that the choice for developmentalism (in her first term) coincided with the end of the commodities boom, those previously latent tensions then surfaced, shattering the governing coalition (Singer 2018) and empowering segments interested in promoting the dismantling of the Developmental State (Ricz 2017).

The Lula administration focused on recovering the state capacities necessary to foster industry by strengthening the BNDES and investing in infrastructure works, condensed in the Growth Acceleration Program (PAC). In addition, special attention was given to social policies, with emphasis on the Bolsa Família Program (conditional cash transfer programme) and the expansion of higher education places in the public and private educational networks.

However, the policies adopted by Lula, labelled as neo-developmental or social-developmental (Bastos 2012), did not subvert the financialization logic. Quite the opposite: many of the adopted policies crossed the interests of the banking and finance sector in Brazil. It is worth mentioning that the Selic interest rate was kept at high levels throughout both Lula's terms.[7] Even in the wake of the 2008 financial crisis, the Central Bank resisted to reduce interest rates, doing so when it was too late.

[7] In the beginning of Lula's first term, in 2003, the Selic rate was 25%. When Lula was about to leave office, the Selic rate had fallen considerably, but it was still operating on high levels, at 10.75%.

Social policies were also circumscribed by the logic of financialization. The Bolsa Família Program dictated that beneficiaries should open an account with Caixa Econômica Federal, leading to the bankability of the poorest strata of the population. In addition, the government fostered payroll loans, especially among retirees and pensioners (Lavinas et al. 2017). Not only did banks expand credit but also companies that were originally non-banking (from supermarkets to clothing companies) created financial branches aimed at granting credit to families. In the case of higher education expansion, although there was an increase in the number of proffered places and public university campuses, there was also strong stimulus to private college enrollment via financing plans (Fies) or partial and whole scholarships (ProUni), fostering the creation of large education conglomerates, with shares on the stock market. Expansion of private credit occurred in the context of high interest rates, putting pressure on household indebtedness. The wealthier classes, in turn, made gains through the expansion of pension funds and by allocating their investments in the purchase of government bonds or in funds linked to Selic, ensuring high profitability in a low risk scenario (Lavinas 2017).

For Lavinas et al. (2017), the dawn of the twenty-first century was marked by "mass financialization", both due to the maintenance of high interest rates, which create incentives for the purchase of government bonds, and by the advance of banking policies and credit incentives. The structural transformation, which gave rise to strong interests in favour of financialization, was already underway when Rousseff was elected.

The Dilma Rousseff Administration—Climax and Crisis of a Development Project

Elected in 2010, Rousseff faced a very adverse scenario imposed by the end of the commodities cycle and the international financial crisis of 2008. The exhaustion of the export-led growth cycle intensified conflicts between workers benefited by rising wages and dissatisfied employers; the effects of deindustrialization (Oreiro and Marconi 2014) hit corporations hard; and the unmet demand for expanded social rights enraged the organized social movements (Bastos 2017). Accosted by the increasingly tense climate, which exposed the discontentment with the commodification of the *res publica*—or the public affairs (Antunes 2018), the Workers' Party (*Partido dos Trabalhadores*—PT) also lost the support of the middle and popular classes.

Studies on the causes for the Rousseff government's ruin and the subsequent events have been piling up, for it was the most dramatic political transition in the history of the New Republic (1985–2016). Avoiding individualizing explanations, which tend to emphasize the president's political mistakes and her little proclivity for dialogue, we resort to multidimensional studies that incorporate domestic and international, cyclical and sociohistorical factors. The social-developmental content of the government's project, clearly distinct from the neoliberal projects of governments prior to 2003 (Paula et al. 2020), was met with growing resistance against inclusive social policies by the political and economic elites, and their fear of left-wing radicalization. The president's decisions to alter distributive mechanisms in favour of work income and productive investment, to the detriment of financial capital (Bastos 2017; Singer 2018), displayed the intention to promote a growth project that is democratically inclusive. However, as we have already observed, it seems that the drive for change was insufficient to alter the institutional conditions and break with the elements that generate Brazilian inequality (Lavinas 2017), changes that would have produced a new growth pattern towards a more inclusive development trajectory.

None of these assessments ignore the weight of the external restrictions that have impacted economic growth and reduced the export sector gains, thus altering the correlation of domestic forces. Lula had sailed through calmer seas in the previous decade of exponential growth in commodities demand. The 2008 international financial crisis had devastating consequences for the Brazilian industry and the export sector (Oreiro and Marconi 2014). In order to increase the competitiveness of Brazilian products, Rousseff resorted to fiscal contraction and monetary easing policies (Selic reduction) to stimulate exchange rate devaluation, measures that laid the foundation of the New Macroeconomic Matrix (NME).[8] This decision was in response to a consensus among industrialists on the exhaustion of the inward-oriented growth model expansion through increasing wages and public social spending (Carvalho 2018). The so-called Agenda Fiesp, a manifesto of the Federation of Industries of the State of São Paulo, defended a "better use for the foreign

[8] The so-called New Macroeconomics Matrix is a set of economic policies put forward during Rousseff's first term (2010–2014) involving fiscal expansion, exchange rate devaluation and tax exemption. The term was coined by Mário Holland, the head Economic Policy Secretariat (Carvalho 2018).

market and investments" assuming that the decrease in the international prices of Brazilian products would have a positive effect on the amount of private investments. Unfortunately, such greater industrial dynamism never materialized. The years 2011 and 2012 showed a decline in industrial production, of 0.9 and 3.7%, respectively. The combination of reduced spending and extensive tax exemptions resulted in a plunge in revenue and the worsening of the economic slowdown.

The flexibilization of the macroeconomic tripod started in early August 2011 with the beginning of the interest rate reduction cycle, which reached 7.5% (historically low level) between 2011 and 2012. Although it was part of the corporate agenda, this measure was then interpreted as "monetary loosening" and met with "surprise" by the markets (Valor Econômico 2012). The criticism made by liberal media economists to Alexandre Tombini's management at the head of the Brazilian Central Bank (BCB) raised doubts about the government's ability to control inflation and ensure a "healthy" business environment.

Exchange devaluation and capital control policies were responses to the adoption of quantitative easing measures by the Federal Reserve System (FED) and the European Central Bank (ECB), which forced an exchange rate appreciation in emerging countries due to the global excess liquidity. In September 2010, during a G-20 meeting, Minister Guido Mantega openly criticized the "currency war" promoted by developed countries as a strategy to escape the economic crisis, which contradicted the mantra for liberalization (Bastos and Hiratuka 2020: 11). In the domestic market, real's appreciation produced inflation acceleration, which, in addition to services inflation, had a negative impact on the purchasing power of wages and household consumption.

In view of the shift in the United States' low-interest monetary policy, in May 2013, and the rapid reversal of market expectations, the direction of capital flows was then inverted, causing massive capital flight and putting pressure on the real's devaluation. The Ministry of Finance announced the elimination of taxes on foreign exchange operations, and the Central Bank, which had already abandoned the policy of interest rate reduction in April 2013, then promoted swap operations to avoid mega currency devaluation and the transmission effects on inflation and exports (Carvalho 2018).

As measurement for the fluctuations in the behaviour of politicians and state institutions, inflation and public debt are crucial to interpreting market signals. The BCB's decisions were continually framed by the media economic coverage as "political" rather than technical, as if the BCB's role as arbiter of the economic policy, via the Monetary Policy Committee (COPOM), had no legitimacy. The veto power of finance over economic policy formulation, consolidated from 1999 onwards with the institutional mandate of the macroeconomic tripod, restricts autonomous state action and prevents the production of an alternative (fiscally expansive) discourse on the economy, whose rules are subject to inflation control and government deficit. For this reason, it would be more accurate to interpret the attacks by the financial and productive sectors on the government as an expression of their fear of the expansion of jobs and rights, even via financial citizenship, which is part of the democratic mandate (Bastos 2017) and not as a problem of technical standards of good management.

The National Financial System (SFN), which regulates financial contracts between public and private agents, is structured around normative and supervising organizations (the National Monetary Council and the Central Bank, respectively) and credit operators. Their management is marked by a clear power asymmetry. While 55% of the available income corresponds to family consumption, the decisions on monetary policy are made by a few institutionalized actors. The monetary authority, the Central Bank, is managed by an "exceptional" technocracy (Best 2018), which operates in political spaces that are exempt from many of the norms of liberal democratic politics, having the power to define and restrict them. Although the government interferes with nominations, analyses of the BCB's occupation profile reveal that, regardless of the government's political bias, whether centre-right or centre-left, the origin of the board members associated with economic policy formulation is external to the government and that they are trained in institutions belonging to the economic mainstream, which is committed to neoliberal policies and therefore opposed to the developmental project (Codato et al. 2016). It is no small matter that the definition of the parameters allowed for inflation has the collaboration of private agents, through the Focus Bulletin, whose interests do not necessarily coincide with those of the government.

Financialization studies often emphasize the power of large corporations and investors who hold large amounts of capital (banks and multinational corporations). This perspective fogs the comprehension of the impacts of financial domination on democratic politics because it ignores the role of middle-income individual investors, who frequently hold treasury bonds and keep savings in complementary private pensions funds. The latter hold large shares in open capital corporations, playing a pivotal role in their governance and investment decisions. Also, middle-class individuals profited from the high interest rates that prevailed in Brazil for over 20 years.

The mainstream perspective on financialization also does not provide a satisfactory explanatory model for the channels of influence of financial actors. When it comes to the representation of the financial sector, for example, there are also barriers to pinpointing the political position of bankers (Dias 2014). Associations such as the Brazilian Federation of Banks (Febraban) and the Brazilian Association of Commercial Banks (ABCC) seem to function more as technical bodies than as political ones. This sector is mainly vocal via mediatic performances by economic analysts from private consulting firms.

The strong bancarization that occurred during the Lula and Rousseff administrations was an important part of the inward-looking growth strategy. The financial inclusion allowed for a significant part of the Brazilian population to access, for the first time, benefits linked to the complex banking system, thus expanding financial citizenship (Costa 2018). The low income groups (LIGs) often have difficulty to access credit when there is no state support, but, on the other hand, they are a potential and rich source of private and public capital for the financial system. State intervention in favour of LIGs can generate a social source of financial power by expanding capital reserve, which, in turn, strengthens state influence upon the international financial order (Seabrooke 2006). The reforms carried out by Rousseff can also be understood under this light. In promoting financial inclusion by expanding the number of bank branches and services around the country, there was an effort to increase the access of the Brazilian middle and low income populations to the financial system, contributing to its decentralization.

However, an isolated analysis of economic factors is not enough to explain the 2015/2016 events. The social upheaval that began with the June 2013 protests[9] affected the president's popularity and put the government in a defensive position, opening a window of opportunity for the departure of business groups from the governing coalition and the construction of a discourse opposed to the economic policy in March. The events and the media coverage of Operation Lava Jato, allegedly aimed at combating corruption (Avritzer and Marona 2017), contributed

[9] For an account of June 2013 protests, see: Bringel (2016).

to criminalize the government. Investigations carried out by the Federal Police and the Public Prosecutor's Office revealed a corruption scheme that charged to negotiate public works contracts, involving public and private companies from the construction and energy sectors and political parties (Paula et al. 2020). With the interruption of construction projects, the impact on the productive sector was tremendous, but it particularly affected the ruling party. The October 2014 elections took place within this context. Dilma's victory was narrow: 51.8% against 48.2% for the centrist Aécio Neves (Brazilian Social Democracy Party—PSDB). The strengthened opposition in both the legislative and executive branches reflected the polarization by income and region that was pointed out in the 2006 and 2010 elections (Singer 2018) and took the chance to question the electoral result. The political-party fragmentation exposes a new, more heterogeneous and complex correlation of forces, which challenges the possibilities of reconciling the executive and legislative branches (Paula et al. 2020).

The appointment, in January 2015, of a representative of the financial sector, Joaquim Levy, to the Ministry of Finance, gave rise to accusations of electoral (and intellectual) fraud. During the campaign, Dilma promised to deepen the building of a New Developmental State and to promote redistributive policies. However, upon taking office, Levy presented a fiscal adjustment programme that included reductions in PAC investments and changes in the rules of labour benefits and increased tax collection as a way to guarantee the primary surplus (Carvalho 2018). In September of the same year, about 100 organizations from industry, commerce, services and agriculture created the National Front Against Tax Increase to launch the campaign "I will not pay for the duck!".[10] Led by Paulo Skaf, president of FIESP, the campaign proclaimed the refusal by the business sector to share the costs of the crisis amid the intense economic slowdown. Rousseff finally lost the support of the industrialist part of the coalition that had brought her to power, giving way to a different national project, opposed in everything to the Worker Party's social development project. Brazil then crossed the bridge towards a deeper export-dependent growth pattern, at a time when state action would have been most necessary.

[10] 'Paying for the duck' is a Brazilian idiomatic expression that means 'unduly paying for something' Translator's note.

Conclusion

Dilma's overthrow by a questionable impeachment process was followed by the ascension of her deputy, Michel Temer (PMDB), and the biggest offensive against the incipient set of public policies for social welfare that had been created within the scope of the 1988 Constitution. Along those two years of interim government, various reforms designed to refrain the state's fiscal expansion capacity were approved, such as the Spending Ceiling Law (Constitutional Amendment No. 95/2016) that froze public spending for 20 years. Observing this dramatic change in course, we ponder to what extent we can associate the Workers' Party governments with the developmental state. We argue that the Workers' Party governments had an agenda to fight inequality based on full employment and the expansion of internal productive capacities, in which the State fulfilled the role of key coordinator. If Rousseff's attempt to promote structural reforms did not succeed in reducing rentism as a privileged way to accumulate capital and thus press for the expansion of private productive investments, political and not merely economic factors must be considered. By challenging the interests of financial capital and failing to ensure that her electoral base understood the efforts to promote structural change, the president lost popular support, even from unionism, traditionally allied to the Workers' Party. Lacking the support of PT's traditional voters, Rousseff became politically vulnerable to the threat of powerful economic groups. Such groups were responsible for consolidating an opposition to the government, boosted by the media and the legislative and judicial branches. The established opposition successfully crafted the narrative that the government was incompetent, technically irresponsible and populist (Bastos 2017).

The consolidation of the structural power of the financial sector in Brazil and globally over the last few decades seems to us to be a fundamental factor to understand the Rousseff government's debacle. Our very notion of the state has been transforming due to the internationalization of economies and the transformation of productive structures. It is true that the Covid-19 pandemic presents new questions about the state's public character. But it cannot be ignored that decades into the neoliberal experience have weakened the type of political power exertion that organizes itself in the form of a State (sovereignty, division of powers, legality and bureaucracy), making it more dependent on private resources and agents, "privatizing" the state (Hibou 2004).

The Workers' Party administrations had doubtlessly transformed the life of ordinary Brazilians for the better. Rousseff's legacy was the expansion of the social protection network, fomenting the formal labour market by encouraging formal labour contracts and a policy of continuous appreciation of the minimum wage, therefore increasing the levels of economic welfare. However, she did not succeed in displacing the emerging individualizing discourse of "entrepreneurship" in the realm of labour, that ended up weakening solidarity among workers (Esquerda Petista 2017). Rousseff's distancing from social and union movements in a context of structural change in Brazilian capitalism proved fatal: while the coup was articulated, resistance waned on the streets.

At the institutional policy level, it is possible to associate the crisis of Brazilian coalition presidentialism[11]—with the soaring costs of building the coalition coupled with the executive's disorder—with the loss of legitimacy of the political system and the crisis of representation that "fell into the Workers' Party's lap", which had been experiencing an unprecedented control on the national executive (Avritzer 2016). Hounded by the structure of political-party alliances, the Workers' Party administrations were unable to consolidate a distributional structure of benefits to their electoral base, nor to reinforce the organizational infrastructure that would allow them to defend their agenda from attacks by the elites (Evans 2019). There was no political room to expand its redistributive agenda.

Acknowledging the structural limits of PT's political position allows us to understand two major ideological elements—the mystification of combating corruption and the lawfare that led former President Lula to prison—that boosted Bolsonaro and his anti-democratic project, supported by the conservative sectors of Brazilian society.

The outcome of this tragedy of dramatic contours unfolds before our eyes, with the advance of the Covid-19 pandemic in Brazil. Registered deaths surpass a thousand every day. On the one hand, unfazed by the massacre, the stock exchange is rapidly recovering from the plunge registered in February/March 2020. On the other, the universal healthcare system, attacked, emptied and underfunded since the 2016 coup, has been proving its capacity to provide healthcare to the population. Despite the omission of the federal administration, resulting in the local governments' anencephalic response to the pandemic and the retention

[11] See: Power (2010).

of resources by the federal government, it is surprising that only three of the 27 Brazilian states (Amazonas, Ceará and Rio de Janeiro) have registered a collapse of their public hospitals during the peak of the pandemic. Rescuing the state is what may save Brazil.

References

Antunes, R. (2018) *O privilégio da servidão: o novo proletariado de serviço na era digital.* Boitempo editorial – São Paulo.

Avritzer, L. (2016) *Impasses da Democracia no Brasil.* Rio de Janeiro – Civilização Brasileira.

Avritzer, L. (2019) *O pêndulo da democracia.* Todavia – São Paulo.

Avritzer, L.; Marona, M. (2017) A tensão entre soberania e instituições de controle na democracia brasileira. *Dados*, 60(2), 359–393.

Bastos, P. (2012) A economia política do novo-desenvolvimentismo e do social desenvolvimentismo. *Economia e Sociedade*, 21(num. Especial), 779–810.

Bastos, P. P. Z. (2017). Ascensão e crise do governo Dilma Rousseff e o golpe de 2016: poder estrutural, contradição e ideologia. Revista de Economia Contemporânea, 21(2).

Bastos, P. P. Z.; Hiratuka, C. (2020). The Foreign Economic Policy of Dilma Rousseff's Government and the Limits of Dependency. *Latin American Perspectives*, 47(2), 25–46.

Best, J. (2018). Technocratic Exceptionalism: Monetary Policy and the Fear of Democracy. *International Political Sociology*, 12(4), 328–345.

Boschi, R. (2011) Instituições, trajetórias e desenvolvimento: uma discussão a partir da América Latina. In: Boschi, R (org.) *Variedades de Capitalismo, Política e Desenvolvimento da América Latina.* UFMG – Belo Horizonte.

Bresser-Pereira, L. C.; Paula, L. F.; Bruno, M. (2019) Financeirização, coalizão de interesses e taxa de juros no Brasil. *Mimeo.* http://luizfernandodepaula.com.br/ups/financeirizacao-coalizao-de-interesses-taxa-de-juros-no-brasil-07.pdf.

Bringel, B. (2016) The Long June: The 2013 Mobilizations and the Future of Social Movements in Brazil. In: Simin Fadaee (org.) *Understanding Southern Social Movements.* Routledge – London.

Camargo, P. (2009) *A evolução do sistema financeiro internacional e as especificidades do Brasil.* UNESP – São Paulo.

Carvalho, L. (2018) *Valsa brasileira: do boom ao caos econômico.* Todavia – São Paulo.

Chesnais, F. (2016) *Finance Capital Today: corporations and banks in the lasting global slump.* Brill Academica Pub – Boston.

Codato, A; Cavalieri, M.; Perissinotto, R.; Dantas, E. (2016) Mainstream econômico e poder: uma análise do perfil dos diretores do Banco Central do Brasil nos governos do PSDB e do PT. *Nova Economia*, 26(3), 687–720.

Costa, F. (2018) Complexidade do Sistema Bancário Brasileiro: interações de pessoas jurídicas e físicas, bancos privados e bancos públicos. Instituto de Economia da Unicamp. *Texto para Discussão 331*. https://fernandonogueiracosta.files.wordpress.com/2018/03/tdie-331.png.

Dias, R. (2014) A representação dos banqueiros no Brasil: um estudo sobre a FEBRABAN. *Teoria & Pesquisa: Revista de Ciência Política*, 23(2), 178–204.

Entrevista Dilma Rousseff. (2017) Revista Esquerda Petista, n°7. Disponível em. https://pt.calameo.com/read/001810147532b6778be30.

Epstein, G. (2005) Introduction: In: Epstein, G (ed.) *Financialization and the World Economy*. Edward Elgar Publishing – Cheltenham and Northampton.

Evans, P. (2019) O desdobramento da tragédia da política no Brasil. *Revista Desenvolvimento em Debate*, 2(7), 127–138.

Fine, B.; Pollen, G. (2018) The Developmental State Paradigm in the Age of Financialization. In: Fagan, H.; Munck, R. (eds.). *Handbook on Development and Social Change*. Edward Elgar Publishing – Cheltenham.

Gerőcs, T.; Szanyi, M. (eds.). (2019) *Market Liberalism and Economic Patriotism in the Capitalist World-System*. Palgrave Macmillan – Cham (Switzerland).

Hall, P.; Soskice, D. (2001) *Varieties of Capitalism: The Institutional Foundations of Comparative Advantage*. Oxford University Press – Oxford.

Hibou, B. (2004) *Privatizing the State*. Columbia University Press – New York.

Ianoni, M. (2017) Interesses financeiros e captura do Estado no Brasil. *Revista de Economia Política*, 37(2), 324–342.

Jackson, G.; Deeg, R. (2006) How Many Varieties of Capitalism? Comparing the Comparative Institutional Analyses of Capitalist Diversity. MPIfG Discussion Paper, 06, 48p.

Lavinas, L. (2017) The Takeover of Social Policy by Financialization. *The Brazilian Paradox*. Palgrave Macmillan – New York.

Lavinas, L.; Araújo, E.; Bruno, M. (2017) Brasil: vanguarda da financeirização entre os emergentes? *Textos para Discussão IE-UFRJ*, 32, 40p.

Minella, A. (2003) Globalização financeira e as associações de bancos na América Latina. *Civitas*, 3(2): 245–272.

Minella, A. (2007) Maiores bancos privados no Brasil: um perfil econômico e sociopolítico. *Sociologias*, 18, 100–125.

Oreiro, J. L.; Marconi, N. (2014) Teses equivocadas no debate sobre desindustrialização e perda de competitividade da indústria brasileira. *Revista NECAT-Revista do Núcleo de Estudos de Economia Catarinense*, 3(5), 24–48.

Paula, L. F. (1998) Tamanho, dimensão e concentração do sistema bancário no contexto de alta e baixa inflação no Brasil. *Nova Economia*, 8(1), 87–116.

Paula, L. F.; Oreiro, J. L.; Basílio, F. (2013) Estrutura do setor bancário e o ciclo recente de expansão do crédito: o papel dos bancos públicos federais. *Nova Economia*, 23(3), 473–520.

Paula, L. F.; Santos, F.; Moura, R. (2020) The Developmentalist Project of the PT Governments: An Economic and Political Assessment. *Latin American Perspectives*, 47(2), 8–24.

Partido do Movimento Democrático Brasileiro. (2015) Uma Ponte para o Futuro.

Power, Timothy. (2010) Optimism, Pessimism, and Coalitional Presidentialism: Debating the Institutional Design of Brazilian Democracy. *Bulletin of Latin American Research*, 29(1), 18–33.

Ricz, J. (2017) The Rise and Fall (?) of a New Developmental State in Brazil. *Society and Economy*, 39(1), 85–108.

Santos, W. G. (2017) *A Democracia Impedida: o Brasil no século XXI*. FGV – São Paulo.

Seabrooke, L. (2006) *The social sources of financial power: domestic legitimacy and international financial orders*. Cornell University Press.

Schneider, B. (2009) Hierarchical Market Economies and Varieties of Capitalism in Latin America. *Journal of Latin American Studies*, 41, 552–575.

Singer, A. (2018) *O lulismo em crise: um quebra-cabeça do período Dilma (2011–2016)*. Editora Companhia das Letras.

Skocpol, T. (1985) Bringing the State Back In: Strategies of Analysis in Current Research. In: Evans, P.; Rueschemeyer, D.; Skocpol, T. *Bringing the State Back In*. Cambridge University Press – Cambridge.

Streeck, W. (2018) *Tempo Comprado: a crise adiada do capitalismo democrático*. Boitempo – São Paulo.

Valor Econômico. (2012) Casa das Caldeiras: BC deixa mercado sem orientação. 7/03. Disponível no link. https://www.valor.com.br/valor-investe/casa-das-caldeiras/2560676/bc-deixa-mercado-sem-orientacao.

Index: Lula (Luiz Inácio Lula da Silva); Dilma Rousseff; Brazil; developmental state; democracy; coalitions; financialization; banks.

CHAPTER 15

Mystification of Power and Development in Pakistan

Nazia Nazeer

Introduction

Over the years, the field of economics has evolved widely and many sub-themes have been developed for instance Keynesianism, Neoclassical economics and Neoliberalism to shape the complex nature of the global political economy. A classical theorist such as Pareto and Mosca debated that elite rule is inevitable and most desirable to administer societal configuration of society. While power elite theorists like Mills (1956) and Dahl (1957) claimed that elite rule carries the highest power elites of society which are connected and function for their power gain. As a result, common people may not get any advantages from the socio-economic structures which they try to develop. Interestingly, it is noticeable that all relevant studies of elite and power theories, from Pareto (1939) to Higley and Burton (1990) were focused on the power systems of developed nations.

N. Nazeer (✉)
National University of Computer and Emerging Sciences, FAST-School of Management, Karachi, Pakistan

T. Gerőcs and J. Ricz (eds.), *The Post-Crisis Developmental State*, International Political Economy Series,
https://doi.org/10.1007/978-3-030-71987-6_15

Yet, all these existing theories and the taxonomies of power elites are not related to developing nations. The developing nations possessed different historical statuses, economical condition, class configurations, cultural and religious characteristics. Also, policy responses to internal conflicts, effects of wars, global instability, technological changes and economic disruptions, such as the huge unemployment occurred in the 1930s, the recession in the 1960s, the oil shocks, economic and financial crises of 2008/09 are certainly different. To better understand the power configuration and complexities in developing nations there is a need to grasp the contestation and involvement among the power elites (landlords, religious groups, bureaucrats, and international capital) that mainly exist in developing nations for such a long time. From the perspective of developing nations, these elites hold an extremely influential power to bring significant policy amendments in the country. Similarly, some development economists, for instance, Rosenstein-Rodan (1943), Scitovsky (1954), Baran (1957), and Gerschenkron (1962) debated that effective contribution plus participation of state help to regularize economic environment for continuous development and industrialization. The advocates of the developmental state from the economic perspective, mainly emphasize on the developmental policies embraced by the state that in return lead to industrialization and economic development (Amsden 1989; Wade 1990; Woo-Cummings 1999; Chang 2002; Kohli 2004).

Therefore, in this context, Pakistan is selected as a case study where a variety of power elites get hold which does not exist in developed nations. Also, the concept of developmental state from economic perspective has been fit with more careful investigation of Pakistan's developmentalist period from 1950 to 1980, which indicate that, overall performance was reasonably stable during this period as compared to liberalization in the 1990s, particularly through industrial development (Burki and Qureshi 2012; Noman 2015; Zaidi 2005). However, despite some successes even in its prime years, the developmental state of Pakistan experienced much less achievement than the East Asian Tigers countries.

Power Contestation and Governance

The history of Pakistan shows that class conflict is one of the main features since the state's independence in 1947. Soon after World War II when the global balance of power was shifted and Pakistan had to join the hegemonic forces, Pakistan decided to form a military alliance with the United

States under the Central Treaty Organization (CENTO), and Southeast Asia Treaty Organization (SEATO) with Russia during the 1950s. Therefore, while analyzing the power configuration in Pakistan the political configuration and national administration are always explained by considering the political structure of the United States or various other Western democracies. Initially from 1947 to 1971, actual administrative power in Pakistan has been carried out by three divisions of elite groups that are the ruling class, the military, the feudal landlords and the civilian bureaucracy (Hussain 1976). But, the major changes occurred in these groups when West Pakistan lost its Eastern Wing and at the same time the nationalization policy was implemented in 1972. Several studies criticize the capitalist structure of Pakistan for this clash among groups, especially between industrialists and landlords (Rashid 1978). Additionally, West Pakistan's corporate elite was given maximum export agreements through their relations with the bureaucratic elite, leaving East Pakistan's corporate elite isolated.

Muhammad Ali Jinnah was the first Governor General of Pakistan and he appointed Liaqat Ali Khan as a Prime Minister in 1947. Liaqat Ali Khan retained this status from 1947 till 1951 using the assistance of bureaucrats who were qualified and employed in the British India civil services. Later, after Liaqat Ali's assassination in 1951, high authorities of the governing Muslim League immediately organized to select a new representative and radical shifts were carried out in the highest ranks. Hence, Ghulam Mohammad was chosen as the Governor General. The seated Governor General Khwaja Nazim-Uddin was downgraded from Prime Minister post and Choudhary Muhammad Ali was selected as minister of finance in Ghulam's position (Rehman 2006). Ghulam governed the state as Governor General from the year 1951 till 1955. Prime Minister Suhrawardy quitted in 1957, and then Ismail Ibrahim Chundrigar of the Muslim League created an alliance regime as Prime Minister in 1957. During the initial years after independence from India, the difficult task of framing strong economic foundation was assigned to the state, as the private sector was still in the primary phase of development with insufficient capital to accelerate industrial growth. The state's main concern was to survive and provide necessities to millions of refugees coming from India (Zaidi 2015).

With no strong political leadership from civilian body in 1951, the Pakistan Military, all together with bureaucrats, arose as the stable and organized institute in the country. The Commander-in-Chief of the

Pakistan Army General Ayub came into power after pressurizing President Iskandar Mirza to quit in 1958. Muhammad Ayub Khan's administrative period is known as the 'Decade of Development'. Pakistan is a traditional agricultural country. Therefore, the first noteworthy effort made by Ayub Khan's regime was the reallocation of land. Land reforms have often been considered as an important factor in economic development particularly in pre-industrial societies. Pursuing large-scale land reforms commenced in 1959, the Green Revolution in agriculture transformed the economic and social relations of production permanently. The Green Revolution along with sufficient US aid increased production of crops. The state introduced new agricultural techniques, installed tube wells and dams, provided more tractors, fertilizer manufacturing, and High Yielding Variety (HYV) Seeds. Also, incentive prices and loans were offered to the farmers through the state price support programme.

Strong development maintained until the year 1960 because manufacturing rose almost 10 per cent per year at an average from 1960 to 1970 (Abbasi 2009). At that time, the main emphasis was towards import-substitution employing tariff protection. The trade policy followed was also very progressive and the state provided general relaxation of restrictive controls on imports. The import policy was focused on the full utilization of industrial capability, support export and a steady reduction in the import of goods manufactured domestically. The government introduced the Export Bonus Scheme which covered all the industrial items, fewer primary commodities and remittances from abroad. As a result, this liberal trade policy facilitated in the stimulation of the high rates of development in the industrial sector. Also, imports of raw materials, spare parts and machinery supported rapid installation and utilization of industrial capacity. However, extraordinary rates of effective protection made domestic industry incompetent. Though, there was tremendous growth marked during Ayub Khan's tenure, but then there was also rising inequality across provinces and classes. The negative effective rates of protection (ERP) turned Pakistani industry ineffective as compared to East Asian countries. The East Asian economies were carefully designed with an effective rate of protection such as tarrif structure, while Pakistani quota and tariff system was not thoroughly planned to develop infant industries and to direct them to attain the subsequent maturity level. The impact of this import dependence led to falling of balance of payment, import of machinery, raw material and outbalance export performance.

All in all, the economic policy package introduced by Ayub Khan's administration was completely capitalistic, and the private sector played an important role. But the fact is that the bureaucracy took an influential, active, practical participation in the development of a private sector that was administered and guided capitalism, or with other words benevolent state capitalism as a form of a developmental state (Zaidi 2015).

The development model pursued by Ayub Khan stimulated manufacturing and industrialization, accumulated agricultural wealth by the successful Green Revolution, emergence of a working class and the appearance of middle classes in the country. These emerging social groups (working class and middle classes) in the Ayub era gave support to Zulfiqar Ali Bhutto to form Pakistan People Party. Bhutto assisted in four of President Ayub Khan's five cabinets and was actively involved in redirecting Pakistan's foreign policy for China in 1963 and also represented Pakistan in the United Nations during 1965 War with India over Kashmir. He disagreed with Ayub Khan on Tashkent Declaration in 1966,[1] and successfully ran the protest movement against General Ayub in 1968 which caused the ultimate downfall of Ayub's regime. Hence, in 1969, General Ayub Khan declared his retirement and announced General Yahya as President and the country was again under martial law. During that time Pakistan consisted of two wings one was East (Currently known as Bangladesh) and second was West Wing (Pakistan). Under President Yahya, Bhutto actively took part in the state's first national elections in 1970, and acquired majority of seats in West Pakistan whereas the Awami league had a greater number of seats in East Pakistan. Since the vote was divided between two wings, this created a political instability which turned out of control. The army under West Wing intervened to control the situation but failed miserably as the Indian army came to the help of the rebels and as a result, the east wing declared independence from the West Wing.

Zulfiqar Ali Bhutto started immediately and introduced policies based on the notions and principles of socialism. Bhutto's democratic regime was different governance that involved the active participation of society and reshaping of economic and social reforms of Pakistan (Shafqat 1996). The Bhutto's administration decided to nationalize all the main industries and sectors and limit private proprietorship. Bhutto's regime is credited

[1] The *Tashkent agreement* was a peace declaration between India and Pakistan signed on the 10 of January *1966* that settled the Indo-Pakistani War in 1965.

with introducing policies that supported the upgrading of science and technology, and education. Numerous medical institutions and colleges were recognized during Bhutto's government. A grant commission for monetary support to universities and higher education institutions were also provided for the progress in all relevant fields (Mahmood et al. 2008).

The state under Bhutto's direction, along with nationalization policy, may not be criticized as a failure to frame visionary and effective micro and macroeconomic policies. Apart from that, its absence of a bureaucratic group with business understanding had severe effects on the economy as well as on the corporate sector. The industrial sector was unsuccessful to flourish despite wide public sector investments; the units nationalized failed to perform satisfactorily. The mode of giving wealth concentration to few upper-class groups did not benefit the society's middle class to increase their standard of living and the nationalization policy of the socialist administration to discontinue the development of private sector failed to succeed to encourage the economic conditions of the middle class and the poor (Zaidi 2015). Zulfiqar Ali Bhutto selected General Zia-ul-Haq as chief of the army staff in the year 1976. The Army under Zia commanded to detain Bhutto on custody of permitting the assassination of his political rival in 1974. In 1979 the Supreme Court of Pakistan dismissed Bhutto appeal and was hanged at Central Jail Rawalpindi.

By keeping in mind an expected reaction of Bhutto's hanging in the country, General Zia announced the elections to revert the state to civilian rule but that promise was broken and he banned all political parties in 1979, prohibited labour strikes, enforced strict censorship on the media and declared military rule in the state. The military takeover by Zia, from 1978 to 1988, transformed the political configuration of Pakistan. Zia tapped the religious elites to proliferate religion Islam and introduced the policy of Islamization in Pakistan in 1978 and announced that all law in the state must be coherent with Islam.[2] Within the year of 1979, the Russia (Soviet Union) invaded Afghanistan and it drastically changed US policies towards Pakistan for the following years. The change in US policies helped Zia to govern Pakistan with the help of US funds.[3] As a result, Zia's administration opened borders for Afghan mujahedeen,

[2] Sharia law comes from a combination of sources including the Qur'an (the Muslim holy book), the *Hadith* (sayings and conduct of the prophet Muhammad) and *fatwas* (the rulings of Islamic scholars).

[3] Almost US$3.2 billion assistance package.

already trained in US armed camps established in Pakistan territory to combat Russian forces. The decision taken by the Zia regime is considered as the radical military and political contract which transformed the structure of Pakistan's economy as well as political portfolio. These decisions not only fetched foreign aid but also generated so many issues like the overburden of Afghan refugees Islamic activism, ethnic diversity, an inheritance of gun culture, drug trafficking, sectarian violence, economic crises and security dilemmas that left the country with critical internal challenges. This deal with international elites put the country in a weaker position; firstly, its resources and land are consumed by external forces for their authoritarian policy interests. Secondly, this type of domestic-international alliance approach gave an advantage to military elites to sustain their power to rule. The US alliance with Pakistan during the Afghan war was an exceptional example of a partnership between two uneven powers. The US, as a superpower, took benefit of Pakistan's need for economic and military support and to extend the possibility of its policy to hold Russian domination. Pakistan, as a weaker state along with regional benefits, grabbed the opportunity given by the US for anti-communist partners in South Asia to achieve economic and military support and to reinforce its position in the region as compared to India (Hilali 2002).

The most important political modification proposed by the Zia regime was the Eight amendments in the Constitution of the country which gave power to the president to dissolve the Pakistan National Assembly and dismiss Prime Minister. This completely changed the balance of power between the president and Prime Minister. Moreover, General Zia regime is also recognized for making Pakistan a nuclear power. Pakistan conducted its nuclear Cold Test in March 1983, followed by the Chaghi nuclear tests conducted in the year May 1998.

General Zia's death in an aircraft crash in 1988, gave the way to the former civil servant Ghulam Ishaq, to be his successor as president. The President directed new provincial and national elections and allowed political parties to contest the ballots. The main political parties in the country at that time were Pakistan People Party (PPP) led by Benazir Bhutto, daughter of former Prime Minister Zulfikar Ali Bhutto, and Pakistan Muslim League (PML) led by Nawaz Sharif, represented General Zia's legacy. Nawaz Sharif, with an industry background, entered in political affairs and became minister of finance in 1980 in General Zia's regime and later became Chief Minister of Punjab province.

The Pakistan People Party (PPP) won the elections and Benazir was appointed as Prime Minister in 1988. Benazir Bhutto wanted to reverse the Eighth Amendment to make a stronger position as Prime Minister but could not get enough political back. But, the disagreements between the military and Prime Minister on the one hand, and between the president and her on the other could not be settled. Hence, in 1990, the president Ghulam Ishaq dissolved the National Assembly and Benazir Bhutto disqualified from the post of Prime Minster. Using his constitutional power the president scheduled national and provincial elections for October 1990 and a countrywide state of emergency was announced.

Nawaz Sharif won the ballot vote in 1990 and elected as the Prime Minister after an alliance with religious parties of the country. Nawaz adopted Zia's policy of Islamization, and he was successful in getting the approval of Shariat Bill from the National Assembly. While doing so he ignored the banking and commercial sector. Eventually, the Prime Minister failed to meet the expectations of his voters, and his alliance with religious parties dissolved. Nawaz also tried to eliminate eight amendments in the constitution but it turned out to be a serious clash between President and Prime Minister. In 1993, President Ishaq by using his constitutional rights dismissed the Nawaz regime and again suspended the National Assembly. Nawaz appeared in the Supreme Court of Pakistan, claimed that the president act is conflicting to legal principles. The supreme court of Pakistan unpredictably accepted Nawaz's appeal and directed that the Prime Minister should retain in his office. After the court verdict, both president and Prime Minister lost their credibility and, the military intervened again and persuaded them to resign from their respective posts in the interest of the country and soon after their resignations the army transferred the power to the caretaker government.

The national elections were announced again in 1993. The Pakistan People (PPP) led by Benazir won the elections and became a Prime Minister for the second term and Farooq Leghari from her party was appointed as a President of the state. Unfortunately, Benazir faced the disgrace when the Benazir's brother Murtaza Bhutto alleged her husband Zardari for corruption. At the same time, Nawaz Sharif (sitting in the opposition) released documents that mentioned Bhutto's excesses. During the Benazir's two terms, numerous contracts with energy corporations for electricity generation were granted. Later, within the year 1998, while 21 western firms were scrutinized by the national anti-corruption agency for suspected bribes to the previous regime, six companies confessed that they had offered bribes. Benazir's husband Zardari in 1989 was suspected to be the main source of these contracts. The charges of corruption against Zardari damaged Benazir reputation and weakened the administration (Nasr 1992). Thus, President Farooq Leghari took action against Benazir and her husband and dismissed government in November 1996.

Benazir appealed in the Supreme Court of Pakistan but the President's decision was sustained by the court and the election were scheduled in 1997. The Pakistan Muslim League headed by Nawaz won the elections. Nawaz got approval from parliament to reduce the power of the President by mean of 13th amendment in the constitution which limits the president's authority to dissolve government at his own decision. In 1998 Nawaz pressurized army for the early retirement of the Chief of the army staff and later army head was replaced by Pervez Musharraf whom Nawaz believed would be more politically aware and compatible. However, in 1999 the Kashmir conflict with India flared again and collision of army forces in Kargil[4] began. The USA intervened again and directed Nawaz to order Pakistani forces to pull back from the disputed area. But, General Musharraf: the Chief of the Army, strongly opposed the Prime Minister's decision to retreat. During the same year, Nawaz tried to expel Musharraf but the plan was thwarted by the other army generals and as a result, Musharraf suspended Nawaz regime and functioning of state parliament. Nawaz was arrested and found guilty and sentenced to long prison. However, due to international pressures, Nawaz was freed and sent to exile to Saudia Arabia for 10 years.

Pervez Musharraf followed similar practices of power as the previous military regimes, such as bringing new political figures from the grassroots system. His government introduced localization of government; and termed it Devolution of Democracy (Khan 2005). To safeguard the army's participation in the governance and decision-making, Pervez Musharraf approved the NSC (National Security Council) Act in 2004. This NSC allowed army to be major national participant in the contest of power control by involving different elite groups (Talbot 2003). Pakistan's political scenery changed radically after the incident

[4]The Kargil Conflict took place between Pakistan and India in May and July 1999 in the Kargil area of Jammu Kashmir. The cause of the conflict was the penetration of Pakistani soldiers and Kashmiri militants into the Indian side of the Line of Control, which is the actual border between the two countries.

of September 11. The USA declared that the attacks were planned in Afghanistan near Pakistan border by Muslim Militant organization with the help of the Taliban regime. The United States demanded Pakistan to assist in operation in Afghanistan. Pervez Musharraf decided to support US troops but his decision was met with violence by Islamist conservatives in Pakistan. Musharraf was forced by the USA to take action against these Islamist conservatives particularly in the tribal areas near Afghanistan; hence, the Pakistan army started a major operation to combat Islamist militants in Waziristan (area located near to Afghan border). The Supreme Court invalidated Musharraf's reelection as president in 2007. Musharraf by using his power dismissed Chief Justice of the time, which ignited a strike of Pakistani lawyers all over the country. The Supreme Court reversed the dismissal of the Chief Justice and was restored on his position. The constitution was again suspended by military administration and a state of emergency was declared. Members of the Supreme Court including Chief justice of Pakistan were removed, and the activities of news media groups were curtailed. In the same year 2007, Benazir and Nawaz were officially allowed to come back to Pakistan and take part in the upcoming elections scheduled in 2008.

Musharraf's party was badly defeated in the 2008 elections. Benazir political party PPP succeeded in the elections and took control of the state but she was assassinated in the same year and in September 2008, Asif Ali Zardari (Benazir's husband) won the presidential elections, managing the coming back of civilian-led democracy (Stachoske 2009). But, this democratic administration was failed to solve those issues which turned out to be the cause of Musharraf's collapse: solving a clash between militants and security forces. In reality, the resistance came from extremist religious groups (Taliban, Al-Qaeda and local *militant groups*) has aggravated and rising security doubts around the world. Elections took place, and the business elite, Muhammad Nawaz, once again took control of the country and formed the government in 2013. In the year 2017, Nawaz Sharif was enforced to resign after being ineligible by the judiciary (Supreme Court of Pakistan)[5] over corruption allegations.

[5] The Supreme Court of Pakistan was established under the country Constitution of 1956. Since then, the Supreme Court has maintained its name and power through the successive legal instruments containing the Constitution of 1973. Judicial analysis in Pakistan came from the principle of judicial review in England. Regime legitimization through judicial authorization in the wake of direct martial law during the 1950s, 1960s,

In 2018, well known international cricket player Imran Khan and his party Pakistan PTI (Tehreek-e-Insaf) appeared as main political party in the general elections and Imran became a Prime Minister on assurance to eradicate corruption and hereditary politics. In Imran Khan's administration, the state has observed important development, particularly in its international relations. The sate made effective efforts to force the Taliban in Afghanistan to have peace talks, improving its relationships with the United States of America. Similarly, the major improvements Pakistan made in the year 2019 were the ties with Saudi Arabia and the United Arab Emirates for foreign aid to lessen the dependency of IMF, and also with Beijing on the China–Pakistan Economic Corridor by proposing scheme in Pakistani Public interest like those that would create employment in the country.

Pakistan's Industrial Policy and the Developmental State

Several causes explain Pakistan's speedy economic development just after independence in 1947 such as the positive effect of development in the global economy, the liberalization policy in the 50s, the economic role of the government and the mobilization of savings (Baqai 1979; Ahmad 1980; Amjad and Mahmood 1982). Although these factors may play a role in development, but industrial development comes from the strong part of the state that helped to raise investments, particularly in manufacturing sector by distributing resources to projects which were crucial for growth (McCartney 2011). Also, industrialization was accelerated by using investment returns, including those accrued from trade.[6] Pakistan's industrial policies are categorized by different periods and have been a vital element of the state's five-year growth strategies. The sectoral GDP growth in different important sectors from 1962 to 2019 can be seen in Table 15.1.

Within 1947 to 1958, the performance of the Pakistan industry was fairly impressive. The main highlight of the 50s was the formation and expansion of large scale manufacturing sector with the yearly rate of 28.7

1970s and in the 1990s is the most noticeable example of the judicialization of politics in Pakistan.

[6] Approximately 40 per cent of trade profits and only 10 per cent from commercial banks.

Table 15.1 Sectorial GDP growth, Pakistan, 1969–2019 (%)

	1969–1970	*1981–1985*	*1986–1990*	*1990–1995*	*1996–2000*	*2001–2005*	*2006–2010*	*2011–2015*	*2015–2019*
Agriculture	0.38	0.07	0.04	0.11	0.12	0.17	0.1	0.21	0.19
Industry	0.23	0.19	0.21	0.11	0.13	0.18	0.25	0.2	0.2
Mining and quarrying	0.005	0.09	0.08	0.02	0.01	0.01	0.02	0.02	0.02
Manufacturing	0.16	0.08	0.06	0.05	0.07	0.12	0.18	0.13	0.13
Construction	0.04	0.03	0.54	0.02	0.01	0.01	0.02	0.02	0.02
Electricity and gas distribution	0.02	0.07	0.12	0.01	0.01	0.02	0.01	0.02	0.01
Services	0.38	0.06	0.06	0.24	0.26	0.39	0.53	0.57	0.6
Transport, storage and communication	0.06	0.07	0.05	0.04	0.05	0.08	0.1	0.13	0.13
Wholesale and retail trade	0.13	0.08	0.05	0.08	0.08	0.13	0.18	0.18	0.18
Finance and insurance	0.01	0.1	0.28	0.03	0.01	0.02	0.05	0.03	0.03
Public administration	0.06	0.05	0.04	0.06	0.03	0.04	0.06	0.06	0.07

Source Author's calculations
Computed from Economic Survey of Pakistan (various issues)

per cent till 1954. But, the agriculture sector, which is the backbone of the country, marked a negative growth rate. One of the reasons for this negative growth was the policies that were implemented by the government that is to transfer income from the agriculture to the fast developing manufacturing sector. Additionally, the boom years of the Korean War lasted from 1950 till 1952, and the decline of the international prices of raw materials showed a clear signal of recession. But Pakistan was failed to respond on time and policies continued and the exchange rate remained high as compared to trading partners (such as India) which devalued its rupee in 1949. In 1952 jute and cotton prices, the main export items of the country, dropped as did export earnings, and Pakistan confronted a serious balance of payments crisis and severely dropping reserves (Zaidi 2015).

During Ayub Khan's government from 1958 to 1968, the state marked an extraordinary development in the manufacturing sector. Both, investment and production rose by almost 20 per cent during 1950 to 1955. This growth continued until 1960s as manufacturing increased by 10 per cent per annum in 1960s (Abbasi 2009). It was the green revolution that was responsible for extraordinary growth rates in the 1960s. Likewise, the focus of the new trade policy in 1959 moved from direct controls to indirect controls on imports. Important steps were taken in import licensing like Export Bonus Scheme introduced in the year 1959, that was counted to be an important factor to the import liberalization process in Pakistan and, the Open General License (OGL) which permitted newcomers to move in the trading sector. Similarly, the government launched a Free List which allowed the import of specific goods without any license (Zaidi 2015). In the year 1965, due to the India Pakistan war, the import list experienced serious obstacles as foreign assistance were restricted, and foreign exchange tightened, the import liberalization policies were halted. Pakistan's industrial experience starting from the 1950s to mid-1960 indicated the successful emergence of private enterprise. Although overall economic growth was extraordinary, there was also a downside of capital development and increase inequalities between East and West Pakistan.

Then, the populist Zulfikar Ali Bhutto's regime came into power in the year 1972 and started a nationalization plan for the manufacturing sector. The economic loss of East Pakistan was intensely experienced. West Pakistan exported almost 50 per cent of its goods to the Eastern Wing and achieved a large amount of foreign exchange from the export of its raw material. The Eastern Wing had more population and most crucial industries involved in exports as compared to West Wing, but the political and capital control was confined to West Pakistan. Additionally, the devaluation of Pakistani rupee by 120 per cent during 1972 carried major dividends through export progress within one year. But, the 1973 OPEC price upsurges badly affected Pakistan's import bill and the balance of payments further deteriorated (Zaidi 2015). This regime stayed unfortunately short survived as a coup d'etat brought in the Zia-Ul-Haq government in 1977, which started economic deregulation, manufacturing rose by only 5.4 per cent average per year from 1970 to 1980. However, manufacturing rose by almost 8.2 per cent per year in 1980s (Zaidi 2005).

The military administration under Zia till 1988, abandoned both state socialism and state capitalism to follow Islamization and the reallocation of economic rents (Sayeed 1996). Besides, the market-friendly policies of deregulation de-control, and denationalization was launched in order to accelerate private investment. Furthermore, the power of the military in the economy intensified as army representatives were employed to major positions (Khan 2000; Noman 1989). Import substitution policy was abandoned because tariffs were dropped and flexible exchange rates announced. Controls on the public account and capital account were also eliminated. All these developments facilitated to encourage industrial exports from industrial sectors as the production of cement, vehicles, steel and fertilizer started to increase. Incentives using direct export subsidies on sales tax and customs duties were introduced in the year 1978–1979 to support manufactured exports. Also, the investment environment improved as the administration gave promises against future nationalization and proposed tax reductions. As a result, manufacturing rose by 9.5 per cent per year between 1978 till 1983. The contribution of private sectors to new industrial investment had increased to almost 90 per cent in 1988 as compared to 25 per cent from 1976 to 1977.

Likewise, the renewal of private industrial investment helped to stimulate the production of traditional industries like cement and cotton textiles. The textiles and clothing industry received importance because of its low gestation and direct profit-making capability. Though, the incentives arrangements did not condition value-adding, hence cotton yarn continued to be a crucial export item despite getting considerable subsidies (Sayeed and Nadvi 2004; Hasan 1998). While exports of cotton yarn and grey fabric increased greatly to make the textile industry the major employer in the state (Sayeed and Nadvi 2004).

Certainly, this input-driven agenda engendered a huge burden on state's reserves, which intensified the current and fiscal account deficits in 1980s. High army expenditures aggravated state's public debt. Defense expenditure increased by almost 9 per cent per year to an average of 6.5 per cent of GDP, while developmental expenditure rose by only 3 per cent per year within this period. Whereas, manufacturing growth decreased during the 90s not only due to the substantial incentives that could not be continued but also due to the absence of technological upgrading policies that limited industrial advancement from lower- to higher-value-added performances. Excluding the year 1997 till 1998, when a tariff rationalization, reduction on sales tax, better sugarcane production and credit provision improved manufacturing growth marginally of about 5.5 per cent per year (Kemal 2004). The manufacturing growth rate per year was dropped by almost 3.5 per cent during 90s. Besides, with unproductivity in the agriculture sector, the slowdown in the manufacturing sector caused a severe decrease in GDP growth after 1988 as poverty and inflation increased. Unfortunately, following governments of Benazir and Nawaz were unsuccessful to minimize the drop. The drop in foreign remittance inflows in the year 1987 till 1990, caused by the Gulf War, intensified state's current account deficit, even though it experienced sound growth in exports. The devaluation of the Pakistani currency and better incentives supported export progress and tightening imports (Sarmad and Hasan 1992, p. 866). In fact, overseas Pakistani nationals and nonresident Pakistanis were permitted to open their foreign currency accounts in Pakistani banks. All these accounts were exempted from wealth and income taxes and those owning foreign currency accounts were also permitted to get loans against such accounts (Khan 2005). Subsequently, from June 1991 till 1996, Pakistan had $4 billion inflow into its foreign exchange balance record (Wizarat 2002, p. 27). From 2000 till 2005, manufacturing sector marked a growth rate of almost 12 per cent per year (Table 15.1). Alike Zia government, General Musharraf's regime, which came into command in 1999, introduced deregulation and decentralization approaches to encourage economic development. Subsiding tariffs plus tariff bands were added by proposals to penetrate export markets particularly in the European Union (EU). Pakistan's integration in EU markets accelerated the opening of duty-free access to apparel articles as nations regulated their fiscal structure consistent with the end of the Multi-Fiber Agreement in 2004 (Rasiah 2012). Import duties of almost 12 per cent had been imposed on apparel imports from

Pakistan to EU till 2005. Though, foreign and domestic investment levels did rise around 20 per cent of GDP, but were noticeably insufficient for sustainable development (see Amjad et al. 2011, pp. 13–30). The Pervez Musharraf's regime also introduced major industrial parks in Karachi: the business hub of the country, and Faisalabad and Lahore. Whereas, following market basics, Pakistan's industrial strategy during the period from 2001 to 2005 focused on product diversification. The total share of industry in GDP improved from 22.6 per cent during 2000 to 26.7 per cent in 2006, rising by double digits annum. Consequently, the state economy raised by almost 7 per cent within this time (Pakistan Economic Survey for 2004–2006). However, both manufacturing and economic development decreased in the following period from 2006 to 2010. This decrease can be ascribed to the deteriorating security condition in the state and the increasing number of terrorist attacks (Looney 2008). Also, the global increase in oil prices and the international financial crisis in 2007 and 2008 affected Pakistan's economy badly. Large-scale power shortage and gas crisis had a severe effect on the manufacturing sector. Engineering firms and Textile mills have, therefore, succeeded to save almost between 15 and 20 per cent of power. In particular, the state's foremost export sales, particularly textiles and apparel, dropped in the year 2006 to 2007, which increased the balance of trade deficit.

The newly-elected Imran Khans administration inherited a high current account deficit from the previous government. Throughout the initial years of Imran Khan's regime, the economic development was slow. Whereas the administration was assessing an almost 6.2 per cent GDP growth during 2019, Pakistan's GDP dropped to nearly 3.29 per cent as compared to 5.8 per cent in the preceding year. The government was enforced to contact the International Monetary Fund (IMF) during its first few months for a $6 billion loan. Yet, the Pakistan economy is predictable to progress marginally from 2021 as improved government revenues from a tax hike permit extended public investment and as further administration reforms required by the IMF begin to provide positive results. Sustained promise to reform, coupled with productive investment particularly in infrastructure and strategic capability development, will be important for the state to trace its previous growth pathway (World Economic Situation and Prospects 2020).

Conclusion

The case of Pakistan supports a conventional understanding that political power and stable regimes are important for economic development particularly in developing countries. Pakistan has never experienced a stable democracy. The army has always been the hegemonic force, ruling over the state's political economy, even when not in power (Zaidi 2014) such as in the year 1971, 1988 and 2008. Eventually, the economic issues are too bound to the structure of its power contestation, which has limited institutional modification. Pakistan's unstable relationship with India (almost three wars between two nations), have had an adverse effect on the state's political, social and monetary environment. Also, it gives the army a substantial political power, intensified by US military assistance (Hasan et al. 1997). Pakistan experienced its maximum growth rate when import substitution strategies were executed, encouraging incentives were provided to the manufacturing sector, the environment to attract huge remittances and the removal of MFA quotas in 2004. Whereas, the unproductive period appears to be after liberalization policies were begun (Haque 2015).

Despite these successes, the speed of Pakistan's growth, during peak eras: the 1950s, 1960s and 2006–2010, was far behind as compared to China, Taiwan and Republic of Korea (Nazeer and Rasiah 2016). Instead of focusing on industrialized diversification and constructing competitiveness globally via creating and distributing rents to help technological catching up, country's government strategies and policies have been formed by clientelist comforts. The government should focus on institutional transformation so that there must be scrutinizing, appraisal and monitoring the incentive structures that were established to support technological upgrading and industrialization in the state. The politicians, military and civil bureaucracy must build solid long term cooperation that could encourage industrial change from low to high value-added performances and lead the nation to move away from its current economic and security pressures.

References

Abbasi, Z. F. (2009). *Analysis of the political economy of industrial policy in Pakistan: The role of the state as an entrepreneur and conflict manager*. Retrieved from http://impact.org.pk/docs/discussion_paper_zfa.pdf.

Ahmed, M. (1980). Import substitution as a strategy of industrialization in Pakistan—A review. *Pakistan Economic and Social Review, 18*(2), 56–64.

Amjad, R., Din, M. U., & Qayyum, A. (2011). Pakistan: Breaking out of stagflation into sustained growth. *The Lahore Journal of Economics, 16*, 13.

Amjad, R., & Mahmood, K. (1982). *Industrial relations and the political process in Pakistan 1947–1977*.

Amsden, A. H. (1989). Asias next giant—How Korea competes in the world-economy. *Technology Review, 92*(4), 46–53.

Baqai, M. (1979). Pakistan's pattern of development and prospects. *Pakistan Economic and Social Review, 17*(3/4), 1–62.

Baran, P. (1973). 1957. The political economy of growth. *New York: Monthly Review*.

Burki, U., & Qureshi, M. A. (2012). Corporate governance in the family-owned businesses in Pakistan: A conceptual framework. *Unpublished work*. Retrieved from http://saicon2011.ciitlahore.edu.pk/Business%20Ethics/11-1196%20umar%20burki.Pdf.

Chang, H. J. (2002). *Kicking away the ladder: Development strategy in historical perspective*. Anthem Press.

Dahl, R. A. (1957). The concept of power. *Behavioral science, 2*(3), 201–215.

Gerschenkron, A. (1962). Economic backwardness in historical perspective (1962). *The Political Economy Reader: Markets as Institutions*, 211–228.

Hasan, P. (1998). *Pakistan's economy at the crossroads: Past policies and present imperatives*. Oxford University Press, USA.

Hasan, P., Kemal, A. R., & Naseem, S. M. (1997). Learning from the past: A fifty-year perspective on Pakistan's development [with comments]. *The Pakistan Development Review, 36*(4), 355–402.

Higley, J., Burton, M. G., & Field, G. L. (1990). In defense of elite theory: A reply to Cammack. *American Sociological Review, 55*(3), 421–426.

Hilali, A. Z. (2002). The costs and benefits of the Afghan War for Pakistan. *Contemporary South Asia, 11*(3), 291–310.

Hussain, A. (1976). Elites and political development in Pakistan. *The Developing Economies, 14*(3), 224–238.

Kemal, A. R. (2004). Exploring Pakistan's regional economic cooperation potential. *The Pakistan Development Review*, 313–334.

Khan, T. A. (2000). Economy, society and the state in Pakistan. *Contemporary South Asia, 9*(2), 181–195.

Khan, M. A. (2005). *We have learnt nothing from history*. Karachi, Pakistan: Oxford University Press.

Khan, M. A., Qayyum, A., Sheikh, S. A., & Siddique, O. (2005). Financial development and economic growth: The case of Pakistan [with comments]. *The Pakistan Development Review*, 819–837.

Kohli, U. (2004). Real GDP, real domestic income, and terms-of-trade changes. *Journal of International Economics*, *62*(1), 83–106.

Looney, R. (2008). *The Musharraf paradox: The failure of an economic success story*. Naval Postgraduate School Monterey CA.

Mahmood, T., Rehman, H. U., Rauf, S., & Rauf, S. A. (2008). Evaluation of macroeconomic policies of Pakistan (1950–2008). *Journal of Political Studies*, *17*, 57–75.

McCartney, M. (2011). *Pakistan—The political economy of growth, stagnation and the state, 1951–2009* (Vol. 103). Routledge.

Mills, C. W. (1981). 1956. *The power elite*. New York.

Nasr, S. V. R. (1992). Democracy and the crisis of governability in Pakistan. *Asian Survey*, *32*(6), 521–537.

Nazeer, N., & Rasiah, R. (2016). Explaining Pakistan's premature deindustrialization. *The Lahore Journal of Economics*, *21*, 351.

Noman, O. (1989). Pakistan and General Zia: Era and legacy. *Third World Quarterly*, *11*(1), 28–54.

Noman, A. (2015). The return of industrial policy and revival of Pakistan's economy: Possibilities of learning, industrial and technology policies. *The Lahore Journal of Economics*, *20*, 31.

Pareto, V. (1939). The mind and society (New York 1935); Gaetano Mosca. *The ruling class*.

Rashid, J. (1978). Economic causes of political crisis in Pakistan: The landlords vs. the industrialists. *The Developing Economies*, *16*(2), 169–181.

Rasiah, R. (2012). Beyond the multi-fibre agreement: How are workers in East Asia faring? *Institutions and Economies*, 1–20.

Rehman, U. (2006). *Who owns Pakistan: Fluctuating fortunes of business Moghuls* (Vol. 37, pp. 632–640). Islamabad: Aekia Communications, Review.

Rosenstein-Rodan, P. N. (1943). Problems of industrialisation of eastern and south-eastern Europe. *The Economic Journal*, *53*(210/211), 202–211.

Sarmad, K., & Hasan, M. A. (1992). External shocks and domestic adjustment in Pakistan 1970–1990 [with comments]. *The Pakistan Development Review*, *31*(4), 857–869.

Sayeed, A. U. (1996). *Political alignments, the state and industrial policy in Pakistan: A comparison of performance in the 1960s and 1980s* (Doctoral dissertation, University of Cambridge).

Sayeed, A., & Nadvi, K. (2004). Industrial capital and pro-poor change. *DFID Drivers of Change Project. Mimeo.*

Scitovsky, T. (1954). Two concepts of external economies. *Journal of Political Economy*, *62*(2), 143–151.

Shafqat, S. (1996). Pakistan under Benazir Bhutto. *Asian Survey, 36*(7), 655–672.
Stachoske, B. (2009). Das politische System Pakistans zwei Jahre nach dem Wechsel: die Zementierung eines kritischen Zustandes?
Talbot, I. (2003). Pakistan in 2002: Democracy, terrorism, and brinkmanship. *Asian Survey, 43*(1), 198–207.
United Nations. (2020). *World economic situation and prospects*. New York.
Wade, R. (1990). Industrial policy in East Asia: Does it lead or follow the market. *Manufacturing Miracles: Paths of Industrialization in Latin America and East Asia*, 231–266.
White, L. J. (2015). *Industrial concentration and economic power in Pakistan*. Princeton University Press.
Wizarat, S. (2002). *The rise and fall of industrial productivity in Pakistan*. Oxford University Press, USA.
Woo-Cummings, M. (1999). Korea: Democracy and reforming the corporate sector. *Economic Reform Today*, 1, 26.
Zaidi, S. A. (2005). *Issues in Pakistan's economy*. OUP Catalogue.
Zaidi, S. A. (2014). Rethinking Pakistan's political economy: Class, state, power, and transition. *Economic and Political Weekly*, 47–54.
Zaidi, S. A. (2015). *Issues in Pakistan's economy: A political economy perspective*. OUP Catalogue.

CHAPTER 16

Conclusion: New Developmentalism in the Twenty-First Century—Perspectives from the Global East and South

Tamás Gerőcs

This volume is a collection of essays that seek to critically engage with the developmental state (DS) paradigm in the twenty-first century from the standpoint of the global semi-periphery. The essays are the outcome of a series of discussions that were organized by the Budapest-based Institute of World Economics as part of the "Role of State in Varieties of Capitalism" (SVOC) conferences. The idea of inviting scholars—especially from the Global East and South—to discuss the role of the developmental state model in the post-2008 global financial crisis as well as at the conjuncture of a global pandemic in 2020 goes back to Judit Ricz's ideas who is the co-editor of this volume. Since the start of the first conference in 2015, participants have been trying to document the extent and

T. Gerőcs (✉)
Institute of World Economics, Centre for Economic and Regional Studies, Budapest, Hungary

T. Gerőcs and J. Ricz (eds.), *The Post-Crisis Developmental State*, International Political Economy Series,
https://doi.org/10.1007/978-3-030-71987-6_16

influence of states' intervention capacities to explore the economic implications of what has been perceived as newly rising authoritarian regimes in the global semi-periphery and ask the question if and how it relates to the paradigm of developmentalism, particularly with respect to new institutional settings. We saw a diversity of approaches in the abovementioned debates that were concentrating around state capitalist varieties by focusing and extending the developmental state approach based on the experience of the Global East and South. The aim of this volume informed by many of those discussions is to reconsider classical modernization theories in a broader geographical context, integrating legacies of path-dependency and the newer political context of populism and rising authoritarianism. With the following discussions we also aim to speak to the state capitalism debates from a developmentalist angle.

The volume is the second in a row that brings the attention of the reader to the abovementioned methodological as well as historical questions. The first book discussed issues related to Market Liberalism and Economic Patriotism in the Capitalist World-System (Gerőcs and Szanyi 2019). One of the questions that we kept asking while organizing conferences and the two respective volumes was whether there is a need for a new paradigm to understand the transformation of developmental state models or the classical theories of developmentalism (Johnson 1982; Amsden 1989; Evans 1989, 1995; Woo-Cumings 1999; Wade 2003; Rodrik 2004) from the pre-crisis era are still valid to inform us about the direction of change, including neoliberal authoritarianism (Bruff 2014) that are spreading in the post-crisis era.

This volume was intended as a forum for exploring ideas related to state intervention and crisis management in present-day semi-peripheral regions from Latin America through Africa and South Asia. The virtue of this volume is that it provides insights both from theoretical and practical perspectives on the potential contours of a post-crisis developmental state model with the possibilities and constraints that states face in their crisis management efforts. Thus, the volume encompasses the experiences of both developing peripheral and more advanced countries, and frames them as part of an overall structural comparison, which we hope will benefit researchers, students, and policy-makers who are interested in the developmental state model in a global and historical perspective focusing on the post-crisis era in the twenty-first century.

This volume has been informed by recent debates about the paradigmatic change taking place in developmental economics in order to go beyond the classical western-centric modernization approaches (see Csaba's chapter in this volume). Therefore, the key framework in our discussions was uneven development of global capitalism from the perspective of the Global East and South. The combined discussions which we deliver here are looking beyond the mere state-centric models to put the future role of the developmental state into a global as well as a historically informed context. The further aim of this volume was to select insightful studies that can help us to recapture the global and historical framework through the experiences of peripheral and semi-peripheral modernization efforts from various regions. We selected cases of both successful catching-up models, such as Taiwan's educational system (Csáki's chapter) or Slovakia's urban-centered economic development (Kollai's chapter) as well as country cases that have been trapped in path-dependency with their low or stagnant middle-income statuses, as cases of Pakistan (Nazeer's chapter), Zimbabwe (Masocha's chapter), or the larger region of North Africa (Szigetvári's chapter) demonstrate. However, we see important success stories in the African context as Ikpe's discussion on Ethiopia informs us.

The point of departure in this analysis is a differentiated approach to the modernizational paradigms of peripheral and semi-peripheral countries, regarding both the structures of their economy as well as their social and class formations and also regarding the regulatory capacities of their respective states to implement developmental policies, such as in the terrain of education or the newer focus on green industrial policies (the latter is discussed by Szalavetz in her chapter). In short, we were interested in the possibilities and constraints semi-peripheral states in the Global East and South face in seeking new strategies for longer term development.

Despite the fact a lot has changed in the structure of the world economy since the late 1970s, and early 1980s, this volume argues that there is still much scope to learn from the experiences of the classical developmental states from that period. This is not in any contradiction with our endeavor to search for new or renewed paradigms that are informed by more recent historical currents regarding the discussions on modernization and new developmentalism in the twenty-first century.

The context of this volume is based on such a methodological as well as conceptual synthesis in which old concepts meet new queries at an enriching intersection that opens up new insights into the problem of modernization not only for academics and students of developmental studies but for development practitioners, as well as the larger public, including policy- and decision-makers. Thus, the volume revisits the historical experiences of post-war developmental states to compare them with economic policy practices in the post-crisis era (Ricz's chapter is important in this respect), and as the reader of this volume can clearly see, there are as many similarities as differences in our historical comparison between the classical and the new modernization projects.

One similar characteristic which immediately strikes in our eyes is that the developmental state paradigm which encompasses interventionist state approaches to economic development particularly in the terrain of industrialization and affiliated public or private services are more embraced by states in semi-peripheral regions, such as in Latin America, Eastern Europe, South Asia, or even in Africa (that is usually associated more with the Global Periphery) than in more developed states in the Transatlantic region.

This is no coincidence, since the most immediate framework of the developmental state paradigm was a model of "catching-up" with the advanced industrial centers. Such modernization paradigm including a critical approach to developmentalism is generally originated in the Latin American school of "dependentsia" which school studied structural constraints, historical legacies of economic and geopolitical dependencies from the colonial past that were treated by the dependency-scholars as structural obstacles for states to modernize or catch up with the more advanced states in the West (Cardoso 1972). One concern of the dependency school has been detected in particular by this volume that is the intensification of capital flows and the rising role of multinational companies that are reshaping both the structures of the world economy as well as the social and economic framework of any national developmental strategies.

Hence, in a corresponding discussion to the structuralist approach, the developmental state paradigm evolved in the 1970s and 1980s to focus on those institutional agencies that can dialectically transform the economic structures that semi-peripheral states depended on. Therefore this paradigm focused on the level of particular state policies through which active intervention promoted industrialization, catching-up models and modernization in general under the egis of developmentalism.

As our discussion in this volume highlighted, one of the key concepts is the "growth-with-equity" approach which stems exactly from this latter tradition. It helped us to revisit the stricter version of classical developmentalism in order to include new institutional elements, such as an extended context of public services in terrains of education, labor-market regulation, taxation systems, or the industry 4.0 (sometimes in partnership with private business interest) as well as broader social, spatial, and ecological concerns. The growth-with-equity approach is also in correspondence with another informative theory that similarly originated from the renewed discussion on developmentalism, which is the concept of the global suppliers' chain (Gereffi and Korzeniewicz 1994; Gereffi 2014). The focus of the latter shifted away from a state-centric approach in order to include non-state actors, most typically business companies into the discussion of corporate governance and upgrading.

Both the suppliers' chain approach as well as the growth-with-equity approach discusses the relationship between economic upgrading—on the level of inter-firm specialization—state developmental agenda and the social and political consequences of all of those performances in the context of "social upgrading" (Scherrer 2018). The question of upgrading was a paradigmatic shift in the discussion especially after the 1980s when both the external and internal environment for the developmental state agenda changed massively due to the new era of globalization with penetrating international financial institution (the role of finance in the Brazilian case is discussed by Ribeiro and da Silva in their chapter), such as the IMF and World Bank under the auspices of neoliberal reformism. Similarly, Vigvári explains the rising role of globally integrated trading systems in his chapter. After the late 1980s throughout the neoliberal era of the 1990s, we witnessed the slow decline of the classical developmental model especially its focus only on the state, and as a matter of fact, this erosion was a parallel process to the consolidation of liberal democracy in many of the countries in our consideration. This was the period when the focus of even the developmental literature shifted away from the state to the role of companies in economic upgrading.

Consequently, the question of the state-centric approach has its limitations. The structures of the world-economy have been greatly transformed since the 1990s in which global supplier chains and service suppliers are crossing over state boundaries. In addition, the scope of states' intervention capacities has been transformed accordingly. Particular enterprises, economic sectors, especially in high-end services, and new reconfiguration of public–private partnerships have opened up new perspectives not only for the developmentalist model, but for scholars to explain and reconceptualize the changing terrain of that agenda.

As many of the authors of this volume have pointed out a new revival of active state intervention has been substantially different from the old developmental paradigm. Broader geographical focus as well as the understanding of new authoritarianism was much needed. On the other hand, a new developmental agenda seems to be on the horizon since the 2000s whose shift has been accelerated by the fact that more active crisis management practices have been expected from the respective states, hence we see the re-emergence of state involvement. But as further questions arise from this, is this shift a mere cyclical phenomenon or a deeper paradigmatic change?

One of the major contributions of this volume to the discussion on new developmentalism is its in-depth investigation of those global forces that are reformulating the states' approaches whether it was during the neoliberal era or the more recent rise of the new "authoritarian" states. One of the important concepts in which the developmental framework is discussed in a multidimensional understanding is the institutions of "multi-level governance" which is our starting point for post-crisis consideration in the new developmental paradigm. Therefore we based our discussions in a critical political economy as a multi-scale approach to the question of institutional settings for development. Multi-level governance encompasses state-market regulations (policies of particular governments), corporate governance of supplier chains, and the structures of the economy (below the state) with a sectoral focus.

The different political reconfigurations of the developmental model in the Global East and South is the manifestation of larger systemic processes that are themselves embedded in the world-economic crisis and which are the outcome of a long transformation of the international order. As some of the authors in this book describe these processes are never predetermined economically, instead the "phases of global transitions" are always contingent upon the balance of different social forces inside the state, but above as well (see for instance Yakovlev's chapter). Therefore, structural changes are almost always subject to the historical conjuncture of world-economic shifts (as Szanyi explains in his chapter), such as the one we witnessed during the global financial crisis in 2008 or during the more recent global pandemic in 2020. On that note, we can see that the state is always more active in phases of global transitions than during times of consolidation as the comparison between the neoliberal era in the 1990s and the interventionist era of the post-crisis period has demonstrated for us. Moreover, important social forces, whether business groups, state institutions, or the abovementioned inter-firm supplier chains are themselves an integral part of those global processes, in that way the global economic changes are also translated into the local institutions through the active mediation of the state. This observation is again in line with the classical developmental state paradigm. Consequently, in studying developmental projects in phases of economic transition, it is not enough to understand the evolving institutional or economic reconfigurations within states' apparatuses, but it is necessary to place the state back into the broader framework of the world economy.

From the perspective of critical political economy, we can highlight the link between the role of those institutions even under authoritarian governance and the reconfiguring social and business alliances that are interlinked through state policies. As this volume argues, the political expression of the developmental state is embedded in the reconfiguration of world-economic structures. However, emergent new beneficiaries of the world-economic integration can still use the state apparatus for their economic as well as political consolidations; hence the political economy perspective explains the form of the new developmental state from the standpoint of new capitalist class alliances. It focuses on different fractions of classes that are the main beneficiaries of various economic policies whether protectionist interventions or neoliberal policies and which groups are able to mobilize the state's capacity to navigate between the geopolitical forces of world-economic change. In this respect, the role of newly rising geopolitical powers, such as China, India, and Russia need special attention in the new developmental paradigm. This volume pays attention particularly to Chinese economic involvement in some of the countries in our concern.

As we can observe in the different chapters of this volume, taking both the world-economic path-dependency approach—that goes back to the structuralist argument of the dependency school—with an agency-based institutional model not only into consideration but more so to a methodological intersection enriches our understanding on a more global and dialectical perspective of the new developmental state. Henceforth, we see a dialectically informed new model of developmentalism in which structure and agency correspond on multi-scale levels in which state intervention can be broadly reconceptualized. This is why we say that our approach that has been built up through this volume is aimed at connecting the classical developmental state paradigm to a new approach in which the emphasis is shifted from an agency only approach to another one which is more embedded in the structural context within which historical legacies and the international power relations, including financial and geopolitical structures are referential.

References

Amsden, Alice. 1989. *Asia's Next Giant: South Korea and Late Industrialization.* Oxford University Press.

Bruff, Ian. 2014. "The Rise of Authoritarian Neoliberalism." In: *Rethinking Marxism* 26(1), 113–129.

Cardoso, Fernando Henrique. 1972. "Dependency and Development in Latin America." In: *New Left Review* 1(74), 83–95.

Evans, Peter. 1989. "Predatory, Developmental and Other Apparatuses: A Comparative Political Economy Perspective on the Third World State." In: *Sociological Forum* 4(4), 561–587.

Evans, Peter. 1995. *Embedded Autonomy: States and Industrial Transformation.* Princeton University Press.

Gereffi, Gary. 2014. "Global Value Chains in a Post-Washington Consensus World." In: *Review of International Political Economy* 21, 9–37.

Gereffi, Gary and Korzeniewicz, Miguel (eds). 1994. *Commodity Chains and Global Capitalism.* Praeger.

Gerőcs, Tamás and Szanyi, Miklós (eds). 2019. *Market Liberalism and Economic Patriotism in the Capitalist World-Systems.* Palgrave

Johnson, Chalmers. 1982. *MITI and the Japanese Miracle.* Stanford University Press.

Rodrik, Dani. 2004. *Industrial Policy for the Twenty-First Century.* Harvard University.

Scherrer, Christoph. 2018. "Relevance of Collective Action for Economic and Social Upgrading." Presentation at the Global Labour University in Berlini March 30.

Wade, Robert. 2003. "What Strategies Are Viable for Developing Countries Today? The World Trade Organization and the Shrinking of 'Development Space." In: *Review of International Political Economy* 10(4), 621–644.

Woo-Cumings, Meredith. 1999. *The Developmental State.* Cornell University.

Index

T. Gerőcs and J. Ricz (eds.), *The Post-Crisis Developmental State*, International Political Economy Series,
https://doi.org/10.1007/978-3-030-71987-6

The manufacturer's authorised representative in the EU is Springer Nature Customer Service Centre GmbH, Europaplatz 3, 69115 Heidelberg, Germany. If you have any concerns regarding our products, please contact ProductSafety@springernature.com

Printed and bound by CPI Group (UK) Ltd, Croydon, CR0 4YY
30/09/2026
02225701-0013